SAUNDERS $79.25   3/8/07

DATE DUE		
JAN 0 5 2009		
JUN 0 5 2009		
JUN 1 0 2014		

THE GREENHAVEN ENCYCLOPEDIA OF

CAPITAL PUNISHMENT

THE GREENHAVEN ENCYCLOPEDIA OF

Capital Punishment

OTHER BOOKS IN THE
GREENHAVEN ENCYCLOPEDIA SERIES:

Ancient Egypt
Ancient Rome
The Civil War
Greek and Roman Mythology
The Middle Ages
The Vietnam War
Witchcraft

THE GREENHAVEN ENCYCLOPEDIA OF

CAPITAL PUNISHMENT

Bruce E.R. Thompson

Mary Jo Poole, *Consulting Editor*

Bruce Glassman, *Vice President*
Bonnie Szumski, *Publisher*
Helen Cothran, *Managing Editor*

GREENHAVEN PRESS
An imprint of Thomson Gale, a part of The Thomson Corporation

Detroit • New York • San Francisco • San Diego • New Haven, Conn.
Waterville, Maine • London • Munich

© 2006 Thomson Gale, a part of The Thomson Corporation.

Thomson and Star Logo are trademarks and Gale and Greenhaven Press are registered trademarks used herein under license.

For more information, contact
Greenhaven Press
27500 Drake Rd.
Farmington Hills, MI 48331-3535
Or you can visit our Internet site at http://www.gale.com

ALL RIGHTS RESERVED.
No part of this work covered by the copyright hereon may be reproduced or used in any form or by any means—graphic, electronic, or mechanical, including photocopying, recording, taping, Web distribution or information storage retrieval systems—without the written permission of the publisher.

LIBRARY OF CONGRESS CATALOGING-IN-PUBLICATION DATA

Thompson, Bruce E.R., 1952–
   Capital Punishment / by Bruce E.R. Thompson
     p. cm. — (Greenhaven encyclopedia of)
Includes bibliographical references and index.
ISBN 0-7377-2174-X
1. Capital punishment—United States—Encyclopedias. I. Title. II. Series.
KF9227.C2T48 2006
345.73'0773—dc22

2004027429

Printed in the United States of America

CONTENTS

Preface, 10

Abbott, Burton, 12
actual innocence, 13
affirmative defense, 13
aggravating circumstances, 15
Alabama, 17
Alaska, 18
Aldridge v. United States, 18
American Bar Association (ABA), 19
American Civil Liberties Union (ACLU), 19
American League to Abolish Capital Punishment, 20
American Society for the Abolition of Capital Punishment, 20
Amnesty International, 20
Amsterdam, Anthony Guy, 20
anesthesia, 21
Antiterrorism and Effective Death Penalty Act, 21
appeals process, 22
Arizona, 23
Arkansas, 25
Assyrian Code, 26
Atkins v. Virginia, 26

B

Barefoot v. Estelle, 28
Beccaria, Cesare, 28
Beck v. Alabama, 30
Bedau, Hugo Adam, 30
Beidler, John X., 31
Bell v. Ohio, 31
benefit of clergy, 32
Bentham, Jeremy, 32
Berns, Walter, 33
Bible, 34
Billington family, 34
Black Code, 34
Blackmun, Harry A., 35
Booth v. Maryland, 36
Bovee, Marvin H., 36
Bradford, William, 36
Branch v. Texas, 37
breaking on the wheel, 37
Brennan, William J., 38
Brooks, Charles, 39
Buenoano, Judias, 39
Bundy, Theodore, 40
burden of proof, 41
burning at the stake, 42

Calcraft, William, 44
California, 44
Callins v. Collins, 47
capital crimes, 47
censorship of reporting on executions, 49
Cheever, George Barrell, 50
Chessman, Caryl, 51
Clark, Stephen, 53
clemency, 53
closure, 55
Coker v. Georgia, 55
Colorado, 56
competence, 57
Connecticut, 57
Constitution of the United States, 58
corporal punishment, 60
cost of capital punishment, 62
crucifixion, 63
cruel and unusual punishment, 64

D

Dallas, George Mifflin, 67
Darrow, Clarence, 68
Death Penalty Information Center (DPIC), 69
death-qualified jury, 70
death row, 70
decapitation, 72
Delaware, 72
deontology, 74
Dershowitz, Alan, 74
determinism, 75
deterrence, 76
dissection, 77
District of Columbia, 78
divine authority, 78
DNA evidence, 79
double jeopardy, 81
Draconian Code, 81
drawing and quartering, 82
due process, 82

E

Eddings. v. Oklahoma, 84
Eighth Amendment, 84
electric chair, 85
Ellis, Ruth Neilson, 88
Enmund v. Florida, 88
equal protection, 89
ESPY file, 90
Evangelium Vitae (The Gospel of Life), 90
evolving standards of decency, 91
executioners, 92
exoneration, 95
extradition, 95

federal death-penalty laws, 97
Felker v. Turpin, 100
film treatment of capital punishment, 100

firing squad, 101
Florida, 103
Ford v. Wainwright, 104
foreign nationals, 105
Foreman, Percy, 106
Fort Leavenworth Penitentiary, 107
Furman v. Georgia, 108

G

Gacy, John Wayne, 110
gallows, 110
gallows reprieve, 111
garrote, 111
gas chamber, 111
Gee Jon, 114
Georgia, 115
gibbet, 116
Gilmore, Gary, 116
Godfrey v. Georgia, 118
Goldberg, Arthur J., 118
Goode, Washington, 119
grand jury, 120
Gregg v. Georgia, 121
guided discretion, 122
Guillotin, Joseph-Ignace, 122
guillotine, 123

H

habeas corpus, 126
Hammurabi, Code of, 128
hanging, 129
hara-kiri, 132
Harris v. Alabama, 132
Hauptmann, Bruno, 133
Hawaii, 135
Haymarket Square riot, 135
Herrera v. Collins, 136
Hill, Joe, 136
Horn, Tom, 137

I

Idaho, 139
Illinois, 140
impalement, 141
imprisonment, 142
In re Kemmler, 144
Indiana, 145
Ingle, Joe, 146
Innocence Project, 146

international criticism of the United States, 147
international use of capital punishment, 149
Iowa, 150

J

Jackson v. Georgia, 151
Joan of Arc, 151
Jurek v. Texas, 153
jury nullification, 153
Justice for All, 154
justification of punishment, 154
Justinian, Code of, 157
juvenile offenders, 158

K

Kansas, 160
Kant, Immanuel, 161
Kemmler, William, 161
Kendall, George, 162
Kentucky, 162
Ketch, Jack, 164
Ketchum, Thomas "Black Jack," 165
Koran, 165

L

last meal, 166
last words, 166
Law of the Twelve Tables, 167
Lawes, Lewis E., 167
Leopold, Nathan F., and Richard A. Loeb, 168
lethal injection, 169
lex talionis, 171
life imprisonment without parole, 171
literature, 172
Livingston, Edward, 173
Locke, John, 174
Lockett v. Ohio, 176
Lockhart v. McCree, 176
Louisiana, 177
Louisiana ex rel. Francis v. Resweber, 178
Loving v. United States, 179
Lowenfield v. Phelps, 179
lynching, 181

M

Maine, 182
Maledon, George, 182
mandatory sentencing, 183
martyrs, 183
Marwood, William, 183
Maryland, 183
Massachusetts, 184
Maxwell v. Bishop, 186
McCleskey v. Kemp, 187
McCleskey v. Zant, 187
McGautha v. California, 188
McVeigh, Timothy, 189
mens rea, 190
mentally ill offenders, 191
mentally retarded offenders, 191
Michigan, 192
military justice, 192
Mill, John Stuart, 194
Mills v. Maryland, 195
Minnesota, 196
Mississippi, 196
Missouri, 197
mitigating circumstances, 199
Model Penal Code, 200
"Monsieur New York," 201
Montana, 201
Montesquieu, Baron de (Charles-Louis de Secondat), 202
moratorium movement, 203
Morgan v. Illinois, 204
multiple executions, 205
murder, 206
Murray v. Giarratano, 207

N

NAACP Legal Defense and Education Fund, 208
National Coalition to Abolish the Death Penalty, 208
Nebraska, 208
Nevada, 211
New Hampshire, 212
New Jersey, 213
New Mexico, 214
New York, 216

North Carolina, 217
North Dakota, 219

Ocuish, Hannah, 220
Ohio, 220
Oklahoma, 222
opposition to capital punishment, history of (1648–1870), 223
opposition to capital punishment, history of (1870–1963), 225
opposition to capital punishment, history of (1963–present), 226
Oregon, 229
Osborne, Thomas Mott, 230
O'Sullivan, John L., 232

Parker, Isaac C., 233
Payne v. Tennessee, 234
peine forte et dure, 234
Pennsylvania, 235
Penry v. Lynaugh, 236
Phillips, Wendell, 237
phrenology, 238
physician participation in executions, 238
Pierrepoint family, 239
Poland v. Arizona, 239
Prejean, Helen, 240
Proffitt v. Florida, 241
proportionality, 241
Protocol 6, 242
public opinion, 242
Puerto Rico, 244
Pulley v. Harris, 244
Purvis, Will, 245

racial discrimination in sentencing, 246
reanimation of corpses, 248
Regulators and Moderators, 248
Rehnquist, William H., 249
relativism, 250
religious views, 251
repentance, 252
retentionists, 254

Rhode Island, 254
rights of the accused, 255
Ring v. Arizona, 255
Roberts v. Louisiana, 256
Romano v. Oklahoma, 256
Roper v. Simmons, 257
Rosenberg, Julius and Ethel, 258
Rudolph v. Alabama, 260
Rush, Benjamin, 261
Ryan, George H., 262

Sacco, Nicola, and Bartolomeo Vanzetti, 264
Salem witchcraft trials, 266
San Quentin State Prison, 267
Sanson family, 267
Sawyer v. Whitley, 270
Schlup v. Delo, 271
Scottish Maiden, 272
Scottsboro Boys, 272
Shays' Rebellion, 274
Simmons v. South Carolina, 274
simulated hangings, 275
Sing Sing Prison, 275
Singleton, Charles, 276
Skipper v. South Carolina, 276
slavery, 277
Snyder, Ruth, 277
social contract theory, 279
Socrates, 280
solitary confinement, 281
South Carolina, 281
South Carolina v. Gathers, 283
South Dakota, 283
Spaziano v. Florida, 284
Spear, Charles, 285
special circumstances, 286
Stanford v. Kentucky, 286
stay of execution, 287
Stewart, Potter, 287
stoning, 288
Supreme Court, 289

Tennessee, 292
Texas, 293

thirty-day rule, 294
Thompson v. Oklahoma, 295
time between sentencing and execution, 295
torture, 296
trial, 296
Trop v. Dulles, 301
Tucker, Karla Faye, 301

United Nations Commission on Human Rights, 302
United States v. Jackson, 302
Universal Declaration of Human Rights, 302
Utah, 303
utilitarianism, 304

Vermont, 306
victim impact statements, 306
victims' rights, 306
viewing of executions, 307
Virginia, 310
visitation privileges, 311
volunteers, 312

Wainwright v. Witt, 313
Walton v. Arizona, 313
war crimes, 314
Washington, 315
West Virginia, 317
Wilkerson v. Utah, 317
Wirz, Henry, 317
Wisconsin, 319
Witherspoon v. Illinois, 319
Woodson v. North Carolina, 320
Wyoming, 320

For Further Research, 322
Index, 325
Picture Credits, 334
About the Author, 335
About the Consulting Editor, 336

PREFACE

Among the most divisive issues in current American society is how we should treat the worst criminal offenders, those whose crimes are judged most heinous, offensive, or harmful to the well-being of the community. Historically, the accepted punishment for such crimes was death, in societies in all places and all ages. A growing movement in the modern era, however, views the death penalty, or capital punishment, as unacceptable on political, religious, or humanitarian grounds, and the death penalty has been successfully abolished in law or practice in more than half the countries in the world. It is legal in the United States, and recent polls indicate more than 60 percent of the population supports its continued use, but controversy has been fueled by forensic advances such as DNA testing, which has exonerated a number of death-row inmates. The current debate involves hard-to-measure concepts such as deterrent value, retributive value, and other fundamental issues of social justice.

Americans have been debating capital punishment since the founding of the nation. The Quakers were the first religious group to take a principled stand against capital punishment, although it was practiced even in the Quaker colony of Pennsylvania. One of the signers of the Declaration of Independence, Benjamin Rush, was an early opponent of the death penalty. Opposition to the death penalty became a widespread movement in America in the years leading up to the Civil War in 1860. Many states considered abolishing capital punishment, and three, Michigan, Rhode Island, and Wisconsin, actually did so. The chief effect of the pre–Civil War abolitionist movement, however, was to transform hangings from large public events to small and exclusive events held behind the walls of prison and jail courtyards.

Following the Civil War and into the twentieth century opposition to the death penalty continued, but the movement achieved few permanent victories. Several states abolished capital punishment only to reinstate it a few years later. However, in response to the abolitionist movement, there was considerable interest in finding more humane methods of execution. The electric chair and the gas chamber each promised to be more reliable and painless than hanging, so by 1950 nearly every state had replaced hanging with one or the other of these two methods.

Beginning in the 1960s opponents of capital punishment changed their tactics. Rather than trying to change state laws one state at a time, they began using legal appeals to challenge the sentences of death row inmates. This tactic brought the pace of executions to a crawl and finally to a stop. From 1968 to 1978 no one was executed in the United States. In 1972, in the landmark *Furman v. Georgia* decision, the U.S. Supreme Court declared that all capital punishment statutes then in effect in the United States were unconstitutional. States hastened to revise their statutes to conform to the requirements laid down by the Court. In 1976, in the *Gregg v. Georgia* decision, the Supreme Court approved the revised statutes, and in 1978, executions under the new laws resumed. As executions resumed, many states adopted lethal injection as their preferred method of execution.

From 1978 to 2000 the number of executions in the United States increased dramatically and capital punishment enjoyed broad public support. Indeed, in 1994 support for the death penalty among Americans reached an all-time high of 80 percent. Since then DNA evidence has proved that several death row inmates were actually innocent, and support for capital punishment has decreased somewhat. In 2000 a moratorium on further executions was declared in Illinois until problems with the state's criminal justice system could be examined and corrected. Opponents of capital punishment have called for similar moratoriums in other jurisdictions as well. Meanwhile, while continuing to allow capital punishment, the Supreme Court has recently placed some important restrictions on its use. In 2002 the Supreme Court declared the execution of mentally retarded offenders to be unconstitutional. In 2005 it declared the execution of offenders who were under the age of eighteen at the time of their crime to be unconstitutional.

Currently capital punishment remains as controversial as ever, and there is no sign that the debate will be settled soon. *The Greenhaven Encyclopedia of Capital Punishment* is an attempt to facilitate debate by providing the background and basic facts around which the debate turns. Besides providing a history of capital punishment, and of the opposition to it, the encyclopedia provides sketches of some of the complex and often colorful figures that people that history. This includes well-known death row inmates, famous executioners, lawyers, judges, and leaders on both sides of the issue. Various methods of execution are explained and their use placed in historical context. The encyclopedia attempts to explore in detail the philosophical underpinnings of the arguments both in support of capital punishment and in opposition to it, tracing these arguments to their roots in such broad theories of social justice as social contract theory, deontology, and utilitarianism. Legal terminology important to the debate is defined and explained. The encyclopedia includes summaries of the Supreme Court decisions that have had the greatest impact on the practice of capital punishment in the United States, including in most cases the reasoning behind these decisions. A unique feature of this encyclopedia is contained in its entries for each state. Besides providing summaries of each state's current death-penalty laws (in those states where capital punishment is practiced), each entry provides a brief history of capital punishment in that state.

This encyclopedia is designed to be convenient for student researchers. Entries are cross-referenced, a bibliography is provided to encourage additional reading, and a complete index guides readers to important content that cannot be easily located by keyword alone.

Abbott, Burton (1928–1957)

Burton Abbott is remembered chiefly because in 1957 he received a stay of execution that arrived just two minutes too late to prevent his execution. Abbott was convicted of the abduction and murder of Stephanie Bryan, a fourteen-year-old girl, in Berkeley, California. Six months after her disappearance, her personal effects were found by Abbott's wife in their basement, and Stephanie's body was found in a shallow grave near Abbott's summer cabin. Although Abbott maintained his innocence, he was convicted and sentenced to death.

Abbott's execution was scheduled for 10:00 A.M. on March 15, 1957, but was delayed while the governor's reprieve board considered a last-minute appeal filed by Abbott's attorney. At 11:00 the board rejected the appeal, meaning that the execution would be allowed to proceed. After a few more moments of discussion, however, the board reversed its decision. A representative tried to reach California governor Goodwin J. Knight to issue a stay of execution, but the governor had gone sailing and could not be reached. Acting on his behalf, the board called San Quentin State Prison directly. Abbott, meanwhile, entered the prison's gas chamber at 11:15. At 11:18 the lethal cyanide pellets were released into the chamber. At 11:20 the reprieve call came. Abbott was probably still alive at that moment, but the warden would not risk having a member of the prison staff enter the

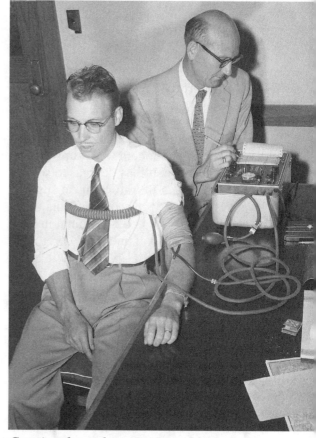

Convicted murderer Burton Abbott, seen here taking a lie detector test in 1955, received a stay of execution just two minutes after he was executed in 1957.

gas-filled room to remove him. Not surprisingly, news of this incident strengthened opposition to the death penalty, which was growing at the time, and Abbott's case is mentioned as an example of the fallibility of the capital punishment process. **See also** stay of execution.

actual innocence

The term *actual innocence* is used to draw a distinction between the legal definition of innocence, determined by a jury's not-guilty verdict, and innocence in the sense that the defendant in fact did not commit the crime of which he or she is accused. A jury's verdict, reached through presentation of evidence and accepted trial proceedings, is held to be fact and ideally reflects the defendant's true guilt or innocence. However, court proceedings and juries are run by humans and are thus fallible, so it is sometimes necessary to talk about whether the defendant actually committed a crime apart from the jury's verdict in the matter. A person is thus considered "actually innocent" if he or she did not commit the crime in question, even if a jury renders a guilty verdict.

In one of its most controversial decisions involving a capital case, the Supreme Court ruled in *Herrera v. Collins* (1993) that it was not the business of appeals courts to correct errors of fact in jury decisions, and that "actual innocence" does not constitute grounds for appeal. Only procedural error is grounds for appeal, unless a motion based on new evidence is filed within thirty days of conviction. An exception is also allowed if a judge determines that the new evidence is so compelling that no reasonable jury would have delivered a conviction had they been given this evidence. (A verdict of not guilty also cannot be appealed on the grounds that the defendant actually did commit the crime, since the jury's verdict is assumed to have settled this question.) However, appeals courts may review cases if it is alleged that a procedural error resulted in the conviction of someone who is actually innocent. A defendant may even file more than one habeas corpus petition (which is not normally allowed) if it can be shown that an error "probably resulted" in the conviction of an innocent person. **See also** appeals process; habeas corpus; *Herrera v. Collins;* thirty-day rule.

affirmative defense

An affirmative defense is an argument offered at trial by a defendant (usually by the defendant's lawyers) that tries to prove that the defendant is innocent of the crime of which he or she is charged. Under American criminal law, a defendant is presumed to be innocent unless proven guilty. When serious felony charges, such as murder, are involved, the prosecution must establish guilt "beyond a reasonable doubt" in order for a jury to return a conviction. The defense is not obligated to do more than question the soundness of the prosecution's evidence. If the jury can be made to believe that the evidence of guilt is open to question, then the verdict must go in favor of the defendant, even if no evidence that the defendant is innocent has been presented. In many capital cases, however, a defense attorney will try to do more than merely discredit the prosecution's case. Some defenses are based on presenting evidence and testimony that establishes that the defendant is innocent. These are called affirmative defenses.

A successful affirmative defense must establish innocence "by a preponderance of the evidence," a less stringent legal measure than the prosecution must meet to establish guilt. But even if the jury decides that an affirmative defense is not successful, the burden of proof on the prosecution does not change. The prosecution must still prove the defendant guilty beyond a reasonable doubt. Conceivably, then, a jury could decide that the defense had failed to prove the defendant innocent yet still vote for acquittal on the grounds that the prosecution had also failed to prove the defendant guilty. It is important to distinguish between affirmative defenses, which, if successful, result in an acquittal or a conviction on a lesser charge, and mitigating circumstances, which, even if proven, do not affect the verdict but only affect the severity of the sentence imposed following the verdict.

Affirmative defenses include the concepts of alibi, self-defense, defense of others, insanity, and intoxication. Some of these defenses are an attempt to show that the defendant did not commit the criminal act at all; others admit that the defendant committed the act but argue that the circumstances under which it was committed render the act excusable.

Alibi. The word *alibi* is a Latin adverb that means "elsewhere." In the English legal tradition, it refers to evidence that a person could not possibly be guilty of a crime because he or she was somewhere else at the time the crime was committed.

Self-defense. A person is justified in using force to repel or prevent an attack, provided the person has good reason to believe that a threat is real and provided he or she uses only the degree of force needed to stop it. When used as an affirmative defense against a charge of homicide, it must be proved that the defendant was acting on a reasonable belief that killing was the minimum amount of force needed to prevent imminent bodily harm or death. It is called "perfect self-defense" if the jury agrees that the defendant's belief was accurate and votes to acquit. It is called "imperfect self-defense" if the jury decides that the defendant had a sincere belief but the belief was inaccurate or unreasonable. In that case, the jury may convict the defendant on a lesser charge than murder.

Defense of others. This is similar to self-defense, except that the defense must prove that the defendant was acting on a reasonable belief that killing was the minimum amount of force needed to prevent imminent bodily harm or death to someone else.

Insanity. Insanity is a legal term, not a term used by psychiatrists or psychologists, who generally prefer the terms *mental illness* or *psychosis*. As a legal term, *insanity* refers to a mental state sufficiently debilitating that a person is incapable of being responsible for his or her actions. Delusional beliefs—for example, the belief that one is confronting a monster or being targeted by assassins—qualify as legal insanity. Other mental disorders, however, are not so clear. As a result, the insanity defense has been one of the most controversial issues in American law. Various standards have been proposed for defining when a defendant qualifies as legally insane.

The most important tests for determining legal insanity are known as the M'Naghten test and the substantial capacity test. Under the M'Naghten test, a person is considered insane if he does not understand what he is doing or does not understand that what he is doing is wrong. Under the substantial capacity test, a person is considered insane if he is incapable of appreciating the wrongness of his actions or incapable of conforming his conduct to the requirements of the law. The M'Naghten test is stricter, since it refers only to the defendant's ability to understand his or her actions. The substantial capacity test is less strict, since it allows a defendant to plead insanity even if he knew what he was doing and understood that it was wrong, provided he can also prove that he was incapable of controlling his actions. A person with delusional beliefs would be considered insane under either of the two tests; a person subject to irresistible compulsions (for example, if he believed he was being given commands by a demonic spirit that he was powerless to disobey) would be considered insane under the substantial capacity test but not under the M'Naghten test. This is because he knew he was acting wrongly, even if he could not stop himself. Since 1984, when John Hinckley, the would-be assassin of President Ronald Reagan, successfully used an insanity defense, states have tended to adopt stricter tests for insanity, more like the M'Naghten test, moving away from the substantial capacity test.

When insanity is used as an affirmative defense against a charge of homicide, it must be proved that the defendant met the legal definition of insanity at the time the crime was committed. Even if the defendant does not suffer from a chronic mental illness, an insanity defense may be possible if it can be shown that the defendant suffered from temporary insanity—that is, a mental condition meeting the legal definition but present only at the time of the criminal act. An insanity defense differs from other affirmative defenses in that, if the defense proves its case, the defendant is not acquitted outright but is instead judged "not guilty by reason of insanity," a verdict that then usually results in commitment to a mental institution rather than release.

Intoxication. Intoxication refers to a mental state induced by drugs or alcohol in which a defendant suffers from diminished mental and physical capacity, such as impaired judgment and lack of self-control. Intoxication is not a valid defense if it can be proven that it was voluntary, since a defendant is then considered responsible for his or her own dangerous or harmful actions. Voluntary intoxication may at best be considered a mitigating circumstance, and may be grounds for a less severe sentence. However, involuntary intoxication may be used as an affirmative defense. When used as an affirmative defense against a charge of homicide, it must be proved that the intoxication rendered the defendant incapable of controlling his or her actions (as with insanity) and either that the ingestion of the intoxicating substance occurred against the defendant's will or without the defendant's knowledge or that the defendant suffered an exaggerated reaction to the substance that could not have been reasonably foreseen. **See also** burden of proof; mitigating circumstances; trial.

aggravating circumstances

Aggravating circumstances are facts related to a crime that make the offense more serious or an accused person more culpable. For example, robbery is a crime, but committing robbery using a lethal weapon is more serious, since the mere presence of a lethal weapon increases the likelihood of loss of life. Thus, the use of a lethal weapon may be considered an aggravating circumstance, and the crime in this case may be referred to as aggravated robbery.

The concept of aggravating circumstances is especially important in modern death-penalty statutes. During the penalty phase of the trial, it must be shown that at least one aggravating circumstance accompanied the crime if the death penalty is to be imposed. Since the circumstances that accompany a crime are considered to be matters of fact, the presence or absence of aggravating circumstances must be decided by a jury. The jury may consider only those aggravating circumstances that are specifically listed in the state's death-penalty statute.

The Supreme Court has not limited or defined the aggravating circumstances that must accompany a murder, so different states have established quite different lists. The only requirements are (1) that an aggravating circumstance cannot be true of *all* murders but must distinguish more serious murders from less serious murders, and (2) that an aggravating circumstance must not be stated in vague terms but must be spelled out in a way that jurors can understand. Although each jurisdiction has its own specific list of aggravating circumstances, and the items on this list can be quite varied, there are some common aggravating circumstances that appear on many lists. Aggravating circumstances fall into three broad categories: facts about the crime, facts about the defendant, and facts about the victim.

Facts about the crime include facts about why and how the crime was committed; that is, circumstances and motive. For example, when a murder is committed in the course of committing some other serious felony, such as robbery, rape, burglary, or kidnapping, the commission of the additional crime is considered by many states to be an aggravating circumstance making the crime of murder more serious. Other typical aggravating facts about the crime include that the murder occurred during an effort to evade arrest or effect an escape from custody, that multiple deaths were caused, that there was significant risk of death to others, or that the killing involved torture or was "wantonly vile." Murder for hire is also often considered an aggravating circumstance, both for the person soliciting the murder and for the person who commits the murder. Many states include specific facts about the method of killing, such as that the killing involved the use of an explosive or incendiary device, that it involved the use of poison, or that it involved the use of an assault weapon. Specific motives for the killing are sometimes listed, such as that the killing was committed for monetary gain, that it was committed to disrupt a legitimate governmental or political function (such as an election), or that it was committed because of the race, religion, or sexual orientation of the victim. Some other aggravating circumstances recognized by some states include lying in wait for the victim, shooting the victim from a moving vehicle, and using the victim as a hostage or shield.

Facts about the defendant include past history and criminal record. Many states consider it an aggravating circumstance that the defendant was previously convicted of murder. Other states broaden this to include a previous conviction for any crime involving the use of violence. Some states consider it an aggravating circumstance that the defendant is currently serving a life sentence; other states consider it an aggravating circumstance that the defendant is currently imprisoned for any serious offense. Obviously the purpose of such laws is to severely punish murders committed by prisoners, but a few states also consider having escaped from prison or being unlawfully at liberty to be an aggravating circumstance.

Facts about the victim are intended to recognize that crimes against certain types of people are especially heinous. Many states consider it an aggravating circumstance that the victim is a police officer. Firefighters and other people who ensure public safety are also often included. Many states include people who are engaged in criminal justice activities, such as judges, court officials, parole officers, jurors, witnesses, and informants. Some states consider it an aggravating circumstance that the victim was an elected official. Along quite different lines, many states consider it an aggravating circumstance that the victim was especially vulnerable to attack. Such victims may include juveniles below a certain age, seniors above a certain age, pregnant women, or people who are handicapped or disabled.

In the past few decades state legislatures have felt political pressure to be "tough on crime." They have often responded by adding new items to the list of aggravating circumstances in their state's death-penalty statute. As a result, these lists have tended to grow. At present, the state with the longest list is Delaware; its death-penalty statute lists twenty-two aggravating circumstances for homicide. **See also** *individual state entries.*

Alabama

Alabama has traditionally permitted juries to impose the death penalty, and continues to do so currently. Prior to 1819, when Alabama became a state, only two executions are recorded, and one of these took place under military, rather than territorial, jurisdiction. Because of strong "home rule" sentiment, Alabama did not have a state prison system until 1839, so prior to that time all responsibility for the punishment of crimes was left to local communities. Between 1820 and 1923, executions (all by hanging) were performed under the jurisdiction of county governments, and some 547 executions are known to have taken place. Alabama was later than most states in centralizing its executions, and did not do so until 1923, when it adopted electrocution as its method of execution. Execution by hanging continued until the electric chair was ready for use. A prison inmate, Ed Mason, built Alabama's electric chair, which was known as the Yellow Mama. The first state execution using the Yellow Mama

Between 1927 and 1965, 153 executions took place in Alabama's electric chair, known as the Yellow Mama.

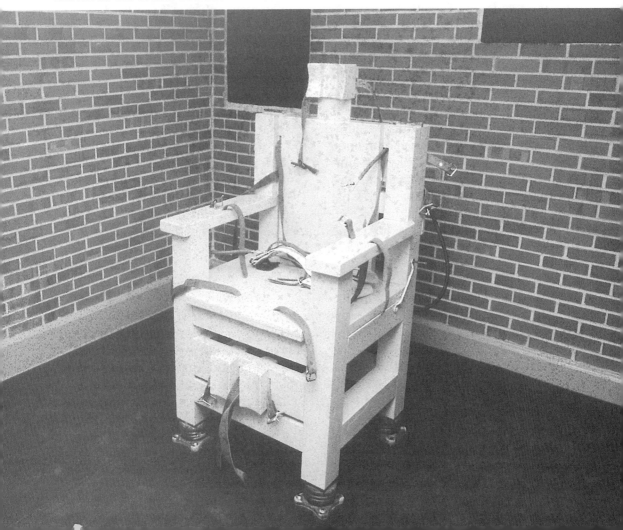

occurred in 1927. Between 1927 and 1965, 153 executions took place in Alabama's Kilby Prison using the electric chair.

In 1965 the Alabama Supreme Court declared the state's death-penalty statute unconstitutional under the Alabama State Constitution, and executions came to a temporary halt. In 1972 the U.S. Supreme Court overturned the death-penalty statutes of all other states as well. A new death-penalty statute was adopted by Alabama in 1976, following the *Gregg v. Georgia* decision, which laid out guidelines for state death-penalty statutes.

The state's current death-penalty statute allows the death penalty to be considered for (1) intentionally causing the death of another person, (2) causing the death of another person in a way that shows extreme indifference to human life, and (3) causing the death of another person in the course of committing another felony that endangers human life.

The death penalty may be imposed if at least one of eight aggravating circumstances is proven to have accompanied the crime. These aggravating circumstances are (1) that the defendant was under sentence of imprisonment; (2) that the defendant was previously convicted of a capital offense or felony involving violence; (3) that many people's lives were put at risk; (4) that the homicide occurred in the course of a rape, robbery, burglary, or kidnapping; (5) that the homicide occurred in the course of evading capture; (6) that the homicide was committed for monetary gain; (7) that the homicide was committed in order to disrupt a governmental function or enforcement of the law; or (8) that the homicide was especially heinous, atrocious, or cruel. The jury must also consider any mitigating circumstances that the defense wishes to present.

In line with the March 2005 Supreme Court decision in *Roper v. Simmons*, a person convicted of a capital offense cannot be executed if he or she was under the age of eighteen at the time of the offense. Alabama does provide for life imprisonment without parole as an alternative to the death penalty. The death penalty may be imposed if ten out of twelve jurors agree to it. The governor has the authority to grant clemency.

Following the hiatus in executions that began in 1965, executions resumed in 1983. Since 1983 there have been 28 executions in Alabama. Alabama replaced electrocution with lethal injection in 2002, although condemned prisoners may still elect to be executed by electrocution if they wish. As of April 2005, 197 people were awaiting execution on Alabama's death row. **See also** *Roper v. Simmons*.

Alaska

Capital punishment has never been used in the state of Alaska. Only eight people were executed (by hanging) in territorial Alaska between 1900 and 1957, and fewer than seven people are known to have been hanged before the region became a U.S. territory, between 1869 and 1900. Alaska abolished capital punishment in 1957, two years before becoming a state. Criminal law in Alaska does, however, provide for a sentence of life imprisonment without parole. **See also** Hawaii.

Aldridge v. United States

This landmark case heard by the U.S. Supreme Court in 1931 confirmed the legality of questioning prospective jurors about possible racial prejudice and bias, a charge on which many death-penalty opponents base their objections. The defendant, Alfred Scott Aldridge, had been accused of the murder of a Washington, D.C., police officer. During jury selection, Aldridge's lawyer attempted to probe prospective jurors for evidence of racial prejudices that might influence their decision about Aldridge, who was African American. The judge in the case refused to allow Aldridge's lawyer to ask such a question. The all-white jury that was eventually seated convicted Aldridge of first-degree murder and sentenced him to death.

On appeal, the Supreme Court overturned both the conviction and the sentence in an 8-to-1 decision. Writing for the majority, Chief Justice Charles Evan Hughes pointed out that the purpose of voir dire (the questioning of prospective jurors) is to determine whether jury members can be fair and impartial. Given the possibility that a prospective juror might harbor a prejudice against blacks, and that the right to question jurors about other forms of prejudice was already recognized, Hughes offered the opinion that questioning prospective jurors about prejudice against blacks was entirely appropriate. By disallowing this question, the judge had violated Aldridge's right to a fair trial. **See also** racial discrimination in sentencing.

American Bar Association (ABA)

The American Bar Association is the principal professional organization of American lawyers and other legal professionals. The influential organization was founded in 1878 and currently includes some 375,000 members. Its many activities include overseeing the accreditation of American law schools and providing ratings and recommendations for judicial candidates, including proposed appointees to the U.S. Supreme Court.

The ABA does not take a position either supporting or opposing capital punishment, but it has been active in seeking changes in some aspects of the administration of capital punishment in the United States. In 1983 the ABA adopted a resolution opposing the execution of juvenile offenders. In 1989 it adopted a similar resolution opposing the execution of mentally retarded offenders. The ABA has also urged changes to state and federal death-penalty laws to prevent discrimination in sentencing. In 1997 the ABA adopted a resolution urging a national moratorium on executions, similar to the one in force in Illinois, until factors leading to the possible execution of innocent defendants can be examined and corrected. **See also** Model Penal Code; Ryan, George H.

American Civil Liberties Union (ACLU)

The American Civil Liberties Union is a nonprofit public-interest organization concerned with the protection and advancement of civil liberties as defined in the Bill of Rights of the U.S. Constitution. The organization was founded in 1920 and currently includes some 275,000 members. Lawyers working for the ACLU take on cases that involve constitutional issues, including freedom of speech, freedom of the press, separation of church and state, and others. The financial resources of the ACLU make possible legal appeals of some cases that might otherwise have to be dropped because the defendant cannot afford the legal expenses.

The ACLU takes the position that capital punishment is unconstitutional because it is a violation of the "cruel and unusual" clause of the Eighth Amendment. A separate branch of the organization, the ACLU Capital Punishment Project, was organized in 1920 to work, through legal channels, for the abolition of capital punishment in the United States. Among its founders were activist Helen Keller and ACLU founder and Harvard Law School professor Felix Frankfurter, who served as an associate justice on the U.S. Supreme Court from 1939 to 1962. **See also** NAACP Legal Defense and Education Fund; opposition to capital punishment, history of (1963–present).

American League to Abolish Capital Punishment

The American League to Abolish Capital Punishment was founded in 1925 by a group of death-penalty opponents including prominent defense lawyer Clarence Darrow and former warden of Sing Sing Prison Lewis Lawes. Originally headquartered in New York City, it moved to Boston in 1949, where it shared office space with the Massachusetts Council for the Abolition of the Death Penalty. The league worked primarily by encouraging the establishment of state anti-death-penalty organizations, which lobbied state legislatures to abolish capital punishment on a state-by-state basis. By 1969 the strategy of challenging the death penalty in federal courts had proven to be more effective, and other organizations that were better able to pursue this national strategy had assumed leadership of the anti-death-penalty movement. The league quietly faded out of existence. **See also** Darrow, Clarence; Lawes, Lewis E.; opposition to capital punishment, history of (1870–1963).

American Society for the Abolition of Capital Punishment

The American Society for the Abolition of Capital Punishment was founded in 1845. It was the first national organization in the United States dedicated to the abolition of the death penalty. It owed much of its national prominence to the fact that its first president, George Mifflin Dallas, was also vice president of the United States (under President James K. Polk). The society was at its most influential in the decades prior to the Civil War. **See also** Dallas, George Mifflin; opposition to capital punishement, history of (1648–1870).

Amnesty International

Amnesty International is a leading international human rights organization, founded in London in 1961 and currently reporting over a million members in 150 countries. The chief focus of Amnesty International is the treatment of political prisoners and prisoners of conscience. The organization works for the release of political prisoners; against the use of cruel, torturous, and inhumane forms of punishment; and for improvements in prison conditions. Its members organize letter-writing campaigns and demonstrations, lobby legislators and other elected officials, and seek to sway public opinion by publicizing cases of human rights violations around the world, including in the United States.

Amnesty International also takes the position that capital punishment is cruel and inhumane and should be abolished worldwide. The organization cites the use of capital punishment in the United States as a violation of human rights. **See also** cruel and unusual punishment.

Amsterdam, Anthony Guy (1935–)

Anthony Guy Amsterdam was the lead attorney for the NAACP Legal Defense and Education Fund during the 1970s. In this capacity, he argued some of the most important death-penalty cases to reach the U.S. Supreme Court.

Amsterdam was born in Philadelphia, Pennsylvania, and received a law degree from the University of Pennsylvania. After graduation he became a clerk for Supreme Court justice Felix Frankfurter. He then served briefly as assistant U.S. attorney in Washington, D.C. In 1962 he accepted a position as professor of law at the University of Pennsylvania. While teaching law, he also began working with the NAACP Legal Defense and Education Fund representing black defendants. In 1963 he took on the case of a man sentenced to death for attempted rape even though his victim had not been injured. This led Amsterdam to take on other death-penalty cases in which it appeared that racial discrimination had played a major role in the determination of the sentence. In 1972 it was Amsterdam's argument before the U.S. Supreme Court in the landmark *Furman v. Georgia* case that led to the invalidation of every death-penalty statute then in effect in the United States. In 1976 Amsterdam represented the defendant in the *Gregg v. Georgia* case. However, in this case he was not able to persuade the Supreme Court not to reauthorize the death penalty.

In 1969 Amsterdam moved to California, taking a position at Stanford University. In 1981 he moved to New York to accept a position at the New York School of Law. He continues to serve as a defense consultant in capital cases. **See also** *Furman v. Georgia*; NAACP Legal Defense and Education Fund.

anesthesia

In 1846 surgeons began using anesthesia in the forms of ether and chloroform to render patients unconscious prior to surgery. Almost immediately some people began advocating the use of anesthesia in executions as well. An essay to that effect written by G.W. Peck appeared in the *American Whig Review* in 1848. In that article, Peck argued that it was "against good manners" and "unbecoming to civilized Christian people" not to use anesthesia in executions now that science had made it available. This proposal appears never to have been adopted, although there was clearly a widespread desire at the time to make executions as humane as possible. It was not until the late twentieth century, with the adoption of lethal injection as a method of execution, that anesthesia came to be regularly used in executions. In an execution by lethal injection, the first drug administered is an anesthetic that causes unconsciousness. **See also** lethal injection.

Antiterrorism and Effective Death Penalty Act

This law enacted by the Congress of the United States in 1996 was intended to increase punishment for terrorist acts and reduce delays between sentencing and execution in capital cases. In the early 1990s many people were willing to argue that the death penalty was not being effectively implemented because inmates sentenced to death could delay their executions by filing a seemingly interminable series of appeals, most of which involved the filing of habeas corpus petitions. Public dissatisfaction with the federal review of death-penalty cases came to a head following the bombing of the Murrah Federal Building in Oklahoma City in 1995, when Timothy McVeigh became the first person in over thirty years to be charged under federal law with a capital offense. In response to the public outcry, Congress passed the Antiterrorism and Effective Death Penalty (AEDP) Act.

The first section of the act increased federal penalties on murders involving the indiscriminate discharge of explosive devices in public places resulting in multiple deaths. The act explicitly made such murders death-eligible under federal law. The second section of the act made changes to the way in which habeas corpus petitions were handled by federal courts. The new law prohibited federal courts from considering a habeas corpus petition if the basis for the petition (i.e., the argument presented in the petition) had been the basis of a previous habeas corpus petition. In other words, once an issue raised by a habeas corpus petition has been decided, that issue may not later be reconsidered. The law also lowered the time limit for the filing of habeas corpus petitions from one year to six months (180 days). That is, from the time that the defendant's conviction and sentence are affirmed by state appeals courts (in a process known as direct review, which is a standard requirement in all death-penalty cases), the defendant has 180 days to file a habeas corpus petition in federal court. However, the passage of this time period is put on hold while state or federal courts are actually engaged in considering appeals by the defendant. In its 1996 *Felker v. Turpin* decision, the U.S. Supreme Court affirmed the constitutionality of the AEDP Act. **See also** *Felker v. Turpin;* habeas corpus.

appeals process

The systematic review of legal proceedings known as the appeals process is intended to ensure that a defendant has received a fair trial, under constitutional guarantees, and that sentences are just. This is a basic element of the judicial system. The merits and flaws of this process are a primary focus of the debate over capital punishment.

Criminal cases are first tried by state or federal courts called "lower courts." It is at these initial trials that a jury is asked to decide on the facts of a case and to determine guilt or innocence. The losing party at such a trial may then exercise the right to appeal the verdict, or require a superior court to review the court proceedings. Appeals can be lodged on various grounds when the petitioner feels that there were procedural errors in the way the initial trial was conducted. An appeal may involve such issues as whether the selection of the jury was appropriately conducted, whether evidence was appropriately introduced (or withheld), and whether instructions to the jury were correct and appropriate. If errors occurred, these errors must be serious enough that the outcome of the trial might have been different if the errors had not been made.

The appeals court that reviews the case does not reconsider the facts of the case as decided by the jury, nor does it consider new facts. The appeals court also does not issue any judgment regarding guilt or innocence. All the appeals court considers is whether the initial trial was properly conducted. Indeed, in a famous ruling in *Herrera v. Collins* (1993), the Supreme Court ruled that a person convicted of a crime does *not* have a right to appeal on the grounds of "actual innocence" (i.e., that he or she did not actually commit the crime), even when new evidence is available. (However, new evidence can be considered in an executive clemency request or introduced in the event that the plaintiff is granted a new trial on other grounds.)

Cases that begin in a state court are appealed first to a state appellate court and then (if a further appeal is made) to the supreme court of that state. Cases heard by a state supreme court can then be heard by the Supreme Court of the United States. Cases that begin in a federal court are appealed first to a federal district court of appeals and then (if a further appeal is made) to the Supreme Court of the United States. In rare cases, a case is considered so important that it is allowed to skip a step and is appealed directly to the U.S. Supreme Court.

Appeals are divided into two types, obligatory and discretionary, depending on the grounds given for the appeal and the court to which the appeal is made. Obligatory appeals are those in which the petitioner has a right to have the case reviewed, so the court has an obligation to review the case. Discretionary appeals are those in which the court may choose to review the case but has no obligation to do so. Nearly all appeals heard by the Supreme Court of the United States are discretionary. Of the roughly five thousand cases that are referred to the Supreme Court each year, the Court chooses to review fewer than two hundred. These are generally cases that involve crucial legal issues or inconsistencies in legal interpretations from one lower-court jurisdiction to another. Thus, each decision by the Supreme Court has an impact on numerous other cases besides the one actually reviewed. **See also** actual innocence; habeas corpus; *Herrera v. Collins;* Supreme Court.

Arizona

Arizona permits juries to impose the death penalty, and has permitted the death penalty for all but two years in its state history. Executions were fairly rare in early Arizona, but in recent times executions have become more common. There were thirty-eight executions in Arizona under territorial jurisdiction and six executions under federal jurisdiction prior to statehood in 1912. The method of execution in all cases was hanging. From 1912 to 1916 there were four executions under state jurisdiction; then, in 1916, voters passed an initiative that abolished capital punishment in Arizona. However, capital punishment was restored just two years later, in 1918, and executions resumed in 1920. From 1920 to 1931, there were twenty executions, all by hanging.

In 1933 Arizona replaced hanging with lethal gas as its method of execution. The first execution by lethal gas took place on July 6, 1934, when two brothers, convicted murderers Fred and Manuel Hernandez, were executed together. From 1934 to 1963, thirty-five people were executed in Arizona's gas chamber. During that time one federal prisoner was executed by hanging, since federal law did not provide for the use of gas chambers.

Following the 1972 *Furman v. Georgia* Supreme Court decision that invalidated all existing U.S. death-penalty statutes as potentially discriminatory, Arizona quickly reinstated capital punishment with a redesigned death-penalty statute on August 8, 1973. The new law, still in effect, allows the death penalty to be considered for premeditated murder; murder occurring during the commission of a sexual offense, a drug-related offense, a serious felony (kidnapping, burglary, arson, etc.), child abuse, or unlawful flight; and the murder of a police officer.

The death penalty may be imposed if one of ten aggravating circumstances is proven to have accompanied the crime. These aggravating circumstances are (1) that the defendant was previously convicted of an offense recognized as death-eligible in Arizona; (2) that the defendant was previously convicted of any other serious offense; (3) that the defendant knowingly created a great risk of death to people other than the victim; (4) that the defendant hired someone else to commit the murder; (5) that the defendant was hired by someone else to commit the murder; (6) that the homicide was especially heinous, cruel, or depraved; (7) that the defendant was in the custody of a correctional facility at the time of the offense, or on authorized or unauthorized release; (8) that the defendant was convicted of one or more other homicides occurring at the same time; (9) that the victim was under fifteen years old or was seventy years or older; or (10) that the victim was known by the defendant to be a police officer acting in the performance of his or her duties. The jury must also consider any mitigating circumstances that the defense wishes to present.

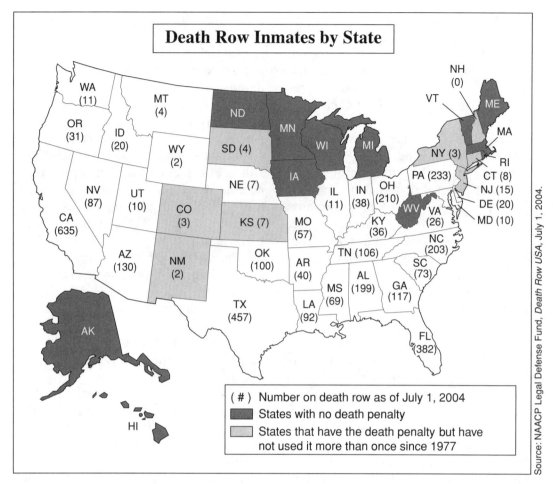

Arizona's law permitting the execution of convicted criminals who were at least sixteen years old at the time of the offense was struck down in March 2005, when the Supreme Court outlawed the execution of juveniles younger than eighteen. Arizona does provide for life imprisonment without parole as an alternative to the death penalty. The governor has the authority to grant clemency, provided he or she receives a favorable recommendation from the Board of Pardons and Paroles. However, the governor is not required to grant clemency. Like most post-*Furman* death-penalty statutes, Arizona's statute allowed for a two-phase trial. However, the jury was supposed to be present only during the guilt phase of the trial. The trial judge alone presided over the penalty phase of the trial and determined the sentence without help from a jury. This aspect of the statute was later declared unconstitutional by the Supreme Court's decision in *Ring v. Arizona* (2002), and had to be revised to include the jury during both phases of the trial.

Though the new Arizona statute was in place soon after the *Furman v. Georgia* decision, nineteen years passed before anyone was executed. In 1992 Donald E. Harding became the first person executed in Arizona since 1963. He was also the last person to be executed by lethal gas in Arizona. In November 1992 Arizona replaced lethal gas with lethal injection as its method of execution, but allowed inmates sentenced before that time to elect either method. Since 1993 twenty people have been executed in Arizona, and all chose lethal injection. As of April 2005, 129 people were awaiting execution on Arizona's death row. **See also** *Furman v. Georgia; Ring v. Arizona.*

Arkansas

Arkansas has traditionally permitted juries to impose the death penalty, and continues to do so currently. Prior to 1913, executions were carried out under the jurisdiction of county governments. Some 231 executions are known to have taken place, mostly by hanging, prior to that time. In 1863, during the Civil War, the U.S. Army seized the Arkansas state penitentiary and used it to house prisoners under federal jurisdiction. Seventy-three executions of federal prisoners occurred at the prison between 1877 and 1896. In 1913 Arkansas centralized executions at the new state penitentiary near Little Rock, which opened in 1910. The penitentiary was known as "the Wells." At the same time, Arkansas replaced hanging with electrocution as its method of execution. A total of 172 executions took place at the Wells between 1913 and 1964, when legal appeals brought the pace of executions to a standstill.

Following the 1972 *Furman v. Georgia* decision, which declared all state death-penalty statutes unconstitutional, Arkansas developed a new death-penalty statute in 1973. The new law currently allows juries to consider the death penalty for homicide, either by the defendant or by an accomplice, when it is committed under special circumstances. The law then provides a list of ten circumstances, including that the murder occurred during the commission of a serious felony, such as a rape, kidnapping, vehicular piracy, robbery, burglary, escape from prison, and drug-related felonies. The killing of a police officer, firefighter, prison official, court official, probation officer, military personnel, or the holder of public office or a candidate for public office also makes a murder death-eligible. Murder-for-hire is death-eligible, for both the murderer and the person who induces the murderer to commit the crime. The killing of someone under the age of fourteen by someone over the age of eighteen is death-eligible. Finally, a homicide committed by firing a weapon from a moving vehicle is death-eligible.

The death penalty may be imposed if at least one of ten aggravating circumstances is associated with the crime. These are similar to the special circumstances above but are considered during the penalty phase rather than the guilt phase. They are: (1) that the defendant was imprisoned at the time of the offense; (2) that the defendant was unlawfully at liberty; (3) that the defendant was previously convicted of a felony in which human lives were placed at risk; (4) that the defendant knowingly created risk of death or injury to people other than the victim; (5) that the defendant was evading arrest or attempting to escape from custody; (6) that the homicide was committed for monetary gain; (7) that the homicide was committed in order to disrupt a governmental or political function; (8) that the homicide was especially heinous, cruel, or depraved; (9) that the homicide occurred because of the unlawful detonation of an explosive device; or (10) that the victim was especially vulnerable to attack (e.g., was disabled or elderly). The jury must also consider any mitigating circumstances that the defense wishes to present.

According to the March 2005 Supreme Court decision in *Roper v. Simmons*, the death penalty cannot be imposed on a person younger than eighteen at the time of the offense. Arkansas does provide for life imprisonment without parole as an alternative to the death penalty. A unanimous jury is required to impose the death penalty. The governor has the authority to grant clemency, but clemency applications are reviewed by the Parole Board, which makes a nonbinding recommendation based on its investigation of the case.

Though the new death-penalty statute took effect in 1973, executions did not resume until 1990. In 1983 Arkansas replaced electrocution with lethal injection as its method of execution, but allowed condemned prisoners sentenced before that time to elect either method. Since 1990 there have been twenty-six executions in Arkansas. As of April 2005, thirty-eight people were awaiting execution on Arkansas's death row. **See also** *Maxwell v. Bishop.*

Assyrian Code

The Assyrian Code was a body of laws discovered by German archaeologists in the ruins of the city of Assur in Mesopotamia. The laws are inscribed on a series of stone tablets, of which only two still survive in good condition, dating from between 1500 and 1000 B.C. The laws are comparable to the older Code of Hammurabi, which was enforced in ancient Babylon. However, the Assyrian Code generally prescribes harsher punishments, and less effort is made to match punishments to their crimes. Death is the mandated penalty for a multitude of crimes, including, among others, the receiving of stolen goods. The penalty is usually imposed directly by the aggrieved party, or by the witnesses to the crime, often without the need for a trial being specified. Husbands are granted considerable discretion in the punishment of their wives for adultery. A husband may put a wife to death, or not, "as he pleases." For crimes that do not warrant the death penalty, facial mutilation (the cutting off of ears and noses) is a commonly prescribed punishment, as is forced labor in service to the king. **See also** Hammurabi, Code of.

Atkins v. Virginia

This capital case heard by the Supreme Court in 2002 revisited the question of whether the execution of a mentally retarded person is cruel and unusual. The defendant, Daryl Renard Atkins, was convicted in 1998 of abduction, armed robbery, and murder committed in 1996. Atkins and an accomplice, William Jones, had abducted the victim, Eric Nesbitt, at an automated teller machine, where they forced him to withdraw money. They then took him to a secluded location and shot him. Each defendant claimed that the other had pulled the trigger, but the jury concluded that Atkins was the shooter. During sentencing, evidence was presented that Atkins was mildly mentally retarded, with an I.Q. of 59. The jury nevertheless sentenced Atkins to death. This sentence was overturned by the Virginia Supreme Court on the grounds that a misleading sentencing form had been used. A second sentencing trial was ordered, at which the jury again condemned Atkins to death. This sentence was then appealed on the grounds that Atkins could not be sentenced to death because of his mental retardation. Citing the 1989 *Penry v. Lynaugh* decision, the Virginia Supreme Court upheld the sentence, but the U.S. Supreme Court agreed to review the case.

In a 6-to-3 decision, the Court ruled that the execution of mentally retarded offenders is cruel and unusual according to contemporary standards of decency and therefore prohibited by the Eighth Amendment. Writing for the majority, Justice John Paul Stevens noted that much had changed since the *Penry v. Lynaugh* decision. At that time, the Supreme Court ruled that, based on a survey of state laws, most of which permitted the execution of mentally retarded offenders, it could not be claimed that execution of the mentally retarded was considered inappropriate or indecent. Hence, execution of mentally retarded offenders was not cruel and unusual by the standards of that time. Following the *Penry* decision, however, many state legislatures took up the issue and revised their death-penalty statutes to prohibit the execution of persons deemed to be mentally retarded. Several other states were in the process of considering legislation, and even in states that permitted execution of mentally retarded offenders, juries rarely imposed a sentence of death on someone shown to be mentally retarded. Stevens argued that this indicated a clear shift away from the execution of mentally retarded offenders in the evolution of public sentiment—enough, in fact, that the practice should now be considered cruel and unusual.

Stevens also argued that there were good reasons for the shift in public sentiment. Unlike persons judged to be legally insane, mentally retarded people are generally able to distinguish between right and wrong. Hence mentally retarded offenders cannot take advantage of an insanity defense, even when their mental and emotional abilities render them incapable of making mature and rational decisions. The Court held that, like children, the mentally retarded should not be held to the same standards of culpability as fully rational adults.

Although this case was decided in favor of the defendant, Daryl Atkins himself could still face execution. In 2005 Atkins's IQ was remeasured at 74 to 76, above Virginia's definition of mental retardation. It is not clear whether the old score was merely wrong or whether intellectual stimulation Atkins might have experienced while assisting his legal counsel led to his improved performance on an IQ test. New legal proceedings will be needed to determine if Atkins is eligible for execution. **See also** mentally retarded offenders; *Penry v. Lynaugh.*

Barefoot v. Estelle

This 1983 Supreme Court decision ruled that the expert testimony of psychiatrists concerning a defendant's likely future behavior (and likelihood of committing another crime) may be presented to jurors in considering a death sentence. The defendant in the case, originating in Texas, was Thomas Barefoot, who had been convicted of capital murder in a jury trial. During the penalty, or sentencing, phase, two psychiatrists, neither of whom had examined Barefoot directly, testified that Barefoot's past history of criminal behavior suggested that he would continue to commit crimes, if given the opportunity. The jury recommended that Barefoot receive the death penalty.

Barefoot's lawyers appealed the sentence and requested a stay of execution until the appeals court could consider whether the testimony of the two psychiatrists had violated the defendant's rights. However, the Texas Court of Appeals refused to issue a stay of execution. Barefoot then sued W.J. Estelle Jr., the director of the Texas Department of Corrections, on the grounds that denying the stay of execution before considering the merits of the case was a violation of proper procedure. Eventually, this case was appealed to the U.S. Supreme Court.

The Supreme Court upheld the Texas Court of Appeals' denial of the stay of execution in a 6-to-3 decision. Writing for the majority, Justice Byron White pointed out that the U.S. Supreme Court, in *Jurek v. Texas* (1976), had already held that it was not impossible for jurors to make reasonable predictions about a defendant's future behavior, so there was no reason to suppose that expert psychiatrists should be any *less* able to do so. Hence, the appeal did not have sufficient merit to warrant consideration, and there was no procedural error in denying the stay of execution prior to considering the merits of the case. Thomas Barefoot was executed by lethal injection on October 30, 1984. **See also** *Jurek v. Texas;* stay of execution.

Beccaria, Cesare (1738–1794)

Eighteenth-century Italian aristocrat Cesare Beccaria is the author of *An Essay on Crimes and Punishments*, probably the single most influential early treatise on criminal justice and the first philosophical critique of capital punishment. Beccaria was born in Milan on March 15, 1738. He was educated in Parma at a Jesuit college and eventually graduated from the University of Parvia in 1758. After graduation he returned to his home in Milan, where he joined a group of young political reformers who called themselves "the academy of fists." Despite the rather violent-sounding name, this was not a group of radical malcontents but a well-connected group of upper-class intellectuals who met regularly to discuss philosophy, including political and economic theory. Allesandro

Verri, a founding member of the academy of fists, worked as an official at the prison in Milan. He arranged for Beccaria to make frequent visits to the prison, where Becarria observed conditions and interviewed prisoners. Beccaria read works by French and British Enlightenment philosophers, including the Baron de Montesquieu and David Hume, who emphasized rationality and the ability of humans to solve problems and improve society. Finally, encouraged by his friends, he wrote a long essay expressing his own ideas, *Dei deletti e delle pene* (*An Essay on Crimes and Punishments*), published in 1764. Despite its sharp criticism of the existing penal system, the book was favorably received, and began circulating widely throughout Europe. The book also became very popular in the American colonies, significantly among leading colonial politicians. Thomas Jefferson, for example, listed it as one of the works that he considered essential to an understanding of society and government.

Beccaria was strongly influenced by the Enlightenment concept of "social contract," a popular idea at the time. This was the idea that individuals in a civil society consent to give up some freedoms to a government in exchange for mutual benefits and protections. In turn, the government must treat its citizens fairly. Prior to Beccaria's essay, little thought had been given to the fairness of punishment. It was merely assumed that punishment for crimes was justified as an act of retribution—that is, criminals were punished to avenge bad acts. Beccaria insisted on a more specific justification. He viewed crimes not as moral transgressions but as acts inconsistent with the proper functioning of society. Likewise, he concluded that the purpose of punishment should not be to exact moral retribution but to prevent crimes from occurring. He wrote, "The end of punishment is no other than to prevent the criminal from doing further injury to society, and to prevent others from committing the like offense." According to this view, laws should clearly define criminal acts and clearly define corresponding punishment. Beccaria argued that punishments should be only severe enough to discourage—that is, deter—criminals, and must be in proportion to the seriousness of the crime.

Beccaria's essay was the first work on criminal justice to take a strong and principled stand against capital punishment. In Beccaria's view, life in prison should be a sufficient deterrent for even the most serious crimes; the death penalty, meanwhile, was both disproportionately severe and not an effective deterrent in any case. Deterrence, Beccaria argued, depended not on the severity of the punishment but, rather, on the certainty that the punishment would be forthcoming. Juries were understandably reluctant to impose a penalty of death; hence, the death penalty was not certain and was therefore less effective as a deterrent than a milder punishment that was certain.

Beccaria applied the theory of the social contract in another important way. A person could reasonably be expected to exchange some degree of freedom for peace and prosperity, he said, but no reasonable person would agree to exchange his or her *life* for peace and prosperity that that person would then be unable to enjoy. Since no people would be willing to enter into a social contract in which they agreed to forfeit their life, it follows that, under the terms of the social contract, no state could acquire the right to punish people with death.

Beccaria's essay was extremely influential in encouraging legal reforms and reforms in the treatment of prisoners. Indeed, Leopold II, grand duke of Tuscany, revised the penal code of Tuscany in 1789 after reading Beccaria's essay, and

Tuscany became one of the first jurisdictions in the world to abolish capital punishment. However, much as social philosophers admired Beccaria's arguments against capital punishment, few were immediately converted by such arguments. Beccaria's chief contribution, then, was to define the debate in terms that are still used after hundreds of years.

After writing his essay, Beccaria briefly took a position teaching economics at the Palatine School of Milan. His lectures on economic theory were published in 1804, ten years after his death. As an economist, Beccaria's ideas often anticipated those of important later economists such as Adam Smith and Thomas Malthus. **See also** international use of capital punishment; justification of punishment; social contract theory.

Beck v. Alabama

This 1980 Supreme Court decision concerned the constitutionality of imposing the death penalty when a jury has not been allowed to consider a verdict of guilty to a lesser (noncapital) offense. The defendant, Gilbert Beck, was accused of capital murder and tried by the state of Alabama. During the trial, the defense admitted that Beck committed a crime but argued that he was not guilty of capital murder per se, but only of a "lesser included offense," that is, a less serious category of homicide. However, under the Alabama death-penalty statute, the jury was not allowed to consider lesser offenses; it was required to choose between guilty or not guilty on the charge of capital murder only. The jury found Beck guilty. Beck's conviction was upheld by Alabama appeals courts, and was eventually appealed to the U.S. Supreme Court, which agreed to hear the case.

The Supreme Court overturned Beck's conviction in a 7-to-2 decision. Writing for the majority, Justice John Paul Stevens offered the opinion that jurors who know that a serious and violent crime has been committed but have "reasonable doubt" as to whether it was a capital offense may be inclined to overlook their doubts in order to return a conviction. Allowing them to consider lesser offenses ensures that they will return a verdict of guilty only to charges that they are confident have been proved beyond any reasonable doubt. **See also** burden of proof.

Bedau, Hugo Adam (1926–)

Hugo Adam Bedau is a prominent American scholar and philosopher, and a noted opponent of capital punishment. Bedau was born in Portland, Oregon, and graduated with honors from the University of Redlands in 1949. He completed a master's degree at the University of Boston in 1951 and a PhD at Harvard in 1961. He taught at Dartmouth and Princeton but eventually settled at Tufts University, where he worked from 1962 to 1997. He retired to the position of professor emeritus in 1997. His chief interest was in ethics and law, especially civil disobedience, social justice, and capital punishment. His 1964 book *The Death Penalty in America* was the first collection of essays to comprehensively examine the issues involved in the death-penalty controversy, and would largely define the debate for the next several decades.

Among Bedau's contributions is his argument that concepts used in the death-penalty debate, such as deterrence and prevention, must be subjected to empirical analysis. For example, claims that capital punishment deters crime are worthless, he believes, unless they can be supported by statistical studies showing the deterrent effect. Similarly, claims that innocent people may have been executed must be supported by documentation. He argues that other issues must be subjected to moral, not empirical, criticism. For example, the concept that punishment should be proportional to the crime is not based on evidence, but only on our sense of morality. We test the concept by considering how it should be applied, as by asking whether rape should be punished by rape, or life exchanged for life. Bedau is also the author of *Death Is Different: Studies in the Morality, Law, and Politics of Capital Punishment* (1987) and numerous other essays and studies. **See also** literature; Prejean, Helen.

Beidler, John X. (1831–1890)

John X. Beidler was perhaps the best known and most successful of the vigilante hangmen known as Regulators, who operated on the American frontier in the second half of the nineteenth century. In places where organized law enforcement was not yet established, the Regulators were often settlers' and ranchers' only resort against robbers and cattle rustlers. However, the Regulators operated without legal authority, serving as arresting officer, judge, jury, and executioner all in one. To protect themselves from retaliation, many of the Regulators wore masks, an image that inspired the masked hero of the popular 1930s–1950s radio and television western *The Lone Ranger*. Beidler, however, was too well known, and too much feared, to bother with a mask.

Beidler was born in Montjoy, Pennsylvania, and moved west with the frontier. He began his career as a Regulator in Kansas, where he headed a posse to capture a gang of robbers. He disabled the entire gang with a single shot, firing a howitzer cannon loaded with lead type from a printer's press. He later moved to Montana, where he was relentless in tracking down and hanging robbers, rustlers, and murderers. In one six-week period he hanged twenty-six men. As the Montana territory became more settled and legal institutions were established, Beidler retired from vigilantism. He opened a saloon and also served as customs collector for Idaho and Montana. He died in Helena in 1890. **See also** lynching; Regulators and Moderators.

Bell v. Ohio

This 1978 Supreme Court decision considered whether a death-penalty statute is unconstitutional if it prevents consideration of certain mitigating circumstances (circumstances that offset the seriousness of the offense). This case was decided at the same time as a parallel case, *Lockett v. Ohio*, which concerned the same issue. The defendant, Willie Lee Bell, was convicted of kidnapping and murder by a three-judge panel. During the penalty phase of the trial, Bell's lawyer argued that Bell, who was sixteen years old at the time of the crime, had acted out of fear of a friend, and that three years of prior drug use had impaired his judgment. Since the Ohio death-penalty statute did not recognize these factors as mitigating circumstances, the judges on the panel chose to ignore these arguments in sentencing Bell to death.

On appeal, the U.S. Supreme Court overturned Bell's sentence in a 7-to-1 decision (with one justice not participating). Writing for the majority, Chief Justice Warren Burger offered the opinion that a death penalty statute could not constitutionally exclude from consideration any mitigating circumstances that might be relevant. The effect of the decision was to make the lists of mitigating circumstances, which are included in most state death-penalty statutes, unnecessary since relevant mitigating circumstances must be considered whether or not they appear explicitly in the statute. Although lists of mitigating circumstances now serve no effective legal purpose, they also do not conflict with the *Bell* decision, so most states have never bothered to revise their statutes to remove them. As a result, while some state statutes no longer provide lists of mitigating circumstances, most states still do. **See also** aggravating circumstances; *Lockett v. Ohio;* mitigating circumstances.

benefit of clergy

This was a legalism used in the Anglo-American legal tradition to provide leniency for first-time offenders convicted of a capital crime. The concept evolved slowly out of medieval legal practices that treated different segments of society under different kinds of laws. In England, following the Norman Conquest in 1066, clergymen and church officials were subject to ecclesiastical law while laymen were subject to the secular civil laws. A clergyman who was convicted in a secular court could have his sentence waived simply by claiming to be a member of the clergy. However, there was no effective way to verify a defendant's claim to be a member of the clergy by checking church records. On the presumption that only clergymen knew how to read—which was mostly true at the time—courts verified such a claim by asking the defendant to read a passage from the Bible. However, by the fifteenth century literacy had spread to the point that many people could claim "benefit of clergy" who were not actually employed by the church. To prevent abuse of the benefit-of-clergy rule, the practice was adopted of allowing defendants, whether members of the clergy or not, to claim clerical status only once. People claiming benefit of clergy were branded on the thumb to show that they had already used this privilege, and were not entitled to do so again. Eventually the literacy requirement was dropped as no longer relevant, and the idea that the clergy were not subject to secular laws was abandoned as well. However, "benefit of clergy" remained a relic of the older legal system, and came to mean that a person convicted of a capital offense could claim leniency if it was a first-time offense, even though the accused was known not to be a member of the clergy.

The benefit-of-clergy rule was widely used even in colonial America. A benefit-of-clergy defense was not allowed for murder but was allowed for lesser offenses, such as burglary and robbery, crimes that in that era often were eligible for a death sentence. Thus, the benefit-of-clergy rule was an effective way to make punishment more proportional to the seriousness of the crime. Following the American Revolution, the new states reformed their penal codes. Most both defined fewer crimes as capital offenses and eliminated the benefit-of-clergy rule. Southern states generally lagged behind northern states in making these reforms. The last state to eliminate the benefit-of-clergy rule was South Carolina in 1869. **See also** capital crimes.

Bentham, Jeremy (1748–1832)

Jeremy Bentham was an eighteenth-century British social reformer and founder of the ethical philosophy known as utilitarianism, a moral theory according to which actions are considered right if they increase society's overall happiness, and wrong if they increase overall unhappiness. In the eighteenth century, Bentham was a partial opponent of capital punishment, arguing that its use should be greatly limited. To this day, utilitarian arguments both for and against capital punishment continue to be raised.

Bentham was a child prodigy who graduated from Oxford University by age fifteen. By age twenty he had completed a law degree and was admitted to the bar in London. His most influential book, *Introduction to the Principles of Morals and Legislation*, was published in 1789. In it he argues that actions and laws are justified to the extent that they tend to increase overall happiness and decrease suffering. The punishment of criminals, he argued, should also be decided on this basis. Since punishment of criminals is obviously going to increase the suffering of the criminals punished, it can be justified only if there is a significant increase in the happiness of others. Punishment can be justified if it deters crime or reforms criminals, thereby producing a safer and happier society, but punishment that has no such effect is morally offensive, since it merely increases overall suffering and is as morally wrong as the crime it is intended to punish. Bentham saw only limited value in capital punishment. Obviously the death penalty could not be used for rehabilitation. So, he believed it should be used only for crimes for which it could be shown to be an effective deterrent.

Bentham designed what he considered a model prison called the Panopticon, but was never able to arrange the funding to have it built. It was designed to put inmates under surveillance by jailers they could never see. Bentham argued that because inmates could never be sure when they were being watched, they would tend to behave better at all times, establishing discipline based on mental uncertainty in the inmate, not on harsh authority.

Bentham also helped to write laws limiting the number of crimes punished by death in England. Among his other social reforms, he helped write laws establishing minimum wages for workers and outlawing child labor in England. **See also** utilitarianism.

Jeremy Bentham is the father of utilitarianism, a moral theory that values those actions that result in happiness for the greatest number of people.

Berns, Walter (1919–)

Walter Berns is a contemporary political philosopher and prominent proponent of capital punishment. Berns was born on May 3, 1919, in Chicago, Illinois. He received a PhD in political science from the University of Chicago in 1951 and went on to a distinguished teaching career at Louisiana State University, Yale University, Cornell University, and Georgetown University. His most influential book on capital punishment, *For Capital Punishment: Crime and the Morality of the Death Penalty*, was published in 1979.

Berns challenges many old assumptions about the purpose of punishment. In particular, he argues that using punishment to rehabilitate criminals, though motivated by humanitarian ideals, leads to a view under which society bears the responsibility for criminals, rather than the view that criminals are responsible for their acts. Berns rejects punishment's deterrent value; rather, he proposes that justice is best served not by trying to reform or deter criminals but by trying to ensure that crimes are met with a fair, consistent, and certain response. In Berns's opinion, the old retributive theory of punishment is best: The purpose of punishment is merely to punish. According to this view, the only just and appropriate punishment for the crime of murder is death. **See also** justification of punishment; literature.

Bible

The Bible is the sacred text of Christianity; portions of the Christian Bible are revered in Islam, and the first five books of the Bible constitute the Torah, the scriptural source of history and law in Judaism. As the most influential document in Western civilization, to which millions of believers turn for moral and ethical guidance, the Bible has figured prominently in the debate over capital punishment from ancient times to the present day. Its verses both support and oppose the death penalty.

The passage from the Bible most cited in favor of the death penalty is Genesis 9:6, "Whoso sheddeth man's blood, by man shall his blood be shed: for in the image of God made he man." Many theologians, notably the Presbyterian minister George Barrell Cheever, interpreted this passage as a command by God requiring civil authorities to punish murder with death. Since man is made in the image of God, murder was a crime against God, as well as being an injury to its victim. Thus, God had endowed civil governments with the responsibility of exacting justice for the crime of murder.

More liberal religious interpretations view this passage not as a command, however, but as a prediction; that is, not as an instruction to governments to shed the blood of murderers but as a warning to murderers that is in the same spirit as another scriptural verse, "All they that take the sword shall perish with the sword" (Matthew 25:52). Other passages cited by proponents of capital punishment include Numbers 35:31, "Take no satisfaction for the life of a murderer, which is guilty of death: but he shall be surely put to death."

Old Testament passages cited by opponents of capital punishment include Leviticus 19:18, "Thou shalt not avenge, nor bear any grudge against the children of thy people"; Deuteronomy 32:35, "To me belongeth vengeance"; and, most famously, the Sixth Commandment, one of the Ten Commandments believed to have been inscribed by God on tablets of stone given to the prophet Moses, rendered in Deuteronomy 5:17, "Thou shalt not kill." **See also** Cheever, George Barrell; religious views.

Billington family

Members of the well-known Billington family served as executioners in England from 1884 to 1905. The first member of the family to be an executioner was James Billington (1847–1901), who had wanted to be an executioner from an early age. He eventually managed to be hired as a hangman in Yorkshire in 1884, and later became the chief executioner in London in 1892. He was assisted by his three sons, Thomas Billington (1872–1902), William Billington (1873–1934), and John Billington (1880–1905). When their father died in 1901, William and John continued to serve as executioners, but after the death of John in 1905, William retired from the profession, leaving the job of chief executioner to be taken up by the Pierrepoint family. **See also** executioners; Pierrepoint family.

Black Code

The Black Code was a group of laws passed by the Kansas territorial legislature in 1858 prescribing the death penalty for people who encouraged black slaves to run away from their masters or assisted them in running away. The purpose of these unusually harsh laws had little to do with stopping runaway slaves. In fact, no one was ever charged with violating these laws. At the time, settlers from eastern states were moving into Kansas, some of whom favored slavery and some of whom opposed it. The proslavery legislature passed the Black Code largely to discourage antislavery settlers from moving into the territory. Other laws were passed that prevented antislavery citizens from holding public office and from serving as jurors. Nevertheless, these efforts to make Kansas unfriendly to people opposed to slavery failed. By the time Kansas became a state in 1861, a majority of its citizens opposed slavery, and Kansas joined the Union as a free state.

At the time the Black Code was enacted, it was unusual for the death penalty to be prescribed for crimes other than robbery, rape, or murder. Assisting a runaway slave was defined as "grand larceny," which was not generally considered a sufficiently serious crime to be punishable by death. **See also** capital crimes; Kansas.

Blackmun, Harry A. (1908–1999)

Harry A. Blackmun was an associate justice of the U.S. Supreme Court from 1970 to 1994. He participated in numerous decisions involving the death penalty, and was more often than not a dissenting voice, disagreeing first with the relatively liberal decisions of the early 1970s but then becoming more liberal himself as the Court became more conservative. By the end of his career, Blackmun, at first a consistent supporter of capital punishment, had become the Court's most outspoken opponent of capital punishment.

Blackmun was born in Nashville, Illinois. He received a scholarship to study at Harvard, where he majored in mathematics. Following graduation in 1929, he entered Harvard Law School, from which he graduated in 1932. He served briefly as a clerk with the U.S. Eighth Circuit Court of Appeals but joined a Minneapolis law firm in 1933. While in private practice, he also taught law at the St. Paul College of Law and at the University of Minnesota. In 1959 President Dwight D. Eisenhower appointed him a judge on the Eighth Circuit Court, where he had previously served as a clerk. There he developed a reputation for thorough and scholarly opinions. In 1970 President Richard Nixon nominated Blackmun to the U.S. Supreme Court, following two unsuccessful nominations of candidates who were rejected by the Senate for their conservative views. Despite a generally conservative record, Blackmun was confirmed.

During the early part of his term on the Court, Blackmun consistently voted in support of capital punishment. In 1970 his majority vote in *Maxwell v. Bishop* prevented the invalidation of numerous capital punishment statutes, and he dissented from the 1972 *Furman v. Georgia* decision that invalidated every capital punishment statute in the country. Blackmun then voted with the majority in the 1976 *Gregg v. Georgia* decision that reestablished capital punishment in the United States. However, by 1987 Blackmun's views had begun to shift. In the 1987 *McCleskey v. Kemp* decision, the Court ruled that mere statistics could not be used to establish that a state's death-penalty statute had been unfairly applied in a particular case. Blackmun dissented in the decision, agreeing with Justice William Brennan that no individual should be sentenced under a law that could be shown—by statistical measures—to have been often applied in an arbitrary and prejudicial manner. Thereafter, Blackmun became increasingly concerned that the death penalty was not being imposed fairly. Finally, in 1994 Blackmun announced, in a strongly worded dissent from the Court's decision not to review the case of *Callins v. Collins*, that he could no longer "tinker with the machinery of death," and that he would henceforth oppose the use of capital punishment. However, that same year Blackmun stepped down from the Supreme Court. He enjoyed a few years of peaceful retirement and died on March 4, 1999. **See also** *Callins v. Collins; Maxwell v. Bishop.*

Booth v. Maryland

This 1987 Supreme Court case addressed the constitutionality of presenting victim impact statements during the penalty phase of a trial. The defendant, John Booth, had been convicted of murdering an elderly couple during an apparent robbery of their home. During the penalty phase of his original trial, the prosecution was allowed to introduce as evidence victim impact statements that described the emotional impact of the crimes on the family of the victims. Booth was sentenced to death; on appeal, the sentence was upheld by the Maryland Court of Appeals. The U.S. Supreme Court then agreed to review the case.

The Court overturned Booth's sentence in a 5-to-4 decision. Writing for the majority, Justice Lewis Powell offered the opinion that, since a defendant often does not know the victim or the victim's family, facts about the impact of the crime on the victim's family are not relevant to the blameworthiness of the crime itself. Introducing victim impact statements, the Court ruled, can therefore only increase the likelihood that the jury will base its decision on irrelevant factors and arrive at an inappropriately harsh sentence. Considered a landmark at the time, this ruling would not stand long; it was reversed in *Payne v. Tennessee* (1991). **See also** *Payne v. Tennessee*; victim impact statements.

Bovee, Marvin H. (1827–1888)

Marvin H. Bovee was a nineteenth-century social reformer and death-penalty opponent in the midwestern United States. He successfully led campaigns to abolish the death penalty in Wisconsin and Iowa.

Bovee was born in Amsterdam, New York, on January 5, 1827. His father was a successful politician who served in the New York legislature and was elected to Congress in 1836. The family moved to Wisconsin in 1843, and Bovee followed his father into a career in politics. In 1853 he was elected to the Wisconsin legislature, where he introduced a bill abolishing capital punishment. The bill passed, making Wisconsin the second state (following Michigan) to permanently abolish capital punishment. Bovee later promoted capital punishment reform in Iowa, Minnesota, and New York. His book *Christ and the Gallows; or, Reasons for the Abolition of Capital Punishment* was published in 1869.

While opposed to capital punishment, Bovee was a practical reformer. Much of his work was directed at restricting the types of crimes for which the death penalty was allowed, and in 1884 he campaigned for presidential candidate Grover Cleveland, a firm advocate of capital punishment. Bovee died on May 7, 1888, in Whitewater, Wisconsin. **See also** Iowa; Wisconsin.

Bradford, William (1755–1795)

William Bradford was an influential lawyer and judge in post-Revolutionary Pennsylvania. His 1792 essay on capital punishment resulted in significant changes in penal law, first in Pennsylvania and eventually throughout the United States.

Bradford was one of a long line of William Bradfords who played significant roles in American history. His great-grandfather established the first printing press in the American colonies in 1685, and his father, who also worked as a printer, became known as "the patriot printer of 1776" for publishing a newspaper that promoted the cause of independence from England. Bradford, however, preferred law to printing, and he began studying law at Princeton. In 1776 he interrupted his studies to join the Continental army during the American Revolution. He served with distinction and rose to the rank of colonel. He also served simultaneously as a representative to Congress from Pennsylvania. The harsh winter of 1777–1778 at Valley Forge and subsequent fighting left Bradford in ill health, so in 1779 he was forced to resign from the army. He returned to the study of law; in 1780 he was appointed to the position of attorney general for the state of Pennsylvania. Eleven years later, in 1791, he was appointed to the Pennsylvania Supreme Court, and in 1794 he became the second attorney general of the United States. However, still in poor health, he died the following year.

In 1792, while serving on the Pennsylvania Supreme Court, Bradford issued a report on the use of the death penalty in Pennsylvania, drawing on his experience as attorney general. The report was published in 1793 as an essay titled "An Enquiry How Far the Punishment of Death Is Necessary in Pennsylvania." In the essay Bradford argued that requiring the death penalty for a multitude of crimes actually made it difficult for prosecutors to obtain convictions, since juries were less likely to return a conviction if they knew the defendant would be executed. In response to Bradford's report, Pennsylvania became the first state to limit use of the death penalty to first-degree murder. Other states followed suit, reforming their penal codes to limit the death penalty to only the most serious crimes. **See also** capital crimes; Pennsylvania.

Branch v. Texas

This 1972 Supreme Court decision was a companion to the landmark *Furman v. Georgia* decision of the same year. The defendant in the *Branch* case was a black man, Elmer Branch, convicted of raping, but not killing, a sixty-five-year-old white woman. For his crime he was sentenced to death. His sentence was appealed on the grounds that racial prejudice had probably contributed to the severity of his sentence, since few whites were sentenced to death for rape. The U.S. Supreme Court agreed to review the case, bundling it with the *Furman v. Georgia* case, which also raised the issue of arbitrary and discriminatory sentencing in capital cases. The Court overturned Branch's sentence, agreeing with the defense that the statute under which Branch was sentenced left jurors free to indulge their prejudices in imposing sentencing, thus violating the constitutional promise of equal protection under the law. **See also** *Furman v. Georgia; Jackson v. Georgia.*

breaking on the wheel

Breaking on the wheel refers to a method of torture and execution that was used in Europe during the Middle Ages. Some instances of its use are also recorded in the American colonial era. The condemned prisoner was first stretched across an ordinary wagon wheel. His limbs were then broken so they could be folded around the rim of the wheel and

A Catholic priest watches as a Protestant man is broken on the wheel. A common form of torture and execution in the Middle Ages, breaking on the wheel was later deemed inhumane.

even interlaced among the spokes. The condemned prisoner, was possibly wheeled around town, but eventually the axle of the wheel was set vertically into the ground, allowing the wheel to rotate parallel to the ground. The condemned prisoner was then left to die slowly. **See also** torture.

Brennan, William J. (1906–1997)

William J. Brennan was an influential associate justice of the United States Supreme Court from 1956 until 1990. In his nearly thirty-five-year term on the Court, he remained a steadfast liberal advocate of expansion of civil liberties and an adamant opponent of the death penalty.

Brennan, the son of Irish Catholic immigrants, was born in Newark, New Jersey. He studied law at Harvard University and then practiced law with a prominent law firm in Newark. He was appointed to the New Jersey Superior Court in 1949, and in 1952 he was appointed to the New Jersey Supreme Court. Four years later, in 1956, he was appointed to the U.S. Supreme Court by President Dwight Eisenhower, who hoped that the appointment would be politically popular with urban Catholic voters and help his reelection campaign. As a member of the Supreme Court, Brennan wrote numerous important decisions, taking a consistently liberal position on civil rights and desegregation, freedom of the press, and strict separation of church and state.

Brennan's views on capital punishment were most strongly felt when he joined the majority in the 1972 *Furman v. Georgia* decision, which overturned death-penalty statutes throughout the country. Other members of the majority objected to death-penalty statutes only because they were not being applied fairly and consistently, but Brennan took the most liberal position that the death penalty per se should be judged unconstitutional. He wrote, "Death is an unusually severe and degrading punishment," and argued that the death penalty was "uniquely degrading to human dignity." Four years later, in 1976, Brennan dissented from the majority opinion in *Gregg v. Georgia*, which allowed states to reintroduce death-penalty statutes that established clear guidelines for jurors in imposing death sentences. Again, Brennan argued that the death penalty per se was no longer "morally tolerable" in a civilized society.

Brennan retired from the Supreme Court in 1990 after suffering a stroke, and died in 1997. **See also** *Furman v. Georgia; Gregg v. Georgia;* Supreme Court.

Brooks, Charles (1942–1982)

Charles Brooks, who was executed in Texas on December 7, 1982, was the first person executed by lethal injection. Brooks was convicted of the 1976 kidnapping and shooting of David Gregory, a Fort Worth auto mechanic. Brooks's accomplice, Woody Loudres, plea-bargained to receive a forty-year prison sentence, but Brooks was sentenced to death. An appeal to the U.S. Supreme Court, based on the disparity between the two sentences, was turned down, and Texas governor Bill Clement refused to grant a reprieve. Texas had adopted lethal injection as a replacement for the electric chair in 1977, but no executions were scheduled until 1982, when the Brooks execution became the first test of the untried method. The execution went smoothly and as planned, confirming for advocates of the death penalty that lethal injection was a humane and reliable method of execution. **See also** lethal injection.

Buenoano, Judias (1943–1998)

Judias (Judi) Buenoano was executed by electrocution in Florida in 1998, the first woman executed in Florida since 1848. A convicted serial killer and arsonist, Buenoano was notorious not only as one of the few women executed in U.S. history but also as Florida's "black widow" for murdering (or attempting to murder) a husband, two lovers, and her son.

Buenoano was born Judias Welty in Quanah, Texas. She had a difficult childhood, which included periods of juvenile detention and reform school. When she was old enough to be on her own, she took a job as a nursing assistant. She gave birth to an illegitimate son, Michael, in 1961, then married and had two more children. From this point forward, her life became an interesting string of accidents and tragedies for which she was the beneficiary of substantial insurance payments. Her husband, James Goodyear, died suddenly in 1971, and the family's house burned down the same year. In 1972 Judi moved with her children to Pensacola, Florida, to live with her new lover, Bobbie Joe Morris. In 1977 she moved her family, renamed Buenoano (Spanish for "Goodyear"), to Colorado following another house fire. There Morris died of an undiagnosed illness. Her son Michael drowned in 1980 after suffering arsenic poisoning, and her new lover John Gentry narrowly escaped death from an automobile explosion in 1983, himself the victim of arsenic poisoning finally traced to Buenoano. Goodyear's and Morris's bodies were exhumed and also found to have been victims of arsenic poisoning. Buenoano was tried and convicted of two of the murders in a sensational trial. She spent thirteen years on Florida's death row before her 1998 execution. **See also** Snyder, Ruth.

Bundy, Theodore (1946–1989)

Theodore (Ted) Bundy was one of the most notorious and prolific serial killers ever executed in the United States. The brutality and sensational nature of his crimes, his ability to prolong his appeals process and delay his execution, and profiles of him suggesting a diabolical personality masked by charisma, intelligence, and the appearance of a model citizen led advocates of capital punishment to point to him as a prime symbol of the need for the death penalty.

Bundy was born in Vermont and raised in Tacoma, Washington. He performed well in school and entered the University of Washington to study law. His only brushes with the law were two arrests on suspicion of burglary and auto theft during high school. In the early 1970s the Pacific Northwest was terrorized by a series of disappearances and murders of young women. Bundy's name appeared on a list of people wanted for questioning after his name was reported in connection with one abduction, but this lead was not pursued and he moved to Utah in 1973. In 1974 and 1975 at least five young women disappeared from the Salt Lake City area and mountain resorts of Colorado, and Bundy's name came up in tracing the whereabouts of suspects in the Washington murders. Evidence connecting Bundy to the crimes was discovered in his automobile after he was pulled over for driving erratically, and he was identified by another woman as the man who had attempted to kidnap her from a Salt Lake City shopping mall. Bundy was charged with multiple counts of murder, and he was extradited to Colorado to stand trial there first.

The case drew national headlines when Bundy escaped from custody in 1977. The target of a nationwide manhunt, Bundy fled to Florida and embarked on a killing spree, including the murders of two women in a Florida State University sorority house, brutal attacks on two other sorority women, and the murder of a twelve-year-old Jacksonville girl. He was finally arrested in Pensacola days later, and tried, convicted, and sentenced to death by the state of Florida.

Bundy spent the next decade on Florida's death row, delaying his execution with multiple unsuccessful appeals, some of which reached the Supreme Court. His success in delaying his execution fueled angry criticism of the appeals process in capital cases, and is cited as a factor in the courts' inclination to restrict the nature of appeals they agree to hear. Bundy finally tried to delay his execution by confessing to numerous murders to which he had not previously been connected (at that point he was officially charged with thirty-six murders, but it is thought that he may have been prepared to confess to as many

Theodore Bundy (center) confers with his attorneys during his 1979 trial. He was convicted and spent a decade on death row before being executed in Florida's electric chair.

as one hundred deaths), but he was ultimately denied a stay of execution and put to death on January 24, 1989, in Florida's electric chair. **See also** appeals process.

burden of proof

The central concept in any criminal proceeding, including those involving the death penalty, is that the defendant is innocent until proven guilty. The state, or prosecuting authority, thus bears what is known as the "burden of proof," a popular term that refers to two, more precise legal concepts. The first legal concept is more properly called "burden of production," which refers to the responsibility of an accuser to present enough evidence to justify going forward with a trial. In a criminal proceeding, the prosecuting attorney presents such evidence at a preliminary hearing. If the prosecutor fails to provide sufficient evidence to show that a crime has been committed, the defendant is assumed to be innocent, and no trial is held.

The second legal concept involved in the notion of burden of proof is more properly called "burden of persuasion." This is the responsibility of one party (the prosecutor in a criminal trial or the plaintiff in a civil trial) to provide enough evidence to have the case decided in his or her favor *at trial*. The purpose of most trials is to settle disputes concerning relevant facts. For example, in a murder trial the question to be settled is whether the defendant in fact committed murder—in other words, whether he or she caused the death of the victim intentionally and maliciously. The dispute is settled by a judge, a panel of judges, or a jury. These "fact finders" are charged with deciding whether the evidence presented is sufficient for the prosecutor's view to be accepted. Again, the burden of proof falls chiefly on the prosecutor. The defendant is presumed innocent, and can be found guilty only if enough evidence is presented to overturn this initial presumption. However, the defense may also choose to offer a stronger argument called an affirmative defense, which is an attempt to prove the defendant innocent. While an affirmative defense is being offered, the burden of persuasion falls on the defense. However, this does not change the burden of persuasion still placed on the prosecution. If *both* sides fail to prove their case, the presumption of innocence prevails, and the defendant is acquitted.

The extent or weight of the burden of persuasion differs depending on the type of trial. There are three levels or weights that the burden of proof may carry. In most civil proceedings, the plaintiff (or party bringing the case) has the burden of establishing his or her position "by the preponderance of the evidence." This means that the plaintiff's position must be shown to be, on balance, more likely than the opposing position. A stronger standard of evidence may be required in some civil proceedings, in which the plaintiff may be required to provide "clear and convincing evidence." This means that the plaintiff's position must be shown to be highly probable or reasonably certain, although some room for reasonable doubt may remain. In criminal cases, including death-penalty trials, a still stronger standard of evidence is required. In criminal cases, the prosecution is required to prove its case "beyond a reasonable doubt." This means that the prosecution must show that there is no real possibility that the defendant is not guilty (i.e., that the guilt of the defendant is a practical certainty). This is the strongest standard of evidence, but practical certainty is nevertheless not the same as absolute certainty; the modern system of criminal justice recognizes that 100-percent certainty is often an impossibility in human affairs.

The presumption of innocence, and the high standard of evidence required at criminal trials, has been an important factor in the outcome of some high-profile court cases. For example, after the 1996 acquittal of former football star O.J. Simpson, on trial for the murder of his ex-wife and her friend, it was revealed that most, if not all, of the jurors believed that Simpson was guilty. But believing that a defendant is guilty is not the same as believing that his or her guilt has been proven "beyond a reasonable doubt." Many of the jurors also believed that the Los Angeles police had mishandled evidence so badly that the evidence against Simpson was not trustworthy. Therefore, they did not think that the evidence presented by the prosecution at trial met the burden of persuasion required of a criminal trial. **See also** affirmative defense; trial.

burning at the stake

Burning at the stake was an ancient method of execution in which the condemned prisoner was tied to a pole and surrounded by wood or other flammable material that was then set on fire. Burning to death is extremely painful, and, as the flames tended to spread slowly, death by this method could be lingering and terrifying as well.

The practice has been used in many societies and eras. The Code of Hammurabi, created by the Babylonian ruler Hammurabi around 1780 B.C., prescribed burning as the appropriate punishment for arson. Christian martyrs were burned at the stake in ancient Rome. Some native North American Indian tribes are known to have burned prisoners captured in battle. Since fire was associated symbolically with the purification of the soul, burning at the stake was the preferred punishment for religious crimes in continental Europe, Ireland, and Scotland from the fifteenth through the eighteenth centuries. The Church of Rome condemned many advocates of the Protestant Reformation to be burned at the stake for heresy, including Girolamo Savonarola in 1498 and Michael Servetus in 1553. Perhaps the most famous burning at the stake was that of the French peasant girl and military patron Joan of Arc, who was executed for heresy and witchcraft in 1431.

Burning at the stake was less frequently practiced in England, where people condemned of witchcraft or heresy were hanged. It was also used less often in colonial America, where it was allowed as a punishment for a slave who had murdered his master and in rare cases as the punishment for a wife who had murdered her husband, a crime known as "petty treason," or to punish arson that resulted in death. In most such cases, the sentence was commuted to simple hanging, or the prisoner was hanged or strangled first and then burned after death. The last recorded burning at the stake in the United States took place in 1825, replaced by hanging thereafter. **See also** Hammurabi, Code of; Joan of Arc.

Calcraft, William (1800–1879)

William Calcraft was an executioner in England from 1829 to 1874; his position was an official post in the English criminal justice system. During his forty-five-year career—the longest of any known executioner—he executed approximately 450 people, making him perhaps the most prolific executioner in history (although twentieth-century British executioner Albert Pierrepoint performed roughly the same number of executions in a much shorter period of time). Calcraft was the last British executioner to hold a salaried position. Later British executioners worked on a fee-for-services basis. Calcraft held a regular position at Newgate Prison, but he also performed executions at Horsemonger Lane Gaol in Surrey and at other prisons throughout England and Ireland. He loved to travel, and the British railway system made it possible for him to take jobs at prisons around the country to supplement his regular income. To further supplement his income, he was also allowed to keep the clothes of the prisoners that he executed, and he often sold these to Madame Tussaud's Chamber of Horrors, a wax museum that occasionally featured lifelike figures of executed criminals.
See also executioners.

California

California has traditionally permitted juries to impose the death penalty, and continues to do so currently. Historically, capital punishment was practiced in the territory of California while the region was part of Mexico. At that time, executions were carried out by means of a firing squad, the method favored under Mexican law. Twenty-six executions are known to have taken place under Mexican jurisdiction. When California came under American control, the firing squad was mostly replaced with hanging. The last execution by firing squad in California took place in 1852.

After statehood was achieved in 1850, capital punishment was authorized in California by the Criminal Practices Act of 1851, and in 1872 capital punishment was made part of the California state penal code. The law required that executions take place in "some convenient private place" (i.e., out of public view). Prior to 1891, executions were carried out under the jurisdiction of county governments, so each county had to provide its own private location. Between 1851 and 1892, 172 executions (by hanging) took place in California. In 1891 the law was changed to require that all executions take place at a state prison. At the time there were two state prisons, one at San Quentin and one at Folsom. San Quentin hosted its first hanging in 1893; Folsom held its first in 1895. Although there was no official rule, it became customary for first-time offenders to be executed at San Quentin, while repeat offenders were executed at Folsom. Between 1893 and 1942, 307 people were hanged at the two prisons, 215 at San Quentin and 92 at Folsom.

In 1937 a gas chamber was built at San Quentin, and the state legislature replaced hanging with lethal gas as the prescribed method of execution for offenders sentenced after August 27, 1937. The first person executed by lethal gas was Robert Cannon in 1938. The last person hanged in California was Lisemba Major, who was convicted of murder in 1936 and hanged at San Quentin in 1942. From 1938 to 1965, 194 people were executed in the gas chamber at San Quentin.

In 1972 the California Supreme Court ruled that the California death-penalty statute was cruel and unusual, under the California state constitution. Voters promptly approved an amendment to the constitution to permit capital punishment, but that same year, in the *Furman v. Georgia* decision, the U.S. Supreme Court invalidated all death-penalty statutes in the country as potentially discriminatory and arbitrary. The state legislature tried to reinstate the death penalty in 1973, but the new statute did not provide for the presentation of evidence of mitigating circumstances, so, following the guidelines laid out in the *Furman* decision, the California Supreme Court ruled that this new statute was still unconstitutional. Finally, in 1977 a death-penalty statute was adopted that met constitutional tests.

Under present California law, the death penalty may be considered for homicide under special circumstances. These special circumstances include that the homicide was premeditated or performed in the course of committing another felony in which human life was endangered. They also include the use of an explosive device, use of armor-piercing ammunition, use of poison, lying in wait, torturing a victim, and firing a weapon from a vehicle.

The death penalty may be imposed if one of twenty-one aggravating circumstances is proven to have accompanied the crime. The list of aggravating circumstances appears similar to the special circumstances noted above, but aggravating circumstances are considered during the penalty phase of the trial rather than during the guilt phase. The aggravating circumstances are (1) that the homicide was committed for monetary gain; (2) that the defendant was previously convicted of murder; (3) that the defendant was convicted of more than one murder in the current case; (4) that the homicide involved the use of a concealed explosive device; (5) that the homicide was committed in the course of evading arrest or attempting to escape from custody; (6) that the homicide involved the use of a mail bomb; (7) that the victim was a police officer; (8) that the victim was a federal law enforcement official; (9) that the victim was a firefighter; (10) that the victim was a witness to a crime; (11) that the victim was a prosecutor; (12) that the victim was a judge; (13) that the victim was a government official; (14) that the homicide was especially heinous, cruel, and depraved; (15) that the homicide involved lying in wait; (16) that the homicide was committed because of the victim's race, religion, or ethnicity; (17) that the homicide occurred in the course of another serious felony; (18) that the homicide involved the use of torture; (19) that the homicide involved the use of poison; (20) that the victim was a member of a jury; or (21) that the homicide was a drive-by shooting. The jury must also consider any mitigating circumstances that the defense wishes to present.

Under California law, a person convicted of a capital offense cannot be executed if he or she was under the age of eighteen at the time of the offense. California does provide for life imprisonment

without parole as an alternative to the death penalty. A unanimous jury is required for the death penalty to be imposed. The governor has the authority to grant clemency, unless the defendant has been convicted twice of a felony. In that case, four members of the seven-member state supreme court must concur in recommending clemency.

The first execution in California following reinstatement was that of convicted murderer Robert Alton Harris, executed in the gas chamber at San Quentin in 1992. The following year, David Mason became the last person to die by lethal gas in California. In 1993 the California legislature adopted lethal injection as an alternative to lethal gas, allowing condemned prisoners to choose between the two methods. However, in 1994 the California Supreme Court ruled that execution by lethal gas was cruel and unusual, but condemned prisoners are still permitted to choose death by lethal gas if they strongly prefer it to lethal injection. The first execution by lethal injection took place in 1996, and all subsequent executions have used that method. Since 1992, two people have been executed in California by lethal gas and eight by lethal injection. As of April 2005, there were 644 people awaiting execution on California's death row, the largest number of any state. **See also** San Quentin State Prison.

Callins v. Collins

A capital case the Supreme Court declined to review in 1994, *Callins v. Collins* is noteworthy nevertheless for the impassioned, lone dissenting comment of Justice Harry A. Blackmun. Blackmun's dissent was remarkable both because it became one of the most often-

Protesters demonstrate outside San Quentin prison as Robert Alton Harris is executed in the gas chamber in 1992.

quoted condemnations of capital punishment and because Blackmun had been, up to that point, a consistent supporter of capital punishment. The justice had become convinced that capital punishment could not be tolerated because it was, he now believed, impossible to be certain that the punishment was applied fairly:

> From this day forward, I no longer shall tinker with the machinery of death. For more than 20 years I have endeavored—indeed, I have struggled—along with a majority of this Court, to develop procedural and substantive rules that would lend more than the mere appearance of fairness to the death penalty endeavor. Rather than continue to coddle the Court's delusion that the desired level of fairness has been achieved and the need for regulation eviscerated, I feel morally and intellectually obligated simply to concede that the death penalty experiment has failed.

As a dissenting opinion, Blackmun's words had no legal force, but they had a strong influence on the nature of the debate, and have often been cited in later majority decisions. **See also** Blackmun, Harry A.; *Rudolph v. Alabama.*

capital crimes

Capital crimes are those crimes for which the penalty of death may be imposed; such offenses are thus sometimes known as death-eligible crimes. Although the penalty of death has generally been reserved for the most serious crimes, historically the crimes that have been judged serious enough to merit the death penalty have varied widely. In ancient Greece, an early Athenian law known as the Draconian Code made nearly every crime a capital offense, but most other societies considered this standard unacceptably harsh. Other ancient legal codes, including the Babylonian Code of Hammurabi and the Roman Law of the Twelve Tables, specified death as the penalty for numerous crimes, not just murder, as long as the crime was considered seriously harmful to the peace and security of society.

In early American colonies, there was a long list of crimes considered capital offenses; however, the lists were somewhat different between the northern colonies and the southern colonies. Many of the northern colonies had been founded by religious groups who had come to the New World seeking freedom to practice their faith without restriction. Many of these sects, such as the Puritans, observed strict moral codes and imposed harsh penalties for so-called moral crimes. Thus the death penalty was often considered appropriate for such transgressions as adultery, bestiality, blasphemy, idolatry, incest, and sodomy. Witchcraft was an important capital crime, and in Massachusetts twenty-six people were executed as witches, mostly during the infamous Salem witch hunt of 1692. In the northern colonies, crimes against property were less likely to be considered capital offenses. In the southern colonies, however, the reverse was true: Burglary, robbery, and housebreaking were considered capital crimes, but moral transgressions were rarely recognized or prosecuted as crimes.

Some crimes were recognized as capital offenses throughout the colonies. Arson was one such crime, and it was the only crime for which free whites were executed by burning at the stake. (Slaves, in contrast, were executed by burning for various crimes.) Rape was also a capital crime throughout the colonies. Petty treason, defined as the murder or attempted murder of a husband by his wife, was also widely recognized as a capital offense. In seaport colonies, especially Virginia and Rhode Island, piracy was an important capital crime.

Indeed, in colonial Rhode Island, more people were executed for piracy than for any other crime.

Following the American Revolution, the new states wrote new constitutions and frequently revised their criminal codes in the process of drafting such constitutions. Many were influenced by works on criminal justice by Cesare Beccaria, Benjamin Rush, and William Bradford, which expressed eighteenth-century Enlightenment ideals of reason and freedom and opposed vengeful punishment based on superstition and religious dogma. The death penalty was consequently limited. Robbery and rape continued to be considered capital crimes, but in practice they rarely resulted in a death sentence unless a murder was also involved.

Meanwhile, the federal government also made espionage and treason capital offenses under federal law. Some state jurisdictions followed suit, making treason a capital offense under state law, but states rarely prosecuted the crime of treason. (There were a few exceptions during the Revolutionary War and the Civil War.)

The definition of capital crimes changed little until 1977, when the U.S. Supreme Court ruled in *Coker v. Georgia* that a death sentence is cruel and unusual punishment for the crime of rape when the victim is not killed. Following this ruling, it has generally been accepted that a death sentence may not be imposed in the United States for any crime that does not involve a victim's death, either as a result of intentional malice or as a result of reckless disregard for human life. Treason and espionage are justified as exceptions on the grounds that they are the ultimate crimes against the state itself. However, the Supreme Court so far has not had a chance to rule on this question, since no one has been sentenced to death for one of these crimes since 1977. Therefore, the status of treason and espionage as capital offenses is currently undetermined.

With the possible exceptions of treason and espionage, the only crimes that are now considered to be capital offenses in the United States are certain categories of homicide. Under the 1972 *Furman v. Georgia* decision, state death-penalty statutes must clearly distinguish homicides that are death-eligible from those that are not. Some states choose to do this by defining a few specific categories of homicide as death-eligible, but most states distinguish death-eligible homicide by means of a list of statutory "special circumstances"—similar to aggravating circumstances—at least one of which must be alleged to be true for the homicide to be considered a capital crime and the process of a death-penalty trial to be put in motion. **See also** murder; special circumstances.

censorship of reporting on executions

In early America, first-person accounts of executions commonly appeared in newspapers and public notices, often far from the site of the execution. It would have been impossible to censor such accounts, as most executions were held in public and could be witnessed by anyone who wished to attend. Beginning in the 1830s, however, public viewing of executions came to be regarded as offensive to public sensibilities, and states began to pass laws prohibiting public executions. Members of the press were still permitted to attend privately conducted executions, and their reports catered to popular tastes for sensational, even lurid, description. Eventually these reports were viewed as virtually as offensive as direct viewing of executions. Moreover, the press loved to report on the errors and difficulties that frequently accompanied executions, since these were what made any one execution different from all the rest. This often made the officials presiding over the executions appear foolish and incompetent.

As a result, officials sometimes tried to discourage press reports of executions. In 1888 New York passed a law prohibiting journalists from reporting on executions. Colorado and Minnesota passed similar laws in 1889. Today such censorship would be ruled unconstitutional, but at the time, the Bill of Rights was more narrowly interpreted as applying only to federal laws. The state laws had little effect and were generally ignored. In 1891 the state of New York attempted to enforce the law by prosecuting several newspaper editors who had printed reports of a sensational quadruple execution. The public outcry against censorship was so intense that the New York legislature was forced to repeal the law.

Officials turned from attempting to prevent reporters from writing about executions to attempting to limit access to the executions themselves. This tack was made easier when hanging, which required more elaborate, large mechanisms and open space, was replaced by electrocution and lethal gas, which took place in small, closed rooms deep within prison walls. Prisons instituted policies prohibiting reporters from bringing cameras to executions. As a result, while there are many photographs of hangings, there are only two known photographs of the use of an electric chair. Both were obtained by reporters who smuggled small cameras surreptitiously into the execution chamber, hidden in their clothes. The first and most famous of these photographs was taken in 1928 at the execution of Ruth Snyder, whose trial for murdering her husband had caused a public sensation. The second was taken in 1949 at the execution of James "Mad Dog" Morelli.

The only court ruling on the constitutionality of limiting press access to executions is a 1991 decision, *KQED, Inc. v. Vasquez*, by the U.S. District Court, Northern District of California. The defendant in the case, Daniel B. Vasquez, was the warden of San Quentin State Prison in 1990 when the prison announced a strict policy prohibiting reporters from bringing recording equipment of any kind with them when viewing executions. This policy included not only audio and video recorders but even sketch pads, pencils, pens, and paper. The San Francisco public radio station KQED challenged the policy in court, claiming that they should be allowed to record the historic execution of Robert Alton Harris, the first person to be executed in California since 1967. The district court ruled that the prison warden's prohibition of audio and video recorders was reasonable but that the prohibition of pens, pencils, and paper was not. The court also ruled that, under constitutional guarantees of freedom of the press, at least some members of the press must be permitted to attend executions, although the court allowed prison officials to continue to determine which members of the press would be permitted to attend.

Technically, since the U.S. Supreme Court never ruled on this or any similar case, this decision is binding only in the Northern District of California. However, most jurisdictions follow roughly the same guidelines. It is generally recognized that, as representatives of the public interest, at least some members of the press must be permitted to witness and report on executions. However, photography is still banned, as are tape recorders and video cameras. **See also** Snyder, Ruth; viewing of executions.

Cheever, George Barrell (1807–1890)

George Barrell Cheever was the most prominent proponent of capital punishment in the United States in the decades before the Civil War. Cheever was born in Hallowell, Maine, in 1807 and educated at Bowdoin College. He then studied theology at Andover Seminary and was ordained as a Congregationalist minister in Salem, Massachusetts. Eventually he became the pastor of the Allen Street Presbyterian Church in New York.

Before the Civil War, two issues were guaranteed to inflame passions and spark controversy. One, of course, was the issue of slavery; the other was capital punishment. Cheever was adamantly opposed to slavery, but he became a vocal advocate of capital punishment. In 1842 he published *Punishment by Death: Its Authority and Expediency* in part as a reply to arguments by opponents of capital punishment. In this book, Cheever focused on refuting the argument that the death penalty had little deterrent effect on criminals. How, he asked, could opponents of capital punishment argue with one breath that the death penalty is too severe and should be abolished in favor of life imprisonment on humanitarian grounds and then with the next breath argue that life imprisonment was more frightening to criminals and therefore served as a better deterrent? In 1846 Cheever published *Defense of Capital Punishment*, a comprehensive treatment of the argument in favor of capital punishment as it was then understood.

As a clergyman, Cheever's advocacy rested on the biblical justification for capital punishment. Cheever held the view that God had placed a clear moral obligation on civil governments to punish murder with death. Against the argument that putting a prisoner to death cut short the time in which he or she might repent, Cheever replied that the expectation of a long life might delay repentance, and that the best way to encourage repentance would be to promise the prisoner a prompt and certain execution.

Cheever did not, however, advocate the death penalty for crimes other than murder, and favored a method of execution that was as painless and humane as possible.

The highlight of the capital punishment controversy in the 1840s was a widely publicized public debate between Cheever and New York legislator John L. O'Sullivan, a vocal crusader against capital punishment, held in New York City in 1843. The debate, conducted over three evenings, addressed the question "Ought Capital Punishment to Be Abolished?" Since the question was stated in a way that made Cheever's position the negative view, Cheever insisted on speaking second, following customary rules of debating. This gave him the opportunity to rebut O'Sullivan's points. On the second evening O'Sullivan assumed that he would be allowed to speak second and arrived without a prepared talk, planning only to rebut Cheever. However, Cheever again refused to speak first, and O'Sullivan was forced to speak extemporaneously. His presentation was somewhat rambling and disjointed as a result. O'Sullivan was better prepared for the final evening, but newspaper accounts still awarded the victory to Cheever. The debates left death-penalty advocates feeling that they had won an important victory and death-penalty opponents feeling that they had been treated poorly. Chiefly, the debates established that capital punishment was a divisive issue on which the two sides could find little common ground. Acrimonious letters to the editor appeared in New York newspapers for months following the debates. **See also** Bible; O'Sullivan, John L.

Chessman, Caryl (1920–1960)

Because of his skill as a writer and his success in delaying his own execution, Caryl Chessman was one of the best-known death row inmates of the twentieth century. He was born on May 27, 1920, in St. Joseph, Michigan, and acquired a record of delinquency as a boy, graduating from petty theft to auto theft and armed robbery. By the time he was a teenager he had been sentenced to a juvenile camp (from which he escaped twice), a reform school, and eventually the state prison, where he spent two years. While in prison, Chessman developed an interest in writing and expressed a desire to become a writer, but when he was released from prison at the age of nineteen, Chessman promptly returned to crime with a group of friends known as the Boy Bandit Gang. Chessman and his gang were eventually captured, following a shootout with police, and Chessman was returned to prison. He escaped briefly but was recaptured and remained in prison until December 1947. In January 1948, less than two months after his release, he was rearrested and charged with kidnapping with intent to perform rape, which was a capital offense. Chessman was convicted and sentenced to death.

Few people have questioned Chessman's guilt, but the trial itself was a procedural nightmare. The judge apparently made several rulings prejudicial to the defense, but the trial could not be reviewed on appeal because no readable transcript of the trial had been made. The elderly court reporter who recorded the trial used an old-fashioned style of shorthand known only to himself. When he died suddenly, before transcribing most of his notes, none of the other court reporters were able to complete his transcription. Despite this gross procedural irregularity, Chessman was never given a new trial.

Chessman made nearly fifty appeals, challenging both his conviction and his sentence. Fifteen of these appeals were reviewed by the U.S. Supreme Court, but

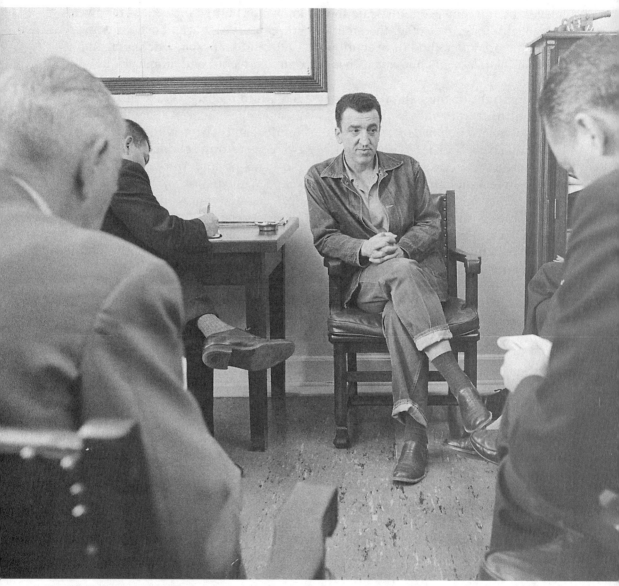

One of the most famous death row inmates of the twentieth century, Caryl Chessman holds a press conference at San Quentin prison in 1960 after receiving his eighth stay of execution.

none of the rulings were decided in his favor. Chessman also received no less than eight stays of execution. He remained on San Quentin's death row for close to twelve years.

While living on death row, Chessman rediscovered his ambition to be a writer. His first book, *Cell 2455 Death Row*, was a best seller and was made into a movie, which was released in 1955. This book and movie were largely responsible for bringing the death penalty to public attention in the 1950s, and made Chessman an international celebrity. His second book, *Trial by Ordeal*, was also a best seller. His third book, *The Face of Justice*, which was less popular, was a thoughtful discussion of the death penalty not focused specifically on his own case. Chessman's writings earned him broad support and sparked an international movement to plead for clemency for him. His supporters ranged from humanitarian Albert Schweitzer to actress Brigitte Bardot.

On May 2, 1960, California governor Edmund Brown refused to grant Chessman a ninth stay of execution, and Chessman was put to death in San Quentin's gas chamber. Brown later repented his decision to let Chessman be put to death. In his 1989 book, *Public Justice, Private Mercy*, Brown called Chessman "a nasty, arrogant, unrepentant man, almost certainly guilty of the crimes he was convicted of." However, he then remarked that he did not think Chessman's crimes deserved the death penalty, and concluded, "I should have found a way to spare Chessman's life." **See also** international criticism of the United States.

Clark, Stephen (1805–1821)

Stephen Clark was executed for arson in 1821, at the age of sixteen. One night in 1820 Clark set fire to a barn in Salem, Massachusetts, and the fire spread to nearby houses. No one was seriously injured, but arson of a dwelling at night was a capital offense in Massachusetts at the time. Although Clark was young and this was his first offense, he was denied clemency and was hanged on a public gallows. His execution was widely viewed as excessively harsh punishment for his crime, and helped spur growing opposition to capital punishment in the United States in the early half of the nineteenth century. **See also** opposition to capital punishment, history of (1648–1870).

clemency

Clemency is the cancellation of charges or voiding of the sentence against someone who has been (or who might be) convicted of a crime, issued by a person with appropriate executive authority. Historically, the power to grant clemency, commonly issued by decisions known as pardons, was vested in the king. Kings as long ago as the ancient Babylonians and Hebrews are known to have exercised such powers. Pardons were traditionally supposed to be used to prevent obvious miscarriages of justice and to give the law flexibility. In the eighteenth century, the Italian social philosopher Cesare Beccaria wrote disapprovingly of the power of clemency, saying that it gave a monarch arbitrary power to overrule the judiciary. After the French Revolution, Beccaria's criticisms won favor, and the president of the new French republic was denied the power to issue pardons. However, French emperor Napoléon I restored the power in 1802. It has generally been felt that the power of rulers to overrule sentences imposed by the courts is, despite its potential for abuse, a necessary element in the checks and balances that are built into a just legal system. However, since the power to grant pardons exists to prevent injustices within the legal system, the granting of pardons supersedes accepted legal processes. A defendant's rights, however, are defined within those ordinary legal processes. Hence, it is sometimes pointed out, no defendant has a *right* to a pardon, not even a defendant who (it is agreed) *deserves* a pardon.

In the United States, the president has the power to grant pardons for federal crimes, and the governors of each state generally have the power to grant pardons for crimes within the jurisdiction of their state. In many states, however, the governor's power is limited, and in most states it is shared with a special administrative body, such as a Board of Pardons, which ensures that the power to grant pardons is not abused. Since the term *pardon* implies a gift bestowed by a monarch, and governors and presidents are not monarchs, the term *clemency* or *executive clemency* is now generally used instead. There are three types of executive clemency, all derived from the power of a ruler (or executive) to grant pardons but very different in their consequences, especially in capital cases.

The first type of clemency is merely a temporary delay in the carrying out of a sentence. This is called a reprieve. A reprieve may occur when a person who has been condemned to death files an appeal but the court does not issue a stay of execution while the appeal is being considered. The issuing of a stay of execution by the court is not automatic but is itself a court decision that must be made after considering the relevant arguments. When an execution is scheduled to occur before the court has had time to consider issuing a stay of execution, it may be appropriate for the governor to issue a temporary delay in the execution to give the courts extra time.

The second type of clemency is the replacement of a more severe sentence with a less severe sentence. This is called commutation of the sentence. Sometimes a commutation is granted only on certain conditions, such as the condition that the prisoner not apply for parole. There is a strong incentive for prisoners to obey these conditions: At the discretion of the governor, a commutation may be reversed and the original sentence reimposed.

Historically, the commutation of a death sentence to a sentence of life imprisonment was fairly common, especially if it was determined that, for one reason or another, circumstances existed that could not be considered by the trial jury. For example, between 1924 and 1966, approximately one-quarter of the death sentences imposed by Florida juries were later commuted by Florida governors. In North Carolina, between 1909 and 1954, the proportion was even higher: Approximately one-third of all death sentences were commuted. In recent years, however, commutation of sentences has become extremely rare. Two factors may be responsible. On the one hand, more careful judicial review of trials may now be overturning unjust sentences before they even come to the attention of an executive clemency board. In other words, it is possible that fewer death row inmates now merit clemency. On the other hand, presently, a majority of the American public so strongly supports the death penalty that many governors may feel it is politically risky to commute sentences, so they may avoid doing it except in rare cases.

The third type of clemency is a full pardon, or exoneration, under which all punishment is canceled. Some legal scholars maintain that a full pardon overturns the conviction as well as the sentence—in other words that a full pardon "blots out guilt." That is clearly the intention in some cases. In the Supreme Court decision *Herrera v. Collins* (1993), Chief Justice William Rehnquist offered the opinion that executive clemency, not the appeals courts, is the appropriate legal recourse when new evidence comes to light proving that a person convicted of a crime was actually innocent. In such cases, clemency is offered because it is now believed that the person convicted was not guilty in the first place. However, a full pardon may also be granted for other reasons. Unlike a reprieve or commutation of a sentence, a full pardon may be granted even before a person has been charged with a crime, thus preventing the matter from ever going to trial.

An amnesty is similar to a pardon, and it has the same basis in law, namely the power of a ruler to void a sentence. However, while a pardon is given to a single person for specific crimes, an amnesty is generally given to a broad group of people for unspecified crimes. **See also** exoneration; *Herrera v. Collins;* Ryan, George H.; stay of execution.

closure

The concept of closure is central to recent arguments advanced by supporters of capital punishment, who maintain that the death of a murderer allows the family of the victim to move beyond their grief and anger, and that they could not do so if the murderer remained alive in prison. Psychologists use the word *closure* to refer to the feeling that a difficult or painful matter has finally been put to rest. Allowing the family of the victim to feel closure is thought to be important because, although no penalty can restore the lost life of the victim, it may be possible for a penalty to help in the healing process by which the family of the victim moves toward a renewed state of psychological well-being. It is also sometimes argued that allowing members of the victim's family to witness the execution will promote closure and encourage healing.

However, the extent to which the execution of a murderer really assists in the healing of the victim's family is unknown. Some family members report feeling a sense of closure after hearing of, or witnessing, an execution, but others report no such feeling, and some even report disappointment that an anticipated feeling of closure remained unrealized. It seems clear that the emotional responses of survivors to the execution of a murderer are highly individual and influenced to a large extent by previously held views on capital punishment. **See also** justification of punishment; victims' rights.

Coker v. Georgia

This 1977 Supreme Court decision concerned whether the death penalty may constitutionally be imposed for the crime of rape. The defendant, Ehrlich Anthony Coker, was convicted of armed robbery and rape committed after he escaped from a Georgia prison, where he was serving a life sentence for various crimes, including murder, rape, kidnapping, and aggravated assault. At the time, Georgia was one of two jurisdictions that still allowed the death penalty for rape, as long as the rape was accompanied by these aggravating circumstances: The defendant was previously convicted of a capital crime, the rape was committed during the commission of another crime, and the crime was "wantonly vile." During the penalty phase of Coker's original trial, the jury agreed that all of these aggravating circumstances were present in this case, and sentenced Coker to death.

On appeal, the U.S. Supreme Court overturned the sentence. Writing for the Court, Justice Byron White offered the opinion that the Eighth Amendment prohibited punishments that were excessively severe or disproportionate. He argued that, while rape was a serious crime—indeed just short of homicide as a violation of the victim's integrity and autonomy—it did not involve taking the victim's life. Hence, taking the defendant's life was not a proportionate penalty. Two justices, William Brennan and Thurgood Marshall, offered the stronger (but concurring) opinion that the death penalty was *never* permissible under the Eighth Amendment.

The Court's opinion was interpreted to mean that rape is nearly as serious a crime as capital murder but not serious enough to warrant the death penalty. Its effect was to dramatically limit the types of crimes for which the death penalty could be imposed. Now, with few exceptions, a crime must involve homicide in order for the death penalty even to be considered. Also, since rape was the crime most subject to discriminatory sentencing—black men convicted of rape were far more likely to be sentenced to death (especially if the victim was white) than white men convicted of the same crime—the *Coker* decision has had the effect of dramatically reducing the proportion of blacks on death row. **See also** capital crimes.

Colorado

Colorado has traditionally permitted juries to impose the death penalty, and continues to do so currently. Six executions are recorded as having taken place in Colorado territory prior to statehood in 1876. Between 1877 and 1933, fifty-eight people were executed in Colorado by means of hanging. In 1933 Colorado replaced hanging with lethal gas as its means of execution. Between 1933 and 1967, thirty-two people were executed in Colorado's gas chamber. The last person to be executed by lethal gas in Colorado was convicted murderer Luis Monge in 1967. Monge was also the last person to be executed anywhere in the United States until the execution of Gary Gilmore in Utah in 1977.

Following the invalidation of the state's death-penalty statute by the 1972 *Furman v. Georgia* decision, Colorado reinstituted capital punishment in 1975. The state's current death-penalty statute allows the death penalty to be considered for the crime of homicide under special circumstances. These special circumstances include that the homicide occurred after deliberation, that it was committed in the course of another serious felony, or that it was committed in a manner that indicated extreme indifference to human life. Causing the death of a person through perjury or suborning of perjury, thus causing an innocent person to be convicted and executed, is a death-eligible offense, as is causing the death of a child for which one is responsible. In Colorado a person can also be charged with capital murder if a death results from the use of a controlled substance distributed by the defendant.

The death penalty may be imposed if at least one of fourteen aggravating circumstances is proven to have accompanied the crime. The list of aggravating circumstances appears similar to the special circumstances noted above, but aggravating circumstances are considered during the penalty phase of the trial rather than during the guilt phase. The aggravating circumstances are (1) that the defendant was under sentence of imprisonment for a prior felony; (2) that the defendant was previously convicted of a felony; (3) that the victim was a police officer, firefighter, court official, elected official, or federal law enforcement officer; (4) that the homicide occurred in the course of a kidnapping; (5) that the homicide was a murder-for-hire and the defendant either performed the murder or solicited another to perform the murder; (6) that the homicide involved lying in wait or the use of an explosive device; (7) that the homicide occurred in the course of another serious felony; (8) that the homicide was committed for monetary gain; (9) that the defendant knowingly created a great risk of harm to people other than the victim; (10) that the homicide was especially heinous, cruel, and depraved; (11) that the homicide was committed in order to evade arrest or escape from custody; (12) that the homicide was committed in a manner that manifested extreme indifference to human life, or that two or more victims were killed during the same criminal episode; (13) that the victim was under twelve years old; or (14) that the homicide was committed because of the victim's race, religion, or ethnicity. The jury must also consider any mitigating circumstances that the defense wishes to present.

Under Colorado law, a person convicted of a capital offense cannot be executed if he or she was under the age of eighteen at the time of the offense. Colorado does provide for life imprisonment without parole as an alternative to the death penalty. A unanimous jury is required for the death penalty to be imposed. The governor is authorized to grant clemency by commuting a sentence of death to a sentence of life imprisonment or to a sentence of not less than twenty years at hard labor.

Following the hiatus in executions that began in 1967, executions did not resume until 1997. By that time Colorado had replaced lethal gas with lethal injection as its means of execution. To date, the only person to be executed by lethal injection in Colorado is Gary Lee Davis in 1997. As of April 2005, three people are on Colorado's death row awaiting execution. **See also** *Furman v. Georgia.*

competence

Competence is a complex legal term with numerous applications. In general, it means having the right qualifications or capabilities to undertake a task. For example, a person is competent to make up a will if he or she understands what property is involved, who will receive it, and how the will affects the distribution of property. Similarly, a witness at a trial is said to be competent if the witness is in a position to know the truth of the matter about which he or she will testify. Even a court can be said to be competent when it has the appropriate jurisdiction, or legal authority, to hear a case. One of the most important applications of the term is to the defendant in a trial. A defendant is said to be competent if he or she understands the nature of the charges and appreciates the severity of the sentence that may be imposed. A defendant must be judged competent if he or she is to undergo trial.

Likewise, a condemned prisoner must be judged competent in order to be executed. A prisoner is judged competent to be executed if the prisoner understands that he or she is being put to death and for what reason. In some cases, prisoners on death row have developed mental illnesses that make their competence to undergo execution questionable. **See also** mentally ill offenders; trial.

Connecticut

Connecticut has traditionally permitted juries to impose the death penalty. However, even though a death-penalty statute is currently on the books, no executions have taken place in Connecticut since 1960, and executions were relatively rare even before that time.

In colonial Connecticut, twenty executions by hanging are recorded—seven for witchcraft, eight for murder, four for sodomy, and one for burglary. In the eighteenth century, Connecticut discontinued executions for crimes such as witchcraft and sodomy. From 1777 to 1936, eighty-eight hangings took place in Connecticut, mostly for murder. In 1935 Connecticut replaced hanging with electrocution as its method of execution, and the first execution using an electric chair took place in 1937. Between 1937 and 1960, only eighteen executions took place. The last person executed in Connecticut was Joseph Taborsky, who was electrocuted in 1960 after being convicted of robbery and murder.

Following the 1972 *Furman v. Georgia* decision, which invalidated Connecticut's old death-penalty statute, the state was quick to reinstate the death penalty, having a new statute in place by 1973. The state's current death-penalty statute allows the death penalty to be considered for homicide under special circumstances. These special circumstances are (1) that the victim was a police officer, corrections officer, or firefighter; (2) that the homicide was a murder-for-hire and the defendant either performed the murder or solicited another to perform the murder; (3) that the defendant was previously convicted of murder; (4) that the defendant was under a sentence of life imprisonment; (5) that the homicide was the killing of a kidnapping victim by the kidnapper; (6) that death was caused by cocaine, heroin, or methadone sold by the defendant; (7) that the homicide occurred in the course of a sexual assault; (8) that two or more persons were killed during the same criminal episode; or (9) that the victim was under the age of sixteen.

The death penalty may be imposed if at least one of seven aggravating circumstances is proven to have accompanied the crime. The list of aggravating circumstances appears similar to the previous list of special circumstances, but aggravating circumstances are considered during the penalty phase of the trial rather than during the guilt phase. The aggravating circumstances are (1) that the murder occurred during the commission of a felony of which the defendant was previously convicted; (2) that the defendant was previously convicted of two or more offenses involving injury to others; (3) that the defendant knowingly created a great risk of injury or death to people other than the victim; (4) that the homicide was especially heinous, cruel, and depraved; (5) that the defendant hired someone else to commit the murder; (6) that the defendant was hired by someone else to commit the murder; or (7) that the homicide was committed with an assault weapon. The jury must also consider any mitigating circumstances that the defense wishes to present.

Under Connecticut law, a person convicted of a capital offense cannot be executed if he or she was under the age of eighteen at the time of the offense. Connecticut does provide for life imprisonment without parole as an alternative to the death penalty. A unanimous jury is required for the death penalty to be imposed. The governor has the authority to grant only temporary reprieves. The power to grant clemency is otherwise vested in a special Board of Pardons.

In 1995 Connecticut replaced electrocution with lethal injection as its method of execution. However, since no one has been executed in Connecticut since 1960, this method of execution has yet to be used. As of April 2005 nine people were awaiting execution on Connecticut's death row. **See also** *Furman v. Georgia; Roper v. Simmons.*

Constitution of the United States

The Constitution of the United States is the primary document on which the government of the United States is based. The Constitution lays out the structure of the government, delineates the powers and responsibilities of each branch of government, and in some cases specifically limits the powers of government. All laws in the United States, including criminal laws, must conform to principles of justice articulated in the Constitution.

The Constitution was written during the summer of 1787 by the delegates of the original thirteen states meeting in a convention in Philadelphia. It was sent to the states for ratification in September, and by June 1788 ten of the thirteen state legislatures agreed to adopt the Constitution. In March 1789 George Washington took office as the first president under the new Constitution, and the United States of America, in its current form, was born. However, concerns that the new federal government had been made too powerful led to the adoption, two years later, in 1791, of a body of ten amendments to the Constitution, known collectively as the Bill of Rights, which

This painting depicts the signing of the U.S. Constitution in 1787. Criminal laws and the practice of capital punishment must conform to principles outlined in the Constitution.

specified individual and states' rights. Seventeen additional amendments have since been added to the Constitution, the latest in 1992.

As the document that defines and limits the powers of government in the United States, the provisions of the Constitution are obviously important to criminal law, including the practice of capital punishment. Four sections of the Constitution are particularly relevant to capital punishment; namely, Section 9 of Article I, the Fifth Amendment, the Eighth Amendment, and the Fourteenth Amendment.

Article I, Section 9. This is the section of the Constitution that guarantees the right of habeas corpus—that is, the right to challenge in federal court the authority of any other court to try a crime and to impose sentence. The right of habeas corpus is the central principle that makes possible the appeal of death sentences for review by federal courts, including by the U.S. Supreme Court.

Fifth Amendment. The Fifth Amendment grants certain fundamental rights to criminal defendants, including the right to refrain from self-incrimination. The Fifth Amendment also guarantees that punishment may not be imposed without "due process."

Eighth Amendment. The Eighth Amendment prohibits the imposition of "cruel and unusual" punishment, and provides the basis for most of the legal challenges that have been brought against the death penalty. Various applications of the death penalty, such as imposing a death sentence for the crime of rape and imposing a death sentence on someone who is mentally retarded, have been prohibited on the grounds that such applications would be cruel and unusual. The Eighth Amendment is central to the argument advanced by opponents of capital punishment that the death penalty itself should be considered cruel and unusual.

Fourteenth Amendment. The Fourteenth Amendment was added to the U.S. Constitution shortly after the Civil War to limit the power of states to discriminate against newly freed slaves. The amendment has since been interpreted as giving federal courts broad powers to review state laws and to apply the protections in the Bill of Rights to state governments. Many of the rights of criminal defendants in capital cases are the result of the "due process" and "equal protection" clauses of the Fourteenth Amendment. **See also** cruel and unusual punishment; equal protection; habeas corpus.

corporal punishment

A phrase often mistakenly used interchangeably with "capital punishment." The two terms have different, but historically related, meanings. The word *corporal* comes from the Latin word *corpus*, meaning "body," so corporal punishment refers to any form of physical punishment that is inflicted on a person's body. This includes whipping and caning, but it also includes displaying a prisoner in a pillory or stocks, as well as more permanent physical punishments such as branding or the chopping off of parts of the body and, ultimately, execution.

Any form of corporal punishment is intended to be painful and humiliating, on the theory that pain and humiliation are the best and most obvious deterrents to misbehavior. The spanking of children by their parents is a mild and widely accepted form of corporal punishment. In modern Western countries, corporal punishment was widely used prior to the eighteenth century, but with the rise of prisons, it dropped out of use as a statutorily defined punishment for specific crimes. Nevertheless, corporal punishment, including pillories and whippings, continued to be used inside prisons to enforce discipline.

The following are traditional methods of corporal punishment, listed in order of increasing severity.

Pillory and stocks. A pillory is a wooden frame with three holes for holding the prisoner's head and hands, leaving the feet free. Stocks are a wooden frame for securing the prisoner's feet, and sometimes both feet and hands, while leaving the head free. A prisoner would be secured in the frame and left for a period of time (which varied with the perceived seriousness of the offense). The frame was always located in a prominent public place, and prisoners were often pelted with rotten fruit, or even stones, thrown by onlookers and passersby. The pillory and stocks were used extensively in England and in colonial America in the seventeenth and eighteenth centuries. Vagrancy and public drunkenness were among the crimes they were used to punish.

Whipping, flogging, or caning. In this type of punishment, the prisoner is tied to a post and stripped to the waist (or entirely naked). He is then struck repeatedly on the back, the shoulders, and (sometimes) the buttocks. The severity of the whipping depends in part on how often the prisoner is struck and in part on what is used to strike him. A lash or whip is a single piece of rope or a strip of rawhide attached to a handle. The rope or rawhide was usually knotted to make the blows more painful. A cat-o'-nine-tails is a lash with nine knotted strips of rope or rawhide attached to the same handle. A scourge or flail is a multitailed lash with metal barbs embedded in the tails. Caning refers to a beating inflicted by means of a bamboo cane. Whipping of some kind or another is undoubtedly the oldest and most common form of punishment in the world. As a form of punishment, it has much to recommend it. It is painful but generally not fatal. By specifying the number of strokes to be administered, it is possible both to match the severity of the punishment to the seriousness of the crime and to ensure that roughly equal punishment is administered to similar offenders. Whipping of one kind or another remains an official punishment in parts of the world; for example, in 1994 an American citizen, Michael Fay, was arrested in Singapore on a charge of vandalism and punished by caning. While provoking some outrage, it also prompted some Americans to wonder whether a return to some forms of corporal punishment might not be a bad idea for some crimes in the United States as well.

Branding. Prior to the development of modern record keeping, it was not possible to keep track of any individual person's criminal history. However, it seemed obvious that a second offense deserved to be punished more severely than a first offense. In order to keep track of a person's criminal history without modern methods of identification and record keeping, offenders were branded on the forehead, cheek, shoulder, or hand with a hot iron. A system of letters was used to identify the crime committed. *M* stood for manslaughter, *T* for thief, *B* for blasphemer, and *A* for adulterer. If a person was unlikely to move to another community, the actual branding could be replaced with the requirement that the appropriate letter be sewn onto a person's clothes. The palm of the right hand eventually became the most common place for brands. As such, a person would be asked to raise his right hand when swearing an oath, displaying his palm to show that he had never been branded and could therefore be presumed honorable. Though the reason has disappeared, this gesture remains in present-day legal procedures.

Mutilation. This includes the cutting off of fingers, hands, ears, and sometimes other parts of the body. The Code of Hammurabi, the legal code created in ancient Babylon, specified various forms of mutilation for certain crimes in poetically obvious ways: the putting out of a prisoner's eyes for causing someone else to be blinded, and the knocking out of a prisoner's teeth for causing someone's teeth to be knocked out. It also specified the cutting off of fingers or even of an entire hand for the crime of theft. Similar forms of mutilation are still practiced in some Islamic countries. In Iran, for example, thieves can still expect to have fingers or hands amputated by means of a small electric guillotine.

The severity of a corporal punishment was supposed to correspond to the seriousness of the crime. For the least serious offenses, the humiliation of the stocks was sufficient; for more serious crimes, a whipping could be added. However, for still more serious crimes, the degree of corporal punishment could be so severe that some prisoners did not always survive the experience. Especially during the Middle Ages, some truly diabolical forms of corporal punishment were designed that clearly no one was likely to survive. Such forms of punishment should not be thought of as methods of *execution*, since their primary purpose was to cause extreme pain and humiliation. Death occurred only as a secondary consequence. In fact, those few people who did survive were then released. In many cases, prisoners were killed outright, but not because they were under sentence of death. Rather, they were killed in order to end their suffering.

In a sense, the death penalty should be seen as an extension of corporal punishment: The most severe forms of corporal punishment ended in death. Hence, seventeenth-century criminal codes that specified the death penalty for most serious crimes must have been seen at the time as humanitarian reforms. They replaced torturous methods of corporal punishment that generally resulted in death with a quick and certain death, omitting the inhumane infliction of suffering. However, this meant that, while the milder forms of corporal punishment were still available for less serious crimes, more serious crimes could only be punished by death, and there was no way to draw fine distinctions among crimes at this end of the scale. The use of imprisonment as a form of punishment was eventually adopted to solve this problem. **See also** benefit of clergy; impalement; imprisonment.

cost of capital punishment

Debates over capital punishment often pit the cost of capital punishment against the cost of life imprisonment. Originally this issue was raised to support capital punishment, because the costs of housing, feeding, and guarding a prisoner for life were far higher than the cost of execution. Today, however, the high costs incurred in death-penalty trials and appeals have made this an issue that is now generally raised by opponents of capital punishment.

The execution of criminals for serious crimes was originally practiced at least in part because there were no suitable alternatives. Prior to the development of penitentiaries in the eighteenth century, communities did not maintain facilities for the long-term housing of convicted criminals. They did not do so because prisons are costly to build and costly to maintain. In order to maintain a prison, a community must make a significant investment in food, clothing, and shelter, as well as in the manpower and security devices needed to prevent escape. Criminals were not usually considered to be worth the expense, so it is not surprising that executions were considered justified simply because they saved a community the trouble and expense of keeping a criminal incarcerated. These factors are still cited as an argument in support of capital punishment.

It is true that the cost of execution per se is minimal compared with the cost of feeding and housing a prisoner over the course of a lifetime. Even execution by lethal gas, which is probably the most costly method of execution since it requires the use of a specially built chamber, averages only a few thousand dollars per execution. Lethal injection, which involves no specialized equipment, costs far less. By contrast, the Federal Bureau of Prisons estimates that the average *annual* cost of housing a prisoner is $21,926.

However, the real expense of capital punishment is not in the execution itself but in the costs involved in a capital prosecution. These costs begin to accumulate as soon as the crime is committed. Investigations into capital offenses are often more painstaking and therefore more expensive than investigations into noncapital offenses. At trial, the cost of both prosecution and defense must typically be borne by the state, and those costs are considerable. Two lawyers represent each side at the jury trial. The trials themselves tend to be longer than noncapital trials since more evidence must be presented, which leads to greater costs involved in investigation and analysis of evidence, in addition to feeding, housing, and compensating the jury. The salaries of judges, clerks, and bailiffs must also be considered. Many of these costs are also incurred, to a lesser extent, in noncapital trials, but capital trials are distinctly more expensive than comparable noncapital ones.

Once the trial is over, capital cases become vastly more expensive than non-capital cases. Every capital trial is subject to automatic appeal, and most involve numerous additional appeals. Each appeal involves court costs that are borne by the state. It is extremely rare for noncapital cases to involve as many appeals as are involved in a typical capital case. Moreover, in most cases, defendants in capital cases are incarcerated for many years during the lengthy appeals process (death row inmates are more likely to die of causes other than execution), so the state pays for the higher cost of the capital prosecution and in many cases for decades of incarceration as well. One 1992 study estimated that the state of California could save $90 million annually by abolishing capital punishment, and that it would cost the state of New York (which did not have the death penalty at that time) about $118 million annually to implement the death penalty.

On the other hand, although it is clear that the modern American system of justice makes the death penalty more costly on average than life imprisonment, the costs are not large in the context of overall state budgets. States have multibillion-dollar budgets and typically prosecute only a few capital cases each year. Supporters of capital punishment (and even some opponents) consider that spending a few million dollars is not enough to make cost a significant issue. **See also** imprisonment.

Jesus of Nazareth was executed by crucifixion, a common form of capital punishment in the ancient world.

crucifixion

Crucifixion is an ancient method of execution in which a person is attached to a wooden cross, usually bound or nailed by the feet and outstretched hands, and put on display in a public place. The condemned prisoner dies slowly of hunger and thirst, and from wounds inflicted during the whipping that is usually administered prior to crucifixion. In some cases the condemned prisoner's legs are broken to ensure or hasten death. From the sixth century B.C. to the fourth century A.D. this was a common form of punishment for crimes against the state, which were generally considered the most serious category of crimes.

Under the Roman Empire, crucifixion was reserved for noncitizens (i.e., slaves and foreigners). It was considered the most cruel and degrading form of punishment that could be administered. The Roman slave Spartacus, who led a rebellion against Rome in 71 B.C., was executed in this manner, along with over six thousand of the slaves who joined him. After the rebellion was put down, the Appian Way, the road into Rome, was lined for miles with crucifixes on which the rebel slaves were left to die. In about A.D. 33 Jesus of Nazareth was executed by crucifixion for the crime of claiming to be king of the Jews. When Christianity was adopted as the state religion of the Roman Empire, crucifixion was banned as a form of punishment, since it was too closely associated with the death of Christ. **See also** Bible; gibbet.

cruel and unusual punishment

The Eighth Amendment of the Constitution of the United States contains a prohibition against "cruel and unusual punishment." Opponents of capital punishment have long argued that the death penalty should be considered a violation of this constitutional prohibition. Even though the Supreme Court has not so far been willing to interpret the Eighth Amendment as prohibiting the death penalty altogether, the prohibition against cruel and unusual punishment has played a significant role in court cases involving the death penalty.

The prohibition against cruel and unusual punishment has a precedent in English law prior to its inclusion in the Eighth Amendment. In 1685 the Catholic king James II of England managed to put down a rebellion led by the Protestant duke of Monmouth. Acts of treason and rebellion are often punished by death, but many of Monmouth's followers were disemboweled alive (which does not immediately result in death) and forced to watch as their bowels were burned before them. Even women who participated in the rebellion were burned alive. Four years later, in 1689, a second rebellion successfully overthrew James II, and he was replaced by the Protestant rulers William III and Mary. With the memory of the bloody executions following the earlier rebellion still fresh, the British Parliament passed a declaration of rights known as the English Bill of Rights. A central provision of this law states, "Cruel and unusual punishment [ought not to be] inflicted," which was apparently the first appearance of the phrase "cruel and unusual" in penal law. The same phrase was then used, after the American Revolution, in the state constitutions of several of the newly independent states. The constitution of the state of Virginia used language identical to the language in the English Bill of Rights. The language of the Eighth Amendment is identical to the language of the English Bill of Rights except that the stronger phrase "shall not be" is used in place of "ought not to be."

The prohibition against cruel and unusual punishment is generally understood not just as a prohibition against torturous punishments but as a prohibition against excessive penalties of any kind. According to some historians, the original purpose of the phrase in the English Bill of Rights was to prohibit *disproportionate* penalties, not necessarily grotesque penalties. In any case, that is the interpretation that modern jurisprudence gives the phrase. For example, Chief Justice William Rehnquist has remarked that punishing illegal parking with life imprisonment would violate the "cruel and unusual" clause of the Constitution, even though life imprisonment is not a form of torture and is an appropriate punishment for certain other crimes.

Whether a particular punishment qualifies as cruel and unusual depends on community standards, or, as Supreme Court justice Joseph McKenna put it, on "current sensibilities." Since sensibilities are bound to change over time, this concept was later extended. In a 1958 case, *Trop v. Dulles*, the Supreme Court ruled that the phrase "cruel and unusual" had to be interpreted in light of "evolving standards of decency." This means that punishments that are considered appropriate and proportionate at one time may come to be considered cruel and unusual at another time as public sentiment changes.

Until 1962, the prohibition against cruel and unusual punishment was assumed to apply only to federal law, not to state law, and the Supreme Court generally refused to review state penal codes. However, in *Robinson v. California* (1962), the Supreme Court ruled that state penal codes were also subject to the provisions of the Eighth Amendment. Since then, the Supreme Court has frequently considered whether state penal codes comply with the prohibition against cruel and unusual punishment.

The issue of cruel and unusual punishment is often raised in death-penalty cases. However, the Supreme Court has generally been reluctant to rule that laws and procedures violate the prohibition. For example, in 1946 condemned prisoner Willie Francis was strapped into the Louisiana electric chair, but due to a mechanical failure, he received only a brief shock even though the switch was thrown several times. He was then returned to his cell until the chair could be repaired. While awaiting a second execution, he appealed to have his sentence overturned on the grounds that he had been subjected to torturous, repeatedly unsuccessful attempts and a lingering execution was cruel and unusual. The Supreme Court did not accept this argument, and Francis was executed in 1947.

In 1972, in *Furman v. Georgia*, the Supreme Court issued a ruling that overturned all existing death-penalty statutes in the United States on Eighth Amendment grounds. However, only two justices held that the death penalty per se was cruel and unusual. Three justices took the position that the death-penalty statutes then in effect were cruel and unusual but only because they produced "arbitrary and capricious" patterns of sentencing. It was the inconsistency that they felt was cruel and unusual. A sentence would have to be considered disproportionate, and therefore cruel and unusual, if a different defendant who was convicted of substantially the same crime received a significantly lighter sentence. However, if death-penalty statutes could be revised to prevent arbitrary and inconsistent sentencing, then there would be no objection to the death penalty itself.

There have been several cases in which the Supreme Court has been asked to place limits on the use of the death penalty. In 1977 the Supreme Court ruled in *Coker v. Georgia* that the death penalty is an excessive punishment for the crime of rape. In 1989, in *Penry v. Lynaugh*, the Court ordered a new trial for Johnny Paul Penry on the grounds that the jury had not been instructed that they could consider Penry's mental retardation as a mitigating circumstance when sentencing him to death. At that time, the Court ruled that Penry's mental retardation per se did not provide grounds for judging his sentence cruel and unusual. However, in 2002 the Court ruled in *Atkins v. Virginia* that standards of decency had changed since 1989 and the execution of the mentally retarded could no longer be considered constitutional. In 1989 the Supreme Court also made two rulings, in *Stanford v. Kentucky* and *Wilkins v. Missouri*, allowing the execution of defendants as young as sixteen or seventeen years old at the time of their crime, on the grounds that community standards of decency at that time did not make the execution of juvenile offenders cruel and unusual. However, in March 2005 the Court outlawed the execution of juveniles in its *Roper v. Simmons* decision, ruling that prevailing public opinion was now against the practice. **See also** Constitution of the United States; evolving standards of decency; *Roper v. Simmons; Trop v. Dulles*.

Dallas, George Mifflin (1792–1864)

George Mifflin Dallas served as the eleventh vice president of the United States under James K. Polk. He remains the highest-ranking public official in U.S. history to publicly oppose capital punishment. Dallas was born in Philadelphia and studied law on his own, although he was probably encouraged by his father, Alexander James Dallas, a prominent lawyer who served as U.S. secretary of the treasury from 1814 to 1816. George Dallas served as an assistant in the Treasury Department, first under Albert Gallatin from 1813 to 1814 and then under his father. In 1813, after joining the Treasury Department, Dallas traveled with Gallatin on a diplomatic mission to Europe, including Russia, Belgium, and Great Britain. The mission ended when Great Britain offered peace terms bringing the War of 1812 to a close. In 1824 Dallas entered politics, first as a Republican, supporting John C. Calhoun. He later switched his support to Democrat Andrew Jackson, and remained a loyal Democrat for the rest of his career. He was appointed to serve as attorney general in Philadelphia in 1835, but the Democrats were voted out of office that year. In 1837 he was given a diplomatic position as minister to Russia, but the position mainly involved attending social events, and Dallas soon tired of it. In 1839 he returned to his law practice in Philadelphia. He became the political rival of fellow Pennsylvanian James Buchanan (who later served a term as president of the United States). The two men frequently found themselves competing for the same political appointments. In 1844 Dallas was selected (over Buchanan) to run for the vice presidency with James K. Polk. Their ticket was successful, and Dallas served as Polk's vice president from 1844 to 1848. Dallas was a particularly active vice president. In his capacity as president of the Senate, he worked on legislation involving the Mexican War and involving difficult tariff and trade issues. In 1845, while he was serving as vice president, he also became the founding president of the American Society for the Abolition of Capital Punishment, the first national organization working to abolish capital punishment.

Following his term as vice president, Dallas briefly retired from public life. However, he returned to serve as minister to Great Britain (taking the place of his old rival Buchanan) in 1856. He remained a loyal Democrat even during the Civil War, despite his opposition to Southern secession. Although he favored the abolition of capital punishment, he opposed the abolition of slavery. He died in 1864. **See also** American Society for the Abolition of Capital Punishment; opposition to capital punishment, history of (1648–1870).

Darrow, Clarence (1857–1938)

Clarence Darrow ranks among the best-known lawyers in American history. He was perhaps the first American lawyer to become a household name, largely through his role in several high-profile court cases. He worked actively to abolish the death penalty in the United States, and his notoriety as a defense attorney in famous murder cases helped keep the issue before the public eye in the first half of the twentieth century.

Darrow was born in Kinsman, Ohio, and studied for a year at Allegheny College in Meadville, Pennsylvania. He took a job as a schoolteacher before completing his degree. He developed an interest in the law and studied for a year

Defense attorney Clarence Darrow sits between his most famous clients, Nathan Leopold (left) and Richard Loeb after the two were convicted of murder in 1924.

at the Ann Arbor School of Law in Ann Arbor, Michigan. He then took a job as a law clerk, again without completing his degree. Nevertheless, a year later, in 1878, he passed the bar exam and established a law practice in Ashtabula, Ohio. In 1888 he moved to Chicago, where he made his living chiefly by representing the city of Chicago and taking on corporate clients.

Darrow's first high-profile case came in 1894 when he agreed to represent Socialist leader Eugene V. Debs and the American Railway Union against the Pullman Company. The case ended inconclusively, but it established Darrow's reputation as a lawyer willing to take on big corporate interests. In defending clients, Darrow frequently tried to turn public opinion against the prosecution by broad emotional appeals, and in seeking publicity for his clients he became famous himself.

In 1924 Darrow defended Nathan Leopold and Richard Loeb, two affluent Chicago teenagers who had committed murder largely to see if they could get away with it. They had confessed to the murder and were clearly guilty. Darrow, however, decided to make the death penalty itself the focus of the trial. Darrow was already an opponent of the death penalty. He was convinced that many people who were sentenced to death were themselves victims of brutal circumstances and emotional disorders. He was also convinced that Leopold and Loeb were mentally ill but that their mental illness did not meet the legal definition of insanity. He had the boys plead guilty, and then brought in a parade of psychiatrists to testify that their disturbed mental condition, as well as their young age, made imposition of the death penalty inappropriate in their case. The strategy worked. The judge sentenced Leopold and Loeb to life in prison rather than sentencing them to death. The trial was one of several high-profile murder trials of the period that gave Americans the opportunity to debate the issues surrounding the death penalty.

In 1925, a year after the Leopold and Loeb trial, Darrow defended schoolteacher John T. Scopes for teaching Charles Darwin's theory of natural selection. Again, he made Darwin's theory rather than Scopes's guilt the focus of the trial. The Scopes trial is probably the trial for which Darrow is still best known. Two years later, he retired. However, he continued to speak and write and to engage in public debates. In particular, he continued to be an active opponent of capital punishment. He served as president of the American League to Abolish Capital Punishment, an organization that he helped found with former Sing Sing Prison warden Lewis Lawes.
See also Lawes, Lewis E.; Leopold, Nathan F., and Richard A. Loeb.

Death Penalty Information Center (DPIC)

The Death Penalty Information Center, founded in 1990 in Washington, D.C., is a nonprofit clearinghouse for current information about the death penalty in the United States. Its staff researches and publishes statistical analyses and fact sheets as well as detailed reports on all aspects of the issue related to costs, deterrence, mental illness, juveniles, race and gender, recent legislation, and court decisions. The center also maintains an Internet Web site that provides current state-by-state statistics on the number of executions performed, the number of prisoners held on death rows, and other information. Funded by private donations and educational foundations, the DPIC attempts to be objective and accurate and officially takes no stand either supporting or opposing capital punishment. Its information and publications are widely quoted as reliable by people on all sides of the issue. **See also** ESPY file.

death-qualified jury

A death-qualified jury is one in which all of the members of the jury are willing, in theory, to impose a sentence of death if they feel the sentence is justified by the facts. The concept that a trial jury should be fair and impartial and capable of deciding the issues put before it without bias or predisposition is central to the judicial system's integrity and the rule of law. This concept comes into play in the jury selection process, called voir dire, of death-penalty cases. At a capital trial, or a trial in which the defendant may be sentenced to death if found guilty, it is necessary to find out during voir dire whether prospective jurors have a bias or predisposition regarding the death penalty itself. A person who is philosophically opposed to the death penalty may not sit on a jury that is asked to consider a death sentence because it is accepted that a person who would never vote for a sentence of death cannot participate fully in jury deliberations.

Similarly, since the 1992 *Morgan v. Illinois* decision, a person who believes that a death sentence is the only acceptable penalty for the crime of murder—a belief that is sometimes held for religious reasons based on passages in the Bible or Koran—may also be excused from a jury that is asked to consider a death sentence. Otherwise, a death-qualified jury is expected to represent the public's wide range of opinion on the death penalty. In *Witherspoon v. Illinois* (1968) and subsequent decisions, the U.S. Supreme Court has ruled that a prospective juror may not be excluded from a jury merely for being somewhat disinclined to impose a death sentence (or somewhat inclined to impose a death sentence) provided that the prospective juror is willing to consider the facts and the law in making the decision. The 1986 *Lockhart v. McCree* decision, however, made clear that a prospective juror with objections to capital punishment *may* be dismissed if the judge feels those objections are sufficiently strong that the prospective juror would be unable to dispassionately "apply the law to the facts of the case." **See also** jury nullification; *Lockhart v. McCree; Morgan v. Illinois; Wainwright v. Witt; Witherspoon v. Illinois.*

death row

An area of a prison in which condemned prisoners are usually held. Convicted criminals who have been sentenced to death in the United States have a special status within state penal systems for both practical and administrative reasons. In practical terms, because these individuals are already facing death, it is assumed that they have little incentive to refrain from disruptive and antisocial behavior in prison, including violent assault and escape attempts, and should therefore be segregated from the larger inmate population. So, condemned prisoners are kept in maximum-security areas of the prison. Furthermore, since physically relocating gas chambers and electric chairs is difficult and costly, states tend to centralize executions at a single state prison, even though condemned prisoners remain technically under the jurisdiction of the county in which their trial was held. Thus, administratively, condemned prisoners are not considered part of the general prison population. For these reasons, condemned prisoners are typically held in separate wings of the prison, where they have no contact with other prisoners. These separate wings are referred to, individually and collectively, as death row.

Life on death row is quite different from life in other areas of the prison. Because death row is a high-security area, cell checks and prisoner counts are conducted frequently. The number of personal items allowed in cells is kept to a minimum. Prisoners are fed in their cells rather than mixing with other prisoners in the prison dining hall, and death row prisoners are not assigned work duties. Outdoor exercise is limited to one hour per day, and typically takes place in small, high-security prison yards separated from the rest of the prison population. Thus, life on death row can seem much like life in solitary confinement, and death row prisoners spend much of their time in solitary pursuits or hobbies, including reading, writing, and crafts. Many devote themselves to assisting with their legal appeals, which may require frequent and lengthy visits with their lawyers. Many death row prisoners have taken such an active interest in their defense that they are allowed extended periods of time to do legal research in the prison library. Some acquire considerable legal expertise, giving rise to the nickname "jailhouse lawyers."

Since the mid-1990s, in response to lawsuits challenging the isolation of death row prisoners, some states have experimented with integrating some death row prisoners into the regular prison population. Prisoners with a record of good behavior have been allowed to eat in dining halls and have even been given work assignments. So far, evidence suggests that, on average, death row prisoners are no more of a risk for escape or for violent and disruptive behavior than the rest of the prison population. They do, however, have a higher than average rate of suicide attempts.

Since 1973 the number of prisoners on death row in the United States has risen steadily from a low of 134 in 1973 to a high of 3,692 in 2002. In 2003 the number dropped slightly to 3,525. The majority of inmates on death row are never executed. Some die of natural causes;

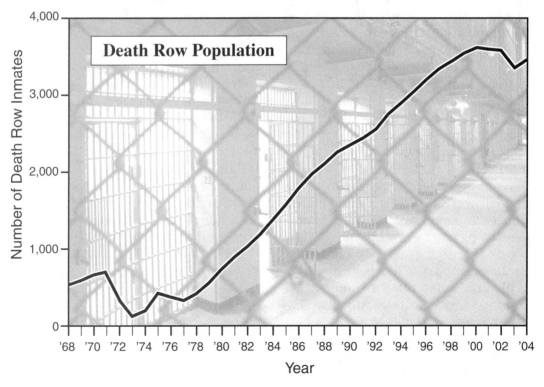

Source: Bureau of Justice Statistics, 1968–2004.

some are pardoned or exonerated. The majority eventually have their sentences commuted to life in prison. **See also** clemency; exoneration; time between sentencing and execution.

decapitation

Familiarly known as beheading, decapitation is a method of execution in which a person's head is severed by an ax, sword, or other sharp blade. Decapitation has been used as a method of execution in both the East and the West since ancient times. It is from this practice that capital punishment derives its name. The Latin word for head is *caput*, which is the root of "de*capi*tation" and "*capit*al."

Among the ancient Greeks and Romans, decapitation was considered a relatively painless and honorable form of punishment, and was used on upper-class citizens instead of more demeaning forms of punishment such as stoning, hanging, or crucifixion. In the Middle Ages and Renaissance, decapitation was also generally reserved for the nobility. In 1792, after the French monarchy was overthrown in the French Revolution, the democratic government of France, in the spirit of egalitarianism, made decapitation the preferred method of execution for all citizens, although, because of the limited number of available guillotines, hanging continued to be the most frequently used method in actual practice.

Historically, official decapitation was normally performed by a skilled professional executioner to ensure that the condemned prisoner did not suffer due to a poorly aimed stroke. However, precisely because decapitation took a great deal of skill, executions often required more than one stroke, and occasionally connecting tissue had to be cut with a sawing motion of the sword or ax. When this occurred, the executioner was blamed for performing the execution badly.

Despite these risks, decapitation generally was considered a humane method of execution, and remained in use after many other ancient forms of punishment had been abandoned. In Germany decapitation using a guillotine was the standard method of execution until the close of World War II, at which point capital punishment was largely abolished. In France decapitation using a guillotine was practiced until 1977 and was not officially banned until 1981, when France outlawed capital punishment altogether. Decapitation was never adopted in the United States, probably because of public distaste for the particularly bloody and gruesome nature of the method. **See also** executioners; guillotine; hara-kiri.

Delaware

Delaware has traditionally permitted juries to impose the death penalty, and continues to do so currently. However, executions have never been common in Delaware. Prior to 1902, executions by hanging were performed under the jurisdiction of county governments, and no official records were kept. The earliest reported execution in colonial Delaware was a hanging that took place in 1662. Judging from newspaper reports, only seven people were executed in Delaware from 1831 to 1902. Twenty-five people were executed in Delaware from 1902 to 1946, all by hanging. In 1958 the Delaware legislature abolished capital punishment, but it was reenacted three years later, in 1961, over the veto of Governor Elbert N. Carvel. No executions took place under this statute.

Following the 1972 *Furman v. Georgia* decision, which invalidated Delaware's death-penalty statute, the state reinstated the death penalty in 1974. The state's current death-penalty statute allows the death penalty to be considered for homicide under special circumstances. These special circumstances include intentionally causing the death of another; causing death in the course of a felony or fleeing from a felony arrest; forcing another person to commit suicide; or causing the death of a police officer, corrections officer, or firefighter. They also include causing the death of someone with a bomb or similar device.

The death penalty may be imposed if one of twenty-two aggravating circumstances is proven to have accompanied the crime. The list of aggravating circumstances appears similar to the special circumstances noted above, but aggravating circumstances are considered during the penalty phase of the trial rather than during the guilt phase. The aggravating circumstances are (1) that the defendant had unlawfully escaped from custody; (2) that the homicide was committed in the course of evading arrest or attempting to escape from custody; (3) that the victim was a police officer, corrections officer, or firefighter; (4) that the victim was a judicial officer or an investigator; (5) that the victim was used as a hostage or shield; (6) that the victim was held for ransom or reward; (7) that the victim was a witness to a crime; (8) that the homicide was a murder-for-hire and the defendant either performed the murder or solicited another to perform the murder; (9) that the defendant was previously convicted of murder; (10) that the homicide occurred in the course of a rape (including sodomy), kidnapping, arson, robbery, or burglary; (11) that the defendant intentionally caused multiple deaths; (12) that the homicide was wantonly vile, involving the use of torture; (13) that the defendant ordered the homicide to be performed or performed the homicide under someone else's direction; (14) that the defendant was under a sentence of life imprisonment; (15) that the homicide was committed for monetary gain; (16) that the victim was pregnant; (17) that the victim was severely handicapped or disabled; (18) that the victim was sixty-two years of age or older; (19) that the victim was younger than fourteen years old, and the defendant was at least four years older than the victim; (20) that the victim was an informant; (21) that the homicide was premeditated and involved substantial advance planning; or (22) that the homicide was committed to interfere with the victim's civil rights. The jury must also consider any mitigating circumstances that the defense wishes to present.

Under Delaware law, a person convicted of a capital offense cannot be executed if he or she was under the age of eighteen at the time of the offense. Delaware does provide for life imprisonment without parole as an alternative to the death penalty. A jury may recommend the death penalty, but sentencing is decided by the judge, who may override the jury's recommendation. The governor has the authority to grant clemency, provided that he or she receives a favorable recommendation from the Board of Pardons. Even with a favorable recommendation, the governor is not obligated to grant clemency. Delaware has a law requiring that all executions take place between midnight and 3:00 A.M.

In 1986 Delaware replaced electrocution with lethal injection as its method of execution, but allowed prisoners already on death row to elect to be hanged instead if they wished. The first execution in Delaware since 1946 occurred in 1992 when convicted serial killer Steven Brian Pennell was executed by lethal injection. Twelve other executions have since taken place, including the last hanging to occur in the United States when William Bailey elected to be hanged in 1996. As of June 2005, nineteen people were awaiting execution on Delaware's death row.
See also *Furman v. Georgia*.

deontology

Deontology is an approach to ethical theories that attempts to focus on moral duties rather than upon the consequences of action. The word *deontology* is derived from the Greek word *deon*, or "duty." The most influential deontological theory was developed by the German philosopher Immanuel Kant during the late eighteenth century. Kant's theory remains one of the most important and influential ethical theories in the world today and is often invoked in the debate over the justification of capital punishment.

Kant claimed that all moral duties could be derived from a single moral principle, which he called the Categorical Imperative. Kant sometimes stated the Categorical Imperative as a rule or procedure for determining whether an action was permissible. According to this rule, a person should act in a certain way only if he was prepared to act *always* in that way (in similar circumstances), and also prepared to see everyone else act always in that way. In short, a person should not do to another what he is not prepared to have done to himself. The great strength of Kant's theory is that it easily accounts for the concept of individual rights (which is very difficult to do under the most important competing moral theory, utilitarianism). Since no one can ever be willing to have his own freedom and autonomy violated, it follows that we have a moral duty to respect the freedom and autonomy of others.

It might seem that the punishment of criminals would be difficult to justify under Kant's theory. After all, no one wishes to be punished, so it would seem that punishing others is not morally permissible. However, under Kant's theory, we assume that all people, including criminals, act according to the Categorical Imperative. Since crimes cause harm to others, it follows that criminals are, by this assumption, willing to have the same harm done to themselves; indeed, their actions suggest that they actually desire to have the same harm done to themselves. We are therefore justified in punishing criminals because, in effect, they are "asking for it." Kant's view thus supports a retributive theory of punishment, and suggests that the death penalty is the most appropriate form of punishment for crimes resulting in the death of others. **See also** justification of punishment; utilitarianism.

Dershowitz, Alan (1938–)

Alan Dershowitz is a prominent defense attorney who has earned a reputation defending some of the most notorious criminal defendants in recent U.S. history. As a law clerk for Supreme Court justice Arthur J. Goldberg, Dershowitz helped formulate some of the legal arguments against the death penalty that were used during the 1970s and 1980s.

Dershowitz was born in Brooklyn, New York, and received his undergraduate degree from Brooklyn College. In 1959 he entered Yale Law School, where he specialized in constitutional and criminal law. After his graduation in 1962 he accepted a position as a law clerk with the U.S. Court of Appeals in Washington, D.C., and a year later he became a clerk for newly appointed Supreme Court justice Arthur J. Goldberg. During the summer of 1963, Goldberg gave Dershowitz the task of researching all conceivable constitutional challenges to the death penalty. Dershowitz threw himself enthusiastically into the task, drafting a memorandum outlining various reasons why the death penalty could be considered cruel and unusual. That memorandum was used as the basis for Goldberg's dissent in a 1963 decision by the Supreme Court not to hear a death-penalty case. Goldberg's dissent inspired

Harvard law professor Alan Dershowitz (center) defended O.J. Simpson during the former football star's 1995 murder trial.

numerous appeals of death sentences in the next few years.

Following his work on the Supreme Court, Dershowitz became a professor of law at Harvard University. While teaching at Harvard, he also took on particularly difficult and controversial civil liberties and criminal defense cases. He defended antiwar activist (and prominent pediatrician) Benjamin Spock on charges stemming from his protest activities, and in 1980 he defended Ricky and Raymond Tison, two brothers sentenced to death for their involvement in a murder that they did not plan or actually commit. In 1995 he participated in the legal defense of former football star O.J. Simpson on murder charges and was successful in convincing the jury that the evidence against Simpson had been sufficiently mishandled to produce reasonable doubt of his guilt. **See also** Goldberg, Arthur J.

determinism

Determinism is the theory that all events, even the most minute, have causes. Since human actions are included in the events of the world, it follows that human actions are also fully caused and are not the result of spontaneous choice. The implication of this view is that there is no "free will."

People who hold the determinist view are inclined to argue that the death penalty—or indeed any punishment that is not aimed at rehabilitation—is unjust. They argue that since human actions are fully caused by previous conditions, acts, or other factors such as genetics and the environment, humans cannot be held morally responsible for their actions. Hence they cannot be justly punished for their actions. However, it would be justified to exert new influences on their behavior to cause their behavior to be appropriate to the society in which they live. **See also** justification of punishment.

deterrence

Nearly every debate over capital punishment touches on whether the death penalty has a deterrent effect on crime. Proponents of capital punishment often argue that fear of death discourages people from committing murder; opponents of capital punishment point to evidence that the death penalty has no clear deterrent effect.

The argument over deterrence is as old as the debate over capital punishment itself. In 1782 King Leopold of Belgium abolished capital punishment, and the murder rate there subsequently went down. This fact was seized upon by opponents of capital punishment in the United States and widely cited as proving that the death penalty had no deterrent effect. Death-penalty advocates argued that this single fact was only weak anecdotal evidence and therefore unconvincing, but it did provide early opponents of capital punishment with an argument against the presumption that the death penalty deters murder.

More recent and more scientific studies are equally controversial. In the 1970s economist Isaac Ehrlich, using a statistical method known as regression analysis, suggested that each execution could be credited with preventing approximately eight murders (on average). His research was based on the relationship of executions and murder rates; in simple terms, he presented evidence that murder rates are lower in jurisdictions where capital punishment is allowed or in use, and concluded that the punishment deters the crime. His results have been challenged on the grounds that many other factors, or variables, may in fact be the reason why murder rates are lower in these jurisdictions, and that it is impossible to isolate capital punishment as the deterrent. Other similar studies measuring and comparing different variables have suggested that capital punishment has no deterrent effect; still other studies make capital punishment appear to be a factor that encourages murder. Thus, deterrence has proven resistant to empirical analysis.

Analysis of comparable jurisdictions—that is, studying jurisdictions that are similar in every way except that one allows capital punishment and the other does not, and then comparing homicide rates—suggests that capital punishment does not have a deterrent effect. For example, Michigan and Illinois are states with approximately the same urban density, racial diversity, and income levels, yet Michigan has a lower murder rate than Illinois even though Illinois allows the death penalty and Michigan does not. A comparison between Missouri and Wisconsin yields the same result. These states also have comparable demographics, yet Wisconsin has the lower murder rate even though Missouri allows the death penalty and Wisconsin does not. Indeed, death-penalty states consistently have higher murder rates than non-death-penalty states. Texas, with the highest number of executions, also has the highest murder rate. Here, too, opponents of capital punishment have suggested that, rather than having a deterrent effect, the death penalty actually encourages murder.

However, a host of factors may be responsible for the differences in murder rates in different states, and it might be argued that states with high murder rates *need* the death penalty to prevent rates from being even higher. Comparisons within the same jurisdiction sometimes support this view. In New York, for example, which did not allow capital punishment from 1978 to 1995, the murder rate dropped following the reinstatement of capital punishment in 1995 (although this proves very little, since murder rates at that time were dropping in most jurisdictions even without changes in the status of capital punishment). In fact, it is not possible to measure the deterrent effect of the death penalty without knowing how many people may have been considering murder in the first place. Thus, while there is no clear evidence that the death penalty deters crime, there is also no clear evidence that it does not. In any case, polls indicate that most Americans do not believe the death penalty deters crime, yet most Americans support capital punishment for its value as retribution or out of lack of faith in rehabilitation. **See also** justification of punishment.

dissection

Dissection is the systematic cutting apart of animal or human bodies for the purpose of studying the anatomical structure of the body. In the eighteenth and nineteenth centuries, the bodies of executed criminals were often dissected.

In Western society, knowledge of human anatomy developed relatively late compared with other scientific knowledge. Although some knowledge of anatomy, based on dissection of dogs and cats, was compiled by the ancient Greeks, it was not until the fifteenth century that dissection of human bodies provided accurate information about humans, and it was not until the eighteenth century that a knowledge of human anatomy was considered essential for the practice of medicine. The science of anatomy was so late in developing simply because of the almost universal horror that people feel at the idea of cutting up a human body. In some cultures it is considered a sacrilegious defilement; in other cultures it is merely considered gruesome.

In the eighteenth century, as physicians came to understand that the dissection of human bodies was the only way to acquire the skills and knowledge necessary for the practice of medicine, there developed an increasing demand for cadavers to dissect. A few grave robbers attempted to meet this demand by illegally digging up recently buried corpses. But for the most part, medical schools turned first to the unclaimed bodies of paupers and the mentally ill and then to executed criminals, the only people considered fit for the indignity. In many cases a representative of the medical school would arrange to be present at an execution and volunteer to dispose of the body afterward, if no friend or family member managed to claim it first. Some condemned prisoners were so concerned about being given to the medical schools that they would designate a trusted friend to take possession of the body after execution. To make this legal, some condemned prisoners even wrote wills that included clauses designating who should be allowed to take possession of their bodies.

In 1752 the British Parliament modified the English penal code to require the dissection of the body as part of the penalty imposed on a condemned criminal. This law had a twofold purpose. First, the law was intended to deter crime by exploiting the general horror of dissection. If simple death could not frighten criminals, perhaps the idea of being cut up after death would keep them honest. Second, the law was intended to provide medical schools with a legal source of cadavers. A version of this law was adopted in some of the American colonies as well, but there dissection was treated not as mandatory but as an optional condition that a judge could impose for particularly heinous or brutal crimes. Only Massachusetts made dissection mandatory, and only for the crime of killing someone in a duel. At his discretion, a judge could also order the loser's body turned over for dissection.

After the American Revolution, the dissection of bodies of executed prisoners became more common. In 1789 a protest in New York City against surgeons dissecting illegally obtained bodies turned into a riot. In response, the state of New York gave judges the power to add dissection to a capital sentence, and several other jurisdictions, including the federal government, did the same. A similar riot occurred in Connecticut in 1824, and again several states responded by granting or reaffirming the power of judges to turn over the bodies of executed prisoners to medical schools for dissection.

In practice, which condemned prisoners were dissected and which were not had little to do with the perceived heinousness of their crimes. Rather, those prisoners who had no family, or whose families were too poor to afford the cost of a burial, were most likely to be turned over for dissection. Some condemned prisoners were even able to turn the demand for medical cadavers to their advantage by preselling their bodies. Franklin Evans, executed in New Hampshire in 1874, received $50 for his body; Charles Tommey, executed in Georgia in 1877, received only $3. Sociologists suggest that racial bias influenced the discrepancy: One reason for the price difference may have been that Evans was white while Tommey was black. Death row prisoners who presold their bodies typically used the money to buy food, drink, and other luxuries for their last days.

So few people are executed in the present day that medical schools would no longer find this practice feasible, and it has been abandoned in the United States to avoid adverse publicity as well. However, modern medical technology has raised new ethical issues related to dissection. For example, today the practice of removing and transplanting the organs of executed criminals is condoned in China but opposed by many people in the West, in part because this would offend capital punishment opponents and in part because of concerns that a judge or jury might be swayed to recommend the death penalty over imprisonment if the need for organ transplantation were allowed to become a factor. **See also** drawing and quartering.

District of Columbia

Capital punishment is not used in the District of Columbia, although executions were permitted prior to 1972. Between 1853 and 1925, sixty-eight executions by hanging were conducted, mostly under federal jurisdiction, since the District of Columbia is under the authority of the U.S. Congress. In 1928 electrocution replaced hanging as the method of execution, and between 1928 and 1957 there were fifty executions using the electric chair. The last person executed in the District of Columbia was Robert E. Carter in 1957. In 1972 death-penalty statutes around the country, including the District of Columbia statute, were overturned by the Supreme Court's decision in *Furman v. Georgia*. Rather than reinstate the statute, the District Council voted to repeal it entirely in 1981. Congress ordered a public referendum on the issue in 1992, and the public endorsed the council's decision by a 2-to-1 margin. **See also** *Furman v. Georgia*.

divine authority

Assuming the religious view that God exists is true, it is naturally acknowledged that God is entitled to condemn someone to death. As the creator of the universe and ultimate source of life, God retains the authority to decide when and how a person shall die, a concept known as divine authority. One issue central to debates on capital punishment is the question of whether anyone other than God has this so-called divine authority to condemn someone to death. Some religions, notably the Quakers, take the view that the authority to decide when and how a person shall die is reserved *exclusively* to God. Applied rigorously, this view leads to the conclusion that the state has no right either to wage war or to condemn criminals to death. Strictly speaking, a person should not kill another person even as an act of self-defense.

However, the concept of divine authority was also used to draw the opposite conclusion. Prior to the Enlightenment in the eighteenth century, it was common for kings to believe that their authority to govern was derived from God. Many rulers claimed to be able to trace their ancestry back to the gods. Emperors of Rome and China even sometimes claimed to *be* gods, which is not to say that they believed they had exceptional powers. They merely believed that they had divine authority to govern. During the Middle Ages, Christian beliefs made it impossible for kings to claim to be, or to be descended from, gods; so, the concept of divine authority was modified into the view that kings were appointed to rule by God through his earthly representative, the pope. (After the Reformation of the fifteenth century, other religious leaders also took on this role.) As the argument goes, a ruler who derives his authority to rule from God also inherits at least some of God's authority to make decisions concerning life and death. For example, a king has the authority to wage war and to condemn criminals to death.

During the Enlightenment, philosophers challenged the concept of the "divine right" of kings. Western democratic nations now generally reject the view that the authority to govern is derived from God, preferring instead the view that the authority to govern derives from the consent of the governed. This means that Western democratic nations that engage in capital punishment must now generally justify their authority to condemn criminals to death on some grounds other than divine authority. **See also** social contract theory.

DNA evidence

DNA evidence collected during criminal investigations can play an important role in capital punishment cases. DNA, or deoxyribonucleic acid, is the complex carbon molecule that makes up the chromosomes, the structures in the nucleus of living cells that carry the organism's genetic code. DNA contains the "instructions" that enable a cell to perform whatever functions that cell performs, from the manufacturing of proteins to the generation of a whole new organism. Most of the DNA that is present in one human being is identical to the DNA in any other human being. However, approximately 0.1 percent of each person's DNA sequence is unique to that individual; with the exception of identical twins, each person's DNA theoretically can be distinguished from the DNA of any other person by sampling the very small portion of the DNA sequence that varies by individual. Furthermore, DNA is present in virtually every biological fluid or tissue, including blood, saliva, semen, skin, hair, fingernails, bones, and teeth. This makes DNA analysis very important in the investigation of crimes: DNA can often be used to link a criminal with the scene of a crime, and, equally important, DNA can be used to establish that a suspect is *not* linked to a crime. A suspect can be shown to be innocent when it can be proven that the suspect's DNA does not match biological specimens left by the perpetrator at the scene of a crime.

Until the mid-1980s, medical technology was not sufficiently advanced, affordable, or reliable to make DNA analysis a useful forensic tool. Then in 1984 scientists invented techniques to isolate and make millions of copies of short, specific segments of the DNA molecule; use these fragments to compile a genetic "fingerprint" unique to a single person; and apply the technique successfully even on old, dried-out samples of blood, semen, and other biological evidence. By the mid-1990s, DNA analysis had become an indispensable element of American criminal investigations and an overwhelmingly persuasive factor in courtroom testimony: When a defendant's DNA and crime-scene DNA samples match, the chance that the crime-scene DNA came from someone

A forensic lab technician examines DNA evidence collected from a crime scene. DNA evidence reduces the likelihood that an innocent person would be sentenced to death.

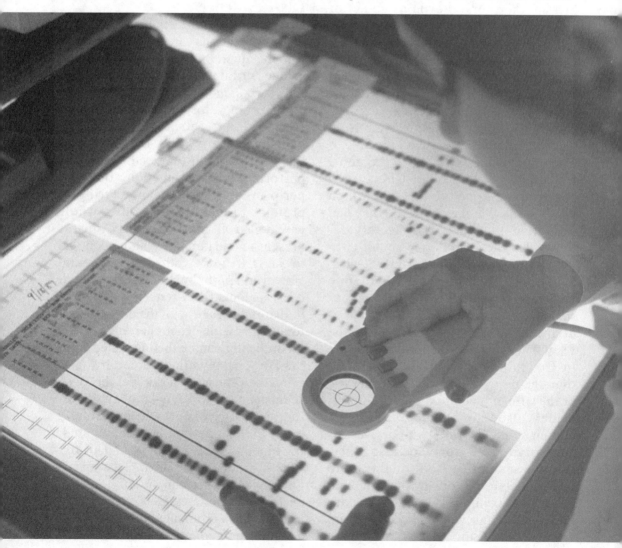

other than the defendant is less than 1 in 10 billion. Today, all fifty states authorize the collection of DNA samples from convicted offenders, and the FBI and all state crime laboratories are building a national database of these genetic fingerprints. If it can be proven in pretrial hearings that a testing laboratory's methods met scientific standards and produced reliable results, then DNA evidence is admissible in court proceedings in most jurisdictions as well. It is expected that DNA testing, administered before indictment, will significantly reduce the chance that an innocent person will be convicted and sentenced to death.

DNA analysis is in demand not only to identify the guilty and eliminate innocent suspects but also to exonerate the innocent already on death row. Because criminal evidence is often kept on file for many years after a defendant has been tried and convicted, it has been possible to reopen many cases in which convicted prisoners maintain their innocence. A group known as the Innocence Project has taken on the task of comprehensively checking DNA evidence from past crimes in which biological evidence has been preserved and bringing appeals on behalf of any inmate when it can be shown that there is no DNA match. As of June 2004, out of 140 exonerations won by the Innocence Project, more than 120 inmates, including 14 death row inmates from various states, have been exonerated by means of DNA evidence and released from prison. **See also** exoneration; Innocence Project.

double jeopardy

The Fifth Amendment to the U.S. Constitution prohibits putting a person on trial twice for the same offense. Being twice at risk of conviction for the same offense is called double jeopardy. The Fifth Amendment states, "Nor shall any person be subject for the same offense to be twice put in jeopardy of life or limb." The granting of this right is intended to limit the powers of prosecutors and to protect defendants from unfair prosecution. The practical effect of the double-jeopardy rule is that prosecutors must be careful not to charge a suspect until clear evidence of guilt is available since, once a person has been acquitted, he or she cannot be charged with the same crime again, even if further evidence proving that the person is guilty later comes to light. Similarly, once a person has been convicted and sentenced to imprisonment, he or she cannot later be charged with the same crime in the hope that a different jury would impose a longer prison term or the death penalty.

The double-jeopardy rule applies only to trials that result in either a standing acquittal or a standing conviction. Trials that end inconclusively, for one reason or another (e.g., because the jury could not reach a verdict), or trials that are overturned on appeal do not count. A second trial in such cases is merely part of the same legal process stemming from the original charges, not a second process stemming from new charges. This point has come up in several death-penalty cases in which a defendant, sentenced to life imprisonment at a first trial, won the right to a new trial on appeal and was convicted again on retrial and this time sentenced to death. Defendants have argued that this constitutes double jeopardy, but the courts have ruled that in winning a new trial, the slate is wiped clean and there is no reason why an even harsher penalty cannot be imposed by a second jury. **See also** Constitution of the United States.

Draconian Code

The Draconian Code was the first known body of written laws for the ancient Greek city of Athens. It was instituted by the Greek lawgiver Draco (or Dracon, as it is sometimes spelled) in 621 B.C. and may have been a revision or expansion of an earlier code. Unfortunately, only a portion of the code survives, namely the portion pertaining to homicide (which was written down for public distribution in 408 B.C.), but it is known that the Draconian Code prescribed the penalty of death for nearly every offense, including even minor offenses. This was considered unusually harsh, even at the time, and in 594 B.C. the archon (ruler) Solon repealed all of the Draconian Code except the homicide laws, replacing them with a more humane criminal code. To this day, the term *draconian* is used to describe laws that are considered excessively harsh.

drawing and quartering

Drawing and quartering was the ultimate punishment ordained for men in England, and occasionally in other parts of Europe, for the crime of treason, from the thirteenth century until the early nineteenth century. (Women convicted of treason were to be burned at the stake.) Many consider the practice among the most barbarous and cruel of all historical methods of execution.

The full punishment involved four phases. First, the condemned man was dragged behind a horse, on a sort of sledge called a hurdle, to the place of execution. There he was hanged by the neck but cut down while still conscious. He was then disemboweled while alive, and his entrails were burned before his eyes. Finally, he was beheaded and his body cut into four parts (quartered), which were typically impaled on posts and put on display in different parts of the city as a warning to others. The purpose of drawing and quartering was not only to cause the death of the condemned prisoner but also to desecrate the condemned prisoner's body, thus increasing the perceived severity of the punishment.

The Scottish rebel and patriot William Wallace was executed by drawing and quartering in 1305, as was the English traitor Guy Fawkes and six coconspirators in the so-called Gun Powder Plot in 1606. At least 10 others were executed by drawing and quartering in the 1600s, some 120 during the 1700s, and another 10 in the 1800s before the practice was abolished as barbaric and replaced by hanging. **See also** burning at the stake; cruel and unusual punishment; torture.

due process

Due process is a legal concept that forms the basis of the majority of death row appeals. The term appears in the U.S. Constitution in two places, once in the Fifth Amendment and again in the Fourteenth Amendment. The Fifth Amendment states that no person shall "be deprived of life, liberty or property, without due process of law." The Fourteenth Amendment states that no *state* shall "deprive any person of life, liberty or property, without due process of law." The language of the Fifth Amendment was intended to be binding only on the federal government, not on state governments. Since the Bill of Rights (the first ten amendments to the U.S. Constitution) was part of the *federal* constitution, it was thought to apply only to the federal government. Following the Civil War, many believed that at least some of the rights guaranteed by the Constitution should apply at every level of government. Hence the language of the Fourteenth Amendment was intended specifically to be binding on the states. It requires that state governments follow the same principles of due process that the federal government is bound to follow. Eventually, this was interpreted as meaning that all of the rights guaranteed in the Bill of Rights are binding on state laws as well as on federal laws.

The purpose of the due process clause is not just to ensure that the law be followed (which must, after all, be assumed) but to ensure that people involved in legal proceedings have an opportunity to respond to those proceedings in an appropriate manner. For example, a person must be notified if he has been charged with a crime, and he must be given the opportunity to defend himself against the charges. He must be permitted to offer his side of the case before he can be subjected to punishment. A defendant must also be told what evidence is being used against him so that he can have the ability to challenge that evidence. In short, due process requires not only that the law be followed in the treatment of suspects but that the law itself be fair and reasonable.

During the 1960s a number of Supreme Court decisions strengthened the meaning of the due process clause. Defendants in federal court had been guaranteed the services of an attorney since 1938, but in 1963 the Supreme Court ruled that the right to an attorney applied to defendants in state courts as well. In 1964 the Supreme Court ruled that defendants in state courts had the right to refrain from self-incrimination. The due process clause is also the basis for court rulings on the use of illegally obtained evidence at trials, in both federal and state courts. The death penalty per se has never been challenged on due process grounds, but numerous death sentences have been individually challenged on the grounds that the defendant's right to due process was violated in some manner or another. **See also** cruel and unusual punishment; equal protection.

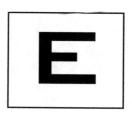

Eddings v. Oklahoma

This was a case heard by the Supreme Court of the United States in 1982. Although the Court originally agreed to hear the case because the defendant, Monty Lee Eddings, was only sixteen years old at the time of his crime, the eventual ruling, based on other considerations, left the question of the execution of minors unresolved.

In 1977 Eddings escaped from a juvenile detention facility and then stole a car and a gun. When he was pulled over by Oklahoma patrol officer Larry Crabtree, Eddings took out the gun and killed Crabtree. Although Eddings was only sixteen years old, he was ordered to stand trial as an adult. During the penalty phase of the trial, Eddings's lawyer argued that Eddings had suffered from an unhappy upbringing and from emotional disturbances. The judge dismissed these considerations, saying that only Eddings's age should be considered as a mitigating circumstance. The judge then sentenced Eddings to death, despite his age.

The case was appealed in the hope that an appeals court might consider sixteen too young to be eligible for the death penalty. Eventually, the U.S. Supreme Court agreed to review the case. In a 5-to-4 decision, the Court overturned Eddings's sentence, but not on the grounds that Eddings was too young. Rather, writing for the majority, Justice Lewis Powell offered the opinion that the trial judge had erred in refusing to consider the other mitigating circumstances (i.e., the unhappy upbringing and the emotional disturbances). This ruling reaffirmed the decision in *Lockett v. Ohio* (1978) that all relevant mitigating circumstances must be considered, but it left the question of the execution of juvenile offenders unresolved. **See also** juvenile offenders; mitigating circumstances; *Roper v. Simmons*.

Eighth Amendment

The Eighth Amendment to the U.S. Constitution, one of the original ten amendments constituting the Bill of Rights, was added to the Constitution in 1791. More than any other provision of the Constitution, the Eighth Amendment is pertinent to the debate over capital punishment, since the most important challenges to capital punishment have been brought on Eighth Amendment grounds. The Eighth Amendment is specifically worded to protect defendants from excessive or disproportionate punishments. It prohibits the imposition of excessive bail or fines, and it prohibits the use of cruel and unusual punishment. Opponents of capital punishment often argue that the death penalty is inherently "cruel and unusual" and is thus unconstitutional; supporters of capital punishment reply that it is not. Several important Supreme Court decisions, notably *Furman v. Georgia*, have concerned this specific issue. **See also** Constitution of the

United States; cruel and unusual punishment; *Furman v. Georgia.*

electric chair

The electric chair is an apparatus used to perform executions by electrocution; that is, by passing a powerful electric current through the condemned prisoner's body. The word *electrocution* is, in fact, a compound of the words *electricity* and *execution*, and it came into the English language because of the use of the electric chair. The electric chair was developed in New York state during the 1880s in the hope that execution by means of electricity would be faster, more painless, and more reliable than execution by hanging.

In a typical execution using an electric chair, the condemned prisoner is strapped into the chair with leather belts, which are placed around the chest, arms, thighs, and legs. The condemned prisoner's head is partially shaved so that an electrode can be attached to the scalp. A second electrode is attached at the base of the spine or to the legs. In early electric chairs the electrodes made contact with the body by means of sponges that were moistened with saltwater to increase conductivity. Later, a special high-conductivity salve was developed. (The same type of salve is used by physicians to enhance the effectiveness of ultrasound equipment, which is used to examine pregnant women.) Once the condemned prisoner is in proper contact with the electrodes, an electric current is passed through the condemned prisoner's body. The condemned prisoner receives a jolt of roughly two thousand volts and ten amperes for a few seconds. A second, weaker current of roughly five hundred volts and four to six amperes is then maintained for about a minute, finishing with a final burst of higher voltage. This pattern is repeated, sometimes several times if necessary.

The strong jolt is intended to knock the condemned prisoner unconscious, but it is the lower voltage that actually kills the prisoner. Death results from paralysis of the heart and chest muscles, which stops the flow of blood to the brain. Heat from the electric current eventually alters the proteins in the internal organs, including the brain, so these organs are literally "cooked," but by this time death has already occurred.

The electric chair has a fascinating early history. It begins when Alfred Southwick, a dentist in Buffalo, New York, read about a man who was killed instantly when he accidentally came into contact with an electrical generator at the city's power plant. In 1882 Southwick and George Fell, a Buffalo physician, persuaded the Buffalo Society for the Prevention of Cruelty to Animals to use electricity to destroy stray and unwanted animals as a more humane alternative to drowning. Southwick and Fell published several scientific papers reporting on the results of using electricity to destroy unwanted animals. Their papers came to the attention of New York's governor, David Bennett Hill, who created a commission to investigate humane alternatives to hanging. Southwick was appointed to the commission. In 1888 the commission recommended that New York replace hanging with a method of execution that employed electricity. A bill to that effect was adopted by the state legislature in 1889. However, the method to be employed had yet to be invented.

Meanwhile, cities around the United States were replacing old oil and gas lanterns with electric lights. Two companies were offering municipal lighting systems, but they used different types of current. Thomas Edison's company used direct current (DC), while the company owned by George Westinghouse used alternating current (AC). DC

A hooded prisoner strapped to an electric chair awaits the fatal jolt of electricity in this 1908 photo.

power, which runs in only one direction, tends to lose strength over long distances. AC power, which switches direction many times per second, remains stable over greater distances. The idea for generating AC electricity was developed by Nikola Tesla, an unappreciated genius who also invented an early version of the radio. Tesla tried to interest Edison in the idea of AC, but when Edison refused to consider it, Tesla sold the idea to Westinghouse instead. Since Westinghouse's municipal lighting system used AC power, it was preferred by most cities. To discourage cities from purchasing the Westinghouse system, Edison began a campaign to convince people that AC power was more dangerous than DC. A former Edison employee, Harold Brown, who insisted that he was no longer affiliated with Edison and was acting only in the public interest, began writing letters to newspapers warning of the dangers of AC power. He staged a number of widely publicized demonstrations in which various animals, from dogs to calves and horses, were killed using AC power. When New York announced that it needed someone to develop a method of executing criminals using electricity, Brown agreed to design a device, insisting that it should employ AC power to be most effective.

Westinghouse was not happy to have his power generators associated with a method of execution and refused to sell Brown the generators he needed. Brown had to resort to subterfuge to get them. Claiming to be an overseas purchaser, Brown bought used generators, had them shipped to Brazil, and then reimported them. Brown was insistent that only Westinghouse AC generators were suitable for use in an electric chair. One of Edison's supporters even proposed the verb *westinghoused* in place of "electrocuted" to describe execution by electricity.

The first person executed using the electric chair was William Kemmler, a Buffalo greengrocer who was convicted of the 1889 murder of his girlfriend. Kemmler's trial was brief, since he had confessed to the crime, but the execution was delayed by an appeal brought on Kemmler's behalf by W. Bourke Cockran, a high-priced lawyer allegedly working without pay. Cockran argued that execution by electricity was cruel and unusual, and therefore prohibited by the Eighth Amendment. The case was taken all the way to the U.S. Supreme Court, but on consideration, the Court could find no reason why the electric chair was worse than hanging, and the electrocution of Kemmler was allowed to proceed.

Although there is no direct proof, historians do not doubt that Cockran was being paid by Westinghouse in a final attempt to prevent his generators from being associated with electrocution. It was probably a waste of money. Kemmler himself had little to gain from the appeal. Even if the appeal had been successful, Kemmler would have been executed, but by hanging rather than electrocution. And Edison's attempt to associate AC power with death was ineffective in any case. Cities continued to prefer AC power to DC power, and eventually even Edison had to adapt to using AC, the modern standard in electric current around the world.

Kemmler's execution was a public relations disaster for the electric chair. A fairly large audience was present for the historic execution, including the press. When the Westinghouse generator was revved up to two thousand volts, a switch was thrown, directing the power through Kemmler's body for seventeen seconds. Kemmler convulsed and turned red, but when the power was turned off, he resumed breathing. The warden, who was detaching the electrodes, hastily reattached them and ordered that the power be turned back on. Unfortunately this could not be done immediately, since the generator had been turned off and its belt was coming loose. Once the generator was repaired and running up to speed, a second jolt of two thousand volts was sent through Kemmler, this time for a full minute. Kemmler jerked spasmodically. His head began to smoke, and the smell of burned flesh filled the room. One later report claims that flames shot from Kemmler's mouth, but this was probably an exaggeration. Horrified newspaper reports declared the new execution method "far worse than hanging." Nevertheless, within a year of Kemmler's execution, four more electrocutions took place at Sing Sing Prison, this time without incident. Encouraged by these successes, other states began adopting the electric chair in favor of hanging.

With practice, electric chair operators learned not to use a sustained flow of power stronger than about six amperes, to avoid scorching the body. However, this is not powerful enough to cause immediate unconsciousness. Hence the flow of power must be modified as the execution proceeds, with a brief but powerful burst at the beginning, followed by a sustained flow of weaker current. Controlling the flow of electricity in the required manner takes a trained electrical technician. For many years, the technician who performed executions in New York was Edwin F. Davis, the electrician who built New York's first electric chairs, following Harold Brown's design.

Whether electrocution is genuinely painless has remained controversial. It has been pointed out that since electrical current paralyzes the muscles, a person executed by electrocution could be in pain but unable to cry out. On the other hand, people who have survived accidental encounters with high-voltage lines generally report that they were instantly unconscious. Whether electrocution is painless or not, observers report that it is no less disturbing to watch than hanging. As a result, some states never adopted the electric chair. Some retained hanging as their method of execution, others adopted the gas chamber instead, and still others abolished the death penalty altogether.

Many of the electric chairs that were built for states at the beginning of the twentieth century remained in use until 1972, when the *Furman* decision officially banned all executions in the United States. (No executions had actually been conducted since 1963, however.) When executions resumed, sometimes decades later, the old electric chairs were considered obsolete or beyond repair. Many states took the opportunity to replace electrocution with lethal injection. Though some states still offer the electric chair as an option, and Florida had a new electric chair built as recently as 1998, use of the electric chair is clearly in decline. Only one state, Nebraska, still uses the electric chair as its exclusive method of execution. **See also** *In re Kemmler*; Kemmler, William; Sing Sing Prison.

Ellis, Ruth Neilson (1926–1955)

Ruth Neilson Ellis was the last woman to be executed in Great Britain, and her execution was among the events that led to Great Britain's placing a moratorium on the death penalty in 1965. There is little doubt that Ellis was guilty of the murder for which she was convicted and sentenced. Ellis was involved with David Blakeley, a race car driver who regularly beat her. When she discovered that he was also involved with another woman, she sought him out and emptied a small-caliber handgun into him on a London street in front of numerous witnesses. When asked on the witness stand what she intended to do when shooting Blakeley, she replied that she obviously intended to kill him. She was hanged on July 13, 1955.

As an abused and wronged woman, Ellis was the object of considerable sympathy, despite her obvious guilt. Misgivings about her execution helped fuel the movement to abolish the death penalty in Great Britain. **See also** international use of capital punishment.

Enmund v. Florida

This 1982 Supreme Court decision concerned the constitutionality of imposing a death sentence on a defendant who, while participating in a crime in which someone is killed, did not kill the victim or intend that the victim be killed. The defendant in the case, Earl Enmund, was convicted in 1975 of participating in a robbery at a farmhouse during the course of which an elderly couple were killed. Enmund, however, only served as the lookout and remained in the car outside the house, so he was not present during the killings. Nevertheless, with the other defendants, he was sentenced to death. His case was appealed on the grounds that the penalty was excessive since Enmund did not participate in the killings and, since the killings were unplanned, did not know that the killings would take place. The Florida Supreme Court ruled that since Enmund had participated in the robbery, he could be held responsible for the killings. The U.S. Supreme Court agreed to review the case.

In a 5-to-4 decision, the Supreme Court ruled that the penalty was indeed excessive given Enmund's role in the crime. Writing for the majority, Justice Byron White argued that participation in a felony during the course of which someone is killed is a serious crime but that nearly all state legislatures, juries, and even prosecutors would not impose the death penalty if participation in the crime were relatively minor. Only a small minority of states allowed the imposition of the death penalty regardless of the degree of participation, and even in these states such a penalty was rarely imposed. Hence, by current community standards, Enmund's sentence could be judged cruel and unusual. Writing in dissent, Justice Sandra Day O'Connor argued that the question of who is a principal in a crime and who merely an accessory should be left to the states to decide. The *Enmund* case significantly changed the way cases with multiple defendants are prosecuted by altering the presumption that everyone involved in the same crime is equally culpable and should receive the same sentence. **See also** cruel and unusual punishment.

equal protection

The concept of equal protection was introduced into the Constitution of the United States by the Fourteenth Amendment, which states that no state shall "deny to any person within its jurisdiction the equal protection of the laws." Ratified soon after the Civil War, the Fourteenth Amendment was intended to ensure that federal and state governments did not discriminate against former slaves, who were now entitled to the rights guaranteed to all citizens of the United States. For many decades, however, the Supreme Court placed a very narrow interpretation on the equal protection clause. In 1883 the Supreme Court ruled that, while the equal protection clause meant that all citizens were entitled, for example, to freedoms of speech, religion, and the right to vote, this principle did not guarantee blacks access to privately owned facilities, such as restaurants, hotels, or theaters. In the 1896 *Plessy v. Ferguson* decision, the Supreme Court ruled that, while blacks should have access to the same *types* of public facilities as whites, they were not guaranteed access to the *same* facilities. As long as the facilities were equal, they could be kept separate. It was not until the landmark 1954 *Brown v. Board of Education* decision that the Supreme Court overturned the *Plessy* ruling by declaring that separate facilities were inherently unequal. With that ruling, the Supreme Court expanded the concept of equal protection.

One of the most important implications of the equal protection clause is that all citizens must be treated equally and have equal access to the judicial system. In its 1956 *Griffin v. Illinois* decision, the Supreme Court ruled that indigent defendants could not be charged a fee for trial transcripts and other materials necessary to their defense since charging for such materials gives indigent people less access to justice than wealthy people. In 1963 the Supreme Court ordered that indigent defendants in state courts must have access to adequate legal representation, even if this means that state funds must be used to pay for legal counsel.

Equal access to justice obviously means that all defendants have a right to be tried by a fair and impartial jury. As early as 1880, the Supreme Court struck down state laws in Virginia and West Virginia that prevented blacks from serving on juries. Unfortunately, the Supreme Court continued to allow jury selection procedures that had much the same effect. However, in 1935 the Supreme Court ruled, in its *Norris v. Alabama* decision, that the conviction of black suspect Clarence Norris had to be overturned because the jury selection process had systematically excluded black jurors and had produced a jury that was racially imbalanced and implicitly racist. Since then, numerous other criminal convictions have been overturned on similar grounds.

The concept of equal protection, and specifically of equal access to justice, poses a potentially serious challenge to the constitutionality of the death penalty. Prior to the 1972 *Furman v. Georgia* decision, it had been noted that the proportion of blacks on death row was far greater than the proportion of blacks in the general population. On average, whites could expect to receive less severe sentences than blacks, even when the crimes committed were more or less similar. Indeed, statistical analysis demonstrated that the death penalty was not consistently applied and that whether or not a defendant would receive a death sentence had more to do with the defendant's race than with the seriousness of the crime committed. It was largely for this reason that the Supreme Court nullified all state capital punishment statutes in *Furman v. Georgia*. Subsequent revisions in death-penalty statutes have been intended specifically to ensure that the death penalty is imposed only with regard to the seriousness of the crime, without consideration for the race of the defendant. How successful these revisions have been is still open to debate. If death rows continue to show the same racial imbalance that they have in the past, it is possible that the Supreme Court could again bring capital punishment to a halt on the grounds that death-penalty statutes still fail to provide equal access to justice as required by the Constitution. **See also** racial discrimination in sentencing.

ESPY file

The ESPY file is an online list of all executions in the United States, beginning in 1608. Work on the file was begun by M.Watt Espy, who based his list on original documents and newspaper reports. In 1977 the University of Alabama Law Center in Tuscaloosa provided space for Espy to continue his work. In 1984 the University of Alabama received a grant to cooperate with the Interuniversity Consortium of Political and Social Research in creating a computer database of Espy's research. The result was the list of executions now available on the Internet. Unfortunately, the ESPY file has not been updated since 1987, and some of the information in it is now known to be flawed. Nevertheless, the file is the most complete and detailed information on executions in the United States currently available. **See also** Death Penalty Information Center.

Evangelium Vitae (The Gospel of Life)

Evangelium Vitae is an encyclical, or statement of doctrine, issued by Pope John Paul II in 1995. In this encyclical the pope effectively reversed the Catholic Church's position on the death penalty. Previously, the church had taken the view that a legitimate government had a moral right to "punish malefactors by means of penalties commensurate with the gravity of the crime, not excluding, in cases of extreme gravity, the death penalty" (from the 1994 *Catechism of the Catholic Church*). In *Evangelium Vitae*, the pope maintains that the purpose of punishment

In his 1995 encyclical Evangelium Vitae, *Pope John Paul II expressed opposition to capital punishment.*

is to ensure public safety while also "offering the offender an incentive and help to change his or her behavior and be rehabilitated." Catholic morality requires that this should be achieved, if possible, without bloodshed, since this is more commensurate with the common good and with respect for human dignity. Hence, the death penalty is justified only when there is no other way to adequately protect society or motivate reform. The pope concludes, "As a result of steady improvements in the organization of the penal system, such cases are very rare, if not practically non-existent." In short, the Catholic Church's view on capital punishment is that, while capital punishment might have been justified in the past, modern prisons render it no longer the best way to achieve the goals of punishment. **See also** Bible; religious views.

evolving standards of decency

The phrase "evolving standards of decency" refers to the criterion that should be used in judging whether or not a punishment qualifies as cruel and unusual. According to this legal principle, whether death as a penalty for certain crimes is cruel and unusual depends on whether the death penalty is accepted by society as appropriate and proportional for those crimes, a standard that may change over time.

The phrase "evolving standards of decency" was first used by Chief Justice Earl Warren in his opinion in *Trop v. Dulles* (1958). The Eighth Amendment to the U.S. Constitution prohibits the use of punishments that are cruel and unusual, which means that punishments must not be excessive but must be proportional to the crimes they are intended to punish. However, comparing the seriousness of a crime with the severity of a punishment is sometimes felt to be an apples-to-oranges comparison, since crimes and punishments are not acts of the same type and there is no clear measure by which the one can be compared to the other.

To solve this problem, Chief Justice Warren wrote that the phrase "cruel and unusual" in the Eighth Amendment "must draw its meaning from the evolving standards of decency that mark the progress of a maturing society." A precedent for Warren's opinion was set in an earlier Supreme Court decision, *Weems v. United States* (1910), in which Justice Joseph McKenna held that the decision of what should count as cruel and unusual should be based on "current sensibilities."

The idea that Supreme Court decisions may be directly influenced by public opinion may seem unacceptably arbitrary, but the justices do not consult opinion polls in making their decisions. Rather, the evidence for what is considered decent and appropriate is drawn from jury decisions and from penal codes passed by state legislatures. **See also** Constitution of the United States; cruel and unusual punishment; *Trop v. Dulles*.

executioners

No matter what method of capital punishment is used, every execution has an executioner, the person who actually pulls a trigger or lever, flips a switch, begins an injection, or performs whatever physical act is required to cause the prisoner's death. Historically, executioners were often local law enforcement officers who had other duties besides the performing of executions. It was common in early America for executioners to be hired on an execution-by-execution basis. Hence, executioners tended to be hired men willing to do an unpleasant job for pay or exchange of goods, or they were citizens who took on the job out of a sense of civic duty. Such people were, in any case, amateurs who rarely underwent training and who sometimes relied on alcohol to steady their nerves. However, in some times and places, executions were performed by professionals, or people whose sole duty was the performing of executions. This was especially likely to be true in places where there were many executions to perform, or when the method of execution required some degree of skill or technical knowledge.

In Europe during the Middle Ages, executions of members of the nobility were typically by decapitation performed using either a sword or an ax. Striking with enough force and accuracy to inflict a precise, quick death blow required a great deal of strength as well as skill, so executions were performed by professional headsmen. Professional headsmen often wore masks to hide their identity, giving rise to the popular image of the bare-chested executioner in a black cowl. Headsmen were valued for their skill, and good headsmen spent much time practicing to keep their skills honed. However, it was not unusual for executions to go badly. Condemned prisoners sometimes paid the headsman a bonus to make the stroke quick and accurate. In some cases, condemned prisoners were even allowed to request the services of a headsman whom they knew and trusted.

In this 1897 photo, hangmen in the town of Liberty, Missouri, prepare a condemned criminal for hanging.

In Gilbert and Sullivan's comic opera *The Mikado*, the Lord High Executioner is a common criminal who has been sentenced to death (for the high crime of "flirting"). The humorous premise of the play is that criminals must be executed in order, so the Lord High Executioner cannot execute anyone else until he has first executed himself. As absurd as this premise seems, it is based on actual practice. In Maryland it was so difficult to find someone willing to serve as public hangman that the colony gave the office to a criminal whose own sentence of execution was then commuted. John Dandy, who was condemned to death for murder, was appointed to the office of executioner in Maryland in 1643. Later Maryland executioners were also convicted criminals, although, unlike the fictional Lord High Executioner of *The Mikado*, these public officials actually performed executions.

Very few names of professional headsmen and hangmen survive, probably because the job of executioner was regarded as an unsavory profession and many professional executioners actually took steps to preserve their anonymity. The best-known professional executioner was Jack Ketch, a seventeenth-century English headsman and hangman (he used both methods). He was so well known that in England his name came to be synonymous with "executioner." In France and England, the job of chief executioner was, for a while, passed down as a family tradition. In France, from 1687 to 1847, the title of executioner was held by a member of the Sanson family, beginning with Charles Sanson in 1687. In England, three members of the Pierrepoint family held the title of chief executioner for much of the twentieth century: Henry Pierrepoint (1874–1922), his brother Thomas (1870–1954), and Henry's son Albert (1905–1992). During the nineteenth century, the two best-known hangmen in America were George Maledon, who performed executions in the Arkansas territory for "Hanging Judge" Isaac Parker, and the anonymous New York executioner known only as "Monsieur New York."

As hanging was replaced by other methods in the United States in the twentieth century, executions increasingly required specialized expertise and technical knowledge. Electric chairs could be built and operated only by an experienced electrician. Gas chambers also required trained operators wearing specialized suits. In New York, executions were performed by Edwin F. Davis, the electrician who built the first electric chair in 1890. His successor was John Hulbert, who was a prison electrician trained by Davis. Hulbert was succeeded by Robert Elliott, who also performed executions in Connecticut, New Jersey, Pennsylvania, Massachusetts, and Vermont as electrocution was adopted by other states. In Mississippi, the chief executioner was an ex-convict named Jimmy Thompson, who transported the state's electric chair from place to place in the back of his pickup truck.

Execution by lethal injection also requires some degree of technical expertise. However, since the American Medical Association (and the Hippocratic Oath) prohibits physicians from inducing death, physicians have not taken the place of electricians as executioners. The practice has been to break up the execution into a series of small procedures so that no one person actually performs all of the execution. The person who procures the lethal chemicals and prescribes the dosage need not actually handle a needle, and the injections themselves can be managed by prison officials with only a little special training. None of these jobs needs to be done by the physician, who is on hand only to pronounce the time of death and perform an autopsy.

See also Ketch, Jack; Maledon, George; "Monsieur New York"; physician participation in executions; Pierrepoint family; Sanson family.

exoneration

If a defendant is convicted of a crime but new evidence is later discovered suggesting that the defendant is innocent, an appeals court may review the case, consider the new evidence, and overturn the conviction if the evidence warrants it. This is called exoneration. (However, if a defendant is acquitted and new evidence is later discovered suggesting guilt, the defendant may not be rearrested and tried a second time, according to the legal concept of double jeopardy.) In order to grant an exoneration, the appeals court must be convinced that it is more likely than not that no reasonable jury would have found the defendant guilty beyond a reasonable doubt had they had a chance to consider the new evidence. Between 1973 and 2005, 119 people on death row have been exonerated on this basis. In two states, Pennsylvania and Illinois, more people on death row have been exonerated than have been executed.

Death Row Exonerations by State (1973–2005)

State	Count	State	Count
Florida	21	North Carolina	5
Illinois	18	Ohio	5
Louisiana	8	Pennsylvania	5
Texas	8	New Mexico	4
Arizona	7	California	3
Oklahoma	7	Massachusetts	3
Alabama	5	Missouri	3
Georgia	5	Indiana	2
South Carolina	2	Nebraska	1
Idaho	1	Nevada	1
Kentucky	1	Virginia	1
Maryland	1	Washington	1
Mississippi	1		

See also actual innocence; double jeopardy.

extradition

Extradition is a legal term that refers to the transfer of a defendant from a jurisdiction where he or she is being held to another jurisdiction to face prosecution. This may refer either to a transfer from one state to another within the United States or to a transfer from one nation to another.

Interstate extradition (i.e., the transfer of a defendant from one state to another) is provided for by the Constitution of the United States, Article IV, Section 2, and is generally regulated by federal statutes. Since some states permit the use of the death penalty while others do not, the extradition of defendants who face charges on capital crimes has sometimes been an issue. It has been argued that states without the death penalty should refuse to extradite prisoners to jurisdictions where they could be sentenced to death. However, the current practice in the United States is for extradition requests to be honored, even if this results in the transfer of a defendant from a non–capital punishment jurisdiction to a capital punishment jurisdiction to face capital charges. Occasionally a prisoner on death row is temporarily extradited to a non–capital punishment state to face further prosecution. In such cases, it has been argued that the original jurisdiction loses the authority to carry out a death sentence. However, courts have consistently ruled that the original jurisdiction does not waive the authority to carry out an execution merely by granting a temporary extradition to a non–capital punishment jurisdiction.

International extradition (i.e., the transfer of a defendant from one nation to another) is provided for by treaties between nations. Such extradition agreements are a standard part of normal diplomatic relations and exist between most countries of the world. However, many countries that no longer permit capital punishment have announced that they will not extradite prisoners to countries where they would face charges that might result in a death sentence. In 1997 Israel turned down just such an extradition request from the state of Maryland. The suspect in the case, seventeen-year-old Samuel Sheinbein, was accused of killing nineteen-year-old Alfredo Enrique Tello and dismembering his body with an electric saw. Sheinbein fled to Israel, apparently because he knew that Israeli law forbid extraditing prisoners to face capital charges. Eventually Sheinbein was tried for the murder in Israel and sentenced to twenty-four years in an Israeli prison. The Israeli public was so outraged by the way in which Sheinbein had taken advantage of the law that in 1999 Israel modified its laws to permit the extradition of detainees on capital charges. However, many other countries, including Canada, continue to refuse to extradite defendants to the United States unless there is a guarantee that they will not be charged with a capital crime. **See also** foreign nationals; international use of capital punishment.

federal death-penalty laws

In the United States, certain crimes qualify as federal crimes and are prosecuted by the federal government rather than by state governments. As in state courts, federal trials may be conducted with a judge and jury and, depending on the charges, may result in death sentences. A crime comes under federal jurisdiction only if it involves crossing state lines, if it is a crime against a federal official, or if it occurs in the District of Columbia (which is directly under federal jurisdiction). Capital crimes can be tried by a federally convened jury only if a grand jury reviews the charges and agrees to let the trial proceed. Because it is more difficult to bring charges in a federal court, the prosecution of ordinary crimes is generally left to state jurisdictions if this is possible. The federal government does not maintain its own facilities for performing executions, and federal law specifies that the method of execution to be employed for a condemned prisoner depends on the state in which the sentencing takes place. If the trial happens to take place in a state that does not permit capital punishment, the judge may move the execution to another state.

Following the 1972 *Furman v. Georgia* Supreme Court ruling, which struck down the federal death-penalty statute, as well as other death-penalty statutes then in effect in the United States, the U.S. Congress did not reenact a federal death-penalty statute until 1988. That law, known as the Drug Kingpin Statute, made murder a capital federal offense when it occurs in the course of furthering the distribution and sale of large quantities of illegal drugs. A more comprehensive death-penalty statute was passed in 1994.

The current federal death-penalty statute allows jurors to consider the death penalty for homicides committed under any of an exceptionally long list of forty-four special circumstances, several of which repeat circumstances already stated in previous provisions. These special circumstances are (1) that the homicide involved poison, lying in wait, or some other circumstance indicating that the killing was willful, deliberate, or premeditated; or that the homicide occurred in the course of an arson, escape from custody, murder of another person, kidnapping, treason, espionage, sabotage, sexual abuse, burglary, or robbery; (2) that the homicide involved the smuggling of aliens; (3) that death resulted from the destruction of an aircraft or motor vehicle; (4) that the homicide was a drug-related drive-by shooting; (5) that the homicide occurred at an international airport; (6) that the homicide was retaliation against the immediate family of a law enforcement officer; (7) that death resulted from a civil rights offense; (8) that the victim was a member of Congress, an executive official, or a Supreme Court justice; (9) that the perpetrator was an escaped federal prisoner already serving a sentence of life imprisonment; (10) that death resulted from an offense involving the transportation of explosives, destruction of government property, or the destruction of property related to foreign or interstate commerce; (11) that the homicide occurred in the course of drug trafficking; (12) that the homicide occurred in a federal facility; (13) that genocide was committed; (14) that the victim was a federal judge or law enforcement official; (15) that the victim was a foreign official; (16) that the perpetrator was a federal prisoner; (17) that the victim was a U.S. national in a foreign country; (18) that the victim was a state or local law enforcement official or someone aiding in a federal investigation; (19) that the victim was a state correctional officer; (20) that the homicide occurred in the course of a kidnapping; (21) that the homicide resulted from a hostage taking; (22) that the victim was a court officer or juror; (23) that the homicide was committed for the purpose of preventing the testimony of a witness, crime victim, or informant; (24) that the homicide was retaliation against a witness, crime victim, or informant; (25) that death resulted from the mailing of injurious articles (e.g., a bomb or disease agent); (26) that the victim was the president or vice president of the United States; (27) that the homicide was a murder-for-hire; (28) that the homicide involved a racketeering offense; (29) that death resulted from the willful wrecking of a train; (30) that death resulted from a bank robbery–related murder or kidnapping; (31) that the homicide involved a carjacking; (32) that the homicide involved rape or child molestation; (33) that the homicide involved sexual exploitation of children; (34) that the homicide occurred in the course of an offense against maritime navigation; (35) that the homicide occurred in the course of an offense against a maritime fixed platform; (36) that the homicide involved a terrorist act against a U.S. national in a foreign country; (37) that the homicide involved the use of a weapon of mass destruction; (38) that the homicide involved torture; (39) that the homicide was related to a continuing criminal enterprise; (40) that death resulted from an aircraft hijacking; (41) that the homicide involved espionage; (42) that the homicide involved treason; (43) that the homicide involved trafficking in large quantities of drugs; or (44) that the perpetrator attempted, authorized, or advised the killing of any officer, juror, or witness in a case involving a continuing criminal enterprise.

The federal death-penalty statute also includes a complex list of aggravating circumstances. Three separate lists are provided: one for homicide committed in the course of espionage or treason; one for homicide committed in the furtherance of drug trafficking; and one for homicide under other circumstances. In the case of homicide committed in the course of espionage or treason, the death penalty may be imposed if one of three aggravating circumstances is proven to have accompanied the crime: (1) that the defendant has previously been convicted of another offense involving espionage or treason for which a sentence of life imprisonment or death could be imposed; (2) that the defendant knowingly created a grave risk to national security; or (3) that the defendant knowingly created a grave risk of death to another person.

In the case of homicide committed in the course of drug trafficking, the death penalty may be imposed if one of eight aggravating circumstances is proven to have accompanied the crime: (1) that the defendant was previously convicted of an offense resulting in death for which the penalty was life imprisonment or death; (2) that the defendant was previously convicted of two or more serious offenses involving trafficking in controlled substances, or the infliction of serious injury or death on another person; (3) that the defendant was previously convicted of an offense involving trafficking in controlled substances for which the penalty was five or more years in prison; (4) that in the course of the offense the defendant used a firearm, or directed, advised, authorized, or assisted someone else in the use of a firearm to threaten or injure someone; (5) that the offense involved the distribution of controlled substances to someone under the age of twenty-one; (6) that the offense involved the distribution of controlled substances near a school; (7) that the offense involved the use of minors as distributors of controlled substances; or (8) that the offense involved trafficking in a controlled substance that the defendant knew was mixed with a potentially lethal adulterant.

In the case of homicide under other circumstances, the death penalty may be imposed if one of fifteen aggravating circumstances is proven to have accompanied the crime. These aggravating circumstances are (1) that death resulted during the commission of another crime; (2) that the defendant had previously been convicted of a violent felony involving firearms; (3) that the defendant had previously been convicted of a felony for which the sentence was life imprisonment or death; (4) that the defendant was previously convicted of two or more serious offenses involving the infliction of serious injury or death on another person; (5) that the defendant created a grave risk of death to other people; (6) that the defendant committed the offense in an especially heinous, cruel, or depraved manner, involving torture or serious physical abuse to the victim; (7) that the defendant procured the commission of the offense by payment or the promise of payment; (8) that the defendant committed the offense for payment or the promise of payment; (9) that the defendant engaged in considerable planning and premeditation, or that the homicide was an act of terrorism; (10) that the defendant was previously convicted of two or more serious offenses involving trafficking in controlled substances; (11) that the victim was particularly vulnerable due to old age, youth, or infirmity; (12) that the defendant was previously convicted of a drug offense for which a sentence of five or more years of imprisonment may be imposed, or was previously convicted of engaging in a continuing criminal enterprise; (13) that the homicide was committed in the course of engaging in a continuing criminal enterprise involving the distribution of controlled substances to people under the age of twenty-one; (14) that the victim was the president of the United States, the president-elect, the vice president, the vice president–elect, the person next in line for the presidency or any person acting legally as president, a foreign head of state, a foreign official in the United States on official business, a judge, a law enforcement officer, or an employee of a federal correctional facility; or (15) that the defendant had previously been convicted of sexual assault or child molestation.

Federal law does not permit the execution of someone who was under the age of eighteen at the time of the crime. Federal law does provide for life imprisonment without parole as an alternative to the death penalty. The president of the United States has sole authority to grant clemency.

Only three people have been executed under federal jurisdiction since the reenactment of capital punishment. The first of these was Timothy McVeigh, who was executed in 2001 for the 1995 bombing of the Murrah Federal Building in Oklahoma

City. Federal death row inmates are held at the federal penitentiary at Terre Haute, Indiana. As of April 2005, there were thirty-six people on death row under federal jurisdiction. **See also** McVeigh, Timothy.

Felker v. Turpin

This 1996 Supreme Court decision specifically concerned the constitutionality of the Antiterrorism and Effective Death Penalty (AEDP) Act, which was passed by Congress in 1996 in response to the 1993 terrorist attack on the World Trade Center in New York City and the 1995 terrorist attack on the Murrah Federal Building in Oklahoma City. The act limited a convicted person's right to file what is known as a habeas corpus petition; that is, an appeal based on the claim that a defendant's constitutional rights were violated during his or her trial. The AEDP Act set a limit of six months (180 days) for the submission of such appeals and forbid courts from considering a second habeas corpus petition filed on substantially the same grounds as a previous petition.

The defendant in the case, Ellis Wayne Felker, was convicted of murder in Georgia and sentenced to death. Felker's lawyers filed appeals on various grounds, including the filing of a habeas corpus petition in federal court. All of the various appeals were unsuccessful. Following the passage of the AEDP Act, Felker's lawyers again lodged a petition for habeas corpus, using substantially the same argument (or grounds) that had been used in the previous petition. The federal appeals court refused to consider the petition on the grounds that, under the AEDP Act, federal courts did not have jurisdiction to consider a second habeas corpus petition lodged on the same grounds as a previous petition. In order to determine the constitutionality of the AEDP Act, the Supreme Court agreed to review the case.

The Supreme Court ruled unanimously that the AEDP Act did not violate Article I, Section 9, of the U.S. Constitution, which prohibits the suspension of the right of habeas corpus. Writing for the Court, Chief Justice William Rehnquist argued that legal tradition has long recognized that the right of habeas corpus is open to abuse, and that it is within the power of Congress to pass laws aimed at preventing "abuse of the writ." The AEDP Act, he continued, placed reasonable restrictions on the right of habeas corpus, consistent with preventing abuse without suspending the right altogether. The decision upheld Felker's original conviction and sentence, and Felker was executed on November 15, 1996. **See also** Antiterrorism and Effective Death Penalty Act; habeas corpus.

film treatment of capital punishment

Capital punishment has figured prominently in film and television dramas virtually since the beginning of the motion picture industry. Death row is a natural setting for dramatic tension and stories related to issues of justice and dying, and audiences have an age-old fascination with the details of crime and punishment. Films are an ideal medium for exploring the ambiguity of human emotional responses to crime: that crimes must be punished, even as the humanity of criminals is recognized. The following films involving the theme of capital punishment are particularly noteworthy or influential, either by generating debate over the morality or justification of the death penalty or by offering great cinematic performances.

M (1931) starring Peter Lorre and directed by Fritz Lang. A child molester is hunted and eventually tried by the criminal underworld of Weimar Germany. The film explores the idea that some crimes are intolerable even to the most hardened of criminals, justifying the death penalty.

The Public Enemy (1931) starring James Cagney. This was one of the first films to explore the factors that produce criminal behavior.

The Last Mile (1932) directed by Samuel Bischoff. This film depicts the last hours of an innocent man awaiting execution for murder. The film was remade in 1959 starring Mickey Rooney.

20,000 Years in Sing Sing (1932) starring Spencer Tracy. A prison inmate is sentenced to death for a killing committed by his girlfriend.

Two Seconds (1932) starring Edward G. Robinson. Seated in the electric chair, an inmate's whole life passes before him.

The Accusing Finger (1936) starring Harry Carey. A district attorney who loves to see defendants sentenced to death is framed for murder and finds himself facing a death sentence.

Angels with Dirty Faces (1938) starring James Cagney. A hardened but sympathetic career criminal ends up on death row.

Cell 2455, Death Row (1955) starring William Campbell. This film is based on the memoirs of Caryl Chessman, one of the most famous death row inmates.

Hold Back Tomorrow (1955) starring John Ayer. Prison guards attempt to make the final hours of a death row inmate a little easier.

Beyond a Reasonable Doubt (1956) directed by Fritz Lang. An opponent of capital punishment has himself framed for murder to prove that it is possible for innocent people to be sentenced to death.

Compulsion (1959) starring Orson Welles. This film is based on the trial of convicted juvenile murderers Nathan Leopold and Richard Loeb in 1924.

In Cold Blood (1967) starring Robert Blake and directed by Richard Brooks. The film of Truman Capote's best-selling book is a gritty portrayal of the two confessed murderers of a Kansas farm family. A modern classic of crime and punishment.

The Traveling Executioner (1970) directed by Jack Smight. This is a black comedy about an executioner who carries an electric chair around in his pickup truck. Based on a true story.

The Executioner's Song (1982) directed by Lawrence Schillar. This is a made-for-television movie based on the life and death of convicted Utah murderer Gary Gilmore, whose sensational campaign to be executed drew national attention to the death-penalty issue.

I Want to Live (1983) directed by Robert Wise. This is the story of Barbara Graham, a woman executed in 1957 who still claimed to be innocent.

Dance with a Stranger (1985) directed by Mike Newell. This is a British film based on the life and death of Ruth Ellis, the last woman executed in England.

The Thin Blue Line (1988) directed by Errol Morris. This is a stylized documentary about an investigation leading to the sentencing of an innocent man to death.

Dead Man Walking (1995) starring Susan Sarandon and Sean Penn. Based on the book by death-penalty opponent Sister Helen Prejean, this film is held up as dramatic support for the abolition of capital punishment. **See also** Chessman, Caryl; Gilmore, Gary; Leopold, Nathan F., and Richard A. Loeb; literature; Prejean, Helen.

firing squad

The firing squad is a traditional method of execution in which the condemned person is shot to death by a row of marksmen. Ideally, the condemned prisoner is shot in the heart, which stops the flow of blood to the brain, causing death in a few minutes due to oxygen starvation to the brain. If no shot actually hits

A U.S. Army firing squad executes a Nazi soldier in 1945.

the heart, the condemned prisoner is allowed to bleed to death from wounds that might even be medically treatable. This outcome, which marksmen seek to avoid, results in a relatively slow and painful death.

Most firing squads are made up of five marksmen using rifles. The shooters stand ten to twenty feet from the condemned prisoner, who wears a hood and a circular target over his heart. In prison executions, the condemned prisoner is generally seated in a chair. At least one of the guns is loaded with blanks and the shooters are not told which guns have live ammunition. This is done so that none of the shooters can know whether his shot caused the condemned prisoner's death. On a signal—usually the word "Fire!"—the members of the squad fire their weapons simultaneously.

The firing squad was the traditional method of execution used in the military, probably because on a battlefield it was easier to form a squad of marksmen than to arrange for other forms of execution. Death sentences for military offenses, such as mutiny and desertion, were traditionally carried out by a firing squad. In civilian jurisdictions, firing squads have rarely been used. Only two states, Idaho and Oklahoma, provide for the use of firing squads, and the method is only available as an option, not as the primary method of execution. Utah, which had allowed the use of firing squads, discontinued their use in March 2004.

By some accounts the first person executed by firing squad in the American colonies was George Kendall in Virginia. He was shot for espionage. In 1977 Gary Gilmore, the first person to be executed in the United States since 1967, was executed by firing squad at his own request.

The firing squad has been criticized for causing slow and painful deaths. Gary Gilmore, for example, took two minutes to die, even though he was hit in the heart by all four of the live rounds that were fired. The question of whether firing squads are cruel and unusual was raised by the U.S. Supreme Court in 1878 in *Wilkerson v. Utah*. In that case the Court ruled that firing squads were not cruel and unusual, and the issue has not been raised since. Perhaps because of its military heritage, the firing squad is considered by some to be a dignified way to die, and some condemned prisoners select it for that reason.

Today, China is the only country other than the United States that uses shooting as a method of execution. However, in China the execution is performed by a single shooter delivering two shots at point-blank range to the back of the head. **See also** Gilmore, Gary; Kendall, George; *Wilkerson v. Utah.*

Florida

Florida has traditionally permitted juries to impose the death penalty, and continues to do so currently. Only five executions are recorded to have taken place in territorial Florida. Florida became a state in 1845, but did not build its first state prison until 1868. The prison, at Chattahoochee, was run by the military until 1871. Executions by hanging, although nominally under state jurisdiction, continued to be handled by county officials until 1923. Indeed, from 1916 to 1923 executions were explicitly conducted under local rather than state jurisdiction. From 1846 to 1923, 103 executions by hanging took place in Florida. Florida's first electric chair was built by prison inmates in 1922, and hanging was abolished in 1923. In 1924 convicted murderer Frank Johnson was the first person executed by electrocution in Florida. From 1924 to 1964, 196 executions by electrocution took place in Florida.

Following the 1972 *Furman v. Georgia* Supreme Court decision, which invalidated all state death-penalty statutes, Florida quickly developed a new death-penalty statute and had it reenacted the same year. Florida's current death-penalty statute allows juries to consider the death penalty for premeditated homicide and for homicide committed in the course of drug trafficking, arson, sexual attack, robbery, burglary, kidnapping, escape, child abuse, elder abuse, abuse of a disabled adult, aircraft piracy, the use of a destructive device or bomb, carjacking, stalking, or murder of more than one person. Juries may also consider the death penalty for the unlawful distribution of drugs that directly cause someone's death.

The death penalty may be imposed for the crime of homicide if at least one of fourteen aggravating circumstances is proven to have accompanied the crime. These aggravating circumstances are (1) that the defendant was already under sentence for a previous felony; (2) that the defendant was previously convicted of a capital offense; (3) that the defendant knowingly caused a great risk of death to many people; (4) that the homicide was committed in the course of a robbery, sexual battery, child abuse, elder abuse or abuse of a disabled person, arson, burglary, kidnapping, aircraft piracy, or the use of a destructive device such as a bomb; (5) that the homicide was committed in order to avoid arrest or effect escape from custody; (6) that the homicide was committed for monetary gain; (7) that the homicide was committed in order to disrupt or hinder a governmental function or the enforcement of laws; (8) that the homicide was especially heinous, atrocious, and cruel; (9) that the homicide was committed in a cold, calculated, and premeditated manner, following a preconceived plan; (10) that the victim was a law enforcement officer; (11) that the victim was a public official engaged in the performance of his or her duties; (12) that the victim was a child under the age of twelve; (13) that the victim was particularly vulnerable; or (14) that the defendant was a gang member. A separate but similar list of aggravating circumstances is given for the crime of drug trafficking that results in someone's death. The jury must also consider any mitigating circumstances that the defense wishes to present.

Under a 1999 Florida Supreme Court decision, a person convicted of a capital offense could not be executed if he or she was under the age of seventeen at the time of the offense. This statute was invalidated by the 2005 *Roper v. Simmons* Supreme Court decision, which outlawed the execution of convicted criminals who were younger than eighteen at the time of the offense. Florida does provide for life imprisonment without parole as an alternative to the death penalty. The governor, with the advice of the Board of Executive Clemency, has the authority to grant clemency. The governor also has the authority to grant reprieves of up to sixty days.

Besides being prompt in passing a new death-penalty statute after the *Furman* decision, Florida was also prompt in resuming executions. Following the 1976 *Gregg v. Georgia* Supreme Court decision that allowed executions in the United States to resume, Florida held its first execution in 1979 with the execution of John Spenkelink. The execution was controversial because newly installed shades over the window that separated the viewing room from the execution chamber created the impression that improper treatment of Spenkelink was being concealed from viewers. It was also controversial because Prison Superintendent David Brierton had suggested offering the condemned prisoner a last drink and Spenkelink was the first prisoner to receive this courtesy. However, the practice was quickly abandoned as a poor idea.

Between 1979 and 1999, fifty-nine people were executed in Florida by electrocution. However, after the execution of Allen Lee Davis, the U.S. Supreme Court once again agreed to consider the constitutionality of electrocution. Without waiting for a decision, Florida made lethal injection an option for condemned prisoners. Terry Sims was the first person to die in Florida by lethal injection in 2000. Fourteen other executions by lethal injection have since taken place. As of April 2005, 384 people were awaiting execution on Florida's death row. **See also** *Furman v. Georgia; Spaziano v. Florida.*

Ford v. Wainwright

This was a case heard by the Supreme Court of the United States in 1986 concerning whether a person who has been sentenced to death may be executed while he or she is judged to be legally insane. The defendant in the case, Alvin Bernard Ford, was sentenced to death for murder in 1974. At the time of his crime, and subsequently at the time of his trial, Ford showed no signs of being mentally ill, and in fact the issue of his mental health was never raised at trial. However, once he was on death row his behavior began to change. His lawyer requested that he be examined by psychiatrists, and one of two psychiatrists who examined him concluded that his mental state no longer met the definition of legal sanity. The state of Florida then began statutorily defined procedures for making an official determination of sanity. Three psychiatrists appointed by the governor made independent examinations of Ford, and each concluded that he was still legally sane. Ford's attorney submitted additional materials for the governor's consideration, and the governor accepted them, without, however, indicating that they would be taken into account. When the governor eventually refused to change Ford's sentence, the case was appealed to the federal district court, which refused to hear the case. However, the U.S. Supreme Court agreed to consider the matter.

In a 7-to-2 decision, the Court ruled first that it was cruel and unusual to execute a person judged to be legally insane and second that Florida's procedure for making a determination of insanity was not adequate to protect the rights of the defendant. Writing for the majority, Justice Thurgood Marshall argued that Florida's procedure placed the ultimate decision solely in the hands of the state's executive branch, which might be subject to political pressure. The defendant was given no opportunity to respond and object to the opinions of the experts appointed by the governor, and there was no assurance that these experts were adequately impartial. The Court ordered that Ford's sanity be reevaluated using a more rigorous procedure.

A trial in 1989 determined that Ford was competent to be executed, but he died of respiratory complications associated with pancreatitis before his sentence could be carried out.

This case had little impact on the execution of inmates judged to be insane. In fact, under common law, no jurisdiction in the United States permits the execution of someone judged to be insane. However, the case did have some impact on the rigor of procedures by which insanity is determined. **See also** mentally ill offenders; Singleton, Charles.

foreign nationals

Foreign nationals, people who visit or live in a foreign country, are subject to the laws of that country; thus, people who commit crimes in a foreign country are subject to the punishments provided for by those laws. This is true of both U.S. citizens traveling abroad and foreign citizens visiting or living in the United States. In particular, a person who commits a death-eligible crime while in a U.S. jurisdiction that permits the death penalty will be subject to a capital trial and may be sentenced to death. This is true even if that person is a citizen of a country that does not permit the death penalty.

However, foreign nationals do have some special rights as provided for in the Vienna Convention on Consular Relations (VCCR), an international agreement adopted in 1963 and ratified by the United States in 1969. Chief among these rights is the right to request assistance (including legal advice and financial assistance) from the consular representative of the country of which the foreign national is a citizen. Of course, if assistance is to be rendered, the consular representative must be notified that a foreign national is being detained. The VCCR specifies that local authorities holding a foreign national must notify the appropriate consular representative "without delay." The International Court of Justice has ruled, in a dispute between Mexico and the United States, that "without delay" means as soon as it is discovered that the detainee is a foreign national. No further legal proceeding should take place until after notification has been given.

Unfortunately, jurisdictions within the United States have been extremely lax in providing consular notification, and the United States has been subject to severe international criticism for its failure to fulfill its obligations under the terms of the VCCR. Since 1976, roughly twenty-one foreign nationals have been executed in the United States. Of these it appears that none were granted the right to consular notification in a timely manner. In some cases, the executions were challenged on the grounds that local authorities had failed to notify the appropriate consular official. So far, U.S. courts have not halted an execution on the grounds that a defendant's right to consular notification had been violated.

As of June 2004, there were 118 foreign nationals on death row in the United States, broken down as follows: California (43), Texas (28), Florida (21), Arizona (3), Nevada (4), Ohio (4), Louisiana (3), Pennsylvania (2), Alabama (1), Oklahoma (1), Oregon (1), Georgia (1), Mississippi (1), Montana (1), Nebraska (1), Virginia (1), and the federal government (2). Fifty-three of these foreign nationals are from Mexico. About thirty other countries have at least one of their citizens on death row in the United States. **See also** international criticism of the United States; international use of capital punishment.

Foreman, Percy (1902–1988)

Percy Foreman was a prominent Texas defense attorney. During his career he handled between a thousand and fifteen hundred death-penalty cases, including some of the most prominent murder cases in the country. Only one of his clients was executed.

Foreman, who was born and spent most of his life in Texas, dropped out of school at age fifteen. However, he eventually won a scholarship to attend the Staunton Military Academy in Virginia and later earned a law degree from the University of Texas. Following graduation, he worked for the district attorney's office in Houston until he was able to establish his own practice.

Foreman was a colorful character who developed a reputation for his flamboyant courtroom style and theatrical tactics. He once defended a safecracker who walked with a wooden leg. Foreman apparently instructed his client to leave his wooden leg at home so that he had to be carried to the witness stand. His aggressive style sometimes led to brawls in the courtroom. Once, when the jury returned a verdict of not guilty, he was beaten by the policemen who had testified against his client. On another occasion a female defendant threatened him with a gun, but he convinced her not to shoot him, saying, "You don't want to shoot me, honey. I'm the only one who can get you off." Foreman was not afraid to charge exorbitant fees for his services. He sometimes joked that, even if he got his guilty clients off, they were punished by his fees. He once said, "I don't represent wealthy clients. If they weren't poor when they come to me, they are when they leave."

Despite his high fees, Foreman often urged law students to take up criminal law rather than civil law on the grounds that civil law was just about money whereas criminal law was about life and liberty. He referred to many of his cases as "misdemeanor murders," pointing out that onetime murderers who kill in the heat of passion are rarely an ongoing threat to society and are among the easiest of criminals to rehabilitate.

Foreman's most high-profile case was the defense of James Earl Ray, the accused assassin of Martin Luther King Jr., in 1969. Recognizing that Ray would probably get a death sentence if the case went to trial, he convinced Ray to plead guilty in exchange for a ninety-nine-year sentence. **See also** Darrow, Clarence.

Defense attorney Percy Foreman presents evidence to the jury during a 1964 trial. Of the nearly fifteen hundred clients Foreman defended, only one was executed.

Fort Leavenworth Penitentiary

Fort Leavenworth, the U.S. Army disciplinary barracks near Leavenworth, Kansas, was originally built in 1874 to house military prisoners. However, between 1895 and 1906 Fort Leavenworth was also used to house civilian prisoners under federal jurisdiction, making Fort Leavenworth the oldest federal penitentiary in the country. Prisoners at Fort Leavenworth were used as labor to build the Leavenworth Penitentiary on a nearby site. Prisoners worked twelve-hour shifts, and many worked while chained to twenty-five-pound iron balls. Leavenworth Penitentiary was used to house civilian prisoners under federal jurisdiction until 1940, at which time the penitentiary again became part of Fort Leavenworth, under the administration of the U.S. Army.

While it was used to house civilian prisoners, Leavenworth Penitentiary was one site where the federal government held death row prisoners. Only three executions of federal prisoners took place there. Executions were carried out by means of hanging. The U.S. Army disciplinary barracks at Fort Leavenworth is still used as death row for prisoners held under military jurisdiction. Between 1950 and 1961, nine soldiers were executed at Fort Leavenworth. **See also** military justice.

Furman v. Georgia

This was a landmark case heard by the Supreme Court of the United States in 1972. The question before the Court was whether capital punishment, as practiced in the United States at the time, violated the prohibition in the U.S. Constitution against cruel and unusual punishment. The decision of the Court supported the view that capital punishment was cruel and unusual. However, the Court's decision was so complex that no simple, unambiguous conclusion can be drawn from it. Nevertheless, *Furman v. Georgia* is undoubtedly the single most important legal decision to date on the issue of capital punishment in the United States, since it forced the rewriting of every death-penalty statute in the country.

The defendant in the case, William Henry Furman, was accused of committing murder in the course of burglarizing a home. A psychiatric evaluation concluded that Furman was not psychotic but that he was not mentally able to participate in the preparation of his own defense. Despite this finding, he was convicted of murder and sentenced to death. Furman's lawyers suspected that racial prejudice had probably played a role in the sentence. Furman was black, his victim white, and comparisons of court records indicated that a white man convicted of the same crime under the same conditions was less likely to have received a death sentence. Furman's lawyers appealed Furman's sentence. However, since the Supreme Court had never been willing to hear a death-penalty case based on the claim that a state's death-penalty statute was itself discriminatory, the lawyers in the case deemphasized the issue of discrimination. When they did raise the issue, toward the end of their argument, they were careful to tie it to the issue of cruel and unusual punishment. They argued that, even though a statistical pattern of discriminatory sentencing could not be used to prove intentional discrimination in a specific case, a statute could still be found to be unconstitutional if it was found to have allowed "arbitrary and capricious" sentencing, since such capriciousness was offensive to community standards of justice and was therefore "cruel and unusual," as the phrase was used in the Eighth Amendment. The U.S. Supreme Court agreed to review the case. At the same time, the Court combined it with two other cases, *Jackson v. Georgia* and *Branch v. Texas*, in both of which a black man had been sentenced to death for raping a white woman.

In a complex 5-to-4 decision, the Court overturned the sentences of the three defendants. However, the justices could not agree on a single statement to represent the opinion of the Court. Instead, the ruling was stated in a short paragraph known as a per curiam opinion. A per curiam opinion merely issues a ruling on the issue before the Court without further comment. Each justice then concurs (agrees) or dissents (disagrees) with the ruling. The per curiam decision in *Furman v. Georgia* is as follows:

> The Court holds that imposition and carrying out of the death penalty in these cases constitute cruel and unusual punishment in violation of the Eighth and Fourteenth Amendments. The judgment in each case is therefore reversed insofar as it leaves undisturbed the death sentence imposed, and the cases are remanded for further proceedings.

Five justices concurred in the ruling. However, only two justices, William Brennan and Thurgood Marshall, argued that the death penalty was *itself* cruel and unusual. Three other justices, William O. Douglas, Byron White, and Potter Stewart, argued only that the death-penalty statutes *currently in effect* gave so little guidance to jurors on when the death penalty should be imposed that juries were free to indulge their prejudices, causing the statutes to be applied in an arbitrary and capricious manner.

Four justices, Warren Burger, Lewis Powell, Harry Blackmun, and William Rehnquist, dissented from the per curiam ruling. As with the concurring opinions, the dissenting opinions were individually written and represented diverse views. However, several of the dissenting justices worried that there was no clear precedent for the decision. They objected that the decision was an instance of judicial lawmaking based on the personal preferences of the justices, rather than on sound interpretation of the Constitution.

The *Furman* decision provides a fascinating example of the way in which Supreme Court rulings affect law in the United States. Technically, the decision affected the lives of only three men, William Henry Furman, Lucius Jackson, and Elmer Branch. However, following the ruling, the Supreme Court issued a memo overturning death sentences in 121 other death-penalty cases that were awaiting consideration. The effect of the ruling was that every death-penalty statute in the country, including the federal death-penalty statutes, was invalidated. Only the law applying to military trials was not explicitly overturned, and even this law was eventually revised in response to the *Furman* decision. States that wished to retain the death penalty were required to revise their statutes in a way that would give juries clear guidance on when the death penalty should be imposed. While the statutes were being revised, no executions could be carried out. This resulted in a four-year ban on executions in the United States, although in fact no executions had been performed in the United States since 1967.

A second consequence of the *Furman* decision was that all death-penalty trials were split into two phases, a guilt phase and a penalty phase, so that appeals for mercy could be offered only after the question of guilt was already settled. This meant that defendants would not have to appear to be admitting guilt by pleading for mercy while the question of guilt was still undetermined.

The state of Georgia was among the first to attempt to revise its death-penalty statute in a way that would meet the standard set by the *Furman* ruling. In 1976 the Supreme Court ruled, in *Gregg v. Georgia*, that the revised state death-penalty statute was not arbitrary and capricious in the way that the previous statute had been. This resulted in a lifting of the ban on the death penalty that had been imposed by the *Furman* decision. Thirty-eight states, the federal government, and the U.S. military eventually developed revised death-penalty statutes in accordance with the *Furman* decision. The remaining twelve states and the District of Columbia either had no death-penalty statute or abolished capital punishment following the *Furman* decision. **See also** *Gregg v. Georgia*; racial discrimination in sentencing; trial.

Gacy, John Wayne (1942–1994)

John Wayne Gacy was a notorious serial killer who was executed in 1994 for the rape and murder of thirty-three boys and young men over a six-year period in Illinois. The lurid nature of his crimes and his sensational trial drew national attention, but his activities on death row are the reason he is associated with the debate over capital punishment.

While on death row, Gacy produced paintings of sad-faced clowns that sold as collector's items for thousands of dollars. He also published two volumes of prison correspondence that sold well. He became so wealthy while on death row that the state of Illinois later sued his estate for a share of the profits. This case, and other examples of financial success by death row inmates, prompted several states to pass laws limiting a convicted offender's profits, justified on the grounds that a criminal should not benefit from his or her crime. Gacy was executed by lethal injection on May 10, 1994, after fourteen years on death row. **See also** rights of the accused.

gallows

A gallows is the apparatus used in conducting an execution by hanging. The gallows for a hanging generally consists of a platform about ten feet above the ground on which the executioner and condemned prisoner stand. Above the platform is a stout beam from which the noose is suspended. The platform itself generally has a single-leaf trapdoor that opens downward when its catch is released. Some gallows, known as upright jerkers, are designed to pull the condemned prisoner upward, however, rather than dropping him or her downward.

Various mechanisms have been used to trigger the gallows. In a standard trapdoor gallows, it was common for the catch on the trapdoor to be operated by a lever that could be pulled by the executioner while standing on the platform. Some gallows were designed to trigger automatically, so no hangman had to feel that he had directly caused the condemned prisoner's death. Some upright jerkers, for example, were designed so that the weight of the prisoner on a platform would release a flow of water (or lead shot), resulting in an automatic triggering of the gallows. In 1905 Francis Barker, a condemned prisoner in Nebraska, invented a release that was activated by electricity and controlled with a push button. By having the button strapped to his left thigh, he was able to operate the gallows himself at his own execution.

Gallows were considered fairly easy to build. When executions were carried out by local officials, it was common for a gallows to be built for a single hanging and then immediately disassembled, on the belief that it would not be needed again for a long time and could easily be rebuilt when it was. **See also** gibbet; hanging.

gallows reprieve

A reprieve given to a condemned prisoner at the last minute. Today, when a prisoner on death row is granted clemency, in the form of either a commuted sentence or an exoneration, he or she is informed immediately. During the eighteenth century, it was common for a condemned prisoner not to be told of a reprieve until the very moment when the execution seemed about to occur. The prisoner would be brought to the gallows, given an opportunity to address the crowd, and even placed in the noose. When it was time for the reading of the death warrant, the sheriff presiding over the event would surprise the crowd and prisoner alike by reading a pardon instead. This gesture was not only theatrical but also served the purpose of causing the prisoner to reflect on the probable consequences of future transgressions. At a time when rehabilitation was considered the most important goal of punishment, the gallows reprieve seemed like an ideal way to teach a moral lesson without actually taking someone's life. However, as the practice became more popular, it also lost some of its impact. The practice was eventually abandoned on the grounds that it took too much of the deterrent value away from executions. Too many prisoners were coming to the gallows expecting a last-minute reprieve. **See also** simulated hangings; viewing of executions.

garrote

A garrote is a string, cord, or wire used to strangle a person to death. The cord is used to cut off the flow of blood in the large veins and arteries of the neck, causing death by oxygen starvation to the brain. The garrote was rarely used as an official method of execution, but executioners would sometimes use a garrote to render a condemned prisoner unconscious when the official punishment involved something particularly cruel, such as breaking on the wheel. Under such circumstances, use of the garrote was considered an act of kindness. **See also** breaking on the wheel.

gas chamber

The gas chamber is an execution device in which death is caused by the inhalation of lethal gas. In the first half of the twentieth century, several states that had not replaced hanging with the electric chair adopted the gas chamber instead. It was hoped that gas would provide a humane method of execution, more painless and reliable than hanging. Some state legislatures were unconvinced that electrocution represented a significant advance over hanging, and hoped that gas would prove to be clearly superior.

A gas chamber is generally not much larger than a phone booth and has one or more walls made of thick glass so that the execution can be observed. The door of the chamber must be tightly sealed with rubber gaskets to prevent leaks and protect onlookers from the gas. In the earliest executions, the gas was pumped into the chamber through a valve, but it later proved more convenient to produce the gas inside the chamber. In modern executions, a bowl of dilute sulfuric acid is placed under the chair on which the prisoner sits. Once the chamber is sealed, some pellets of sodium cyanide are released into the bowl. The chemical reaction of the pellets in the acid produces enough hydrogen cyanide gas to fill the chamber. Hydrogen cyanide bonds with hemoglobin in the blood, preventing the blood from carrying oxygen. Death is caused in approximately ten minutes by oxygen starvation to the brain. Prisoners are sometimes instructed to cooperate by

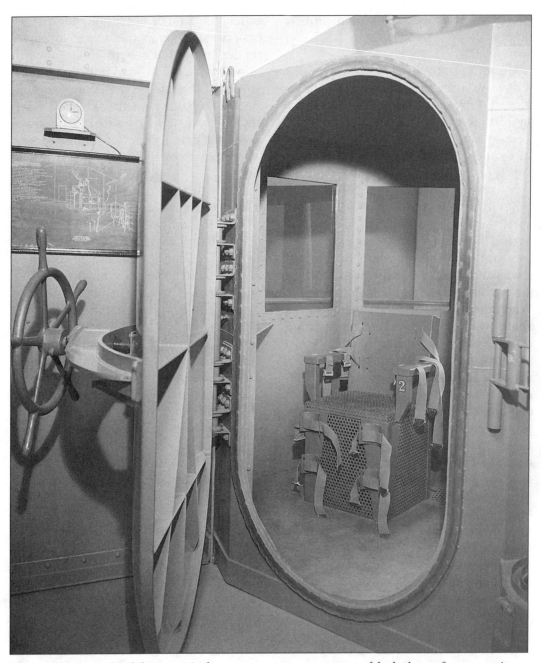

Throughout much of the twentieth century, many states used lethal gas for executions. Pictured in this 1960 photo is the gas chamber at San Quentin prison.

breathing deeply to hasten the effect of the gas. Once the prisoner is dead, the gas is vented out of the chamber with an exhaust fan, and a spray of ammonia is used to neutralize traces of cyanide clinging to the prisoner's clothes and hair.

Using gas as a method of execution was first considered during the late nineteenth century. Some humane societies used gas as a means of destroying unwanted animals, and as early as 1896 the Medical Society of Allegheny County in Pennsylvania was supporting the use of gas to execute criminals. However, at the time, electrocution received more serious attention.

It was not until 1921 that the Nevada state assembly decided to replace hanging and the firing squad with a more modern form of execution. It passed a statute designating lethal gas as the preferred method. The statute did not specify the type of gas to be used or how it was to be administered. In fact, the manner of execution envisioned by Nevada lawmakers was quite different than the one that was finally employed. The lawmakers imagined that the prisoner would be exposed to the lethal gas while asleep in his cell. The prisoner would not be told the exact night the execution was to take place and so would presumably be spared the anxiety created by the elaborate ceremonies that were so much a part of executions by hanging or by electric chair.

Prison officials quickly realized, however, that the legislators' vision was impractical. Poisonous gas could not safely be released into a prisoner's cell at night. Clearly, a small, airtight chamber would be needed. Major Delos A. Turner, a medical corps officer with the army, designed the gas chamber used by the state of Nevada. The decision to use hydrogen cyanide gas was made by the state's food and drug commissioner in part because the gas, which was used as a pesticide on orange trees, was available from a supplier in Southern California.

The first execution using a gas chamber took place at the Nevada state prison in Carson City on February 8, 1924. The condemned prisoner was a Chinese immigrant named Gee Jon, who was convicted of the murder of Tom Quong Kee, a gangster working for a rival gang. The fact that the execution took place during the winter both helped and hindered the execution. The Los Angeles company that had agreed to supply hydrocyanic acid (the liquid form of hydrogen cyanide gas) refused to ship the chemical to Nevada since it had to be kept below 22 degrees Fahrenheit to remain liquid. The supplier was afraid that the chemical would warm up and explode during the trip. Nevada prison officials drove to Los Angeles and took personal responsibility for transporting the chemical back to Carson City. In February they were able to do so without incident. However, the gas chamber itself was in an unheated area of the prison. Rather than being a comfortable room temperature, it was only 52 degrees Fahrenheit inside the chamber. When the hydrocyanic acid was pumped into the chamber, much of it did not turn into gas but merely pooled on the floor. It took three hours before the liquid fully evaporated and the chamber could be vented. Despite these problems, Gee Jon died in what appeared to be a gentle and painless manner. Overall, the first execution by lethal gas was declared a success.

Even so, other states did not immediately adopt the gas chamber. It was nearly a decade later, in 1933, when Colorado and Arizona replaced hanging with the gas chamber. Wyoming followed suit in 1935, and California, Missouri, and Oregon followed in 1937. The last state to replace hanging with the gas chamber was Maryland in 1955. North Carolina, which had adopted the electric chair in 1909, switched to the gas chamber in 1935. Mississippi and New Mexico switched from the electric chair to the gas chamber in 1954 and 1955, respectively.

Whether execution by lethal gas is painless remains controversial. In many executions by gas, the condemned prisoner appears to fall asleep and die peacefully. However, there are also accounts of condemned prisoners gagging, gasping for breath, and going into convulsions.

The gas chamber is sometimes criticized as the only method of execution that poses a serious risk to witnesses. During an execution in Arizona, witnesses fled in panic when they mistook the odor of ammonia, which was on hand to neutralize the poisonous gas, for a leak in the chamber. In fact, no witnesses have been harmed during a gas chamber execution, but the care that must be used in handling toxic chemicals makes gas chamber executions among the most expensive and most technically difficult to perform.

Because they are expensive and difficult to perform, executions using gas are most cost-effective when more than one execution is performed at a time. For this reason, several states have gas chambers that seat two condemned prisoners. Historically, the most notorious use of gas in executions occurred during World War II when the Nazis used gas to exterminate most of the Jewish population of Europe. The four gas chambers at the concentration camp Auschwitz-Birkenau resembled dormitory showers and could accommodate several hundred people at a time. In 1944, when the Jewish extermination was in full swing, as many as nine thousand people a day died in those gas chambers. The Nazis originally used carbon monoxide gas in their gas chambers, since it could be produced cheaply by running an automobile engine. However, they later switched to a pesticide called Zyklon-B, which was more effective and not much more expensive to produce. Zyklon-B is a form of hydrogen cyanide, similar to the gas used in American gas chambers.

No states now use the gas chamber as their primary method of execution. By the 1990s, most gas chambers in the United States had become old and unreliable. Rather than have new ones built, those states that had used lethal gas as a method of execution merely switched to lethal injection. Only California and Arizona still offer the gas chamber as an optional method of execution. **See also** Gee Jon; San Quentin State Prison.

Gee Jon (1894–1924)

Gee Jon was executed in Nevada in 1924 after being convicted of murder in a feud between two rival Chinese American gangs. Gee's execution is notable because it was the first execution in the United States in which a gas chamber was used.

Gee was born in China, but immigrated to San Francisco's Chinatown. Chinese American society in the late nineteenth and early twentieth centuries was isolated, by culture and by language, from the rest of American society. It was run by family organizations, but also by criminal gangs known as tongs. Rival tongs were in violent competition with each other, and killings of rival tong members were common. Gee was a member of the Hop Sing tong, which ran illegal gambling operations in California and Nevada. In Nevada, on August 27, 1921, Gee and fellow Hop Sing member Hughie Sing shot and killed Tom Quong Kee, an elder member of a rival tong. Gee, who was believed to be the shooter, was convicted of murder and sentenced to death. Sing was also sentenced to death, but his sentence was later commuted to life in prison.

Because Nevada had recently replaced hanging with execution by lethal gas, Gee became the first person executed in the United States in a gas chamber. Gee's execution was considered a reasonably successful test of the new method of execution. It took place on February 8, 1924. **See also** gas chamber.

Georgia

Georgia has traditionally permitted juries to impose the death penalty, and continues to do so currently. The first person executed in Georgia was Alice Ridley, an indentured servant from Ireland who was hanged for murdering her master. From 1735 to 1924, executions in Georgia were carried out by public hanging and were handled by local officials. Roughly 530 executions are known to have taken place. In 1924 Georgia officially replaced hanging with electrocution as its method of execution, and ordered that executions take place at the state prison at Milledgeville. However, a few executions by hanging occurred after that time, one as late as 1931, for condemned prisoners who were sentenced prior to the effective date of the new law. A double hanging in 1926 of convicted murderers Willie Jones and Gervis Bloodworth had to be moved from Butler to Columbus, since public executions were now illegal and the Butler gallows could be observed from the roof of the local drug store. The first electrocution took place in 1924, and from 1924 to 1937, 162 executions took place at the Georgia State Prison in Milledgeville. In 1938 the electric chair was moved to a new state prison at Reidsville, where it continued to be used until 1964; 256 executions took place at Reidsville.

Following the 1972 *Furman v. Georgia* ruling, which struck down Georgia's death-penalty statute, the Georgia General Assembly quickly passed a new death-penalty statute in 1973. Georgia's current death-penalty statute allows jurors to consider the death penalty for homicide under special circumstances. These special circumstances include that the homicide was intentional (i.e., involved "malice aforethought") or that the homicide was committed during the commission of another felony. Aircraft hijacking and treason are also recognized as death-eligible crimes in Georgia.

The death penalty may be imposed if at least one of ten aggravating circumstances is proven to have accompanied the crime. The list of aggravating circumstances appears similar to the special circumstances noted above, but aggravating circumstances are considered during the penalty phase of the trial rather than during the guilt phase. These aggravating circumstances are (1) that the defendant was previously convicted of a capital felony; (2) that the homicide occurred in the course of another capital felony, aggravated battery, or first-degree burglary or arson; (3) that the defendant knowingly created a great risk of death to more than one person in a public place by means of a device (such as a bomb) that would normally endanger more than one person; (4) that the homicide was committed for monetary gain; (5) that the victim was a judicial officer, district attorney, or solicitor general acting in the performance of his or her duties; (6) that the defendant ordered the homicide to be performed or performed the homicide under someone else's direction; (7) that the homicide was wantonly vile, involving torture or beating of the victim; (8) that the victim was a police officer, corrections employee, or firefighter, acting in the performance of his or her duties; (9) that the defendant was in custody or had escaped from custody; or (10) that the defendant committed the homicide in order to avoid the arrest either of himself or of another. The jury must also consider any mitigating circumstances that the defense wishes to present.

Under Georgia law, a person convicted of a capital offense cannot be executed if he or she was under the age of eighteen at the time of the offense. Georgia does provide for life imprisonment without parole as an alternative to the death penalty. The State Board of Pardons and Paroles, not the governor, has sole authority to grant clemency.

Executions in Georgia did not resume until 1983. The old electric chair at Reidsville was retired from service and a new electric chair built for the prison in Jackson. Another twenty-three people were executed by electrocution, but in 2000 Georgia replaced electrocution with lethal injection as its method of execution. In October 2001 the Georgia Supreme Court declared executions by electrocution unconstitutional under the Georgia state constitution. Since that time, all executions in Georgia have been by lethal injection, even for prisoners originally sentenced to electrocution. So far, eight people have been executed by lethal injection in Georgia. As of April 2005, 112 people were awaiting execution on Georgia's death row. **See also** *Coker v. Georgia; Furman v. Georgia; Gregg v. Georgia.*

gibbet

Originally the word *gibbet* was synonymous with the word *gallows*, but was introduced into English from the French at the time of the Norman Conquest in 1066, whereas the word *gallows* came into English much earlier, from the Old Norse. Eventually, a distinction was drawn in English between a gallows, which was a device used for performing an execution by hanging, and a gibbet, a post with an extending arm used for displaying the bodies of executed criminals following their execution. Sometimes live criminals could be displayed on a gibbet, hung by the wrists using a rope or chain, as a form of public humiliation. A crucifixion cross is actually a type of gibbet, and was sometimes referred to in English as a gibbet.

The Halifax gibbet was somewhat different. It was a device built in the town of Halifax, England, that was used for beheading condemned prisoners with a falling blade. It was, in fact, the forerunner of the guillotine. The Halifax gibbet had a raised platform, so it resembled a gallows, but it was not really a "gibbet." A similar device was later built in Edinburgh and named the Scottish Maiden. **See also** gallows; Scottish Maiden.

Gilmore, Gary (1940–1977)

The execution of convicted murderer Gary Gilmore was notable for several reasons, but primarily because it was the first execution to be held in the United States after a decadelong hiatus from 1967 to 1977. It is also notable because Gilmore refused to appeal his sentence even though the Utah law under which he was sentenced had not yet been determined to be constitutional. In addition, Gilmore chose to be executed by firing squad, becoming one of very few inmates undergoing this method of execution in modern times.

Gilmore was born in Texas on December 4, 1940, but he grew up in Portland, Oregon. Even as a child he was excessively impulsive and foolhardy. He made a game of waiting on railroad tracks for approaching trains and then jumping aside at the last minute. By age fourteen he had dropped out of school, and at age fifteen he was arrested for running a car theft ring. Released on those charges, he was soon arrested again for theft, and he spent the next several years in jails and reformatories.

At age eighteen he was sent to the Oregon State Correctional Institution for auto theft. While he was in prison, his father died. Gilmore expressed his grief by becoming violent and had to be controlled with antipsychosis drugs. When he was released from prison at the age of twenty-one, he assaulted a man with a lead pipe to steal eleven dollars, and was sent back to prison. When Gilmore found

In 1977 convicted murderer Gary Gilmore became the first person to be put to death after the death penalty was reinstated following a decadelong hiatus.

out that his brother had been killed by a knife wound in the stomach, he again became violent and was put into solitary confinement. He used this time to read, write poetry, and develop his considerable artistic talent, even winning some contests with his art. In 1972 he was granted early release and given the opportunity to study art at a local community college, but in less than a month Gilmore committed an armed robbery and was again sent to prison.

When he was released in 1976, Gilmore moved to Utah to be near a cousin with whom he had corresponded while in prison. However, he was still unable to control his impulsive behavior. In order to pay for a new truck, he held up a service station and murdered the attendant. The next night he held up a motel and murdered the manager. For these crimes he was promptly convicted and sentenced to death.

Gilmore was sentenced under a new and untested Utah death-penalty statute similar to the one in Georgia that was declared to be constitutional by the U.S. Supreme Court in the landmark 1976 *Gregg v. Georgia* decision. Even though the Utah statute was untested, Gilmore refused to appeal the sentence. He believed he was incapable of living outside of prison, yet could not face the prospect of life in prison again. Lawyers acting without his consent filed an appeal to have the case reviewed, but the Supreme Court refused to hear the case, noting that it saw no reason to grant relief to a defendant who had no complaint. Indeed, Chief Justice Warren Burger remarked that Gilmore's only complaint against the state of Utah was "with respect to the delay on the part of the State in carrying out the sentence." The Utah law was, however, declared constitutional by the Utah Supreme Court, on appeal from a different defendant, just months before Gilmore's execution.

Gilmore elected to be executed by a firing squad. At the time, Utah was one of only three states to permit execution by firing squad. The sentence was carried out on January 17, 1977. All four of the bullets fired by the squad hit Gilmore in the heart. **See also** firing squad.

Godfrey v. Georgia

This was a case heard by the Supreme Court of the United States in 1980 concerning whether the judge in the case had sufficiently explained the phrase "outrageously or wantonly vile, horrible or inhuman" so that its meaning was clear enough to guide jurors in determining a sentence of death. The defendant in the case, Robert Franklin Godfrey, was convicted of murdering his wife and his mother-in-law with a shotgun. Under the Georgia death-penalty statute, a jury could sentence a murderer to death if they judged that the murder was accompanied by one or more aggravating circumstances. Included in the list of possible aggravating circumstances was that the murder could be described as "outrageously or wantonly vile, horrible or inhuman." The jury in this case agreed that Godfrey's murders fit this description and sentenced him to death. This sentence was appealed on the grounds that the jury had been allowed to misunderstand the intended meaning of the statute. The Georgia Supreme Court rejected the appeal, but the U.S. Supreme Court agreed to review the case.

In a 6-to-3 decision, the Supreme Court ruled that the judge's instructions to the jury had not been adequate to explain the meaning of the statute. Writing for the Court, Justice Potter Stewart pointed out that the phrase "outrageously or wantonly vile, horrible or inhuman" was defined by the Georgia statute to mean murder involving torture or beating of the victim prior to death. These two murders clearly did not fit that description. Stewart argued that the language in the Georgia statute was clear and unambiguous enough to be considered constitutional, but in this particular case instructions to the jury had not been adequate to explain the statute's meaning. The Court ordered that Godfrey's sentence be reconsidered. **See also** aggravating circumstances.

Goldberg, Arthur J. (1908–1990)

Arthur J. Goldberg was an associate justice of the U.S. Supreme Court from 1962 to 1965. Although his time on the Supreme Court was relatively brief, he had an enormous influence on the way in which the Supreme Court decided death-penalty cases, and laid the groundwork for the landmark decisions that eventually revolutionized death-penalty statutes in the United States.

Goldberg was born in Chicago, Illinois, and was educated at Northwestern University, where he received a law degree in 1929 at the age of twenty. He represented striking workers during the Great Depression, and continued to focus on labor law for the next two decades, eventually becoming one of the most respected experts in labor law in the country. In 1961 President John F. Kennedy appointed him secretary of labor, but less than two years later a Supreme Court seat became available, and Kennedy nominated him to fill the position.

On joining the Court, Goldberg knew little about criminal law. Nevertheless, he quickly came to believe that death sentences were being imposed in discriminatory and arbitrary ways in the lower courts. It was clear to Goldberg that, as he wrote, "the impact of the death penalty was demonstrably greatest among disadvantaged minorities." In the summer of 1963 he assigned a young law clerk, Alan Dershowitz, to the task of researching all of the constitutional arguments that might be made against capital punishment. Together, they prepared a memo that provided a comprehensive outline of Eighth and Fourteenth Amendment objections that might be raised against capital punishment. A brief portion of this memo was used by Goldberg in a dissent (in which Justices Douglas and Brennan joined) over a decision not to hear a death-penalty case, *Rudolph v. Alabama*, in 1963. The dissent by Goldberg made defense attorneys around the country aware that some members of the Supreme Court were interested in hearing death-penalty cases and were already sympathetic to the lines of reasoning outlined in Goldberg's memo. This sparked an intense effort by defense attorneys to bring death-penalty cases before the Supreme Court. The large number of cases brought during the 1960s and early 1970s caused significant changes in the way in which capital punishment was practiced in the United States, and even briefly brought an end to the practice altogether.

Goldberg resigned from the Supreme Court in 1965 to accept an appointment as ambassador to the United Nations, a position from which he hoped to help bring an end to the Vietnam War. (It is also known that he was pressured to resign by President Lyndon Johnson, who was keen to appoint a personal friend, Abe Fortas, to the Supreme Court in Goldberg's place.) Goldberg served as UN ambassador until 1968. He then made an unsuccessful run to be governor of New York and eventually returned to private practice in Washington, D.C. He died on January 19, 1990. **See also** Dershowitz, Alan; *Rudolph v. Alabama.*

Goode, Washington (1819–1849)

Washington Goode was a free black sailor who was executed for murder in 1849. His trial and execution were followed closely by the Boston press and helped motivate the anti–capital punishment movement of the pre–Civil War period.

Little is known about Goode's life prior to his arrest. He worked as a ship's cook aboard the *Nancoockee* and, while not at sea, lived in a boardinghouse that catered to sailors. Goode and another black sailor, Thomas Harding, were apparently seeing the same woman, Mary Ann Williams. Goode had destroyed a handkerchief given to Williams by Harding. This angered Harding, and the two men were known to be looking for each other. Each had been heard making threatening remarks about the other. On the night of June 28, 1848, Goode and Williams had a public altercation at a tavern, while Harding was in another room. Goode left the tavern, and Harding left soon afterward. A few moments later, Harding was dead of a knife wound and a fractured skull. Witnesses who saw Harding killed believed the attacker was Goode, but in the dark it was hard to tell. Goode was arrested for the killing.

There had not been a capital trial in Boston in over a decade, and there was strong sentiment against the death penalty at the time. As a result, Goode's trial became a sensation in Boston and attracted nationwide attention. When Goode was convicted and sentenced to death, the most prominent death-penalty opponents in the country, including Wendell Phillips and Charles Spear, organized to try to save him. They appealed to Governor George Briggs to commute his sentence on the grounds that Goode was clearly not a habitual criminal but only a product of a rough environment who had acted chiefly on the passion of the moment. Briggs declined to commute the sentence.

Goode considered hanging a dishonorable way to die. In the days leading up to his execution, he tried repeatedly to kill himself in other ways. He tried suffocating himself with his blanket and poisoning himself by eating various substances found in his prison cell. On the night before his execution, he managed to obtain a piece of glass and slashed his veins near the elbow. A prison doctor rushed to his cell and saved his life by stopping the bleeding. Goode was executed by hanging the following morning, May 25, 1849. **See also** Phillips, Wendell; Spear, Charles.

grand jury

A grand jury is a group of people, usually made up of experienced judges, attorneys, and investigators, who determine whether criminal charges should be brought to trial. A decision by a grand jury allowing a case to go to trial is called an indictment. Grand juries were originally used in English law as a safeguard against the powers of the monarch. Requiring that a grand jury review and approve the charges against a person before a trial may be held prevented the monarch from harassing a citizen with unjustified charges. As a guard against federal power, the Fifth Amendment to the U.S. Constitution requires that criminal charges brought in federal court for "a capital or otherwise infamous crime" must be approved by a grand jury. Curiously, even though most of the limits placed on the power of the federal government by the Bill of Rights have been extended to apply to state governments as well, the requirement that serious criminal charges be approved by a grand jury has not been. Thus, states rarely convene grand juries.

Because grand juries do not determine guilt or innocence but only whether a trial should be held at all, grand juries are not subject to many of the restrictions that are in place to protect the rights of a defendant. Unlike a regular court, a grand jury has broad powers to compel testimony. A grand jury may consider evidence that has been illegally obtained and may subpoena documents without proving that they are relevant to the case under consideration. (However, use of such evidence by a grand jury does not guarantee that it will be admissible at trial.) Perhaps because of these powers, federal grand juries have evolved into investigative bodies that do much of the work at the federal level that is done at the local level by a district attorney's office.

The number of people who sit on a grand jury ranges from twelve to twenty-three. It is called a "grand" jury because this number is larger than the six to twelve people who sit on a regular, or "petit," jury. **See also** federal death-penalty laws.

Gregg v. Georgia

This was a case heard by the Supreme Court of the United States in 1976 concerning the constitutionality of the death penalty. Following the 1972 *Furman v. Georgia* decision, which overturned all of the death-penalty statutes in the United States then in effect, the *Gregg v. Georgia* decision, which reaffirmed the constitutionality of the death penalty, is the most important Supreme Court decision on capital punishment. It permits the death penalty but places strictures on how it may be implemented.

The defendant in the case, Troy Leon Gregg, was convicted of two counts of armed robbery and two counts of murder, and was sentenced to death under a new Georgia death-penalty statute that had been passed to replace the old statute overturned in 1972 by the landmark *Furman v. Georgia* decision. The new Georgia statute differed from the old statute in a number of important respects. First, the statute provided for a two-phase trial in which conviction and sentencing were handled separately. This allowed the defense to reserve testimony about mitigating circumstances, which might be seen as implying an admission of guilt but might also lead to a lighter sentence, until the penalty phase of the trial. In the penalty phase of the trial, guilt was presumed to have been already established, so testimony seeming to imply guilt could no longer harm the defendant. Second, the statute provided a specific list of aggravating circumstances, at least one of which had to be present for a sentence of death to be imposed. These circumstances included the murder of a police officer or firefighter, murder-for-hire, and murder following an escape from custody. The statute also provided a list of mitigating circumstances that should be considered by the jury, including the defendant's age, emotional state, and subsequent cooperation with law enforcement officials. Finally, the statute required the mandatory review of death sentences by the state supreme court to ensure that the sentence was justified by the evidence, not influenced by social prejudice, and was comparable to sentences given to other defendants in similar cases.

Gregg's attorneys naturally appealed the sentence, since at the time the constitutionality of any death-penalty statute was in doubt. The Georgia Supreme Court reversed Gregg's sentence on the two counts of armed robbery but allowed the sentence to stand for the two counts of murder. The case was then appealed to the U.S. Supreme Court, which agreed to hear the case, along with two similar cases, *Jurek v. Texas* and *Proffitt v. Florida*.

In a 7-to-2 decision, the Supreme Court allowed Gregg's sentence of death to stand. Writing for the majority, Justice Potter Stewart affirmed that the death penalty per se was constitutional and that, even in light of "evolving standards of decency," it could not be considered cruel and unusual as long as it was imposed in a consistent manner proportional to the severity of the crime. Stewart then argued that the Georgia death-penalty statute met the required standard by providing for a two-phase trial, by giving jurors specific guidelines to follow in imposing a death sentence (i.e., by providing the jurors with "guided discretion"), and by requiring a mandatory review to ensure consistency.

The *Gregg v. Georgia* decision had the effect of reintroducing the death penalty into the United States after a decadelong hiatus. After 1976, many states passed death-penalty statutes similar to Georgia's, incorporating two-phase trials, specific lists of aggravating and mitigating circumstances, and mandatory review procedures. Gregg, however, was not executed. He escaped from prison with four other death row inmates on July 28, 1980, and was killed that evening in a bar fight in North Carolina. **See also** *Furman v. Georgia; Jurek v. Texas; Proffitt v. Florida;* trial.

guided discretion

The phrase *guided discretion* appears in the U.S. Supreme Court's 1976 *Gregg v. Georgia* decision. It is used to describe death-penalty statutes that, while giving juries discretion to decide whether or not to impose a sentence of death also lay out clear criteria defining a death-eligible crime to guide the jury's deliberations. A guided-discretion statute does not make the death penalty mandatory, which would eliminate the jury's discretion altogether, but it does clearly delineate (by providing a list of aggravating circumstances) when a crime is sufficiently serious that a sentence of death *may* be imposed. The goal of guided-discretion statutes is to allow juries the discretion to weigh various factors in making their decision yet prevent jurors from making decisions based on their own prejudices concerning a defendant's race, religion, or political views, rather than on the seriousness of the crime itself. The *Gregg* decision (as well as the 1976 *Woodson v. North Carolina* and *Roberts v. Louisiana* decisions, which prohibited the use of the death penalty as a mandatory sentence) established that death-penalty statutes in the United States must be guided-discretion statutes. **See also** *Gregg v. Georgia; Roberts v. Louisiana; Woodson v. North Carolina.*

Guillotin, Joseph-Ignace (1738–1841)

Joseph-Ignace Guillotin is the man after whom the guillotine is named. Although, as a French legislator, he was instrumental in having the guillotine designed and built, he is not generally given credit for inventing it, and, contrary to some popular misconceptions, he was not executed on it.

Guillotin was a brilliant and highly educated man. He was born in Saintes, France, and received his first degree from the University of Bordeaux. He became a Jesuit and spent several years as a professor of literature at the Irisnah College in Bordeaux. At about the age of thirty he decided to change careers. He left the Jesuits to study medicine at Reims, and earned a degree in medicine in 1770. He then joined the medical faculty at the University of Paris. In 1784 he was asked to serve on a committee to investigate Franz Mesmer and his alleged health treatments involving so-called animal magnetism, which were popular with Parisian socialites at the time. Following the French Revolution in 1789, he was elected to the Constituent Assembly of the new republic, where he became a voice for progressive social reform.

Guillotin was opposed to capital punishment. He initially argued that it should be abolished altogether. When he realized that he would not be able to prevail on effecting a complete abolition of capital punishment, he argued that the method of execution should be as painless as possible. Under the new French republic, he argued, all citizens should enjoy the same rights that had previously been reserved solely for the nobility. One of those rights was the right to a quick and humane execution. In 1791 Guillotin persuaded the assembly to pass a law designating beheading as the method of execution for anyone condemned to death in France. At that point a working guillotine had not yet been designed and built, but by the following year a working prototype had been constructed and was ready for use. Guillotin may have suggested the general concept, but it was left to others to design and build the actual machine.

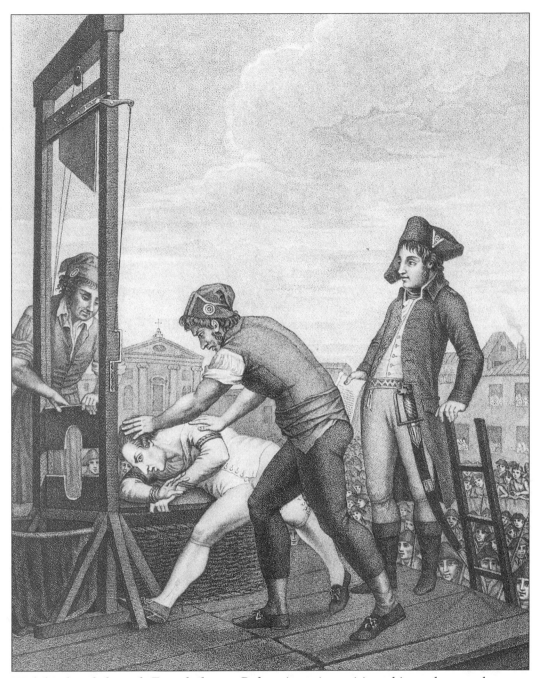

With his hands bound, French despot Robespierre is positioned into place at the guillotine in 1794.

The same year that Guillotin's law was passed, the assembly was dissolved and Guillotin retired from public life. He was briefly imprisoned under Robespierre, but he was released when Robespierre fell from power. He died peacefully of natural causes in 1814. **See also** guillotine.

guillotine

The guillotine is a device used for decapitating (beheading) convicted criminals with a heavy falling blade. It is closely associated with the Reign of Terror during the French Revolution, and became by law the preferred method of execution in France in 1791. However, it was never the most common method. In the countryside outside of Paris, where guillotines were not easily available, hanging continued to be the most commonly used method of execution.

The guillotine was not intended to be an instrument of terror. In fact, it was the result of an effort to make France's treatment of criminals more humane. Joseph-Ignace Guillotin, a physician and member of the new French government, argued that France should extend the privilege of a humane execution to all citizens, not just the nobility. The nobility had traditionally been executed by beheading, so, at Guillotin's urging, the French assembly voted to make execution by beheading available to all citizens. Unfortunately, execution by decapitation generally required the services of a skilled professional, and there were not enough such professional executioners to extend the practice of decapitation so widely. The guillotine offered a solution to this problem. Using a guillotine, even an untrained executioner could manage a clean, painless execution in nearly every case.

Guillotin did not invent the guillotine, but he may have suggested the general concept. The idea of using a falling blade was not new. The idea had already been tried in Scotland in a device known as the Scottish Maiden, which was itself copied from a device used in Halifax, England, known as the Halifax gibbet. Nevertheless, the guillotine was an important advance in the technology of executions, since it included three vital improvements. First, the blade was angled to give it a slicing rather than a chopping action. Second, the prisoner's head was held firmly in place by a collar to prevent the condemned prisoner from flinching. This ensured that the blade would strike in the intended place. Finally, the blade was not stopped by a chopping block on which the condemned prisoner's head rested but slid past the collar in which the prisoner's head was held. This helped to keep the blade sharp, and ensured that only a single stroke would be needed. In later models, the falling blade was stopped by a system of springs that caught the blade at the ends. All in all, the guillotine worked more like a powerful pair of scissors than like a traditional executioner's ax. The condemned prisoner's head was not so much chopped off as snipped off.

The first guillotine was designed by Antoine Louis, a surgeon who was a friend of Guillotin's. It was built by Tobias Schmidt, a German harpsichord maker. The notorious chief executioner of Paris, Charles-Henri Sanson, was also one of the principal people involved in the project. He offered advice and conducted preliminary tests (using sheep) of the effectiveness of the new machine. There is a legend that the deposed king Louis XVI, who was later executed with the first guillotine, proposed the new blade design. However, this story is probably not true, and most historians believe it was Schmidt who proposed the angled blade. A hundred years later, in 1890, further refinements were added by Leo Berger, a carpenter and assistant executioner. These refinements included a release mechanism for the blade and the system of springs used to catch the falling blade.

The first execution using the guillotine took place in 1792 with the execution of highwayman Jacques-Nicolas Pelletier. After the dissolution of the French assembly in 1791, the guillotine was used to execute political prisoners as well as common criminals. It is estimated that by 1799 fifteen thousand people had been executed on the guillotine. Eventually, leaders of the Reign of Terror, including Robespierre, were themselves executed on the guillotine.

Following the execution of Louis XVI, the guillotine was generally known as *la louisette* or *le louison*, although it is not clear whether this name was used in honor of the former king or in honor of Antoine Louis, the designer of the device (or both). In any case, by 1800 it was more commonly being called *le guillotine* in honor of the man who had proposed its use. Guillotin's children were so embarrassed to be associated with the device that, after unsuccessfully protesting the use of the word, they eventually had their own names changed.

Although the guillotine is most closely associated with France and the French Revolution, several other European countries also used the guillotine as a method of execution, including Greece, Switzerland, Sweden, and Germany. Indeed, Germany used it extensively during World War II, killing between sixteen and twenty thousand people. In England and the United States, the guillotine was never adopted. Despite its appeal as a humane method of execution, these countries viewed it as simply too gruesome. The last execution by guillotine occurred in France in 1977. Four years later, France abolished capital punishment, including the use of guillotines. **See also** decapitation; Guillotin, Joseph-Ignace; Sanson family; Scottish Maiden.

habeas corpus

A writ of habeas corpus is an order issued by a court requiring that a person who has been detained or imprisoned in some manner be brought to court so that the legality of that detention can be determined. The Latin phrase *habeas corpus* means "you should have the body," referring to the issue of who is allowed to have possession of a person's body. Since the right of habeas corpus prevents governments from abusing their power to arrest and imprison people without a court hearing, it is considered one of the most fundamental human rights recognized in the Western legal tradition. Because it is so important, habeas corpus is also sometimes called the Great Writ.

The issuing of writs of habeas corpus by courts is among the oldest legal practices. Some legal scholars believe it has its roots in the Magna Carta, the thirteenth-century document that forms the basis of British law. Originally, writs of habeas corpus were used to force people to appear in court for such purposes as giving testimony. By the late fifteenth century, however, they were used to require civil authorities to justify the holding of prisoners. This use of habeas corpus was officially recognized in the Habeas Corpus Act, passed by the British Parliament in 1679.

In American law, the power to issue writs is granted to federal courts by Congress. The very first law passed by the first Congress of the United States in 1789 was a law authorizing federal courts to issue writs, including writs of habeas corpus. While Congress can grant and modify the power to issue writs, Article I, Section 9, of the Constitution of the United States guarantees that the right of habeas corpus cannot be suspended except when the public safety is endangered "in Cases of Rebellion or Invasion." President Abraham Lincoln attempted to suspend the right of habeas corpus during the Civil War, but in *Ex Parte Merryman* (1861) the Supreme Court ruled that the power to suspend habeas corpus rests solely with Congress, not with the president. When Congress voted to grant Lincoln the power to suspend habeas corpus at his discretion, the Supreme Court ruled unanimously, in *Ex Parte Milligan* (1866), that Congress could not do so. The most recent Supreme Court decision on access to the right of habeas corpus concerned the detention of prisoners captured in Afghanistan and held at the Guantánamo Bay Naval Station in Cuba. Lawyers representing President George W. Bush had argued that, as foreign nationals being held outside the United States, the prisoners could not petition for writs of habeas corpus in U.S. courts. In *Rasul v. Bush* (2004) the Supreme Court ruled that all prisoners held under the authority of the United States may petition for habeas corpus relief in federal courts, regardless of their citizenship and regardless of the specific location at which they are detained.

It is the right of habeas corpus that nowadays provides the basis for most of the postconviction reviews that are brought in death-penalty cases. There is an important difference between a petition for a writ of habeas corpus and a standard appeal. When a case is reviewed on appeal, the court is asked to decide whether correct procedures were followed to guarantee the defendant's rights. When a writ of habeas corpus is being considered, the court is asked to decide more fundamental issues concerning whether the lower courts had proper jurisdiction to conduct a trial in the first place. A standard appeal decides whether laws and procedures were correctly followed; a habeas corpus hearing decides whether those laws and procedures—even when correctly followed—are legitimate.

Throughout most of the nineteenth century, the right of habeas corpus played a relatively minor role in the review of criminal laws. It was assumed that a prisoner could challenge the jurisdiction of a court but could not challenge the actual laws and procedures under which that court operated. It was also assumed that federal courts did not have the power to review the cases of prisoners held under state jurisdiction. Following the Civil War, Congress and the courts began to interpret the right of habeas corpus more broadly. In 1867 Congress expressly granted federal courts the power to review state cases and to rule on whether state laws are consistent with the U.S. Constitution, with federal statutes, and with treaties into which the United States had entered. Then, in a series of rulings, federal courts gradually extended the right of habeas corpus to cover review of laws and procedures as well as narrow jurisdictional issues. The reasoning behind this expansion was that a court could not really be said to have proper jurisdiction if the laws and procedures under which it was operating were invalid. Since imprisonment was being used as a method of punishment, the right to habeas corpus was interpreted not only as allowing prisoners to challenge their detention but as allowing prisoners to challenge any form of punishment, including a sentence of death.

By the mid-twentieth century, the right of habeas corpus had become a flexible tool giving courts broad power to review both state and federal laws. Indeed, some people began to feel that the right of habeas corpus was being abused. Between 1940 and 1970 the number of habeas corpus petitions in federal courts rose from roughly one hundred per year to over fifteen thousand per year. Moreover, since the grounds on which laws and procedures could be challenged seemed endless, it appeared that a clever lawyer could delay the execution of his or her client indefinitely, merely by filing an endless stream of habeas corpus petitions. Since the 1970s, there has been a tendency for court decisions and some federal laws to restrict the right of habeas corpus. Restrictions on the right of habeas corpus are of three types, namely, restrictions on the order in which appeals and petitions may be lodged, restrictions on the number of appeals that may be lodged, and restrictions on the time period in which petitions must be lodged.

Order of appeals and petitions. To prevent conflicts between state and federal jurisdictions, a rule has developed under which a defendant must pursue all appeals available under state law before lodging habeas corpus petitions in federal court. Several rulings in the 1940s and 1950s formalized the requirement, known as the "exhaustion requirement," on the principle that states have primary responsibility for correcting errors made in trials under state jurisdiction. In the 1963 *Fay v. Noia* decision, the exhaustion requirement was somewhat relaxed when the U.S. Supreme Court ruled that failures to pursue state appeals did not necessarily mean that a prisoner could not then petition for a writ of habeas corpus in federal court. However, in the 1991 *Coleman v. Thompson* decision, the Supreme Court reversed this ruling, saying that if a defendant had an opportunity to raise an issue in state court but failed to do so, the defendant could not later petition for habeas corpus relief in federal court. In effect, defaulting on opportunities to lodge state appeals should be considered tantamount to waiving the right of habeas corpus in federal courts.

Number of petitions. In the 1991 *McCleskey v. Zant* decision, the U.S. Supreme Court ruled that a prisoner is entitled to only one habeas corpus petition. Subsequent petitions will be heard only if they raise a substantially new issue and there is a good reason why the new issue was not raised in the earlier petition. In 1996 Congress strengthened the rules limiting subsequent petitions by passing the Antiterrorism and Effective Death Penalty Act, which requires that defendants seek permission from the courts before filing a second habeas corpus petition, and mandating that courts refuse to hear cases unless a substantially new issue is raised. That is, prior to the passage of this law, while courts usually did refuse to hear second petitions, they could choose to hear them even if a substantially new issue were *not* raised; following the passage of the law, federal courts could hear a second petition only by ruling that a new issue had been raised.

Time to submit petitions. The original 1789 law authorizing courts to issue writs of habeas corpus placed a one-year limit on petition requests. The 1996 Antiterrorism and Effective Death Penalty Act shortened this to six months (180 days). However, like the time clock in a football game, this limit is subject to time-outs. The time does not elapse while appeals are being considered by a court, and prisoners may also request a thirty-day pause if they can provide a sufficient reason.

In 1996 the Supreme Court ruled in *Felker v. Turpin* that the restrictions on the right of habeas corpus introduced by the Antiterrorism and Effective Death Penalty Act did not violate the U.S. Constitution. These restrictions have made it more difficult for inmates on death row to obtain habeas corpus hearings, and may be largely responsible for the sharp rise in the number of executions in the United States since 1996. **See also** Antiterrorism and Effective Death Penalty Act; appeals process; *Felker v. Turpin*.

Hammurabi, Code of

The Code of Hammurabi is one of the oldest recorded codes of law. It was issued in approximately 1780 B.C. in the ancient Middle East during the reign of the Babylonian king Hammurabi. It survives because the code was carved into stone for public display, apparently the first time a code of justice was made publicly available for all (literate) citizens. The laws recorded were probably not developed by Hammurabi himself but represented a long legal tradition that Hammurabi sought to make available.

The code was primarily concerned with how a transgressor should compensate a victim. As such, the most common penalty prescribed by the code is the payment of fines, especially for damage to property (including slaves) and for breach of contract. However, crimes for which compensation is not possible (or was not considered sufficient) are punished by retaliation instead. A wide variety of crimes are punishable by death. Some of the crimes for which death was the prescribed punishment include theft, buying or selling stolen goods, kidnapping, harboring fugitive slaves, and disorderly conduct at a tavern. A builder could be put to death if his building collapsed and resulted in the death of the owner or the owner's son. In most cases, the manner of death is not specified, but in some cases it is. A person caught looting during a fire was to be thrown into the fire. Drowning was the penalty for adultery and various other moral transgressions.

Although the code may be considered excessively harsh by modern standards, it was extremely influential. Certain elements of biblical law are clearly derived from the Code of Hammurabi, and the principles of justice on which the code was based are still recognized today. The idea that the law should be made available so that citizens can know what behavior is considered criminal and how it will be punished represents one of the best and most enlightened ideas in the history of jurisprudence. **See also** Draconian Code; justification of punishment.

hanging

Hanging is a method of execution in which a rope is tied around a condemned prisoner's neck and the condemned prisoner is then suddenly suspended in midair. Death is caused by asphyxiation, or lack of oxygen, to the brain, but the exact cause of the asphyxiation may vary with the method of hanging used. In most hangings, the rope around the condemned prisoner's neck is tied in a characteristic manner known as a hangman's noose, which is designed to let the rope slip freely through a large knot formed of multiple coils. The condemned prisoner's hands and feet are tied together and a hood is usually placed over the person's head, which prevents viewers from seeing the effects of strangulation and asphyxiation on the condemned prisoner's face. Hanging is one of the oldest methods of execution known. It is even mentioned in the Bible in Deuteronomy 21:22–23 and elsewhere. It is historically one of the most common methods ever used. Although exact figures are unknown, it seems certain that more people have been executed by hanging than by any other method.

Hanging was certainly the preferred method of execution in colonial America. The first hanging recorded in the colonies was that of Daniell Frank, which took place in Virginia in 1622. Frank was convicted of stealing cattle. The first woman hanged in the colonies was Jane Champion, who was hanged in Virginia in 1632. The crime of which she was convicted is not recorded. After the American Revolution, hanging was the only method of execution used in the United States until the invention of the electric chair in the 1880s. It is estimated that about 13,350 people have been executed by hanging in the United States since 1622.

When it was first used, hanging was one of many painful and undignified methods of execution. Other comparable methods included crucifixion and impalement. Like these, hanging was considered a low form of execution, suitable for use on slaves and common criminals. The idea was not to cause a quick and painless death but to make a show of publicly humiliating the condemned prisoner in order to deter crime by others.

However, it was discovered that hanging, when done correctly, could be relatively quick and painless. A large knot in the rope, correctly placed below the left ear, can crush or dislocate the vertebrae of the neck, causing the condemned prisoner to lose consciousness instantly. Brain death can follow rapidly, in as little as three to six minutes. Even if the neck is not broken, constricting the blood vessels that carry oxygen to the brain can cause unconsciousness within a few seconds and death in under fifteen

A crowd of spectators watches as four conspirators are hanged in New York during the Civil War. Hanging is one of the oldest forms of capital punishment.

minutes. Because hanging could be a relatively merciful method of execution, its popularity tended to grow, and it remained in use for hundreds of years after crueler alternative methods had been abandoned.

The problem with hanging is that the results are notoriously variable, and a successful execution depends on many factors, including the weight of the condemned prisoner, the length of the fall, the elasticity of the rope, the placement of the knot, and even the quality of the hinges on the trapdoor through which the condemned prisoner falls (if a trapdoor gallows is used). Since hangings were often performed by local sheriffs with little experience, hangings frequently did not go as expected. In 1901 Thomas "Black Jack" Ketchum was executed by hanging, and the force of his fall caused his head to be ripped from his body. In 1930 Eva Dugan, a fifty-two-year-old woman, was also beheaded by the force of her fall. Dugan's botched execution prompted the state of Arizona to abandon hanging and build a gas chamber. In 1876 in Ohio, James Murphy had to be hanged twice, since the rope broke on the first attempt. However, the most typical type of error occurred when the force of the drop was not strong enough to render the condemned prisoner unconscious. In those cases the condemned prisoner would die slowly and painfully, by being choked to death. Because of the variable results, considerable effort was put into trying to improve the technology of hanging to make it more predictable and reliable. In the twentieth century, hanging in the United States was largely replaced by the electric chair or the gas chamber.

Hanging can take one of four different forms.

Short drop. Hangings that involve a fall of less than three feet are called short-drop hangings. These hangings can be performed without the use of an elaborate scaffold or gallows. The condemned prisoner is merely hanged from a tree branch or roof beam while standing on a ladder or cart, or sitting on a horse. The support is then removed. Since the drop is too short to cause immediate unconsciousness, condemned prisoners in a short-drop hanging usually die slowly of strangulation. Lynchings (unauthorized illegal hangings) are generally performed using this method, and people who commit suicide by hanging themselves usually only achieve a short drop.

Standard drop. When executioners take the time to build a proper gallows, a much longer drop is possible. In the United States during the nineteenth century, a drop of four or five feet was usual. While a drop of this length was usually enough to knock the condemned prisoner unconscious, it was usually not long enough to break the condemned prisoner's neck. As a result, there were still numerous cases in which condemned prisoners died slowly, and even one case in which the condemned prisoner, who was thought to be dead, revived on the way to the graveyard and had to be taken back to be hanged again.

The upright jerker. In 1831 a different kind of gallows was invented for the execution of Charles Gibbs, who was convicted of piracy. Rather than using a stationary rope tied to a beam, the rope was run through two pulleys and attached to heavy weights that could be dropped suddenly, pulling the condemned prisoner upward. The advantage of this design was that the force applied to the condemned prisoner's neck depended not on the condemned prisoner's own weight but on the weight attached to the rope, which could be heavier than the condemned prisoner. This should have made the outcome of executions far more predictable and subject to control. Since it seemed like such a good idea, use of the upright jerker spread rapidly from the 1830s to the 1870s. However, since it required the use of pulleys, the upright jerker was more technically complicated than a standard gallows, and in the hands of inexperienced local sheriffs, the results were still frequently less than satisfactory.

Long drop. Hangings that involve a fall of five feet or greater are called long-drop hangings. Long drops were used in England and were adopted by some U.S. states in the early twentieth century at about the same time that other states were abandoning hanging in favor of the electric chair. In a long-drop hanging, the length of the drop is determined by the condemned prisoner's body weight to ensure that enough force is generated by the fall to break the condemned prisoner's neck. A fall of five feet is the minimum, and is used for condemned prisoners weighing 220 pounds or more. Lighter condemned prisoners must fall farther to achieve the same force, so a condemned prisoner as light as 120 pounds must fall about eight feet. Modern executions by hanging have all employed the long-drop method.

Following the decadelong hiatus in executions in the United States that began in 1967, there have been only three executions by hanging in the United States. Only two states, Washington and Delaware, still offer hanging as an option. Westley Allan Dodd was hanged in Washington in 1993 and Charles Rodman Campbell was hanged in Washington a year later in 1994. William (Billy) Bailey was hanged in Delaware in 1996. All three executions went smoothly. **See also** gallows; Ketchum, Thomas "Black Jack."

hara-kiri

Hara-kiri (sometimes spelled hari-kari) is a form of ritual suicide traditionally practiced in Japan and to a lesser extent in China. The term *hara-kiri* is considered somewhat vulgar and colloquial; the more formal term is *seppuku*. Although the execution is self-administered, it is historically, nevertheless, an execution and thus a form of capital punishment, with a parallel, in the United States, where some gallows were rigged to allow the prisoner to perform his or her own hanging in the same spirit. The ritual of hara-kiri involves disemboweling oneself by plunging a dagger into the left side of one's abdomen, slicing to the right and then upward. At this point, a witness (traditionally a close friend) may strike off the head with a single blow of a *katana* (the traditional sword of a samurai warrior), to prevent further suffering. The practice was started in feudal Japan by defeated warriors who would commit suicide to avoid being taken by the enemy. From about 1500 to 1868, hara-kiri was used as a form of execution reserved for the nobility and for samurai warriors. A person who had been disloyal to his lord would receive a jeweled dagger from his lord with which to perform the ritual. After 1700, the actual disembowelment was often merely simulated.

Hara-kiri as a form of execution was abolished in Japan in 1868, at the end of a civil war that restored the rule of the emperor and brought many changes to Japanese society. However, traditionalists continued to practice hara-kiri as a form of political protest or as a response to a perceived dishonor. Forty men committed hara-kiri in 1895 to protest the return of the Liaotung peninsula to China after it had been captured by Japanese forces. In 1945, following the surrender of Japan at the end of World War II, many Japanese military officers who felt dishonored by the Japanese defeat committed hara-kiri. **See also** gallows.

Harris v. Alabama

This was a case heard by the Supreme Court of the United States in 1995 concerning how much weight a judge must give to an advisory jury when considering a sentence of death. The defendant in the case, Louise Harris, was convicted in Alabama of soliciting the murder of her husband by asking her lover to hire someone to commit the murder. Although soliciting murder is a death-eligible offense, the jury found that the mitigating circumstances in the case were sufficient for them to recommend that Harris be sentenced only to life imprisonment without parole. However, under Alabama law at the time, the trial judge was not bound by the jury's recommendation during the penalty phase of the trial. In this case, the judge overrode the jury's recommendation and imposed a sentence of death. The sentence was then appealed on the grounds that Alabama law did not specify how much consideration should be given by the judge to the jury's opinion. Eventually, the U.S. Supreme Court agreed to review the case.

In an 8-to-1 decision, the U.S. Supreme Court ruled that it did not matter how much or how little consideration the

Alabama law required judges to give to a jury's recommendation. Writing for the majority, Justice Sandra Day O'Connor pointed out that some states (at the time) allowed judges to impose sentence without consulting a jury at all. If these laws could be considered constitutional, then there could be no constitutional objection to laws requiring only minimal weight be given to a jury's recommendation. Harris's sentence was therefore upheld.

This decision has since been superseded by the 2002 *Ring v. Arizona* decision, under which questions of fact raised during the penalty phase of a trial must be decided by a jury, which places significant limits on a judge's ability to override a jury's opinion. **See also** *Ring v. Arizona.*

Hauptmann, Bruno (1899–1936)

Bruno Hauptmann was executed by electrocution in New Jersey in 1936 after being convicted of one of the most notorious crimes of the twentieth century, the kidnapping and murder of the infant son of aviator Charles Lindbergh. His case increased support for capital punishment in the United States, though it also raised the issue of anti-immigrant sentiment as a factor in death-penalty sentencing.

Hauptmann was a German immigrant who had fled Germany to escape criminal charges. In the United States he worked as a carpenter, but could find little work because of the economic depression of the early 1930s. In March 1932 Hauptmann allegedly built a ladder using some floorboards taken from his attic and used it to enter the Lindberghs' house through the window of the nursery on the second floor. He kidnapped the Lindberghs' twenty-month-old child, leaving behind a ransom note.

The investigation into the kidnapping turned into what can only be described as a media circus, in part because Lindbergh was an internationally known hero. So many state police showed up to investigate, carelessly tramping through the house and grounds, that valuable clues, including fingerprints and tire tracks, were destroyed. Various publicity-seeking crooks, including gangster Al Capone, claimed to have information, and much time was wasted following false leads supplied by people who actually knew nothing. One con artist, Gaston Means, actually claimed to be the kidnapper and was paid $100,000 by a wealthy socialite who was trying to be helpful. Means was caught and convicted of fraud, but turned out to know nothing about the actual kidnapping.

Meanwhile, someone using the name Cemetery John made contact with an agent working for Charles Lindbergh. Cemetery John was able to prove that he was the real kidnapper by correctly describing the pajamas that the baby was wearing when kidnapped. He was paid $50,000, including $20,000 in gold certificates (money that could be exchanged for gold). He gave directions for finding the baby and left with the money. His directions, however, turned out to be false. The baby was already dead, and its body was found not far from the Lindbergh home on May 12, 1932, about a month after the ransom had been paid. The child had been killed the night of the kidnapping.

Hauptmann managed to elude capture for about two years. However, in 1933 the U.S. Treasury discontinued the use of gold certificates as currency, so much of the ransom money became easily identifiable. In September 1934 Hauptmann was caught after spending one of the gold certificates to buy gasoline. The remainder of the ransom money was found in his house, and the wood used to make the ladder used in the kidnapping was matched to missing floorboards in Hauptmann's attic. Lindbergh's agent identified Hauptmann's voice and accent as belonging to "Cemetery John." Hauptmann, however, claimed that he was merely holding the money for a fellow immigrant who had returned to Germany and died while there. The jury did not believe him. Hauptmann was sentenced to death and executed using New Jersey's electric chair on April 2, 1936. He asserted his innocence to the end. The view that he was framed is a favorite with conspiracy theorists, al-

Bruno Hauptmann went to the electric chair in 1936 for kidnapping and killing Charles Lindbergh's infant son.

though there is little doubt that Hauptmann was involved in the kidnapping in some capacity or other. **See also** opposition to capital punishment, history of (1870–1963).

Hawaii

Capital punishment has never been used in the state of Hawaii, although there were forty-seven executions (by hanging) in territorial Hawaii between 1856 and 1957. The last person executed in Hawaii was Mariano Flores in 1941. Hawaii officially abolished capital punishment in 1957, two years before becoming a state.

Haymarket Square riot

The 1886 Haymarket Square riot in Chicago was one of the most violent confrontations between police and workers in the early days of the labor movement. It led to the trial of nine men on charges of murder, four of whom were subsequently executed. The trial was highly controversial, and evidence has since been presented that indicates that all four of the men were innocent of the charges for which they were executed.

On May 1, 1886, a labor strike against the McCormick-Harvester plant in Chicago turned violent when striking workers tried to prevent scab laborers from entering the plant. Police shot at the strikers, killing one. To protest this killing, union leaders called for a demonstration in Haymarket Square on May 4. Fifteen thousand demonstrators showed up. Various labor leaders gave speeches, and Chicago's mayor, Carter Harrison, made a brief appearance to express his support. When the mayor was gone, a squadron of 180 police officers arrived and ordered the crowd to disperse. The leaders reluctantly began to comply when a dynamite bomb was thrown at the police. Seven policemen were killed, as well as two demonstrators, and 130 policemen were injured. Police fired into the crowd, causing more injuries, and the demonstrators fled in panic.

The police killings caused public outrage around the country. Much of the outrage was directed at anarchists and Communists, who tended to be associated with the labor movement. Since there was no evidence to indicate who had actually thrown the bomb, suspicion was directed at the organizers of the demonstration. Eventually, nine men were indicted on charges of murder. They were George Engel, Samuel Fielden, Adolph Fischer, Louis Lingg, Oscar Neebe, Albert Parsons, Rudolph Schnaubelt, Michael Schwab, and August Spies. Seven of these men were arrested, but Parsons and Schnaubelt could not be found. Parsons dramatically showed up at the courtroom as the trial began and seated himself with the other defendants, but Schnaubelt, who was charged with actually throwing the bomb, probably fled the country.

From the beginning, the judge in the case, Joseph Eaton Gary, showed a clear bias in favor of the prosecution. He refused to disqualify potential jurors who knew the dead policemen, forcing the defense to use peremptory challenges to have these jurors dismissed. The case against the defendants consisted solely of evidence that they had all, at one time or another, advocated radical political views. No evidence was presented to identify the bomber, to link the defendants with the bomber, or even to link the defendants with each other. Nevertheless, Judge Gary instructed the jury that the defendants could be found guilty of murder as part of a conspiracy even if the principal conspirator was not identified. All of the defendants were found guilty. Neebe was sentenced to fifteen years in prison; the rest were sentenced to death. Fielden and Schwab later had their sentences commuted to life imprisonment. Lingg killed himself with a small bomb before being executed, leaving Engel, Fischer, Parsons, and Spies to be hanged on November 11, 1887.

In 1892 a new governor, John P. Altgeld, was elected in Illinois. Upon reviewing the trial, Governor Altgeld promptly pardoned Fielden, Neebe, and Schwab, and declared the four executed defendants to be innocent as well. Unfortunately for Altgeld, popular sentiment against the defendants was still strong. Altgeld was defeated in his reelection campaign and never again held public office. **See also** Sacco, Nicola, and Bartolomeo Vanzetti.

Herrera v. Collins

This was a case heard by the Supreme Court of the United States in 1992, and decided in 1993, concerning whether a person convicted of a crime is entitled to a new trial whenever new evidence that might support the person's innocence is found. The defendant, Lionel Torres Herrera, was convicted in 1981 of the murders of two Texas police officers and sentenced to death. In 1983, while Herrera was still awaiting execution, Herrera's nephew provided a statement that his father, Raul Herrera Sr., had told him that he had actually killed the two officers. Herrera's lawyers immediately filed for a writ of habeas corpus to obtain a new trial; however, under Texas law, motions for new trials based on new evidence had to be filed within thirty days of the conviction. Since nearly two years had elapsed, the motion was denied. The case was appealed on the grounds that the thirty-day limit on discovery of new evidence was a violation of the "due process" clause of the Fourteenth Amendment. Eventually, the Supreme Court agreed to hear the case.

In a 6-to-3 decision, the Supreme Court ruled that Herrera should not be given a new trial based on the evidence presented. Writing for the majority, Chief Justice William Rehnquist argued that it was not the job of appeals courts to overturn findings of fact made during the original jury trial. While "truly persuasive" evidence might convince an appeals court to order a new trial, the evidence presented by Herrera fell short of what was needed. Moreover, it was reasonable for states to set limits on the presentation of new evidence, even limits as short as thirty days. Hence, the appeals court was right to deny Herrera a new trial. Rehnquist pointed out that executive clemency, not the appeals court system, was the appropriate mechanism for preventing miscarriages of justice.

The decision in this case was among the Court's most controversial. In dissenting from the decision, Justice Harry Blackmun said that the Court's action was "perilously close to simple murder," and even read his dissenting opinion aloud in open court to emphasize his disagreement. Even three justices who concurred in the Court's opinion took the position that, although Herrera had not presented sufficient evidence to be granted a new trial, it was indeed the role of the courts to prevent the execution of the innocent.

At the time of this decision, the Supreme Court was attempting to limit what was perceived to be the excessive number of appeals made by death row inmates. The *Herrera v. Collins* decision severely limited the grounds on which habeas corpus petitions could successfully be filed. Herrera was executed on May 12, 1993, still maintaining his innocence. **See also** actual innocence; habeas corpus; thirty-day rule.

Hill, Joe (1879–1914)

Joe Hill was a union organizer, songwriter, and legendary folk hero who was executed for murder in 1914. It is believed by some that he was innocent, and his execution—as well as his life—is associated with dissident labor and anarchist movements and has become a symbol of the injustice with which American society sometimes treats its poorest members.

Hill, whose original name was Joel Hagglund, was born in Sweden in 1879. In 1902 he immigrated to the United States, where his name was changed to Joseph Hillstrom. This was then shortened to Joe Hill. Around 1910 he became involved with the labor movement as an organizer for the Industrial Workers of the World, or IWW, also known as the Wobblies. The Wobblies used songs—usually new lyrics written to familiar tunes—to motivate their members at meetings and rallies. Hill traveled around the country with hoboes and migrant workers performing Wobbly songs and adding songs of his own to the repertoire. His most famous line, sung to the tune of "In the Sweet Bye and Bye," was "You'll get pie in the sky when you die."

On the evening of January 10, 1914, Hill was wounded by a bullet in Salt Lake City, Utah. He told the doctor who dressed his wound that he had been in an altercation for having apparently insulted a friend's wife. However, he did not identify the friend or his wife. That same evening two men, John G. Morrison and one of his sons, were found shot to death. Another son, who had witnessed the shooting, reported that they were shot by two men who had shouted, "We have got you now!" Morrison fired a shot and hit one of the two assailants. Hill was arrested for the murders.

Because Hill was already well known, the trial attracted national attention. The IWW sent two lawyers, Soren Christensen and Orrin Hilton, to defend Hill. They tried to submit evidence that Morrison, a former police officer, had many enemies among those he had arrested, and that previous attempts had been made on his life. The judge refused to admit this evidence. The lawyers argued that Hill had no motive for the killings. However, some sources claim that Morrison had used his authority as a police officer to break IWW strikes and that his name was on a hit list put together by IWW leaders. Otto Applequist, another Wobbly activist, may have been the second shooter. In any case, the jury found Hill guilty and he was sentenced to death. Hill's attorneys appealed the case at the state level, but the appeal was turned down. A nationwide campaign, in which even Helen Keller became involved, was launched to have the state commute his sentence. However, Utah governor William Spry refused to grant clemency unless Hill identified the couple who could corroborate his alibi. Hill refused.

Hill was executed by firing squad on November 19, 1914. Following his death, a new song, "I Dreamed I Saw Joe Hill Last Night," appeared among the songs sung by union organizers. It remains among the best-known anthems of the union movement and has been sung by numerous performers, including Woody Guthrie and Pete Seeger. **See also** Sacco, Nicola, and Bartolomeo Vanzetti.

Horn, Tom (1861–1903)

Tom Horn was hanged in Wyoming in 1903 after being convicted of murder. Horn was a notorious hired gunman, a real-life model on which the myths and legends of the Wild West are based, but historians now believe that he may not have committed the crime for which he was executed.

At the age of fourteen, Horn left his Missouri home to work for the pony express mail service. When the railroad put the pony express out of business, he tried panning for gold in Arizona. He found little gold, but met a friend who taught him the art of tracking. The pair became scouts for the U.S. Army in its military campaigns against the Apache tribes of the Southwest. After the surrender of Geronimo in 1886, Horn briefly became a cowboy, but was eventually hired by the Pinkerton Detective Agency, where he used his tracking skills to hunt down bandits and bank robbers.

Some time in the early 1890s, Horn left the Pinkertons and became a hired gunman for cattle barons in southern Wyoming. Horn was reputedly paid by the large cattle ranchers to murder homesteaders and sheep ranchers. It was said that he would kill just about anyone for $600.

In 1902 someone shot and killed a fourteen-year-old boy, Willie Nickell, who was working on his father's ranch. It was speculated that Horn shot the boy mistaking him for his father. No direct evidence linked Horn to the shooting, but, posing as a cowboy, U.S. marshall Joe LeFors got Horn drunk one evening, and teased a confession out of him. With this confession as evidence, a jury convicted Horn and sentenced him to death, even though the details of the confession did not match the location where the murder occurred. The jury apparently believed that, even if Horn was not guilty of this murder, he was guilty of others, and that this was a good opportunity to get rid of him.

While awaiting his execution, Horn spent time braiding rawhide lariats, a craft at which he was a master. This has given rise to the legend that he wove the rope used to hang him, which is, however, not true. Horn was hanged on November 20, 1903. The hanging did not go well. The gallows was designed with a release mechanism that was triggered when a tank of water emptied to the point that the weight of the water no longer counterbalanced the weight of the condemned prisoner. Such mechanisms were supposed to spare the human executioner from directly performing the execution. Many gallows of this period were designed with similar devices. In this case, however, the water trickled from the tank too slowly, leaving Horn to stand on the platform for several minutes waiting in suspense. While waiting Horn is reported to have remarked, "You're the sickest bunch of sheriffs I ever saw." **See also** hanging.

Idaho

Idaho has traditionally permitted juries to impose the death penalty, and continues to do so currently. From 1864 to 1888, fourteen executions took place under territorial jurisdiction, all by hanging. Another twelve hangings took place after Idaho became a state in 1890. The last person hanged in Idaho was Raymond Snowden in 1957. Idaho never adopted either the electric chair or the gas chamber.

Following the 1972 *Furman v. Georgia* ruling, which struck down Idaho's death-penalty statute, the state quickly passed a new death-penalty statute in 1973. Idaho's current death-penalty statute allows jurors to consider the death penalty for (1) homicide perpetrated by means of poison, lying in wait, or torture; (2) homicide of a police officer, executive officer, officer of the court, firefighter, judicial officer, or prosecuting attorney; (3) homicide committed by someone under sentence for a previous murder; (4) homicide committed in the course of battery on a child under twelve, arson, rape, robbery, burglary, kidnapping, or mayhem; (5) homicide committed by someone incarcerated in a penal institution; or (6) homicide committed in the course of escaping or attempting to escape from a penal institution.

The death penalty may be imposed if one of ten aggravating circumstances is proven to have accompanied the crime. These aggravating circumstances are (1) that the defendant was previously convicted of another murder; (2) that the defendant was convicted of one or more other homicides occurring at the same time; (3) that the defendant knowingly created a great risk of death to many people; (4) that the homicide was a murder-for-hire and the defendant either performed the murder or solicited another to perform the murder; (5) that the homicide was particularly heinous, atrocious, and cruel; (6) that the homicide was committed in a way that manifested utter disregard for human life; (7) that the homicide was committed in the course of an arson, rape, robbery, burglary, kidnapping, or mayhem; (8) that the defendant is a continuing threat to society; (9) that the victim was a police officer or other public official and the homicide was committed because of the victim's official duties; or (10) that the victim was a witness and the homicide was committed because the victim was a witness. The jury must also consider any mitigating circumstances that the defense wishes to present.

Under Idaho law, a person convicted of a capital offense could be executed if he or she was at least sixteen at the time of the offense. In March 2005 the Supreme Court decision in *Roper v. Simmons* abolished the execution of juveniles, however, and set the minimum age at offense at eighteen. Idaho does provide for life imprisonment without parole as an alternative to the death penalty. Only the state's Commission of Pardons and Paroles has the authority to grant clemency, although the governor may grant reprieves that may not extend beyond the next meeting of the commission.

In 1978 Idaho replaced hanging with lethal injection as its method of execution. Idaho also allows execution by firing squad in cases in which lethal injection is judged impractical. Since the reauthorization of the death penalty, only one execution has taken place in Idaho. Keith Wells was executed by lethal injection in 1994 after voluntarily dropping all his appeals. As of April 2005, twenty people were awaiting execution on Idaho's death row. **See also** *Furman v. Georgia*.

Illinois

Illinois has traditionally permitted juries to impose the death penalty, and continues to do so currently. According to surviving records, one person, a black slave, was burned for witchcraft in the Illinois region in 1779, one of only four executions to take place in Illinois prior to statehood. Only three executions took place in territorial Illinois. Illinois became a state in 1818, and between 1821 and 1928, 246 people were executed in Illinois, all by hanging and all for the crime of murder, or murder in conjunction with another felony, such as robbery or rape. In 1927 Illinois replaced hanging with electrocution as its method of execution, although hangings continued until the end of 1928, when the electric chair was ready for use. Between 1928 and 1962, ninety-seven executions by electrocution took place in Illinois.

Following the 1972 *Furman v. Georgia* ruling, which struck down Illinois' death-penalty statute, the state passed a new death-penalty statute in 1974. The state's current death-penalty statute allows jurors to consider the death penalty for homicide under special circumstances. These special circumstances include that the homicide was intentional, that the defendant knew his or her conduct would cause someone's death, or that the defendant knew his or her conduct had a high probability of causing someone's death. Causing someone's death while committing a felony involving the use of force also makes a homicide death-eligible.

The death penalty may be imposed if one of eighteen aggravating circumstances is proven to have accompanied the crime. The list of aggravating circumstances appears similar to the special circumstances noted above, but aggravating circumstances are considered during the penalty phase of the trial rather than during the guilt phase. These aggravating circumstances are (1) that the victim was a police officer or firefighter; (2) that the victim was on the grounds of a correctional facility either as an employee, an inmate, or a visitor; (3) that the defendant was previously convicted of two or more murders; (4) that the homicide occurred in the course of hijacking a public conveyance, such as an airplane, train, or bus; (5) that the homicide was a murder-for-hire and the defendant either performed the murder or solicited another to perform the murder; (6) that the homicide occurred in the course of another felony; (7) that the victim was under twelve years old and the homicide resulted from brutality indicative of wanton cruelty; (8) that the victim was a witness; (9) that the homicide occurred in the course of drug trafficking; (10) that the defendant was incarcerated in a correctional facility; (11) that the homicide was committed in a cold, calculated, and premeditated manner, following a preconceived plan; (12) that the victim was a medical attendant employed by the government; (13) that as the leader of a gang engaged in drug trafficking, the defendant ordered the homicide; (14) that the homicide involved torture; (15) that the homicide resulted from firing a gun from a motor vehicle; (16) that the victim was sixty years old or older and the homicide resulted from brutality indicative of wanton cruelty; (17) that the victim was known by the defendant to be disabled; or (18) that the victim was a community policing volunteer. The jury must also consider any mitigating circumstances that the defense wishes to present.

Under Illinois law, a person convicted of a capital offense cannot be executed if he or she was under the age of eighteen at the time of the crime. Illinois does provide for life imprisonment without parole as an alternative to the death penalty. The governor has the authority to grant clemency, but receives nonbinding recommendations from the State Prison Review Board.

In 1982 Illinois replaced electrocution with lethal injection as its method of execution. The first execution following the reenactment of the death penalty occurred in 1990 with the execution of Charles Walker for robbery and murder. Since 1990, twelve people have been executed by lethal injection in Illinois. Since the 1972 *Furman* decision, Illinois has been one of two states in which more people were removed from death row by exoneration (i.e., by being proved innocent) than by being executed.

Presented with this evidence that the Illinois criminal justice system was sentencing innocent people to death, in 2000 Governor George Ryan was persuaded to declare a moratorium on executions and appointed a commission to study problems in the prosecution of capital offenses in Illinois. The commission returned several recommendations, but as Ryan was preparing to leave office, the state legislature still had not enacted any of the commission's recommendations. Rather than leave office with the issue unresolved, Ryan commuted the sentences of all 167 of the inmates then on death row. Although some of the commission's recommendations have since been adopted, Ryan's successor, Rod Blagojevich, did not lift the moratorium put in place by Governor Ryan. Hence, while new inmates have been put on death row, no executions are currently scheduled. As of April 2005, ten people were awaiting execution on Illinois' death row. **See also** Ryan, George H.

impalement

Impalement was an ancient, torturous form of punishment, usually imposed for the crime of heresy against the church, that nearly always resulted in death. The punishment involved forcing a wooden or metal spike through the condemned

Fifteenth-century Hungarian prince Vlad Tepes gained notoriety for impaling his enemies on stakes.

prisoner's body, usually entering through the rectum. In some cases the spike was heated prior to insertion. This method of torture was fairly common during the Middle Ages in Europe, and the ingenious devices invented to facilitate its use can still be seen in many museums. Even though death usually resulted from impalement, the purpose of impalement was not to cause death but to cause the maximum possible pain in order to encourage repentance and confession. In a few rare cases, people are known to have survived the treatment.

The most notorious practitioner of this method of torture was a Hungarian prince, Vlad Tepes (1431–1476), known as Vlad the Impaler (and also known as Dracula, which means "son of Dracul," since his father was named Vlad Dracul). His legendary cruelty made him the model for Bram Stoker's vampire in the novel *Dracula*. However, historians now believe that Prince Vlad's reputation for cruelty was probably undeserved. He used impalement as a method of punishment no more frequently or gleefully than other European princes of the same era. **See also** corporal punishment; torture.

imprisonment

Imprisonment, as a method of punishing criminals, involves confining criminals in a guarded facility in which their movements and activities are controlled to varying degrees, for varying lengths of time depending on the seriousness and repeat nature of the offense. Prisoners generally sleep and spend much of their time in small, locked rooms called cells. Cells may be assigned to individuals or shared by two or more prisoners. Prisoners are permitted time to exercise in fenced yards and are allowed outside their cells to eat and to do work that contributes to the function of the prison. In most modern prisons, job training, counseling, and other rehabilitation services are also provided.

Today, imprisonment is accepted as the standard punishment for most criminal offenses. In fact, however, the imprisonment of criminals is a relatively modern idea and has been practiced only since the eighteenth century. Prior to that time, the standard punishments included flogging, branding, forced labor, the stocks, and public execution. People might be held temporarily in a jail while awaiting punishment, but confinement was not in itself part of the sentence; rather, it was a means of preventing prisoners from fleeing until the sentence could be carried out. The only category of crime that sometimes led to long-term imprisonment was nonpayment of debts. The appropriate punishment for this crime was the payment of the debt, so, paradoxically, debtors were confined in so-called debtors prisons to prevent them from escaping their responsibility until the debt was paid. Not surprisingly, imprisonment often made it impossible for debtors to earn money, so it was common for debtors to be held for long periods of time. As imprisonment came to be considered a form of punishment, the practice of holding debtors in prison was abolished.

Before the eighteenth century, dungeons, jails, the Tower of London, the Bastille of Paris, and other places viewed today as prisons, certainly were degrading because conditions there were awful. However, they were not *designed* to be degrading since a prisoner's pain, suffering, and humiliation had to occur in public to count as punishment. The concept of imprisonment itself as punishment developed as the purpose of punishment changed from retribution and deterrence to rehabilitation. In America, this change was largely due to the influence of Dr. Benjamin Rush, who argued that brutal punishments, including forced labor, merely produced hardened criminals. The ideals of the American Revolution, including a concern for human rights and a mistrust of governmental power, also contributed to the desire for more humane and enlightened treatment of criminals. It should not be surprising that the idea of imprisonment is relatively new. Feeding, clothing, and housing imprisoned criminals can be expensive, so imprisonment is likely to be adopted only by a society that is affluent enough to afford the expense. Moreover, the idea that being fed, clothed, and housed at public expense could be considered a form of *punishment* is not altogether obvious. Imprisonment is likely to be adopted only by a society that is trying to redefine its understanding of social justice. However, in the eighteenth century, Europe and America met these conditions. Both societies were relatively affluent, and both were deeply concerned with coming to a new understanding of social justice.

The first facility in the United States intended to rehabilitate criminals was the Walnut Street Jail in Philadelphia. The jail was constructed in 1773, and by 1776 it was overcrowded and underfunded. No attempt was made to separate prisoners by age, gender, or type of offense, and the feeding of prisoners had to be supplemented by charitable contributions. In 1790, after the American Revolution, the jail was put under new management and designated a "penitentiary," or house of penitence. A new cell block was built to hold some prisoners in solitary confinement, which at the time was thought to be a humane way to provide prisoners with time for reflection and meditation.

Aside from solitary confinement, the chief method of reform was to impose upon prisoners a highly regulated and authoritarian way of life, similar to life in a monastery. The idea was to teach discipline and self-control, virtues considered necessary to life in society. It was assumed that criminals lacked discipline and self-control but that with practice they could acquire these virtues and be safely returned to society.

The Walnut Street Jail was not architecturally suited to achieve its lofty mission. Even with the additional cell block, it was too small to accommodate the number of prisoners sent for rehabilitation, and overcrowding quickly made a life of monastic discipline difficult to achieve. Nevertheless, the problem appeared to be not with the idea of imprisonment per se or with the goal of rehabilitating prisoners but with the inadequacies of the facility. To address these problems, Pennsylvania built two new penitentiaries, one in Pittsburgh in 1821 and one in Philadelphia in 1829. However, it was the Auburn Prison, built in New York in 1819, that provided the model that was followed by most subsequent penitentiaries.

Unlike the Pennsylvania prisons, which were designed to provide prisoners with seclusion and opportunities for quiet, individual work, the Auburn Prison was designed for shared activities, including a common dining facility, and production-line labor that required prisoners to work collaboratively. Prison organization was still highly regulated and authoritarian, but the object was to teach social skills as well as discipline and self-control.

In the late nineteenth and early twentieth centuries, most states added probation and parole programs to their prison systems. Since the purpose of a prison sentence was to teach prisoners how to function in society, inmates who were not guilty of serious crimes, or who had displayed model behavior in prison, could be released into society under supervision. Probation and parole were seen as accomplishing the same goal as a prison sentence, but without the cost and inconvenience of keeping a person incarcerated.

Ever since the Auburn model was developed, there have been attempts to improve upon it. Prisons have added counseling, vocational training, psychiatric services, libraries to encourage reading and education (as well as access to legal materials), and numerous other programs and services designed to address the problems that lead to criminal behavior. Despite these changes, it is generally admitted that prisons have not succeeded in becoming true rehabilitation facilities. The number of former prisoners who commit new crimes is typically as high as 70 percent. This rate, known as the recidivism rate, suggests that imprisonment is not a particularly effective means of rehabilitating criminals. It has even been pointed out that prison creates the ideal conditions for criminals to swap trade secrets, thus producing more proficient and dedicated criminals. However, imprisonment is so widely accepted as a punishment for serious crimes that it is hard to imagine a return to the widespread use of punishments intended to produce pain and public humiliation.

The increased acceptance of imprisonment as a form of punishment has been the single most significant factor in the declining use of the death penalty throughout the world. Painful and humiliating punishments were necessarily limited in duration and intensity, unless they were so grotesque that they were really forms of torture. As such, punishments based on pain and humiliation could be used to punish only relatively minor crimes. Serious crimes seemed to require a more severe penalty, but, before there were prisons, death was the only punishment that was both sufficiently severe and sufficiently humane to be considered an appropriate punishment for most serious crimes. Hence the death penalty was widely used to punish many types of crimes. Long-term imprisonment provided a reasonable alternative, being both long-lasting and humane. Thus, as imprisonment became a common penalty, fewer and fewer crimes were included in the category of capital crimes. **See also** corporal punishment; San Quentin State Prison; Sing Sing Prison; solitary confinement.

In re Kemmler

This was a case heard by the Supreme Court of the United States in 1890 concerning whether death by electrocution was "cruel and unusual" and therefore prohibited by the Eighth Amendment of the U.S. Constitution. The defendant, William Kemmler, had used a hatchet to murder his girlfriend and had been convicted of murder. The state of New York had just adopted the electric chair as its method of execution, so Kemmler was sentenced to death by electrocution. Lawyers representing Kemmler appealed the sentence on the grounds that electrocution constituted cruel and unusual punishment. The New York appeals courts upheld the sentence, but the U.S. Supreme Court agreed to review their decision.

The decision of the Supreme Court, written by Chief Justice Melville Weston Fuller, was that electrocution was not cruel and unusual as that phrase is meant in the Constitution. Fuller expressed the view that a punishment could be considered cruel only if it was painful and lingering. Death per se was not cruel. The electric chair as a method of causing death might be considered "unusual" in the sense that it had never been used before, but death itself was not unusual. Fuller was clearly unwilling to declare a new method of execution unconstitutional solely on the grounds that it was *new*. Such a decision could make progress impossible. Rather, he noted that the electric chair was actually an attempt to make executions more humane, and was therefore consistent with the intention of the Eighth Amendment. **See also** cruel and unusual punishment; electric chair; Kemmler, William.

Indiana

Indiana has traditionally permitted juries to impose the death penalty, and continues to do so currently. Only one execution is recorded as having taken place in territorial Indiana. Between 1816, when Indiana became a state, and 1896, executions were carried out under the jurisdiction of local authorities. Some fifty-seven executions by hanging are known to have taken place then. Although bigamy, horse stealing (on a second offense), and dueling (if the loser was killed) were considered capital crimes, all executions of whites were for the crime of murder, or murder in conjunction with robbery or burglary. One black man was legally hanged for rape. The number of blacks executed for rape might have been higher except that blacks accused of rape were generally lynched before receiving a trial. There were forty-one recorded lynchings in Indiana, fifteen blacks and twenty-six whites.

In 1897 Indiana revised its criminal code, and executions were thereafter carried out directly under the jurisdiction of the state. Between 1897 and 1907, thirteen people were executed by hanging. In 1913 Indiana replaced hanging with electrocution as its method of execution. Between 1914 and 1961, fifty-eight people were executed in Indiana's electric chair.

Following the 1972 *Furman v. Georgia* ruling, which struck down Indiana's death-penalty statute, the state passed a new death-penalty statute in 1974. Indiana's current death-penalty statute allows jurors to consider the death penalty for homicide under special circumstances. These special circumstances include that the homicide was intentional; that it occurred while committing or attempting to commit arson, burglary, child molestation, consumer-product tampering, kidnapping, rape, robbery, or carjacking; that it occurred in the course of a drug-related offense; or that it resulted in the death of a viable fetus.

The death penalty may be imposed if one of sixteen aggravating circumstances is proven to have accompanied the crime. The list of aggravating circumstances appears similar to the special circumstances noted above, but aggravating circumstances are considered during the penalty phase of the trial rather than during the guilt phase. These aggravating circumstances are (1) that the homicide was committed in the course of arson, burglary, child molesting, criminal deviant conduct, kidnapping, rape, robbery, carjacking, criminal gang activity, or trafficking in cocaine or narcotics; (2) that the homicide occurred because of the unlawful detonation of an explosive device with intent to cause injury or damage to property; (3) that the homicide involved lying in wait; (4) that the defendant was hired by someone else to commit the murder; (5) that the defendant hired someone else to commit the murder; (6) that the victim was a corrections employee, probation officer, parole officer, community corrections worker, home detention officer, firefighter, judge, or law enforcement officer; (7) that the defendant was previously convicted of murder; (8) that the defendant had previously committed another murder even if he or she was not convicted of it; (9) that the defendant was in the custody of a correctional facility, on probation, or on parole; (10) that the defendant dismembered the victim; (11) that the defendant burned, mutilated, or tortured the victim while the victim was still alive; (12) that the victim was under twelve years old; (13) that the victim was battered, kidnapped, subjected to confinement, or sexually abused; (14) that the victim was known to the defendant to be a witness against the defendant on a separate matter and the homicide was committed to prevent the victim's testimony; (15) that the defendant committed the homicide by intentionally discharging a firearm either into an inhabited building or from a vehicle; or (16) that the victim was pregnant and the homicide resulted in the intentional killing of a viable fetus. The jury must also consider any mitigating circumstances that the defense wishes to present.

Under Indiana law, a person convicted of a capital offense cannot be executed if he or she was under the age of eighteen at the time of the crime. Indiana does provide for life imprisonment without parole as an alternative to the death penalty. The governor has the authority to grant clemency only if he or she receives a favorable recommendation from the Parole Board, but the governor is not required to grant clemency on the board's recommendation.

In 1986 a sixteen-year-old girl, Paula Cooper, was sentenced to death for murder. She was the youngest person ever sentenced to death in Indiana, although at the time Indiana's death-penalty statute allowed children as young as ten years old at the time of their crime to be sentenced to death, the lowest minimum age of any state in the United States. Cooper's sentence was later overturned, but in 1987 the Indiana legislature revised the law, raising the minimum age to sixteen years old at the time of the offense. In 2002 the minimum age was raised again, to eighteen.

Under Indiana's new death-penalty statute, three people have been executed by electrocution. The first was Steven T. Judy in 1981 and the last was Gregory Resnover in 1994. Resnover and a companion, Tommie J. Smith, were convicted of the killing of a police officer. In 1995 Indiana replaced electrocution with lethal injection as its method of execution, and in 1996 Smith became the first person executed by lethal injection in Indiana. Since 1996, there have been seven executions by lethal injection. As of April 2005, thirty-three people were awaiting execution on Indiana's death row. **See also** *Furman v. Georgia; Roper v. Simmons.*

Ingle, Joe (1948–)

Joe Ingle is a United Church of Christ minister who specializes in ministering to inmates on death row. In his capacity as spiritual adviser, he has been present at executions throughout the southern United States. He is a vocal opponent of the death penalty.

Ingle began his death row ministry in the mid-1970s. At that time he helped found the Southern Coalition on Jails and Prisons, an organization that works to promote prison reform. The coalition currently has branches in eight southern states. He also started a Visitation on Death Row program to help relieve the isolation that many death row inmates feel, and cofounded the Tennessee Coalition Against State Killing. For his work ministering to death row inmates and for his efforts opposing capital punishment, he was twice nominated for the Nobel Peace Prize, in 1988 and 1989. **See also** Prejean, Helen.

Innocence Project

The Innocence Project is a nonprofit legal clinic that is attempting to examine DNA evidence from past crimes in order to identify cases in which an innocent person was wrongly convicted. The project was initiated by attorneys Barry C. Scheck and Peter J. Neufeld in 1992. It operates in conjunction with the Ben-

Attorney Barry Scheck (left), cofounder of the Innocence Project, looks on as one of his clients addresses the media. The project has used DNA evidence to exonerate a number of innocent death row inmates.

jamin N. Cardoza School of Law, and much of the work is done by law students, who volunteer their time to obtain valuable experience with cases in criminal law. Even though the Innocence Project limits its cases to those in which biological evidence has been preserved, its backlog currently exceeds one thousand cases. Approximately 140 defendants have been exonerated through the efforts of the Innocence Project, 120 on the basis of DNA evidence and analysis. Several of these have been death row exonerations, including Nicholas Yarris, freed from Pennsylvania's death row in September 2003 (but still in prison on other charges), and Ryan Matthews, freed from Louisiana's death row in June 2004. **See also** DNA evidence.

international criticism of the United States

As the only major Western democracy to retain and regularly use capital punishment, the United States has been the target of widespread international criticism for its retention of capital punishment. During the mid-twentieth century, several high-profile capital cases in the United States may have been partly responsible for moving world opinion against capital punishment. For example, during the Cold War, the executions of convicted spies Julius and Ethel Rosenberg in 1953 provoked worldwide criticism. In the 1950s Caryl Chessman, a death row prisoner condemned for robbery and attempted rape, gained a worldwide following with his articulate memoir about life on death row. In 1958 the case of Jimmy Wilson, a black defendant who was sentenced to death in Alabama for stealing $1.95 from a white woman, drew international condemnation. So many letters of protest were received by U.S. embassies—as many as a thousand a day—that eventually the U.S. secretary of state, John Foster Dulles, asked Alabama governor James Folsom to commute Wilson's sentence. Folsom agreed.

International criticism of the United States with regard to the death penalty tends to focus on two specific issues. These two issues are the execution of foreign nationals without adequate notification given to consular authorities and the execution of juvenile offenders.

The issue of consular notification. It is a recognized principle of international law that visitors to a country are subject to the laws of the country they are visiting. However, it is also a requirement of international law that when a foreign national is arrested and charged with a crime, the government of his or her country should be informed (through its consulate) of the arrest and charges and should be given an opportunity to provide assistance and legal advice. Jurisdictions within the United States regularly ignore this requirement. For example, in 1999 the International Court of Justice issued a ruling that the state of Arizona should refrain from executing two German citizens, Walter and Karl LeGrand, until the court could consider complaints by the German government that it had not received adequate consular notification. Arizona ignored the ruling and proceeded with the executions. So far, U.S. courts have not been willing to delay executions based on claims by foreign governments that they did not receive timely notification of a defendant's arrest.

The issue of juvenile offenders. The United Nations takes no official position condemning capital punishment per se, but the UN does have an official position condemning the execution of juvenile offenders. Resolution 39/118, passed in 1984, requires states that permit capital punishment to refrain from executing pregnant women or people who were under the age of eighteen at the time of their crime. Until 2005 the United States was in violation of this resolution, a fact noted in the majority opinion in *Roper v. Simmons*. The 2005 *Roper* decision outlawed the execution of juvenile offenders in the United States. Other international agreements also condemn the execution of juvenile offenders, including the Convention on the Rights of the Child and the International Covenant on Civil and Political Rights. When the United States signed and ratified the International Covenant on Civil and Political Rights, it expressed reservations about the clause condemning the execution of juvenile offenders. Some treaties explicitly allow nations to opt out of certain provisions of the treaty merely by expressing reservations to those provisions. This treaty, however, does not follow that model, and the Inter-American Court of Human Rights has ruled that signatories to this treaty are not permitted to selectively opt out of its provisions as they see fit. The United States has ignored this ruling.

In 2001 lawyers for Michael Domingues, who was sentenced to death for a murder in Nevada committed while he was sixteen years old, appealed his sentence on the grounds that state laws are required to conform to U.S. treaty obligations. A law to this effect was passed by the Congress in 1867, and remains in effect today. Nevertheless, the U.S. Supreme Court refused to review the case, and indeed no Supreme Court decision has so far overturned a state law on the grounds that it fails to meet the requirements of treaties that the United States has entered into with other nations. **See also** extradition; foreign nationals; international use of capital punishment; juvenile offenders.

international use of capital punishment

Capital punishment has traditionally been practiced by most countries around the world. Indeed, during the eighteenth century the young United States was considered unusually progressive for the mildness of its criminal laws and for the rarity with which the death penalty was used, especially for crimes other than murder. However, the Enlightenment spirit that had been so influential in the formation of U.S. criminal law also exerted itself in other parts of the world. Apparently the first jurisdiction in the world to formally abolish capital punishment was Russia under the empress Catherine II, who abolished the practice in 1767. In Europe, the Italian state of Tuscany abolished capital punishment in 1786, and Austria abolished capital punishment in 1787. However, all three of these states later reestablished capital punishment under later leaders.

During the nineteenth century, the abolitionist movement that resulted in the abolition of capital punishment in Wisconsin and Iowa was also effective in South America and Europe. The first nation to permanently abolish capital punishment was Venezuela in 1863. In 1867 Portugal became the first European country to abolish capital punishment. Costa Rica, Brazil, and Ecuador also abolished capital punishment at about this time.

During the twentieth century, use of the death penalty around the world continued to decline. Mexico held its last execution in 1937. Following World War II, Germany, Austria, and Italy abolished capital punishment. Capital punishment was a contentious issue in many places, but by the 1950s and 1960s many countries simply stopped conducting executions. Denmark and Belgium stopped conducting executions in 1950. The Netherlands joined them in 1952 and Ireland in 1954. New Zealand conducted no executions after 1957. In 1965 Britain declared a moratorium on executions and in 1969 officially abolished capital punishment. In recent years, the international trend away from capital punishment has continued to accelerate. Between 1986 and 2004, the number of countries listed by the human rights organization Amnesty International as "abolitionist," either by law or in practice, rose from 64 to 117. Even though the worldwide trend has been away from the use of capital punishment, approximately half the countries in the world still retain the death penalty.

With respect to use of the death penalty, at present countries may be divided into four groups. The first group are countries that have no laws providing for the death penalty for any crime. Amnesty International currently lists seventy-nine countries in this group. The group includes Australia, Cambodia, Canada, Djibouti, the Dominican Republic, East Timor, and all the countries of the European Union, including France, Germany, and the United Kingdom, to name only a few. The second group are countries that have laws permitting the death penalty only for extraordinary crimes, which are crimes committed during time of war or under other exceptional circumstances. Amnesty International lists fifteen countries in this category, including Mexico and several South American countries, such as Argentina, Bolivia, Brazil, and Chile. Israel and Turkey also fall in this group. The third group are countries that have laws providing for the death penalty for ordinary crimes, chiefly murder, but have not conducted an execution in the past ten years. These countries seem to have policies and practices in place that prevent the carrying out of executions even when a sentence of death is imposed. Some have signed international agreements not to conduct executions and to work toward the official abolition of capital punishment. Amnesty International lists twenty-three countries in this group, including the

Russian Federation and Papua New Guinea, as well as various African and South Asian countries such as the Congo, Mali, Niger, and Sri Lanka. The fourth group are countries that still retain the death penalty for ordinary crimes and regularly carry out executions. Amnesty International lists seventy-eight countries in this group, including Afghanistan, China, India, Iran, Uganda, the United States, and Vietnam. Within this group, just four countries are responsible for over three-quarters of all the executions that take place in the world each year. These countries are China, Iran, the United States, and Vietnam. The year 2004 was the first time that Amnesty International listed fewer countries in the fourth group than in the first group. **See also** international criticism of the United States; Protocol 6.

Iowa

Iowa does not currently permit juries to impose the death penalty. In 1851 Iowa restricted the death penalty to first-degree murder and treason, and in 1872 an anti–capital punishment campaign led by social reformer Marvin Bovee, and supported by Iowa's large Quaker population, resulted in the abolition of capital punishment. However, capital punishment for first-degree murder was restored in 1878 and remained in effect until 1965, when the legislature again voted to abolish it. Even while capital punishment was in effect, only forty-one people were executed in Iowa. The last person executed under Iowa law was Charles Kelly in 1962. However, the last person executed in Iowa was Victor Harry Figuer, who was executed in 1963 under federal law. **See also** Bovee, Marvin H.

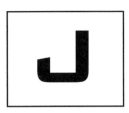

Jackson v. Georgia

This was a case heard by the Supreme Court of the United States in 1972, and was a companion case to the landmark *Furman v. Georgia* case. The defendant in the case, Lucius Jackson, was a black man convicted of raping a white woman while holding a pair of scissors to her throat. Although the woman was not killed, Jackson was sentenced to death. His sentence was appealed on the grounds that racial prejudice had probably contributed to the severity of his sentence. The U.S. Supreme Court agreed to review the case, bundling it with the *Furman v. Georgia* case, which also involved arbitrary and prejudiced sentencing in capital cases. The Court overturned Jackson's sentence, agreeing that the statute under which Jackson was sentenced left jurors free to indulge their prejudices in imposing sentencing, thus violating the constitutional promise of equal protection under the law. **See also** *Branch v. Texas; Furman v. Georgia.*

Joan of Arc (1412–1431)

Joan of Arc was a French peasant girl who, guided by voices that she claimed were sent by God, brilliantly rallied and rode at the head of French armies during the Hundred Years' War. After her capture by the English, she was tried for heresy and witchcraft and executed at the age of nineteen, perhaps the most famous person to be burned at the stake in history.

Joan was born in Domremy in the Lorraine region of France. Her father was a tenant farmer. At the time much of what is now France was controlled by the English, and the French army was near collapse. Guided by voices that she claimed to be of St. Michael, St. Catherine, and St. Margaret, Joan presented herself to Captain Robert de Baudricourt in 1428 and asked to be given command of a unit of men. At first Baudricourt did not take her seriously, but being desperate, he eventually decided to give her some clothing and a unit of just six men. With this base, she mustered several hundred additional recruits at Blois and marched to Orléans, which was being besieged by the English. With her small army she was able to disrupt the siege and force the English to withdraw. Over the next three years she led French forces to several more remarkable victories, which reinspired the French and made her a national hero. Stories of her divine voices undoubtedly served to inspire her troops with courage and confidence. Joan was eventually captured at Compiègne when she fell from her horse while fighting a rear-guard battle to allow the rest of her army time to retreat.

In the Middle Ages, the church was the supreme authority in Europe, and a person's claim to communicate directly with God without the mediation of the clergy was generally viewed as heresy. Church officials in Burgundy (which was under English control) ordered Joan to

Condemned as a heretic and witch, Joan of Arc is burned alive at the stake.

answer seventy specific charges based on her claim to be acting under divine guidance. Eventually Joan agreed to sign a statement acknowledging that the authority of the church was greater than that of her "voices." She was then sentenced to perpetual imprisonment. A few days later, however, Joan announced that St. Catherine and St. Margaret had reprimanded her for signing the document and that she no longer accepted its provisions. As a result, she was turned over to civil authorities to be burned. On May 30, 1431, she was allowed to make confession and receive communion—courtesies generally denied to condemned heretics. She was then led to a town square, where she was tied to a stake and burned. Twenty-five years later, in 1456, the Vatican reviewed her trial and declared her to be innocent. In 1920 she was officially elevated to sainthood by the Catholic Church. **See also** burning at the stake.

Jurek v. Texas

This was a case heard by the Supreme Court of the United States in 1976, and was a companion case to the landmark *Gregg v. Georgia* case, which concerned the constitutionality of a newly enacted state death-penalty statute. The defendant in the case, Jerry Lane Jurek, was convicted of the murder of a ten-year-old girl and sentenced to death under a new Texas death-penalty statute that had been passed to replace the old statute overturned in 1972 by the *Furman v. Georgia* decision. The Texas statute was similar to the statute enacted in Georgia, so the Supreme Court bundled this case with the *Gregg v. Georgia* case. In a 7-to-2 decision, the Supreme Court ruled that the new state death-penalty statutes were constitutional, and it allowed the death sentences to stand. This decision opened the way for a continuation of executions in the United States after a ten-year hiatus. Jerry Lane Jurek, however, was not executed. On a later appeal, his conviction was overturned on evidence that he had not been properly advised of his rights. At retrial, Jurek agreed to plead guilty in exchange for a sentence of life imprisonment. **See also** *Gregg v. Georgia; Proffitt v. Florida.*

jury nullification

Jury nullification is the term used to describe the situation in which members of a jury knowingly and deliberately refuse to convict a defendant, despite their belief that the defendant is guilty of breaking the law, either because they feel that the law itself is unjust or because they feel that the application of the law in this case would be unjust. The term means that the law is nullified with respect to the particular case being considered. Juries do not have the authority to overturn laws permanently, as some courts can do. While jury nullification does not occur only in capital trials, some of the most important implications of jury nullification are in death-penalty cases.

The authority of juries to nullify law in specific cases has its roots in England's Magna Carta, but the power of juries has never been clearly defined. In 1670 colonial leader William Penn was tried for preaching to an unlawful assembly, but four members of the jury refused to convict him, even though they were imprisoned without food for four days. One of the jurors, Edward Bushnell, later protested this treatment before the Court of Common Pleas, and the court ruled that jurors could not be punished for their verdicts. This ruling, which is still recognized as setting precedent in American law, gave juries the effective power to nullify law. Prior to the Civil War, northern juries regularly exercised this power by refusing to convict defendants under the 1850 Fugitive Slave Law.

However, while juries clearly have the power to nullify law, it has not been established that they have a *right* to do so. The most important case on this issue was a capital case, *Sparf and Hansen v. United States* (1895), in which the defendants had been sentenced to death for the crime of murder on the high seas, after the judge had instructed the jury that there was no basis in law for a lesser sentence. On appeal to the Supreme Court, the Court ruled that the role of the jury is merely to decide the facts of the case, and that the judge has no obligation to inform the jury of their power to simply nullify the law. Based on this ruling, a judge may even prohibit the defense attorney from pleading with the jury to exercise their power to nullify the law.

Jury nullification is most likely to occur when one or more members of a jury are opposed to a law on moral or religious grounds. Some effort is made to prevent jury nullification in capital cases by systematically excluding from the jury any prospective jurors who declare themselves to be categorically opposed to the death penalty. A jury that is willing to apply capital punishment statutes is referred to as a death-qualified jury. Precisely what grounds may be used to exclude jurors from death penalty cases has been slowly clarified by the Supreme Court, beginning with the 1968 *Witherspoon v. Illinois* decision, and modified by the 1989 *Wainwright v. Witt* decision. **See also** death-qualified jury; *Wainwright v. Witt*; *Witherspoon v. Illinois*.

Justice for All

Justice for All is a nonprofit all-volunteer organization headquartered in Houston, Texas. The organization generally supports victim's rights legislation and supports the death penalty. It was founded in 1993 to advocate changes in the criminal justice system on the premise that the current system does not do an adequate job of protecting the lives and property of law-abiding citizens. Justice for All tries to effect positive changes in the criminal justice system by educating its members and by exerting peaceful social and legislative influence. **See also** victims' rights.

justification of punishment

In the nineteenth century, the British social philosopher John Stuart Mill advanced the argument that, since punishment by its very nature causes distress to the person punished, and since it is normally considered wrong to cause distress to others, punishment would have to be considered wrong unless there are strong reasons to justify it. Other philosophers generally agree with Mill's assertion that punishment, ultimately including capital punishment, must be justified, but there is considerable disagreement about what constitutes legitimate justification and how to determine and measure such criteria.

Theories of how punishment is to be justified fall into two broad categories, which may be called forward-looking (or externalist) theories and backward-looking (or internalist) theories. Forward-looking theories attempt to justify punishment on the grounds that punishment has beneficial future consequences. Such theories are sometimes called "externalist" since the justification for punishment focuses on considerations that are external to the punishment: on what the punishment achieves rather than on the punishment itself. Backward-looking theories attempt to justify punishment by referring back to the crime. Such theories are sometimes called "internalist" since the justification for punishment focuses on the inherent justice of the punishment itself, even if its effects are not necessarily desirable.

Three forward-looking theories for the justification of punishment have been proposed. Some philosophers appeal to a combination of justifications, but it is still usually possible to assign forward-looking arguments to one of these three categories.

Deterrence theory. Deterrence theorists hold that the primary reason for punishing criminals is to discourage people from committing crimes. This certainly seems to be the most intuitive justification, and is surely the rationale that parents would give for spanking or threatening to spank their children. The Italian social philosopher Cesare Beccaria considered deterrence to be the primary justification for punishment, and the ancient Greek philosopher Plato considered it to be an important (but not primary) justification. Presumably, punishment discourages crime because people want to avoid the pain and discomfort that punishment causes. However, some modern proponents of deterrence theory, such as sociologist Emile Durkheim, have argued that it is not so much the fear of punishment that deters crime as the fact that punishing criminals expresses social disapproval for the actions punished. Most people want to avoid the disapproval of others, and may be deterred more because punishment is shameful than because it is painful.

Deterrence theorists are likely to support capital punishment, but only if it can be shown that the threat of death significantly deters crime. Since, in fact, the evidence that the death penalty has a deterrent effect is not particularly convincing, many deterrence theorists are opposed to capital punishment.

Aside from its intuitive appeal, the chief argument in favor of deterrence theory is that it does not depend on religious or moralistic judgments of right and wrong. The goal is merely to prevent actions that everyone agrees are harmful to society by imposing penalties to discourage those actions. However, there are some problems with deterrence theory. The first problem is that deterrence theory does not fit well with the idea that punishment should be proportional to the crime—in other words, that more serious crimes should be punished more severely than less serious crimes. Rather, under deterrence theory, the severity of the punishment would be dictated by how much punishment is needed to deter the crime, and this in turn could be determined by how frequently the crime is committed. Hence a frequently committed crime, such as jaywalking, might need to be punished much more severely than a relatively rare crime, such as aggravated murder. A second problem with deterrence theory is that, in practice, it is extremely difficult to know how effective a punishment has been at deterring crime. In order to know this, one would have to know how many people had considered committing a crime but decided not to on the grounds that they did not wish to be punished. It is possible to measure how many crimes did occur, but it is not possible to measure how many crimes did not occur. Because of these problems, many social philosophers reject deterrence as a primary justification for punishment, although nearly all admit that deterrence plays at least some role in the justification of punishment.

Rehabilitation theory. Rehabilitation theorists hold that the primary reason for punishing criminals is to get them to reform and become good citizens. Plato considered this to be the primary justification for punishment. People who have held this view often consider the criminal to be the victim of some form of mental or spiritual "illness." In this view, punishment is seen as therapeutic. Rehabilitationists are, of course, universally opposed to capital punishment, since killing a person cannot produce reform.

The argument in favor of rehabilitation theory is that it is a humane approach to punishment since it is largely concerned with the well-being of the people who have committed crimes. For this reason, rehabilitation theory was popular with social philosophers during the late nineteenth and early twentieth centuries as the practice of psychiatry and psychology seemed to offer scientific insights into the personality of criminals. However, it now appears that punishment is not a particularly effective method of getting people to reform. There are various methods that tend to promote reform of criminals, but these appear to be such things as general education, job training, and the development of social connections. Punishment per se apparently does not promote reform, so the rehabilitationist theory does not really justify punishment.

Incapacitation theory. Incapacitation theorists hold that punishment is primarily justified as a means of preventing criminals from doing further harm. Incapacitationists see a limited value to the death penalty for the small number of criminals who cannot be prevented from committing violent crimes as long as they are alive, although they are quick to point out that effective high-security prisons should make the death penalty unnecessary.

Recently, incapacitation theory has become more popular with philosophers as the problems with the other forward-looking theories have become apparent. However, incapacitation theory has problems as well. It may make sense to incapacitate a violent criminal to prevent him or her from harming others, but for minor crimes, such as speeding or shoplifting, it makes far less sense. Incapacitation will also prevent a person from going about useful activities and may therefore be excessively harsh and do more harm than good. Moreover, most accepted punishments, such as the payment of fines, could not be justified under this theory.

The forward-looking theories have been characterized as more enlightened or progressive than the backward-looking ones. However, philosophers such as Walter Berns have begun to reexamine the older backward-looking theories. Here, too, arguments fall into three groups.

Expiation theory. Expiation theory was the view held in early colonial America. Under this view, a crime stains or disgraces an entire community. The community has an obligation to punish the crime in order to expiate, or remove, the disgrace. By punishing transgressions, the community shows that it disapproves of, and is not complicit in, the crime. In early colonial America, where this view was held, death was considered an appropriate form of punishment for a wide variety of crimes, including such "moral" crimes as adultery, bestiality, and homosexuality, as well as murder.

Expiation theory is currently not endorsed by social philosophers. The view rests upon metaphysical or religious views that are not generally held today. Moreover, the theory seems to justify the punishment of "crimes" that are nowadays considered to be matters of private conscience.

Retribution theory. Retribution theorists hold that punishment is justified by the general principle that justice requires balance. According to this view, a crime creates a sort of inequality or imbalance in human relations; punishment strives to restore or rectify the balance. The so-called *lex talionis*, or law of retaliation, which appears in the Bible and in the Code of Hammurabi, is a naive expression of retribution theory. The *lex talionis*, associated with the phrase "an eye for an eye," says that a criminal should be made to suffer whatever loss was suffered by his or her victim. Clearly, in this view, death is the only appropriate punishment for the crime of murder. Modern retributionists recognize that the *lex talionis* should not be treated as a literal law but only as an allegorical expression of the general principle that punishment is what a criminal *deserves*. The harm done to a victim may be a primary consideration in deciding what a criminal deserves, but it is not the only consideration. Other considerations might include the intentions of the criminal. For this reason, retributionists are likely to think that death is the appropriate penalty for first-degree murder, but are flexible enough not to require the death penalty for all crimes resulting in someone's death.

The chief argument for retribution theory is its appeal to fundamental fairness. However, there are several objections to retribution theory. The most important is that the idea of retribution requires that we compare or equate the severity of a punishment with the seriousness of a crime even though there is no common scale by which these two can be measured. It is also sometimes objected that the emotional impulse that makes retribution seem just is really identical to the desire for revenge, which is an unworthy emotion that should not be the basis for justice in a civilized society.

Reparation theory. Reparation theorists hold that the purpose of punishment should be to repair or undo the harm caused by a crime, or to reverse any unfair advantage that a criminal may have obtained as a result of the crime. Under this view, payment of fines is justified as a way of compensating society for the harm done by a crime. Reparationists are also inclined to favor punishment that involves community service rather than imprisonment. Reparationists may see some value in the death penalty, but only insofar as it satisfies the emotional needs of the victim's family (i.e., insofar as it repairs some of the emotional damage done by the crime by producing a feeling of closure).

Like retribution theory, reparation theory appeals to a fundamental sense of fairness. The objection to reparation theory, however, is that many crimes cause damage that cannot be repaired, or at least cannot be repaired by the person who committed the crime. A crime that causes extensive damage may be so expensive to repair that a relatively poor person would not be able to bear the cost. And, of course, it is outside the power of a murderer to restore life to his or her victim. Hence, reparation appears to be a limited and, at best, supplementary justification for punishment.

It is, perhaps, possible to take the view that different forms of punishment serve different goals and are therefore justified by different theories. Similarly, it may be that different theories of punishment apply to different categories of crime. However, the fact that people cannot seem to discover a single, coherent rationale for the practice of punishing criminals is disturbing to philosophers. Some have even suggested that punishment cannot be justified and that we should therefore discard the concept. Rather than punishing criminals, they suggest that we should focus our efforts on correcting the social problems that give rise to crime. **See also** Beccaria, Cesare; deterrence; *lex talionis;* proportionality.

Justinian, Code of

The Code of Justinian, or *Corpus Juris Civilis*, was the final and most comprehensive codification of Roman law. It is important not only because it was the model upon which the laws of virtually all modern European countries were based, but also because it is the first "modern" body of laws in the sense that it shows a humane concern with the rights of individuals. The death penalty is also used far less extensively in the Justinian Code than it had been in previous codes of law.

In 528 Emperor Justinian appointed a commission of ten legal scholars to compile and update Roman law. The result of their work was published in 529, along with an extensive index, which made the code easier to use, and instruction manuals for training lawyers in their use. The work of these scholars was based on an earlier updating of Roman law, the Code of Theodosius, which was a summary of imperial edicts issued since the time of Emperor Constantine in 312. The Code of Theodosius was published in 438, but had become out of date by the time of Emperor Justinian.

The Code of Justinian marks an important change in the law. It is far more lenient and egalitarian than previous laws had been. The code specifically protects people in weaker social positions, generally favoring debtors over creditors, wives over husbands, and even slaves over masters. Where the earlier Code of Theodosius had listed some eighty crimes that were punishable by death, the Justinian Code lists far fewer, and the intent is clearly that the death penalty be reserved for the most heinous of crimes. **See also** Draconian Code; Hammurabi, Code of; Law of the Twelve Tables.

juvenile offenders

A juvenile offender is someone who commits a crime prior to the age of maturity, defined in the United States as the offender's eighteenth birthday. Historically, less than 2 percent of people executed in the United States have been juvenile offenders. The youngest juvenile offender executed in the United States (who was not a slave) was Hannah Ocuish, who was convicted of murder and hanged in 1786 at the age of twelve.

The earliest execution of a juvenile in colonial America occurred in 1642 when Thomas Graunger was executed at age sixteen in Plymouth colony for the crime of bestiality. In the modern era, because of the lengthy appeals process associated with capital punishment prosecutions, juvenile offenders sentenced to death all reached adulthood by the time of their execution.

Prior to 1973, death-penalty statutes in different states specified widely different minimum ages for the perpetrator of a crime to be eligible for the death penalty. Indiana's death-penalty statute had the lowest minimum, allowing a defendant as young as ten years old to be executed. (However, no one that young was ever actually sentenced to death in Indiana.) Montana's statute set the minimum at twelve, and Mississippi set the minimum at thirteen. Various states set minimums ranging from fourteen to seventeen years old. A few states did not allow the execution of juvenile offenders at all (by setting the minimum age at eighteen) while other states did not specify a minimum.

This lack of consistency escaped scrutiny by the U.S. Supreme Court, largely because few juvenile offenders were actually sentenced to death. It was not until the 1980s that the Supreme Court issued some rulings that had the effect of making state death-penalty statutes less variable. Indeed, in the early 1980s, the Supreme Court appeared reluctant to take up the issue. In 1982 the Court agreed to consider the case of *Eddings v. Oklahoma*, in which the sentence of Monty Lee Eddings, who had killed a law enforcement officer at the age of sixteen, was challenged. The Court overturned the sentence, but not on the grounds that Eddings was too young to receive a death sentence. Hence, the Court's ruling left the issue of age unresolved. The Court then refused to hear several other appeals based on the age of

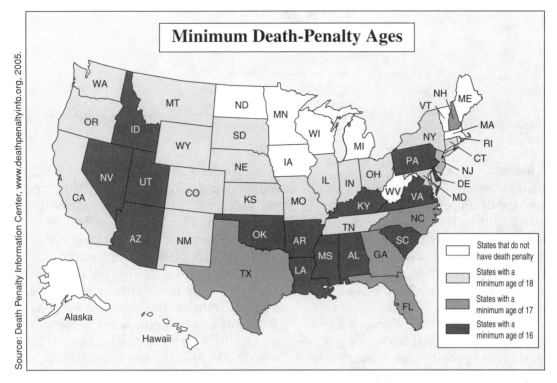

the defendant. Finally, in 1988 the Supreme Court issued a ruling in *Thompson v. Oklahoma* that William Wayne Thompson, who participated in the murder of his brother-in-law at the age of fifteen was too young at the time of his crime to be eligible for the death penalty.

The following year, in 1989, the Supreme Court issued two further rulings, *Stanford v. Kentucky* and *Wilkins v. Missouri*, in which it was decided that, since sixteen- and seventeen-year-olds are granted some degree of adult responsibility (such as driver's licenses), they may be expected to shoulder adult culpability for crimes. Thus, the execution of a defendant as young as sixteen or seventeen did not count as "cruel and unusual" under current standards of decency and was not forbidden by the Constitution.

Following the 1988 *Thompson v. Oklahoma* ruling, fourteen juvenile offenders were executed in the United States. Sean Sellars, who was executed in 1999 in Oklahoma, is the only one who was sixteen at the time of his crime. The other condemned criminals were all seventeen. At that time the United States was one of only five nations in the world that executed people who were younger than eighteen at the time of their crime. The other four countries were Iran, Pakistan, Saudi Arabia, and Yemen.

In March 2005 the Supreme Court abolished the death penalty for juveniles in a narrow 5-to-4 decision in the case of *Roper v. Simmons*, ruling that persons under the age of eighteen cannot be considered fully responsible for their actions. It also overturned the death sentences of seventy-two juvenile murderers who were on death row. This ruling invalidated the provision allowing for execution of minors in the death-penalty statutes of twenty-three states, nineteen of which had juvenile offenders on death row at the time. Their sentences were accordingly overturned. **See also** *Eddings v. Oklahoma; Roper v. Simmons; Stanford v. Kentucky; Thompson v. Oklahoma.*

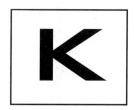

Kansas

Kansas currently permits juries to impose the death penalty, although Kansas has traditionally not been a death-penalty state. Only twenty-four people have been executed in Kansas under state jurisdiction. Another nineteen people have been executed in Kansas under federal and military jurisdiction.

The death penalty was part of the criminal code when Kansas became a state in 1861. Nine people were executed (by hanging) under state jurisdiction between 1862 and 1870. For the next thirty-seven years no one was executed by the state of Kansas, and in 1907 the Kansas legislature abolished capital punishment altogether. Capital punishment was reinstated in 1935, at a time when New York and Chicago gangland crimes were common news. However, no one was executed under state jurisdiction until 1944, when Clark Knox was hanged for murder. From 1944 to 1965, fifteen executions took place, all by hanging. A number of executions under military jurisdiction also took place in Kansas during that period.

Following the 1972 *Furman v. Georgia* Supreme Court decision, which invalidated all state death-penalty statutes, Kansas was slow to reinstate the death penalty. In 1994 Kansas finally adopted a new death-penalty statute and replaced hanging with lethal injection as its method of execution. The current death-penalty statute in Kansas allows juries to consider the death penalty for homicide under special circumstances. These circumstances include that the victim of the homicide had been kidnapped for ransom, that the homicide was committed while the defendant was in custody, that it was committed during the commission of a rape or criminal sodomy, or that multiple deaths were caused. The killing of a law enforcement officer also makes the homicide death-eligible, as does the killing of a child under the age of fourteen who had been kidnapped with sexual intent. Murder-for-hire is death-eligible as well, either for the murderer or for the person who suborns the murder.

The death penalty may be imposed if at least one of eight aggravating circumstances is proven to have accompanied the crime. The list of aggravating circumstances appears similar to the special circumstances noted above, but aggravating circumstances are considered during the penalty phase of the trial rather than during the guilt phase. These aggravating circumstances are (1) that the defendant had been convicted of a previous felony involving great bodily harm, disfigurement, or dismemberment of another person; (2) that the defendant knowingly caused a great risk of death to more than one person; (3) that the homicide was committed for monetary gain; (4) that the defendant authorized or employed another person to commit the crime; (5) that the homicide was committed in order to prevent arrest or prosecution; (6) that the homicide was especially heinous, atrocious, or cruel; (7) that the defendant was serving a sentence of imprisonment for another felony; or (8) that the victim was a witness. The jury must also consider any mitigating circumstances that the defense wishes to present.

Under Kansas law, a person convicted of a capital offense cannot be executed if he or she was under the age of eighteen at the time of the offense. A jury may not impose a sentence of life imprisonment without parole, but the governor, who has sole authority in granting clemency, may commute a death sentence to life imprisonment without parole.

No one has so far been executed under the new statute. In 2001 the Kansas Supreme Court declared some portions of the Kansas death-penalty statute to be flawed and ordered all inmates then on death row to be resentenced. However, as of June 2005 there were seven people on death row in Kansas. **See also** Fort Leavenworth Penitentiary.

Kant, Immanuel (1724–1804)

Eighteenth-century German philosopher whose ethical theories remain among the most important and influential in the world today. In particular, Kant's theories of moral duty and ethical behavior have been used to justify capital punishment.

Kant was born in East Prussia, the son of a saddle maker. He studied at the University of Konigsberg and, after several years as a private tutor, took a position at that university teaching logic and metaphysics. His life was singularly uneventful, spent almost entirely on teaching and writing. As a philosopher he attempted to reconcile the separate traditions of European rationalism with British empiricism, and was generally thought to have succeeded in this effort. In ethics his most important works are *The Critique of Practical Reason* and *Groundwork for the Metaphysic of Morals.*

Kant never questioned the legitimacy of capital punishment. He believed that punishment was justified, not by the consequences that it produced, but simply because criminals deserved to be punished. Kant's ethical theory is based on a principle known as the Categorical Imperative, according to which we must treat persons with a consideration for their own goals and values, being careful not to act toward others as we would not wish to be treated ourselves. However, if we assume that criminals also act according to this principle, we find that they act in ways that undermine their own values. For example, a person who steals acts as if the concept of property has no value by failing to consider the value that others may place in possessing property. In so doing he acts as if his own property is also without value. Hence he *deserves* to have his own property confiscated, since he apparently places no value in it. Similarly, a murderer acts without consideration for the value of life, so no wrong is done to him by taking away his own life. **See also** deontology; justification of punishment.

Kemmler, William (1862–1890)

William Kemmler is famous for being the first man to be executed by means of an electric chair. His execution took place on August 6, 1890, at New York's Auburn Prison.

Kemmler made his living as a greengrocer, selling vegetables on the streets of Buffalo, New York. He had a modestly successful business that employed several men and boys besides himself. However, Kemmler was an alcoholic with a violent temper. One day in 1889 he caught his girlfriend, Tillie Ziegler, who lived with him, packing some clothes into a trunk. He accused her of planning to leave him, and when she confessed that she was planning to run away with one of Kemmler's employees, he got a hatchet from the barn and hacked her to death with it. He probably regretted the murder as soon as he had done it, since he immediately went next door and told his neighbor what had happened.

Kemmler was quickly convicted and sentenced to death. Because the state of New York had just adopted electrocution as its method of execution, Kemmler became the first person to be sentenced to die in the electric chair. However, lawyers acting on Kemmler's behalf appealed the sentence on the grounds that electrocution amounted to cruel and unusual punishment. The appeals court heard testimony from various experts on electricity, including Thomas Edison. Edison and the other witnesses assured the judges that death by electrocution was instantaneous and far less cruel than death by hanging. The case, *In re Kemmler* (1890), was eventually reviewed by the U.S. Supreme Court, which agreed with the lower courts that the execution should be allowed to proceed.

However, Kemmler's execution did not go smoothly. The first seventeen-second burst of electricity was apparently not enough to kill him, since Kemmler started breathing again once the power was turned off. Prison officials hastily reattached the electrodes and gave Kemmler a second and longer burst of electricity. The second burst was so powerful and sustained that Kemmler's flesh was scorched and discolored from being literally cooked by the heat. Witnesses were horrified by the spectacle, and the execution was held up by opponents of capital punishment as evidence that the death penalty is cruel and inhumane. **See also** electric chair; *In re Kemmler.*

Kendall, George (?–1608)

The first recorded execution in colonial America took place in 1608 in the early days of the Jamestown colony. The person executed was Captain George Kendall, who, along with John Smith, was one of the leaders sent by the London Company to establish a colony in the New World. Some accounts indicate that Kendall was executed for mutiny involving "a dangerous conspiracy." The precise nature of this conspiracy is not stated, but it was revealed to the other colonists by a blacksmith, James Read, who was himself sentenced to be hanged for striking one of the colony's leaders. Independent evidence suggests that Kendall may have been spying for Spain. However, a later memoir by members of the colony tells the story quite differently. According to the later account, Kendall and Edward Maria Wingfield, another leader of the colony, attempted to steal a boat stocked with badly needed supplies, presumably for a return trip to England. They planned to leave while Smith was away on a hunting expedition, but Smith returned in time to prevent them. The account remarks that this event cost Kendall his life, but it is not explained how he died. The implication is that he was not executed but, rather, that he was shot to death while trying to escape. **See also** Virginia.

Kentucky

Kentucky has traditionally permitted juries to impose the death penalty, and continues to do so currently. Only four executions took place in Kentucky prior to statehood in 1792. All were by hanging. From 1795 to 1905, some 226 executions by hanging took place under the authority of local governments. In 1906 Kentucky centralized executions at the Branch Penitentiary in Eddyville. Hanging continued to be the only method of execution used until 1911. Between 1906 and 1911 seventeen executions by hanging took place at the Branch Penitentiary. In 1911 Kentucky introduced electrocution as an optional method of execution. Between 1911 and 1962, 171 executions took place in Kentucky, 162 by electrocution and 9 by hanging. The last hanging took place in 1938.

Following the 1972 *Furman v. Georgia* ruling, which struck down Kentucky's death-penalty statute, the state passed a new death-penalty statute in 1975. Kentucky's current death-penalty statute allows jurors to consider the death penalty for homicide under special circumstances. These special circumstances are (1) that the homicide was intentional or, even if the intended victim escaped death, the defendant's conduct resulted in the death of someone other than the intended victim; (2) that the death of the victim resulted from wanton conduct (specifically including, but not limited to, the operation of a motor vehicle) that created a grave risk of death to others; or (3) that the victim was kidnapped and died as a result of the kidnapping.

The death penalty may be imposed if one of eight aggravating circumstances is proven to have accompanied the crime. The list of aggravating circumstances appears similar to the previous list of special circumstances, but aggravating circumstances are considered during the penalty phase of the trial rather than during the guilt phase. These aggravating circumstances are (1) that the defendant was previously convicted of a capital offense or had a substantial history of convictions for violent crimes; (2) that the homicide or kidnapping occurred in the course of first-degree arson, robbery, burglary, rape, or sodomy; (3) that the defendant knowingly created a great risk of death to more than one person in a public place by means of a device (such as a bomb) that would normally endanger more than one person; (4) that the homicide was committed for monetary gain; (5) that the defendant was incarcerated in a penal institution and the victim was an employee of the institution acting in the performance of his or her duties; (6) that the defendant intentionally caused multiple deaths; (7) that the victim was known to the defendant to be a public official, police officer, sheriff, or deputy sheriff acting in the performance of his or her duties; or (8) that the defendant was under a restraining order not to disturb or approach the victim, including an order issued as a condition of probation or parole. The jury must also consider any mitigating circumstances that the defense wishes to present.

Under Kentucky law, a person convicted of a capital offense cannot be executed if he or she was under the age of sixteen at the time of the crime. This provision, however, was overturned in March 2005 by the Supreme Court's decision in *Roper v. Simmons*, which abolished the death penalty for persons younger than eighteen at the time of the offense. Kentucky does provide for life imprisonment without parole as an alternative to the death penalty. The governor has sole authority to commute a death sentence to a term of life imprisonment without parole.

The first execution to take place in Kentucky following the reenactment of capital punishment did not take place until 1997 with the execution of Harold McQueen. This was also the last electrocution to take place in Kentucky. In 1998 Kentucky introduced lethal injection as an optional method of execution, and Edward L. Harper, executed in 1999, elected to be executed by lethal injection. Only these two executions have taken place in Kentucky since the reenactment of capital punishment. As of April 2005, thirty-seven people were awaiting execution on Kentucky's death row. **See also** *Furman v. Georgia*.

Ketch, Jack (?–1686)

Jack Ketch (or Catch, as it was sometimes spelled) was a well-known executioner in England during the seventeenth century. When and where he was born is unknown, but he served as executioner in London from sometime before 1678, when his name first appears, until his death in 1686. He performed executions on many Roman Catholics accused of participating in the conspiracy known as the Popish Plot of 1678. He also executed participants in the Rye House Plot of 1685. His most famous execution was of James Scott, the duke of Monmouth, who was beheaded for treason in 1685.

Ketch used various methods of execution, including both hanging and beheading. In some cases, the sentence included whipping prior to execution, and Ketch diligently performed these whippings himself, earning a reputation for cruelty. He also oversaw executions by drawing and quartering.

Ketch was apparently not a skilled headsman, and indeed had a reputation for incompetence. The execution of Lord William Russell in 1683 required more than one stroke—accounts differ as to whether two or three were required—and was followed by the publication of a pamphlet, allegedly written by Ketch himself, denying that he had been drunk or that he had bungled the execution on purpose. The pamphlet also denies that Russell paid him in gold to perform the execution well. The execution of the duke of Monmouth also did not go well, requiring multiple blows. Ketch even tried to abandon the effort after a few unsuccessful strokes and had to be forced to finish.

Hangmen in New Mexico place the noose around the neck of Thomas "Black Jack" Ketchum in 1901. Ketchum's head was severed from his body by the force of the fall.

Jack Ketch was so notorious that his name became a synonym for "executioner," and was used with this meaning until well into the nineteenth century. Even today the name of any executioner in a Punch and Judy puppet show is always Jack Ketch. **See also** executioners.

Ketchum, Thomas "Black Jack" (1866–1901)

Thomas "Black Jack" Ketchum was hanged in 1901 after being convicted of train robbery and of killing two lawmen in a shootout. His execution is remembered because it was a particularly gruesome hanging: Ketchum's head was pulled off his body by the force of his fall.

Ketchum had an undistinguished career as a train robber. In New Mexico he and his gang, which included his brother Sam, robbed the same train four times at almost exactly the same spot. Each time they took only small amounts of money. During the fourth robbery his brother was shot, and he later died of his wounds. A posse chased the remainder of the gang to a canyon near Cimerron, New Mexico, where a shootout ensued, resulting in the deaths of Sheriff Edward Farr and his deputy W.H. Love. Ketchum was captured and sentenced to death.

On the gallows, Ketchum's last words were "Let 'er rip!" These turned out to be prophetic words, as his head was ripped from his body by the force of his fall. Some sources claim that Ketchum was excessively overweight, but this appears not to be true. A photograph taken of Ketchum on the gallows shows that he was a tall man—about six feet—but rather slender. **See also** hanging.

Koran

The Koran (or Qur'an) is the book comprising the sacred scriptures of Islam. The text consists of 114 chapters, called suras, of varying lengths. The work is traditionally attributed to the prophet Muhammad, who either wrote the suras himself or delivered them orally and they were recorded by his followers. Like the Christian Bible, the Koran is considered by adherents of its religion to be the sacred authority on matters ranging from laws for the governance of society and the family to prayers, history, and statements of dogma.

It is clear that the Koran allows capital punishment. In one passage the Koran forbids killing "except through due process of law." The Koran actually specifies a penalty of death for certain important crimes deemed to be crimes against Islam itself. These crimes are robbery, adultery, and apostasy, or the renunciation or abandonment of the faith. Some Islamic legal scholars believe that these crimes *must* be punished with death, since the death penalty is specified by the Koran itself. Murder is treated separately, in the category of crimes against persons. The Koran includes a passage stating the *lex talionis*, or law of retaliation originally found in the Code of Hammurabi, and specifies that crimes against persons should be punished on this principle. Punishment is to be inflicted by the victim or the victim's family, but should be supervised by public officials. The punishment should be equivalent to the harm done by the crime, so the punishment for murder may be death. However, the victim's family may be (and are encouraged to be) merciful and request a lesser penalty, such as the payment of compensation, or blood money, instead. **See also** religious views.

last meal

One of the rituals of execution still practiced in the United States is allowing a condemned prisoner to choose a last meal. Although few people today attach a religious meaning to the last meal, the custom may be derived from an association of the last meal with the Christian Last Supper of Christ. In theory, condemned prisoners are allowed to order whatever they like, and every attempt is made to provide what is requested. In practice, most states designate a budget for last meals, and some states are more generous than others. The final decision of what to serve is made by prison officials, and substitutions and reductions in quantity are often made. David Allen Castillo, for example, who was executed in Texas in 1998, requested twenty-four tacos for his last meal but was actually served four. Sometimes the meal is provided by a local restaurant, but in most cases it is prepared in the prison kitchen. Most prisoners request fairly simple and familiar meals. The most common choice is a hamburger with french fries. In 1992 Ricky Ray Rector, a severely mentally retarded man, was executed by the state of Oklahoma. His last meal included a piece of pecan pie, which he set aside, saying he would save it for after the execution. **See also** last words.

last words

Reporters attending executions often make a point of recording a condemned prisoner's final pronouncements, perhaps in the hope that they will contain special wisdom or insight. Few do. Here is a brief selection of famous last words.

George Jacques Danton, beheaded in 1794: "Sanson, you will show my head to the people. It is worth showing."

Thomas "Black Jack" Ketchum, hanged in 1901: "Let 'er rip!" His head was torn from his body by his fall.

Joe Hill, executed by firing squad in 1914: "Fire! Go on and fire!"

Erskin Childers, executed by firing squad in 1922: "Take a step or two forward, lads. It will be easier that way."

Carl Panzram, a serial killer executed by hanging in 1930: "Hurry up, you Hoosier bastard. I could hang a dozen men while you're fooling around!"

Gary Gilmore, executed by firing squad in 1977: "Let's do it."

John Spenkelink, electrocuted in 1979: "Capital punishment: them without the capital get the punishment."

Jesse Bishop, executed by lethal gas in 1979: "Commute me or execute me. Don't drag it out," as officials struggled to get the gas chamber mechanism to work properly.

Jeffrey Barney, electrocuted in 1986: "I'm sorry for what I done. I deserve it. I hope Jesus forgives me. I'm tingling all over."

Edward Earl Johnson, electrocuted in 1987: "I guess nobody is going to call."

Jimmy Glass, electrocuted in 1987: "Yeah, I think I'd rather be fishing."

Ted Bundy, electrocuted in 1989: "Give my love to my family and friends."

Edward Ellis, executed by lethal injection in 1992: "I just want everyone to know I think the prosecutor and Bill Scott [a fellow inmate who testified against Ellis] are some sorry sons of bitches."

Robert Alton Harris, executed by lethal gas in 1992: "You can be a king or a street sweeper, but everybody dances with the Grim Reaper."

Warren Bridge, executed by lethal injection in 1994: "See ya."

See also last meal; repentance.

Law of the Twelve Tables

The Law of the Twelve Tables was the earliest written body of law for the ancient Roman republic. It was established by a committee of lawgivers known as the Ten Consuls in about 450 B.C. The laws provide the foundation for later Roman law, and so, indirectly, for much of the Western legal tradition. The primary purpose of the laws appears to have been to define relations, especially commercial relations, between the patrician and plebeian classes. The laws are significant in that they grant clear rights to the lower plebeian class in their dealings with the patrician class.

In the Law of the Twelve Tables, the death penalty is prescribed only for the crime of treason. However, the tables are not a comprehensive body of law, and the Twelfth Table endorses the unwritten customary law of "the people" as the law to be followed in all other matters. Under the customary law, the death penalty was available for a much wider group of crimes. **See also** Draconian Code; Hammurabi, Code of.

Lawes, Lewis E. (1883–1947)

Lewis E. Lawes was the warden of New York's infamous Sing Sing Prison from 1919 to 1941, longer than any other warden. In that time, he managed to transform Sing Sing from one of the most reviled and violent prisons in the country to a model of prison reform.

Lawes was the son of a prison guard, and took a job as a prison guard himself at the age of twenty-two. He took an interest in the theory and practice of penology and rose through the ranks to supervisory and eventually administrative positions in New York's penal system. In 1919 he was appointed warden of Sing Sing Prison. Lawes instituted numerous reforms designed to make the treatment of prisoners more humane and respectful. He drastically reduced the use of corporal punishment and allowed prisoners to decide for themselves how to spend leisure time. He tried to make himself available to prisoners who wished to discuss problems, and he frequently risked his own reputation by allowing furloughs for inmates to attend important family events, such as funerals. His wife, Kathryn, worked in the prison hospital and often helped prisoners write letters. She was so well loved by the prison inmates that when she was tragically killed in an automobile accident in 1937, a delegation of prisoners appealed to Lawes to allow them to pay their respects. Lawes allowed the entire prison population, with no guards present, to walk single file to his house, which was a short quarter of a mile away, past his wife's casket, and then return single file to the prison. Not a single prisoner tried to escape, and all returned to the prison without incident.

Sing Sing Prison was the site of New York's electric chair, and, as warden of Sing Sing, Lawes dutifully presided over numerous executions. He was, however, a vocal opponent of capital punishment. He considered the death penalty an ineffective deterrent, unnecessary for the protection of society, and arbitrarily applied in any case. He wrote books and articles on the subject, gave speeches and interviews, and testified before the New York state legislature. He also served as president of the American League to Abolish Capital Punishment, which he helped found with prominent defense attorney Clarence Darrow. Lawes retired as warden of Sing Sing in 1941 but remained an active campaigner against the death penalty until his death in 1947. **See also** American League to Abolish Capital Punishment; Sing Sing Prison.

Leopold, Nathan F. (1906–1971), and Richard A. Loeb (1907–1936)

Nathan F. Leopold and Richard A. Loeb were sentenced to life imprisonment plus ninety-nine years after being convicted of a virtually unmotivated murder, one of the most sensationalized crimes of the twentieth century. They were not sentenced to death, but only because the brilliant and well-known defense attorney Clarence Darrow made capital punishment itself a central issue at their trial.

Leopold and Loeb had been friends and lovers for four years when, in 1924, they conceived the idea of committing a perfect murder, mostly for the intellectual challenge of it. Both boys were acknowledged geniuses. At eighteen, Leopold was the youngest student to complete a bachelor of philosophy degree from the University of Chicago, and at seventeen Loeb was the youngest graduate of the University of Michigan. They were also both from wealthy families and had no need of money. For this reason, they thought that police would never suspect them if their perfect murder appeared to be a kidnapping for ransom. On May 20, 1924, the two boys rented a car and persuaded a distant acquaintance, Bobby Franks, to get in it with them. They then stabbed him in the head with a chisel, stripped his body, and stuffed it into a drainpipe. The next day they sent a ransom note to his parents.

Their crime proved to be far from perfect. A pair of distinctive horn-rimmed glasses were found near the body, which led police to Nathan Leopold. Reporters then found letters that Richard Loeb had typed on the same typewriter used to compose the ransom note. Confronted with this evidence, the two boys confessed to the murder.

The trial was a media sensation, in part because of the social status of the defendants but also because Leopold's father hired famous defense attorney Clarence Darrow to defend the boys. Darrow had the boys plead guilty, and then threw all his effort into preventing them from being executed. Of his defense, he said, "While the State is trying Loeb and Leopold, I will try capital punishment." Darrow opted for a trial before a single judge, waiving the right to a jury trial, since he thought a judge would be more likely to understand the testimony of psychiatrists brought in to testify to the boys' mental state. Psychiatry was becoming an accepted science, but was still widely mistrusted by the general public. Darrow's summation portrayed his clients as children helpless to resist the compulsions of their diseased brains and condemned the death penalty so eloquently that the judge was reportedly

Chicago police discover the body of fourteen-year-old Bobby Franks in 1924. Leopold and Loeb confessed to the murder and were sentenced to life in prison.

moved to tears. In any case, the judge sentenced the boys to life imprisonment for murder, plus ninety-nine years for kidnapping, a sentence that was thought at the time to be long enough to prevent any possibility of parole.

Loeb was later killed in a prison fight when he tried to sexually assault another prisoner. Leopold made parole after thirty-four years in prison. He married and moved to Puerto Rico, where he died in 1971, reportedly still haunted by memories of his crime. **See also** Darrow, Clarence; juvenile offenders.

lethal injection

Lethal injection is a method of execution in which a combination of lethal drugs are introduced into the condemned prisoner's bloodstream. The first drug is a strong sedative to induce unconsciousness. Subsequent drugs cause death while the condemned prisoner is unconscious.

The current standard procedure begins with the insertion of an IV (intravenous) needle into each of the prisoner's arms. Only one needle is actually needed, but the second is inserted as a backup. One of the needles is connected to a harmless saline-drip solution located in an adjacent room. At this point the execution begins. A curtain is raised so that witnesses can observe the prisoner through a glass window. A bag of sodium thiopental is added to the IV drip, which quickly causes the prisoner to fall asleep. Once the prisoner is asleep, pancuronium bromide is put into the IV line. This is a muscle relaxant that stops the prisoner's breathing by disabling the chest muscles and the diaphragm. Finally, potassium chloride is introduced into the IV. This stops the prisoner's heart.

Lethal injection is currently the favored method of execution in nearly every state, since it is almost entirely

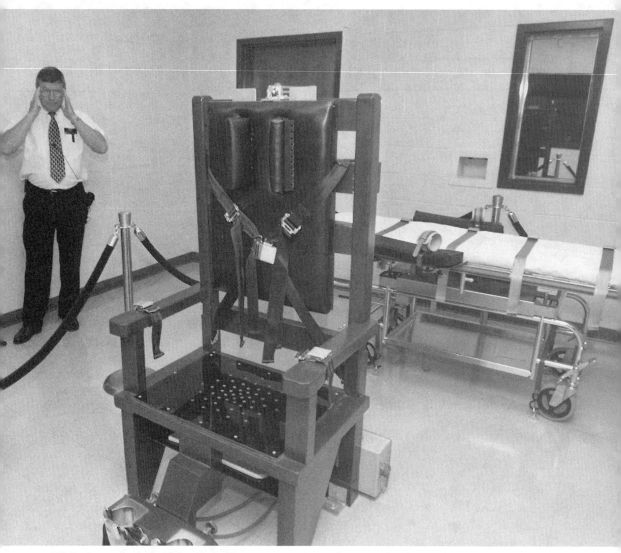

This execution chamber in a Tennessee prison features both an electric chair and a lethal injection gurney. Lethal injection is today the preferred mode of execution nationwide.

painless and, unlike decapitation, hanging, electrocution, or gas, is not particularly distressing to witness. It is also relatively cheap. Aside from the lethal drugs themselves, the supplies needed for execution by lethal injection include only standard medical supplies. The training and expertise needed to administer the drugs is also minimal. As a result, executions can be performed by prison staff, and (in most cases) without error.

One reason lethal injection was adopted so rapidly and so universally is that many states needed to update their execution equipment anyway. During the 1960s and 1970s, executions in the United States were extremely rare. Indeed, from 1967 to 1977 no executions took place at all. During this long hiatus in executions, many of the elderly electric chairs and gas chambers around the country had fallen into disrepair. Faced with the prospect of repairing or replacing expensive equipment, many states decided to move to a new method of execution that promised to be easier, cheaper, and more humane.

Oklahoma and Texas were the first states to adopt lethal injection in 1977, the year a ten-year nationwide moratorium on executions ended, and most other states soon followed suit. However, the first execution by lethal injection did not take place until December 1982, when convicted murderer Charles Brooks was executed in Texas.

Although lethal injection employs standard medical equipment and procedures, the code of ethics of the American Medical Association forbids physicians from causing death. Hence, lethal injections are performed by prison staff, not by medical professionals. Since prison staff are not as experienced with IV needles as doctors and nurses, and since some prisoners have collapsed veins due to years of intravenous drug use, finding a usable vein has, in some cases, been difficult. During the execution of Raymond Landry in Texas, the needle popped out of his arm and sprayed toxic solutions at observers. However, as prison staff have become more experienced, incidents of this sort have decreased. **See also** Brooks, Charles; physician participation in executions.

lex talionis

This is a legal phrase meaning "law of retaliation," or justice by retaliation. It refers to a principle of justice in which a person who committed a crime should be made to suffer the same harm that he or she has caused to others. Naturally, the *lex talionis* would prescribe death for the crime of murder.

The *lex talionis* appears to be one of the guiding principles of the Code of Hammurabi, written about 1780 B.C., in which the following two laws appear:

196. If a man put out the eye of another, his eye shall be put out.

200. If a man knock out the teeth of his equal, his teeth shall be knocked out.

This principle also appears in the Bible; for example, in Deuteronomy 19:21, in which the phrase "an eye for an eye, a tooth for a tooth," appears.

Although many philosophers and legal scholars accept the notion that punishment should be based on proportional retaliation for crimes, modern writers are quick to point out that the *lex talionis* per se is too crude and simplistic to have practical value. Many crimes, such as jaywalking, forgery, and public nudity, simply do not offer a convenient form of retaliation. But even when straightforward retaliation is possible, it is often difficult to ensure proportionality. If a famous violinist causes someone to lose a finger, should he have his own finger cut off, given that this will destroy his ability to play the violin? In addition, a person who has performed multiple murders can be killed only once, so his punishment can never be proportional to his crime. Finally, modern sensibilities rebel at the idea that we should rape and torture prisoners, even if they are themselves guilty of rape and torture. Because of these problems, modern writers view the *lex talionis* not as a literal law or principle of justice but as a metaphor expressing a general approach to justice. **See also** Hammurabi, Code of; justification of punishment; proportionality.

life imprisonment without parole

A sentence in which life imprisonment is assigned as a minimum term of imprisonment, which means that the prisoner is never eligible for parole. The term of a prison sentence is generally understood to be the maximum period of time that a prisoner may be confined. Depending on a prisoner's behavior, he or she may be considered for release before the full term of the sentence has been served. Even sentences of life imprisonment are generally understood as maximum sentences, and most people who have received life sentences do not actually spend the remainder of their lives in prison. The release of prisoners before their full sentence has been served is called parole. Some criminal statutes specify a minimum as well as a maximum term of imprisonment. Under such sentences, a prisoner is not eligible for parole until after the minimum sentence has been served.

During the 1980s and 1990s, state legislatures responding to public support for stiffer criminal sentencing issued stricter guidelines than had previously been in force. During this time, many states adopted life-without-parole laws, making life imprisonment the minimum sentence for certain crimes. In some cases these laws even took away the governor's discretion to commute sentences or to offer pardons for people convicted of these specific crimes. The life-without-parole laws had two distinct purposes. Some of the laws were primarily written to discourage repeat offenders. Often called "three strikes" laws, these laws made a sentence of life without parole mandatory after a specified number of felony convictions, provided one of the convictions was for a violent crime. In some states the number was two convictions and in others it was four, but the usual number was three, so the laws were called three strikes laws because of the rule in baseball that you are "out" after three strikes. Other life-without-parole laws were intended explicitly to provide an alternative to the death penalty. These laws made the sentence of life imprisonment without parole available or mandatory for a first offense for crimes that might otherwise receive either a standard life sentence or a sentence of death. The idea was to provide a sentence sufficiently harsh that it amounted to taking away a prisoner's life but without taking the irreversible step of actually putting the prisoner to death.

A sentence of life imprisonment without parole is viewed by many as a favorable alternative to capital punishment but is not without controversy, as some convicted criminals have argued that life in prison is a crueler punishment than death. **See also** imprisonment.

literature

The issue of capital punishment has been the subject of important works of literature, both nonfiction and fiction. Whether the work defines moral or ethical principles, provides a historical or sociological overview of the practice, or dramatizes an individual's crime and punishment, the body of capital punishment literature has been instrumental in stimulating public and scholarly debate and swaying public opinion. One of the most influential early nonfiction treatises is Cesare Beccaria's *An Essay on Crimes and Punishments* (1764). Important modern examples include Hugo Adam Bedau's The *Death Penalty in America* (1964) and Walter Berns's *For Capital Punishment: Crime and the Morality of the Death Penalty* (1979).

A new kind of death-penalty literature captured the public imagination in 1966 with the publication of Truman Capote's "nonfiction novel" *In Cold Blood*, which launched a genre known as literary true crime. Such books are sophisticated accounts of actual crimes, including the investigation that led to the capture of the perpetrators and often the legal proceedings that followed. Capote's book recounts the facts of the Clutter family murders, which took place in 1959, following the case all the way to the execution of confessed murderers Richard Hickock and Perry Smith in 1965. The following is a representative list of modern literary true-crime works that involve capital punishment issues:

Sacco and Vanzetti: The Anarchist Background (1991), by Paul Avrich

The Sleeping Lady: The Trailside Murders Above the Golden Gate (1991), by Robert Greysmith

Bodies of Evidence: The True Story of Judias Buenoano, Florida's Serial Murderess (1993), by Chris Anderson and Sharon McGehee

Crime of the Century: Richard Speck and the Murder of Eight Nurses (1993), by Dennis L. Breo and William J. Martin

A Woman's Right to Self-Defense: The Case of Aileen Carol Wuornos (1994), by Phyllis Chesler

Boston Strangler: The Wrongful Conviction of Albert Desalvo and the True Story of Eleven Shocking Murders (1995), by Susan Kelly

Killer Clown: The John Wayne Gacy Murders (1997), by Terry Sullivan and Peter T. Maiken

The Executioner's Song (1998), by Norman Mailer

There are many classic works of pure fiction involving the theme of capital punishment. The following are novels in which the theme of capital punishment figures prominently:

An American Tragedy (1925), by Theodore Dreiser

The Transgressors (1994), by Jim Thompson

The Chamber (1995), by John Grisham

A Lesson Before Dying (1997), by Ernest J. Gaines

True Crime (1997), by Andrew Klavan

The Ballad of Frankie Silver (1999), by Sharyn McCrumb

The Green Mile (1999), by Stephen King

Reversible Errors (2003), by Scott Turow

A final important category of death-penalty literature has been personal memoirs, written by death row inmates and by others who have been involved with executions in various capacities. Here is a list of some important memoirs:

Cell 2455 Death Row (1955), by Caryl Chessman. This death row memoir made Chessman an international celebrity.

Dead Man Walking (1993), by Helen Prejean. Written as fiction, this is actually the memoir of a nun who served as a spiritual counselor to death row inmates.

Death Blossoms: Reflections from a Prisoner of Conscience (1997), by Mumia Abu-Jamal. The memoir of a death row inmate who claims that he is incarcerated as a political prisoner.

Death at Midnight: The Confession of an Executioner (1998), by Donald A. Cabana. The memoir of a prison warden responsible for conducting executions.

See also Beccaria, Cesare; film treatment of capital punishment; Prejean, Helen.

Livingston, Edward (1764–1836)

Edward Livingston was an important American lawyer and lawmaker and a noted opponent of capital punishment. He is chiefly known for his important revisions to Louisiana's judicial procedures during the early nineteenth century.

Livingston was born in Clermont, New York, and studied law at Princeton University. He graduated in 1781. In 1785 he set up a law practice in New

York City, where he soon rose to prominence. In 1795 he was elected to Congress and served two terms before being appointed both to the position of U.S. district attorney for New York state and to the position of mayor of New York City in 1801. Unfortunately he contracted yellow fever in 1803, and during his illness his financial affairs were mismanaged by an incompetent (or dishonest) clerk. Livingston recovered to find himself deeply in debt. He resigned his offices and moved to New Orleans, which, as part of the Louisiana Purchase, had recently been acquired by the United States.

In New Orleans, Livingston was appointed by the territorial legislature to revise the code of judicial procedures. This was an important and difficult task. The laws then in effect in Louisiana were based on French and Spanish laws, which were in turn based on Roman law. These laws had to be made consistent with U.S. law, which was based on the very different English legal tradition. Revising the code of judicial procedures was one step in achieving this reconciliation. In 1821 the state legislature handed Livingston the still more difficult task of revising the criminal code. Livingston, who was an opponent of the death penalty, produced a code in which capital punishment was not employed. He provided for terms of imprisonment in which prisoners could be rewarded for good behavior and voluntary hard work with better food and living conditions. This code, known as the Livingston Code, was never adopted, but it was published in both English and French in 1833 and had a strong influence on criminal codes throughout the world, especially in Central America.

In 1823 Livingston was again elected to Congress, this time representing the state of Louisiana. He served from 1823 to 1829. He was then elected to the Senate, was later appointed secretary of state under President Andrew Jackson, and served as minister to France. At the end of his life he returned to New York, where he died in 1836. **See also** Louisiana; Rush, Benjamin.

Locke, John (1632–1704)

John Locke was one of the most influential philosophers of the seventeenth century. He had an enormous influence on all branches of philosophy but especially in epistemology (the theory of knowledge) and in social and political philosophy. His version of the social contract theory provided the philosophical underpinnings of the English rebellion against James II in 1688, the American Revolution in 1776, and the French Revolution in 1789. Although he shared the same religious background and philosophical views as many of those who opposed capital punishment, Locke himself was a supporter of capital punishment and justified its use based on philosophical principles known as social contract theory.

Locke was born in Wrington, England. His father, a liberal Puritan, fought in the English Revolution, which overthrew Charles I in 1642. John Locke studied classics and classical languages at Oxford, but, dissatisfied with strict classical studies and with Scholastic philosophy, he also taught himself political theory and science, making friends with some of the most eminent scientists of the day. In 1667 he became the personal assistant to the Earl of Shaftsbury, serving as medical adviser and as a general secretary. In that capacity he helped draft the constitution of the colony of Carolina in America. Shaftsbury was an important leader of the opposition party in Parliament, and Locke was closely associated with him. Tensions between Catholics and Protestants became more acute in the 1680s, and in 1681 Shaftsbury left England for his safety and fled to Holland.

Seventeenth-century English philosopher John Locke based his justification of capital punishment on the social contract theory.

Locke followed two years later. In Holland, Locke served as adviser to William of Orange, who in 1688 overthrew James II to become the king of England. With the Protestants again in power, Locke returned to England in 1689. For the remainder of his life he lived quietly in London and Oates, working on his philosophical writings, which were strongly influenced by his practical experience in politics.

Locke's views on capital punishment are contained in his *Second Treatise on Government*, published in 1690. As a social contract theorist, Locke believed that all of the powers of government derive from the consent of the governed. Without government, people lived in what could be described as a "state of nature." In that state of nature, people had certain natural rights (i.e., rights that were an inherent part of the natural state.) Locke listed life, liberty, and property as among the most fundamental of these rights. Given these rights, Locke believed that each person in the state of nature also had the right to *defend* his life, liberty, and property, with lethal force if necessary. A person who takes the life, liberty, or property of another has broken the natural law and proven himself to be a threat. All others in the state of nature are therefore within their rights to (a) defend themselves from further transgressions by that person and (b) deter others from similar transgressions, by depriving the transgressor of life, liberty, and property in proportion to the seriousness of his or her transgression.

When people band together to form societies, they give up some of the rights that they possessed in the state of nature and vest those rights in the government. They do not give up the most fundamental rights, which Locke believed were "inviolable" and could not be surrendered. (Thomas Jefferson later used the word *unalienable* to describe these most fundamental of rights.) But they do give up some of the less-fundamental rights, such as the right to punish transgressors. The government then inherits these rights, and may exercise them as long as it does so in the interest of (and with the consent of) its citizens. Since people in the state of nature possessed the right to use lethal force in defense of their rights, it follows that a legitimate government may also use lethal force in defense of the rights of its citizens. Hence legitimate governments are entitled to put criminals to death, if this proves to be a proportionate and effective means of securing a peaceful and safe society. **See also** social contract theory.

Lockett v. Ohio

This was a case heard by the Supreme Court of the United States in 1978 concerning whether a state's death-penalty statute can limit consideration of mitigating circumstances. The defendant, Sandra Lockett, was charged with aggravated murder for participating in a pawnshop robbery in which the owner was killed. Lockett had been responsible for driving the getaway vehicle and was not in the pawn shop during the robbery. Nevertheless, Lockett was convicted of aggravated murder. Despite her limited role in the crime, and the fact that her previous criminal record included only minor juvenile offenses, the judge reluctantly sentenced her to death, pointing out that the Ohio death-penalty statute gave him "no alternative."

On appeal, the U.S. Supreme Court overturned Lockett's sentence. Writing for the majority, Chief Justice Warren Burger offered the opinion that a judge must be allowed to consider any relevant mitigating circumstances and that it was unconstitutional for a state statute to place limits on which circumstances could be considered. This case was decided at the same time as a parallel case, *Bell v. Ohio*, which concerned the same issue. **See also** aggravating circumstances; *Bell v. Ohio;* mitigating circumstances.

Lockhart v. McCree

This was a case heard by the Supreme Court of the United States in 1986 concerning whether jurors with moral objections to the death penalty may be excluded from a jury asked to consider a death sentence. The defendant in the case, Andria McCree, was charged with murdering the owner of a store in the course of robbing the store. During jury selection, several prospective jurors were dismissed on the grounds that they had moral objections to the death penalty. McCree's lawyer objected to their dismissal but was overruled. At trial, McCree was convicted of the murder and sentenced to death. The case was appealed on the grounds that, according to the 1968 *Witherspoon v. Illinois* Supreme Court decision, prospective jurors may not be dismissed merely for holding moral objections to the death penalty. The U.S. Eighth Circuit Court of Appeals agreed that jury selection had violated the *Witherspoon* decision and vacated McCree's conviction and sentence. The Supreme Court then agreed to review the case.

In a 6-to-3 decision, the Supreme Court reversed the appeals court's decision and reinstated McCree's conviction and sentence. Writing for the majority, Justice William Rehnquist reaffirmed the language of the *Witherspoon* decision, saying that a jury should be permitted to represent a broad spectrum of attitudes and predispositions. However, he pointed out that a jury must also be capable of deciding the questions put before it. He argued that the jury actually seated in the McCree trial met these two criteria, so McCree's rights were not violated. **See also** *Witherspoon v. Illinois.*

Louisiana

Louisiana has traditionally permitted juries to impose the death penalty, and continues to do so currently. Prior to the Louisiana Purchase in 1803, Louisiana was chiefly under French control. Between 1722 and 1779, sixty-one executions are recorded. A variety of methods were used. Under French law at the time, breaking on the wheel was a common method of execution, and eleven executions using this method are recorded in Louisiana. In 1769 six men were shot for treason, and burning was also fairly common. Hanging was apparently the most common method of execution, although in many cases the method of execution is simply not recorded. The majority of executions in early Louisiana were the result of slave revolts. In 1730 eight black slaves were executed by breaking on the wheel for participating in a slave revolt. In 1776 three black slaves were hanged. In 1795 a major slave revolt ended with the execution of twenty-three black slaves. Slave revolts continued after Louisiana became a possession of the United States. In 1811 a slave revolt ended with the execution of sixteen black slaves under U.S. territorial jurisdiction. Louisiana became a state in 1812, after which hanging became the sole method of execution. However, slave revolts continued to be a major cause of executions. In 1837 fourteen black slaves were executed following a slave revolt, and in 1840 another twenty-eight black slaves were executed. Between 1808 and 1941, 478 executions by hanging took place in Louisiana. In 1941 Louisiana replaced hanging with electrocution as its method of execution. Between 1941 and 1961, sixty-seven people were executed in Louisiana's electric chair.

Following the 1972 *Furman v. Georgia* ruling, which struck down Louisiana's death-penalty statute, the state quickly passed a new death-penalty statute in 1973. Louisiana's current death-penalty statute allows jurors to consider the death penalty for homicide under special circumstances. These special circumstances are that the defendant had a specific intention to kill or cause bodily harm and, in addition, (1) the homicide occurred in the course of committing a kidnapping, escape from custody, arson, rape, burglary, robbery, or a drive-by shooting; (2) the intended victim was a firefighter or police officer engaged in the performance of his or her duties; (3) there was more than one intended victim; (4) there was payment given or received for the homicide; (5) the victim was under twelve years old or was sixty-five years or older; (6) the homicide occurred in the course of a drug transaction; or (7) the homicide occurred in the course of "ritualistic activities" (i.e., is a ritual murder).

The death penalty may be imposed if one of twelve aggravating circumstances is proven to have accompanied the crime. The list of aggravating circumstances appears similar to the previous list of special circumstances, but aggravating circumstances are considered during the penalty phase of the trial rather than during the guilt phase. These aggravating circumstances are (1) that the homicide occurred in the course of a rape, kidnapping, burglary, arson, escape from custody, drive-by shooting, or robbery; (2) that the victim was a firefighter or police officer engaged in his or her duties; (3) that the defendant was previously convicted of murder, rape, burglary, arson, escape from custody, armed robbery, or kidnapping; (4) that the defendant knowingly created a great risk of death or injury to more than one person; (5) that there was payment given or received for the homicide; (6) that the defendant was under sentence of imprisonment for an unrelated felony involving the use of force; (7) that the homicide was especially heinous, atrocious, or cruel; (8) that the victim was a witness against the defendant in another matter; (9) that the victim was a corrections officer or employee of the Department of Public Safety and Corrections engaged in the performance of his or her duties; (10) that the victim was under twelve years old or was sixty-five years or older; (11) that the homicide occurred in the course of trafficking in a controlled dangerous substance; or (12) that the defendant was engaged in ritualistic activities. The jury must also consider any mitigating circumstances that the defense wishes to present.

Under Louisiana law, a person convicted of a capital offense cannot be executed if he or she was under the age of sixteen at the time of the crime. This provision was invalidated in March 2005 when the Supreme Court abolished the death penalty for juveniles under the age of eighteen at the time of the offense. Louisiana does not provide for life imprisonment without parole as an alternative to the death penalty. The governor has the authority to grant clemency only if he or she receives a favorable recommendation from the Board of Pardons, but the governor is not required to grant clemency on the board's recommendation.

The first execution following the reenactment of capital punishment took place in 1983 with the execution of Robert Williams. Since 1983 there have been twenty executions by electrocution in Louisiana. In 1990 Louisiana replaced electrocution with lethal injection as its method of execution, although electrocutions continued through 1991. The first execution by lethal injection took place in 1993 with the execution of Robert Sawyer. Since 1993 there have been seven executions by lethal injection in Louisiana. As of April 2005, ninety-one people were awaiting execution on Louisiana's death row. **See also** breaking on the wheel; Livingston, Edward.

Louisiana ex rel. Francis v. Resweber

This was a case heard by the Supreme Court of the United States in 1947 concerning whether more than one attempt to execute a condemned prisoner was cruel and unusual punishment. The defendant in the case, Willie Francis, had been convicted of the 1944 murder of Andrew Thomas, a druggist in St. Martinsville, Louisiana. Francis, who was black, was fifteen years old at the time of the crime. In 1946 Francis was strapped into an electric chair at the Louisiana state penitentiary. The chair delivered a two-minute burst of electricity and then quit working, leaving Francis alive and well. Prison officials rescheduled the execution for the following week. However, attorneys acting for Francis sought to block the execution on the grounds that subjecting Francis to a second session with the electric chair constituted cruel and unusual punishment. The Supreme Court agreed to review the case.

In a 5-to-4 decision, the Court allowed Francis's execution to proceed. Writing for the majority, Justice Stanley F. Reed argued that the defense had failed to show why a second attempt at execution was any more cruel and unusual than the first. Justice Felix Frankfurter, usually a critic of capital punishment, provided a critical swing vote for this decision. Francis was executed by electrocution on May 9, 1947, slightly over a year after the original execution attempt. **See also** cruel and unusual punishment; electric chair.

Loving v. United States

This was a case heard by the Supreme Court of the United States in 1996 concerning whether Congress, rather than the president, must establish the aggravating circumstances to be considered by military courts considering a sentence of death. The defendant in the case, army private Dwight J. Loving, was convicted of killing two cab drivers near Fort Hood, Texas. He received a court-martial and was sentenced to death under the death-penalty provisions of the Uniform Code of Military Justice. In 1984 the Uniform Code of Military Justice was revised by an executive order issued by President Ronald Reagan to bring its death-penalty provisions in line with the requirements for death-penalty statutes laid out in the 1976 *Gregg v. Georgia* Supreme Court decision. In particular, Reagan's executive order provided a list of aggravating circumstances that may be considered by military courts during the penalty phase of a trial, a list that is usually created (in state death-penalty statutes) by legislation, not by executive order. However, in this case the U.S. Congress had specifically authorized the president to make modifications to the Uniform Code of Military Justice, and President Reagan acted on that authorization. Loving's sentence was appealed on the grounds that it was a violation of constitutional separation of powers for the executive branch to establish the list of aggravating circumstances used at military trials, and that Congress did not have the power to delegate law-making authority to the president. However, the military appeals court rejected this argument and upheld Loving's sentence. The Supreme Court then agreed to review the case.

In a unanimous opinion, the U.S. Supreme Court upheld Loving's sentence. Writing for the Court, Justice Anthony M. Kennedy argued that, in establishing the list of aggravating circumstances to be used at military trials, the president was not making law (which is a function reserved solely for the legislative branch) but merely establishing the rules under which a law already in force is to be executed (which is a function regularly performed by the executive branch).

As of June 2005, Dwight Loving was still one of seven men awaiting execution under military jurisdiction. **See also** military justice.

Lowenfield v. Phelps

This was a case heard by the Supreme Court of the United States in 1988 concerning whether the "special circumstances" used by a state death-penalty statute in the definition of death-eligible crimes may also be used as "aggravating circumstances" to be considered during the penalty phase of a capital trial. The defendant in the case, Leslie Lowenfield, a foreign national from the South American country of Guyana, was convicted in Louisiana of killing five people during a single crime spree. Under the Louisiana death-penalty statute, "intent to kill or inflict great bodily harm upon more than one person" is one of the special circumstances that makes a murder death-eligible. At the same time, "knowingly creating a risk of death or great bodily harm to more than one person" is one of the aggravating circumstances that a jury may consider during sentencing. The jury found Lowenfield guilty of three counts of murder, and sentenced

This 1916 lynching of a black man in Texas drew an enormous crowd. Lynching was very common in the American South into the mid-twentieth century.

him to death. The case was appealed on the grounds that the jury had used substantially the same circumstances both to decide the question of guilt and to determine the sentence. The appeals court upheld the conviction and the sentence, and eventually the U.S. Supreme Court agreed to review the case.

In a 6-to-3 decision, the Supreme Court also upheld Lowenfield's conviction and sentence. Writing for the majority, Chief Justice William Rehnquist argued that the purpose of both special circumstances and aggravating circumstances is to delineate what is meant by a death-eligible crime, so there is no reason that the two lists should not overlap. What is important, he continued, is that during sentencing the jury considers whether there are also mitigating circumstances sufficient to call for leniency despite the fact that a capital crime has been committed. **See also** aggravating circumstances; mitigating circumstances; special circumstances.

lynching

The term *lynching* refers to an illegal execution by hanging. The word is probably derived from the name of Charles Lynch, who, during the American Revolution, set up an unauthorized "court" at which he and two other men, Thomas Calloway and Robert Adams, presided as "judges." They tried people for the crime of being British sympathizers. They sentenced the "guilty" to be strung up by their thumbs until they cried, "Liberty forever!" No one was executed by this "court," but the term *lynch law* came to be associated with "justice" imposed by citizens acting outside the law. Lynch courts often operated in the territorial American West before true legal jurisdictions could be established. The first executions by lynch courts took place in California during the gold rush of the 1850s.

Following the Civil War, lynchings were conducted by the racist vigilante group the Ku Klux Klan to intimidate freed blacks. This practice continued in the South through the first half of the twentieth century. Even as southern states banned public executions, some southern whites felt so strongly that the crime of rape should continue to be punished by public hanging that accusations of rape were often "tried" outside the regular system of justice to ensure that the sentence could be carried out in public. Photographs taken at lynchings indicate that these were not furtive nighttime events conducted by mobs; many were held in broad daylight, often with women and children present.

Of the 4,729 lynchings known to have taken place in the United States between 1882 and 1950, 3,436 of the condemned were black men, most of whom had been accused of rape, although in the absence of a legitimate trial, it is doubtful that many were actually guilty. **See also** hanging; viewing of executions.

Maine

Maine does not currently permit juries to impose the death penalty, and Maine has a long history of distrust of capital punishment. Only five executions took place in colonial Maine. In 1835 Maine introduced an unusual death-penalty reform known as the Maine Law to prevent executions from taking place due to heightened public anger at the time of the crime and trial. Under the law, someone sentenced to death had to be held in prison (at hard labor) for a year following conviction, and then could be executed only if the governor ordered the execution to proceed. In 1887 Maine abolished capital punishment altogether, following a hanging in which the condemned prisoner was strangled slowly rather than dying of a snapped neck. From 1780 to 1885, thirteen people were executed by the state of Maine, all by hanging. Three people were also hanged under federal jurisdiction. **See also** federal death-penalty laws.

Maledon, George (1834–1911)

George Maledon was the best-known hangman of the American West. He was the chief executioner working for "Hanging Judge" Isaac Parker in the western Arkansas territory.

Maledon was born in Bavaria but came to the United States as a child when his parents immigrated. He grew up in Detroit, where he worked as a carpenter. Eventually he left Detroit and took a job as a guard at Fort Smith in Arkansas. He fought in the Union army during the Civil War, but after the war he eventually returned to his position at Fort Smith. He agreed to serve as hangman, and soon distinguished himself as a careful and competent executioner. He was paid $100 per execution, which covered his fee as well as burial costs. Using his skills as a carpenter, he built a gallows that could accommodate twelve men at a time. However, six was the largest number of men he ever executed at once. That execution in 1875 made him something of a celebrity in the eastern press, who dubbed it "the dance of death."

Maledon had a busy career. Fort Smith had jurisdiction over the violent and lawless Indian Territory (which later became the state of Oklahoma), and the federal judge in the territory was the infamous "Hanging Judge" Isaac Parker. Maledon executed nearly all of the men who were sent to their deaths by Judge Parker.

In 1895 Maledon's eighteen-year-old daughter, Ann, was murdered by her lover, Frank Carver, in a lover's quarrel. Carver was sentenced to death, but successfully appealed the sentence and escaped being hanged by his victim's father. Maledon retired as a hangman a few years after Judge Parker's death in 1896. He then toured the country, exhibiting his ropes, newspaper clippings, and photographs to the public. He died on May 6, 1911, at the Old Soldiers' Home in Johnson City, Tennessee. **See also** executioners; Parker, Isaac C.

mandatory sentencing
A mandatory sentence is one in which the law requires a specific sentence for a specific crime, giving the trial judge and jury no discretion. Support for mandatory sentencing laws grew in the United States during the 1970s and 1980s perhaps in response to rising crime rates and the perceived judicial leniency. The 1972 *Furman v. Georgia* decision invalidated death-penalty statutes on the grounds that they were being applied too arbitrarily. Following the decision ten states voted to make the death penalty mandatory for certain crimes, reasoning that a mandatory sentence could not be applied arbitrarily and that making the death penalty a mandatory sentence would therefore satisfy the objections to capital punishment raised by the *Furman* decision. However, in the 1976 *Woodson v. North Carolina* decision, the U.S. Supreme Court ruled that a mandatory death sentence is cruel and unusual under the U.S. Constitution and that juries must be permitted to consider possible mitigating circumstances. **See also** guided discretion; *Woodson v. North Carolina.*

martyrs
A martyr is someone who is executed, or otherwise severely persecuted, for maintaining a strong belief, usually of a religious nature. The word comes from the Greek *martys*, meaning "witness"; by the early Christian era it connoted self-sacrifice as well as bearing witness. The Latin translation was adopted to refer to Christians who were executed for their beliefs during the Roman Empire. Many of these Christian martyrs were canonized by the church, and many are closely associated with the manner of their execution. For example, St. Thomas is often depicted holding a spear or lance, since he was martyred by being impaled on a spear. St. Sebastian is depicted shot full of arrows, since the emperor Diocletian ordered that he be killed with arrows. When the arrows failed to kill him, he was beaten to death. **See also** impalement; stoning.

Marwood, William (1820–1883)
William Marwood was an executioner in England from 1874 to 1883, taking over the position of chief executioner in England from William Calcraft. In fact, when Marwood was first hired, his knowledge of hangings was purely theoretical. He had never assisted in a hanging. Nevertheless, he persuaded officials at Lincoln Prison that he knew how to make some improvements in the way hangings were done. Apparently, he was right. Marwood is the hangman who first developed the concept of the "long drop," that is, the idea of basing the length of the prisoner's fall on the prisoner's body weight. Marwood discovered that a fall of six to ten feet (depending on the prisoner's weight) could cause what appeared to be nearly instantaneous death due to a broken neck. During his nine-year career, he executed 176 people. **See also** executioners; hanging.

Maryland
Maryland has traditionally permitted juries to impose the death penalty, and continues to do so currently. Between 1638 and 1773, forty-seven executions took place in colonial Maryland, mostly for the crime of murder, although one woman, Rebecca Fowler, was hanged in 1685 for witchcraft. Most of the executions were hangings, but a Native American was executed by shooting in 1669 and another woman, Esther Anderson, was burned for murder in 1746. Two slaves were hung in chains on a pillory and left to die of exposure in 1743. In 1773 four slaves were hanged for murdering their master. Between 1781 and 1922, 170 executions took place under

the authority of local governments. The first nonpublic execution took place in 1913, although public executions were not officially abolished and moved to the state penitentiary until 1923. Between 1923 and 1957, seventy-five more executions by hanging took place in Maryland. In 1955 Maryland replaced hanging with lethal gas as its method of execution, but this applied only to people sentenced after the new law took effect. The first execution by lethal gas took place in 1959 and the last in 1961. Only four people were executed in Maryland's gas chamber.

Following the 1972 *Furman v. Georgia* ruling, which struck down Maryland's death-penalty statute, the state passed a new death-penalty statute in 1975. Maryland's current death-penalty statute allows jurors to consider the death penalty for homicide under special circumstances. These special circumstances include that the homicide was willful, deliberate, or premeditated (especially including the use of poison or of lying in wait); that the homicide was perpetrated by means of arson; that the homicide was committed in the course of rape or other sexual offense, mayhem, robbery, carjacking, burglary, kidnapping, or escape from custody; or that the homicide was perpetrated by means of a destructive device (e.g., a bomb).

The death penalty may be imposed if one of ten aggravating circumstances is proven to have accompanied the crime. The list of aggravating circumstances appears similar to the special circumstances listed above, but aggravating circumstances are considered during the penalty phase of the trial rather than during the guilt phase. These aggravating circumstances are (1) that the victim was a police officer acting in the performance of his or her duties; (2) that the defendant was incarcerated in a correctional facility; (3) that the homicide was committed in order to escape from custody or evade arrest; (4) that the homicide occurred in the course of a kidnapping or abduction; (5) that the victim was an abducted child; (6) that the defendant was hired by someone else to commit the murder; (7) that the defendant hired someone else to commit the murder; (8) that the defendant was under sentence of death or life imprisonment for a previous crime; (9) that the defendant was convicted of one or more other homicides occurring at the same time; or (10) that the homicide occurred in the course of a carjacking, robbery, arson, rape, or other first-degree sexual offense. The jury must also consider any mitigating circumstances that the defense wishes to present.

Under Maryland law, a person convicted of a capital offense cannot be executed if he or she was under the age of eighteen at the time of the crime. Maryland does provide for life imprisonment without parole as an alternative to the death penalty. The governor has the authority to commute a death sentence to a term of imprisonment of any length.

In 1994 Maryland replaced lethal gas with lethal injection as its method of execution. The first execution since the reenactment of capital punishment took place the same year. Since 1994 there have been only three executions in Maryland, all by lethal injection. As of April 2005, nine people were awaiting execution on Maryland's death row. **See also** *Furman v. Georgia.*

Massachusetts

Massachusetts has traditionally permitted juries to impose the death penalty, but does not currently have an active death-penalty statute. In colonial Massachusetts, between 1630 and 1777, 145 people were executed by hanging for various crimes, including murder, piracy, witchcraft, and housebreaking.

A girl writhes on the floor of a courtroom in Salem, Massachusetts, as if under the spell of the woman (before the judge) on trial for witchcraft.

Two executions by burning are recorded, one for murder and one for arson. During the famous Salem witchcraft trials, one man was put to death by pressing (*peine forte et dure*) for failing to acknowledge the jurisdiction of the court. Those accused of witchcraft were hanged. At the time of the American Revolution, a few people were executed by firing squad for military desertion. From 1778 to 1898, another ninety-seven executions, all by hanging, took place under state jurisdiction. Twenty-one executions by hanging also took place under federal jurisdiction, mostly for the crime of piracy.

In 1898 Massachusetts replaced hanging with the electric chair as its method of execution. The electric chair was located at the state prison in Charlestown, and was first used to execute convicted murderer Luigi Storti in 1901. Between 1901 and 1947, sixty-five people were executed by electrocution in Massachusetts. No executions have taken place in Massachusetts since that time.

Following the 1972 *Furman v. Georgia* decision, which invalidated the Massachusetts death-penalty statute as well as every other death-penalty statute in the country, Massachusetts has made some attempts to reenact a death-penalty statute, but none so far has satisfied the state's supreme judicial court. In 1975 the supreme judicial court ruled that a mandatory death penalty for murder with rape was unconstitutional. In 1979 the Massachusetts legislature passed a death-penalty statute similar to those in other states, but the supreme judicial court declared it to be unconstitutional under the state's constitution. In 1982 voters approved an amendment to the state's constitution designed to allow the death penalty, but in 1984 the supreme judicial court declared the amendment to be inconsistent with other provisions of the state constitution. The reasoning behind the ruling was that, since a death sentence may only be imposed by a jury, the new law created too much incentive for defendants to plead guilty in order to avoid a jury trial, thereby giving up their right to due process and trial by jury. As of this publication, Massachusetts remains without a death-penalty statute. **See also** *peine forte et dure;* Salem witchcraft trials.

Maxwell v. Bishop

This was a case heard by the Supreme Court of the United States in 1969. The original issues raised in this case were whether the Arkansas death-penalty statute gave jurors too much discretion in sentencing and whether capital cases could be tried using only a single-phase trial. These issues were central to several other cases that were decided about the same time. In the end, this case was decided on the much narrower grounds that some prospective jurors had been inappropriately excused during jury selection. Although this case set no important legal precedent, it is interesting for historical reasons: This case nearly resulted in a wholesale invalidating of death-penalty statutes around the country. Had things gone slightly differently, this case rather than the *Furman v. Georgia* case, which was decided three years later, might have been the most important death-penalty decision made by the U.S. Supreme Court in the twentieth century.

The defendant in this case, William Maxwell, was a black man who had been sentenced to death for rape in Arkansas. Lawyers working for the Legal Defense Fund appealed the sentence, arguing that the Arkansas death-penalty statute resulted in discriminatory sentencing. Specifically, they claimed that the statute gave jurors too much discretion to decide the sentence based on their own prejudices rather than on the facts of the crime, and they claimed that the single-phase trial required defendants to plead for mercy (thus appearing guilty) even before their guilt had been established. Eventually the U.S. Supreme Court agreed to review the case.

After hearing the arguments in the case, eight of the nine members of the Supreme Court voted to invalidate the Arkansas death-penalty statute. However, different justices had different reasons for this opinion. Five justices—William O. Douglas, Abe Fortas, Thurgood Marshall, Earl Warren, and William Brennan—eventually agreed to require a two-phase trial in death-penalty cases; John Harlan II considered joining them in this opinion but could not quite make up his mind. Two other justices, Potter Stewart and Byron White, felt the case should be decided on different grounds. Only Justice Hugo Black believed that the Arkansas death-penalty statute should be left in place. In any case, before a decision could be announced, Abe Fortas was forced to resign because of a scandal involving his financial dealings. This destroyed the five-vote majority, and Harlan declined to become the fifth vote. The court agreed to reconsider the case the following year. However, by that time Earl Warren had retired and was replaced as chief justice by Warren Burger, and Harry Blackmun had joined the Court to replace Abe Fortas. Both of these justices agreed with Hugo Black that the statute should be left in place. Stewart and White still wanted the statute overturned, but could not be persuaded to join the opinion written by Douglas. Unable to form a majority in either direction on the really crucial issues, the justices finally agreed to decide the case in the defendant's favor on the grounds that some prospective jurors had been dismissed in a way that violated the Supreme Court's earlier 1968 ruling in *Witherspoon v. Illinois*. Given the potentially earth-shaking issues that were originally at stake, the decision was a notable anticlimax. **See also** *Furman v. Georgia; Witherspoon v. Illinois*.

McCleskey v. Kemp

This was a case heard by the Supreme Court of the United States in 1987 concerning the extent to which statistics could be used in determining whether a law violates the equal protection clause of the Fourteenth Amendment. The defendant, Warren McCleskey, who was black, had been convicted for the 1978 murder of a white Atlanta police officer and sentenced to death. Lawyers representing the Legal Defense Fund appealed the sentence, arguing that the Georgia death-penalty statute was being applied in a manner that permitted undue influence of racial prejudice. A statistical analysis by David Baldus, professor of law at the University of Iowa, showed that, in Georgia, defendants accused of killing whites were 4.3 times more likely to receive a death sentence than defendants accused of killing blacks. The Supreme Court agreed to review the case.

In a 5-to-4 decision, the Court ruled that the Georgia death-penalty statute could not be overturned on statistical evidence alone. Writing for the majority, Justice Lewis Powell argued that the law could be overturned only if it could be shown that the state legislature had enacted the law with a discriminatory intent. Otherwise, to overturn McCleskey's specific sentence, it would need to be shown that the judge or jury had acted with discriminatory intent in his case. Baldus's statistics could not establish that either was true. Justice Powell did suggest that such statistics might be used by the Georgia legislature to improve existing law, but that they were not relevant to the courts, which had to make decisions on specific cases. In dissent, Justice William Brennan argued that statistics *could* be used to demonstrate a significant risk of discrimination in the application of the law, and that this was enough to show that the law did not provide for equal protection as required by the Fourteenth Amendment. **See also** equal protection; *McCleskey v. Zant*; racial discrimination in sentencing.

McCleskey v. Zant

This was a case heard by the Supreme Court of the United States in 1990, and decided in 1991, concerning when a defendant on death row may file habeas corpus petitions. The defendant, Warren McCleskey, had been sentenced to death after being convicted of the 1978 murder of an Atlanta police officer. In 1987 his sentence was appealed on the grounds that the Georgia death-penalty statute was being applied in a discriminatory manner, but this claim, made in *McCleskey v. Kemp*, was decided by the U.S. Supreme Court in favor of the prosecution. In 1990 McCleskey's lawyers appealed again on the substantially different grounds that statements by McCleskey made to fellow inmates and used against him at trial had been obtained improperly. The Supreme Court agreed to hear the case in order to clarify when defendants may file appeals based on the right of habeas corpus.

In a 6-to-3 decision, the Court ruled that McCleskey's appeal should be rejected. Writing for the majority, Justice Anthony M. Kennedy argued that, given the outcome of the trial, an appeal on the grounds of improperly obtained evidence should have been pursued immediately if it had any merit and evidence would have to be presented that the error had actually prejudiced the defendant's case. McCleskey's appeal, coming after an earlier appeal, was clearly an afterthought and was not accompanied by evidence showing that the conviction of a defendant who was actually innocent had resulted. Hence, the appeal should be rejected.

This case was one of several cases decided during the early 1990s in which the Supreme Court attempted to place limits on appeals by death row inmates. Kennedy's decision laid out specific conditions for the filing of writs of habeas corpus, especially when these were preceded by previous filings. The ruling substantially limited when and how such appeals could be filed. **See also** habeas corpus; *McCleskey v. Kemp.*

McGautha v. California

This was a case heard by the Supreme Court of the United States in 1971 concerning whether juries may be given absolute discretion in determining whether a defendant should be given a sentence of death and also whether a trial in which the sentence is decided at the same time as the question of guilt or innocence adequately protects a defendant's right to due process.

This case actually bundled together two cases from different jurisdictions. The defendant in one of the cases was Dennis C. McGautha, who was tried for murder and sentenced to death in California; the defendant in the other case was James E. Crampton, who was tried for murder and sentenced to death in Ohio. The death-penalty statutes in both states gave jurors complete discretion to consider whatever aggravating and mitigating circumstances they considered relevant in determining whether a defendant should be put to death. The states' statutes differed, however, in at least one respect. The California law provided for a two-phase trial in which the question of guilt or innocence had to be decided first and then the question of sentencing was taken up separately. Ohio's law provided for only a one-phase trial, so the question of sentencing was decided at the same time as the question of guilt. Both sentences were appealed on the grounds that the state statutes gave the jury too much discretion to consider aggravating circumstances and the state laws were therefore likely to produce arbitrary and inconsistent results. Crampton's sentence was appealed on the additional grounds that the single-phase trial required a defendant to offer evidence of mitigating circumstances surrounding a crime yet at the same time maintain that the defendant had committed no crime to which mitigating circumstances might be considered relevant. Because of the similarities and differences in the two cases, the U.S. Supreme Court agreed to review them together.

In a 6-to-3 decision, the Supreme Court upheld the convictions and sentences of both McGautha and Crampton. Writing for the majority, Justice John M. Harlan II argued that it was the business of state legislatures, not the courts, to decide what guidance (if any) to give to jurors in determining a sentence of death. On the question of bifurcated trials, Harlan pointed out that the adversarial justice system frequently put defendants in the position of having to make difficult decisions concerning what strategy to follow in mounting a defense. He argued that it was not fundamentally unfair to require that a defendant choose between maintaining his innocence and pleading for mercy. Writing in dissent on the first point, Justice William Brennan argued that it was precisely the business of the courts to maintain standards of uniformity in the administration of justice and that the courts had every reason to invalidate laws that were likely to yield inconsistent and arbitrary results. Writing in dissent on the second point, Justice William Douglas maintained that forcing a defendant to choose between arguing his innocence and arguing for leniency was indeed fundamentally unfair and robbed the defendant of his right to due process. The dissenting opinions in this case are especially important because the following year, 1972, these opinions became the basis for the *Furman v. Georgia* decision, which overturned the *McGautha* decision and had the effect of invalidating every death-penalty statute then in place in the United States. **See also** *Furman v. Georgia.*

McVeigh, Timothy (l968–2001)

Timothy McVeigh, the convicted bomber of the Alfred P. Murrah Federal Building in Oklahoma City in 1995, was executed by lethal injection in 2001 for the murders of eleven federal law enforcement officers who died in the bombing. A total of 168 people were killed in the attack, but prosecutors chose to try McVeigh for the deaths of the eleven federal officers

Oklahoma City bomber Timothy McVeigh (center) consults with his attorneys. McVeigh's 2001 execution by lethal injection was the first by federal authorities since 1963.

because such charges made the crime a capital offense under federal law. (Had McVeigh not been convicted and sentenced under federal law, he would then have faced charges of murder for the civilian deaths under Oklahoma law.) McVeigh's execution has been the only execution under federal jurisdiction since 1963.

Even as a young college student, McVeigh held extreme right-wing political views, including advocating the violent overthrow of the federal government. He also had a fascination with guns, which may have led him to enlist in the army. McVeigh served as a soldier in the Gulf War of 1991. He was apparently an exemplary soldier and was awarded a Bronze Star for his service. While in the army, he met Terry Nichols, who shared McVeigh's extreme political views. After leaving the army, McVeigh moved to Michigan, where Terry Nichols and his brother also lived. The three became members of a paramilitary organization called the Patriots, which advocated overthrowing the federal government. McVeigh and Terry Nichols began making plans to achieve this goal.

On April 19, 1995, a Ryder truck containing a load of gasoline-soaked ammonium nitrate fertilizer exploded next to the Murrah Federal Building in Oklahoma City. The explosion caused an entire side of the nine-story building to collapse into rubble and resulted in the deaths of 168 people, including the children in the building's day-care center. At first it was assumed to be an attack by foreign terrorists, but a trail of clues eventually led to Timothy McVeigh. He was identified as one of two men who had rented the Ryder truck, and his fingerprint was found on the receipt issued for the purchase of the fertilizer that was used to create the explosion.

McVeigh confessed to the crime and made little effort to avoid the death penalty, justifying his actions as a patriotic response to illegal and immoral federal abuses of power. His relatively brief trial took place in Denver, Colorado, in 1997. McVeigh was convicted and sentenced to death. The execution by lethal injection took place at a federal prison in Indiana on June 11, 2001. **See also** federal death-penalty laws.

mens rea
Mens rea, a Latin phrase meaning "guilty mind," is a legal term that refers to the mental state by virtue of which a criminal action qualifies as a crime. Any crime has two aspects, the criminal act itself (i.e., the physical activity by which someone is wronged or harmed) and the mental state (i.e., the intention or purpose of the person performing the act). A criminal action is not a crime unless it is accompanied by the appropriate mens rea, or guilty purpose. For example, taking a pen that is not yours does not qualify as theft unless you *meant* to take it. Pocketing the pen out of habitual reflex may be regrettable, but it is not a crime (unless you then intentionally decide to *keep* the pen). In the same way, causing the death of another does not qualify as murder unless there is an intention to cause death, referred to in legal terms as "malice aforethought." Causing the death of another may qualify as negligent homicide, but even here there is mens rea, namely a conscious disregard for the fact that a dangerous situation exists. Important distinctions between crimes that may seem quite similar are often drawn in terms of their mens rea. In particular, various grades of homicide are distinguished in this way. No jurisdiction in the United States considers the death penalty to be an appropriate punishment for a killing that is merely negligent or accidental. **See also** murder.

mentally ill offenders

Mental illness can refer to a variety of mental conditions ranging from mild chronic depression to severe schizophrenia. Mental illness should not be confused with legal insanity, although the two concepts are related. Legal insanity refers to a mental condition, possibly temporary, under which a person is incapable of understanding the moral significance of his or her actions, or (under some definitions) is incapable of controlling such actions. Certain forms of mental illness, such as paranoid schizophrenia and some forms of compulsive behavior, do produce legal insanity, but other forms of mental illness, while important and distressing to sufferers, do not have legal significance.

A defendant who is judged to be sufficiently mentally ill at the time of his or her crime to be considered legally insane is regarded as innocent under the law. Some states recognize a special verdict, "guilty but mentally ill," under which a jury declares that the defendant suffers from a debilitating mental illness but was not legally insane at the time of the crime. However, even in states in which this verdict is recognized, a defendant who truly meets the legal definition of insanity is still judged to be innocent. Thus, defendants who are considered legally insane at the time of their crime cannot be sentenced to death. Similarly, a defendant must be judged legally competent to stand trial, so defendants who are considered legally insane before they are tried cannot be sentenced to death.

Some inmates, however, develop mental illnesses while they are awaiting execution on death row. In some cases, these mental illnesses are sufficiently severe to meet the legal definition of insanity. In the Anglo-American legal tradition, a person cannot be punished if he or she does not understand the reasons for the punishment. Hence, it is considered to be a principle of common law that an inmate may not be executed while he or she is judged legally insane. This principle was specifically endorsed by the U.S. Supreme Court in 1986 in the *Ford v. Wainwright* ruling. However, the common law custom of not executing the insane was developed before effective treatments for psychosis were discovered. This puts prison psychiatrists in the position of treating a prisoner for mental illness in order to facilitate the prisoner's execution. In January 2004 a mentally ill prisoner, Charles Singleton, was executed despite the fact that, without his antipsychotic medications, he clearly met the legal definition of insanity and would not have been judged competent to undergo execution. **See also** affirmative defense; *Ford v. Wainwright;* Singleton, Charles.

mentally retarded offenders

A person who scores significantly below average on an accepted, standardized intelligence test is considered mentally retarded. On the best known of such tests, the Stanford-Binet Intelligence Scale, a score of 100 is average, so a person who scores below 70 would be considered well below average. A person who scores between 50 and 70 is considered mildly mentally retarded. Such a person has difficulty learning new skills and as a result is likely to do poorly in school. However, such people do learn, and do develop emotionally. They are capable of functioning as adults and of living independent, productive, and satisfying lives. People who score below 50 are considered moderately to severely mentally retarded. Such people can also live productive and satisfying lives but will probably require assistance and support even as adults. Mental retardation should not be confused with mental illness, which refers to various emotional abnormalities that are unrelated to intelligence. It is also important to remember that mental retardation does not necessarily affect emotional development. A person described as having the "mental age" of a six-year-old has the reading, writing, and mathematical skills typical of a six-year-old but does not necessarily have the emotional responses of a six-year-old.

The issue of mental retardation and capital punishment arose only in the mid-twentieth century, when measurement of intelligence using standardized tests first became common. When empirical measurement of defendants' intelligence was accepted as reliable, defense attorneys began using evidence of low intelligence in arguments for leniency, and in many cases juries were inclined to grant leniency on that basis.

The Supreme Court of the United States has made two significant rulings concerning the execution of mentally retarded offenders. In the 1989 *Penry v. Lynaugh* decision, the Supreme Court ruled that juries should be instructed that mental retardation could be considered as a mitigating factor, but it also ruled that being mentally retarded did not make a defendant ineligible for the death penalty. The *Penry* decision resulted in widespread protests, and in response to these protests many states added clauses to their death-penalty statutes prohibiting execution of the mentally retarded. By 2002 enough laws had been changed that the Supreme Court decided to revisit the issue. In the *Atkins v. Virginia* decision, it ruled that by "evolving standards of decency" (i.e., changes in law and public sentiment since the time of the *Penry* decision), execution of the mentally retarded could no longer be considered constitutional. As such, the United States no longer permits execution of the mentally retarded. **See also** *Atkins v. Virginia; Penry v. Lynaugh.*

Michigan

No executions have ever been performed in the state of Michigan. However, four executions did take place in territorial Michigan, prior to statehood in 1837, and eight executions are recorded in preterritorial Michigan, before Michigan became part of the United States. In 1846 Michigan became the first English-speaking jurisdiction to abolish capital punishment (for all crimes except treason, which has never been prosecuted under Michigan law). In 1964 a provision prohibiting the death penalty was added to the state's constitution. **See also** opposition to capital punishment, history of (1648–1870).

military justice

The U.S. military has the authority to impose the death penalty on members of the armed services. Originally, this authority was granted solely for crimes of a specifically military nature, and most of these were death-eligible only when committed during times of war. Crimes that were not specifically of a military nature fell under civil jurisdiction. However, over time the jurisdiction of U.S. military courts (courts-martial) has expanded to include all crimes committed by military personnel, including crimes not specifically of a military nature.

The law that granted the military the authority to punish crimes of a military nature was passed by the first U.S. Congress in 1789, and was known as the Articles of War. The Articles of War defined fourteen offenses of a military nature that could be punished by death, including desertion, mutiny, and assaulting an officer. In 1806 Congress considered abolishing the military's authority to impose the death penalty, but the proposal was defeated and the issue has never since been raised. In 1863, during the Civil War, Congress significantly expanded the military's authority, giving military courts jurisdiction to try crimes of a nonmilitary nature when those crimes were committed by military personnel during times of war. In 1916 the military's authority was expanded again, allowing military courts to try nonmilitary crimes by military personnel even during peacetime. However, murder and rape were excluded. In 1950 Congress passed the Uniform Code of Military Justice, which replaced the old Articles of War. This law gave military courts jurisdiction over even rape and murder, when committed by military personnel.

The Uniform Code of Military Justice was the only law in the United States providing for a penalty of death that was not explicitly overturned by the Supreme Court's 1972 *Furman v. Georgia* decision. The question of whether the *Furman* decision applied to military law remained unresolved until 1983, at which time the Court of Appeals for the Armed Forces (the highest appeals court in the military jurisdiction) ruled, in *United States v. Matthews*, that military capital sentencing procedures were unconstitutional. In 1984 the death penalty was reinstated when President Ronald Reagan issued an executive order establishing procedures for military trials that brought them in line with the requirements laid out in the 1976 *Gregg v. Georgia* Supreme Court decision, which had established guidelines for capital trials in the rest of the country.

The Uniform Code of Military Justice defines sixteen offenses as death-eligible. Nearly all of these are of a specifically military nature, and are death-eligible only when committed during time of war (when they might endanger the lives of others). The sixteen offenses are desertion, assaulting or willfully disobeying a superior commissioned officer, mutiny, sedition, misbehavior before the enemy, subordinate compelling surrender, improper use of a countersign, forcing a safeguard, aiding the enemy, spying, espionage, improper handling of a vessel, misbehavior of a sentinel or lookout, murder, felony murder, and rape.

A military trial (or court-martial) for a capital offense differs somewhat from a civilian trial. The trial is convened by a high-ranking officer who appoints the jury. The jury must consist of at least five members but may include more, of which at least two-thirds must be officers. The remainder may be enlisted personnel. The defendant cannot plead guilty or ask for a bench trial (a trial in which there is no jury).

As with most civilian trials, the death penalty may be imposed only if the jury unanimously decides that at least one aggravating circumstance accompanied the crime (and there are no mitigating circumstances sufficient to counterbalance it). However, because of the specifically military nature of the crimes, the aggravating circumstances are somewhat different than those listed in other jurisdictions. For crimes other than murder and rape, it is considered an aggravating circumstance if (1) the offense was committed in the presence of the enemy; (2) the offense was intended to harm the national security of the United States, even if no harm was caused; (3) the offense actually harmed the national security of the United States, even if no harm was intended; (4) the offense substantially endangered the lives of others; or (5) the offense was committed in order to avoid hazardous duty. In the case of rape, it is considered an aggravating circumstance if (1) the rape occurred in a place where U.S. forces are engaged in combat or in a place where the United States, or one of its allies, is serving as an occupying force; (2) the victim was under the age of twelve; or (3) the defendant also attempted to maim or kill the victim. In the case of murder, it is considered an aggravating circumstance if (1) the murder occurred in a place where U.S. forces are engaged in combat or in a place where the United States, or one of its allies, is serving as an occupying force; (2) the defendant was serving a sentence of thirty years or more for a previous crime; (3) the murder was committed in the course of a robbery, rape, arson, sodomy, burglary, kidnapping, mutiny, sedition, or piracy of an aircraft or vessel; (4) the murder was committed for promise of payment; (5) the defendant hired or coerced another to commit the murder; (6) the murder was committed while attempting to avoid arrest or escape from custody; (7) the victim is the president of the United States, either sitting or elect; the person next in line for the office of president, either sitting or elect; any member of Congress, either sitting or elect; or any judge of the United States; (8) the victim was known to the defendant to be an armed forces officer, a law enforcement officer, a security officer (either civilian or military), or a firefighter; (9) the murder was preceded by the intentional infliction of maiming or pain to the victim; (10) more than one murder occurred; or (11) the defendant was the actual perpetrator of the killing (not merely an accomplice).

The president of the United States has the authority to grant clemency to someone sentenced by a military court, and indeed no death sentence is carried out without the personal authorization of the president. Though firing squads have traditionally been associated with military executions, executions at Fort Leavenworth following a formal court-martial were actually carried out by means of hanging. The last execution under military jurisdiction took place on April 13, 1961, when Private John A. Bennett was hanged for rape and attempted murder. Hanging has since been replaced by lethal injection as the method of execution, but no executions have taken place under military jurisdiction since 1961. As of June 2005, there were seven people on death row at Fort Leavenworth. **See also** Fort Leavenworth Penitentiary.

Mill, John Stuart (1806–1873)

John Stuart Mill was one of the most influential philosophers of the nineteenth century. His writings in philosophy include highly regarded works on logic and scientific method as well as works on ethics and the philosophy of government. His essay *On Liberty*, published in 1834, is still one of the most widely read works on political and social philosophy. In that essay he argues that the chief purpose of society is to promote the happiness of individuals. Mill was a noted humanitarian and reformer who favored equal rights for women and advocated improved conditions for workers. He was also the chief proponent of the ethical theory known as utilitarianism. However, unlike other prominent utilitarians, Mill was a supporter of capital punishment.

Mill was born in London and educated by his father, James Mill, himself a noted intellectual and social reformer. John Stuart Mill was a child prodigy who mastered Greek by the age of three and Latin by the age of eight. By the age of fifteen he had studied history, mathematics, and logic and turned his attention to social philosophy. At the age of seventeen he took a position with the East India Company, where he worked until 1858. In 1865 he was elected to Parliament, despite his refusal to campaign for the seat. (He was defeated in the following election.) In 1868, as a member of Parliament, Mill gave a speech in support of capital punishment. In that speech he argued that the death penalty should be retained, but only as a punishment for the most atrocious of crimes. Characteristically, his argument appealed to the principle of humaneness. In the case of criminals who were beyond reform and who could not be permitted to live in society, the only alternative to death would be to keep them alive under conditions that would normally be considered cruel (i.e., life imprisonment at forced labor). For criminals who have proven themselves to be unworthy of life, he argued, it would actually be a kindness to put them to death. **See also** Bentham, Jeremy; Kant, Immanuel; utilitarianism.

Mills v. Maryland

This was a case heard by the Supreme Court of the United States in 1988 concerning whether jurors must unanimously agree on the presence of a mitigating circumstance if that circumstance is to be considered in sentencing. The defendant in the case, Ralph Mills, murdered his cell mate while he was imprisoned at the Maryland Correctional Institution and was convicted of the crime. During the penalty phase, the jury unanimously agreed that Mills had committed the crime while incarcerated in a penal institution, which is considered an aggravating circumstance under the Maryland death-penalty statute. Various jurors felt that there were sufficient mitigating circumstances to override this aggravating circumstance, but the jurors could not unanimously agree on the presence of any single mitigating circumstance. The judge instructed them that if they could not agree

Unlike most other utilitarians, John Stuart Mill supported the death penalty as punishment for particularly heinous crimes.

on the same mitigating circumstance, they should return a sentence of death. In response to this instruction, the jury sentenced Mills to death. The case was then appealed on the grounds that the Maryland death-penalty statute does not require unanimous agreement on a single mitigating circumstance. As long as the jurors agree that there are some circumstances sufficient to balance the aggravating circumstances, they need not necessarily agree on which circumstances each juror has in mind. The Maryland Court of Appeals, however, rejected this argument and reaffirmed the sentence. The U.S. Supreme Court then agreed to review the case.

In a 5-to-4 decision, the Supreme Court reversed the appeals court's decision and ordered Mills to be resentenced. Writing for the Court, Justice Harry A. Blackmun argued that jurors must be permitted to consider whatever mitigating circumstances seem relevant. In this case, the judge's instructions seemed to prevent some jurors from considering circumstances that seemed relevant to them merely because other jurors (or even only a single other juror) did not consider those circumstances to be relevant. **See also** *Bell v. Ohio;* mitigating circumstances.

Minnesota

Minnesota does not currently permit juries to impose the death penalty. Only one execution is recorded under territorial jurisdiction, that of a Native American named Yu-ha-gu, who was hanged for murder in 1854. Twenty-six people were hanged in Minnesota under state jurisdiction between 1860 and 1906. More than half of all executions in Minnesota took place on a single day, December 26, 1862, when thirty-eight Sioux warriors were executed under federal jurisdiction, on orders signed by Abraham Lincoln, for participating in an uprising against the U.S. Army. This was the largest multiple hanging in U.S. history. The last person executed in Minnesota was William Williams, who was executed in 1906 for murder. It was a botched execution. The rope used to hang Williams was too long, so he landed on the ground below the gallows. He was then hauled into the correct position, but without the fall to break his neck, it took him nearly fifteen minutes to strangle to death. Despite a ban on press attendance at executions, the story was leaked to the press, sparking public outrage. Minnesota abolished capital punishment in 1911. **See also** multiple executions.

Mississippi

Mississippi has traditionally permitted juries to impose the death penalty, and continues to do so currently. In early Mississippi, all executions took place by means of hanging, and nearly all were for the crime of murder or robbery with murder. Only two executions by hanging took place in territorial Mississippi. Mississippi became a state in 1817, and between 1818 and 1940, 255 people were hanged in Mississippi. In 1940 Mississippi replaced hanging with electrocution as its method of execution. Between 1940 and 1954, sixty-three people were executed in Mississippi's electric chair. Most states that used an electric chair also held their executions at a centralized location, generally the state penitentiary. Mississippi was an exception. In Mississippi, executions continued to be performed in the county where the crime had taken place until 1954. The state's electric chair was moved from county to county, as needed, in the back of a pickup truck that belonged to the state's traveling executioner, an ex-convict named Jimmy Thompson. In 1954 Mississippi again changed its method of execution, replacing electrocution with lethal gas. The gas chamber was permanently installed at the Mississippi state penitentiary, and thereafter executions in Mississippi took place at that location. Between 1954 and 1964, thirty-one people were executed in Mississippi's gas chamber.

Following the 1972 *Furman v. Georgia* ruling, which struck down Mississippi's death-penalty statute, the state passed a new death-penalty statute in 1974. Mississippi's current death-penalty statute allows jurors to consider the death penalty for homicide under special circumstances. These special circumstances are (1) that the victim was known to the defendant to be a police officer, corrections officer, or firefighter acting in his or her official capacity; (2) that the defendant was under sentence of life imprisonment; (3) that the homicide was committed by means of an explosive device; (4) that something of value was given or received in payment for the homicide; (5) that the homicide occurred in the course of a rape, burglary, kidnapping, arson, robbery, or sexual battery; (6) that the homicide occurred in the course of child abuse; or (7) that the victim was known to the defendant to be an elected official.

The death penalty may be imposed if one of eight aggravating circumstances is proven to have accompanied the crime. The list of aggravating circumstances appears similar to the previous list of special circumstances, but aggravating circumstances are considered during the penalty phase of the trial rather than during the guilt phase. These aggravating circumstances are (1) that the defendant was under sentence of imprisonment; (2) that the defendant was previously convicted of a capital offense or of a felony involving violence; (3) that the defendant knowingly created a great risk of death to many people; (4) that the homicide occurred in the course of a rape, arson, burglary, kidnapping, aircraft piracy, sexual battery, sexual intercourse with a child under twelve, other nonconsensual sex, child abuse, or unlawful detonation of an explosive device; (5) that the homicide was committed in order to evade arrest or escape from custody; (6) that the homicide was committed for monetary gain; (7) that the homicide was committed in order to disrupt a governmental function or the enforcement of the law; or (8) that the homicide was especially heinous, atrocious, or cruel. The jury must also consider any mitigating circumstances that the defense wishes to present.

Under Mississippi law, a person convicted of a capital offense cannot be executed if he or she was under the age of sixteen at the time of the crime. This provision was invalidated by the 2005 Supreme Court decision in *Roper v. Simmons*, which abolished capital punishment for persons younger than eighteen at the time of their offense. Mississippi does provide for life imprisonment without parole as an alternative to the death penalty. The governor has sole authority to grant clemency, but may ask the State Parole Board to make a clemency recommendation based on its own investigation of the case.

The first execution following the reenactment of the death penalty took place in 1983 with the execution of Jimmy Lee Gray. In 1984 the Mississippi legislature voted to replace lethal gas with lethal injection, but this applied only to condemned prisoners sentenced after the new law took effect. As a result, executions by lethal gas continued until 1989. Between 1983 and 1989, four more people were executed in Mississippi's gas chamber. In 1989 the legislature amended the law to abolish the use of lethal gas regardless of the date of an inmate's sentence. So far, two people have been executed by lethal injection in Mississippi. As of June 2005, seventy people were awaiting execution on Mississippi's death row. **See also** electric chair; *Furman v. Georgia*; Purvis, Will.

Missouri

Missouri has traditionally permitted juries to impose the death penalty, and continues to do so currently. Only two executions are recorded in territorial Missouri, one in 1810 and one in 1821, both by hanging. Missouri became a state in 1821. Between 1824 and 1937, 240 people were executed by hanging in

Missouri. These executions were conducted by local sheriffs in the county where the crime occurred. Nearly all were for the crime of murder. Missouri did not centralize its executions at the Jefferson City Correctional Center until 1937. At that time, Missouri also changed its method of execution from hanging to lethal gas. Between 1938 and 1968, thirty-six people were executed under state jurisdiction in Missouri's gas chamber.

Following the 1972 *Furman v. Georgia* ruling, which struck down Missouri's death-penalty statute, the state passed a new death-penalty statute in 1975. Missouri's current death-penalty statute allows jurors to consider the death penalty for a homicide that is committed knowingly and after deliberation. The death penalty may be imposed if one of seventeen aggravating circumstances is proven to have accompanied the crime. These aggravating circumstances are (1) that the defendant was previously convicted of first-degree murder or had a substantial history of convictions for violent crimes; (2) that the homicide occurred in the course of committing another homicide; (3) that the defendant knowingly created a great risk of death to more than one person in a public place by means of a device (such as a bomb) that would normally endanger more than one person; (4) that the homicide was a murder-for-hire and the defendant either performed the murder or solicited another to perform the murder; (5) that the victim was a judicial officer, prosecuting attorney, circuit attorney, police officer, or elected official; (6) that the defendant ordered or procured the homicide on behalf of another person; (7) that the homicide was wantonly vile, involving torture; (8) that the victim was a police officer or firefighter acting in the performance of his or her duty; (9) that the defendant had unlawfully escaped from custody; (10) that the homicide was committed in order to avoid someone's arrest or effect someone's escape from custody; (11) that the homicide occurred in the course of a rape, sodomy, burglary, kidnapping, or other felony; (12) that the victim was a witness; (13) that the victim was an employee of a penal institution acting in the performance of his or her duties or an inmate in a penal institution; (14) that the homicide occurred in the course of hijacking a public conveyance such as an airplane, train, ship, or bus; (15) that the homicide was committed in order to conceal another felony; (16) that the homicide was committed in order to prevent someone from initiating or aiding in the prosecution of a felony; or (17) that the homicide occurred in the course of criminal gang-related activity. The jury must also consider any mitigating circumstances that the defense wishes to present.

Under Missouri law, a person convicted of a capital offense cannot be executed if he or she was under the age of eighteen at the time of the crime. Missouri does provide for life imprisonment without parole as an alternative to the death penalty. The governor has sole authority to grant clemency, but is required to get a nonbinding recommendation from the Board of Probation and Parole before making a decision.

In 1988 Missouri added lethal injection as an optional method of execution. The choice between lethal gas and lethal injection is to be made not by the condemned prisoner but by the director of the Department of Corrections. The first execution following the reenactment of the death penalty occurred in 1989, when George Mercer was executed by lethal injection. Since 1989, there have been sixty-one executions in Missouri, all by lethal injection. As of April 2005, fifty-six people were awaiting execution on

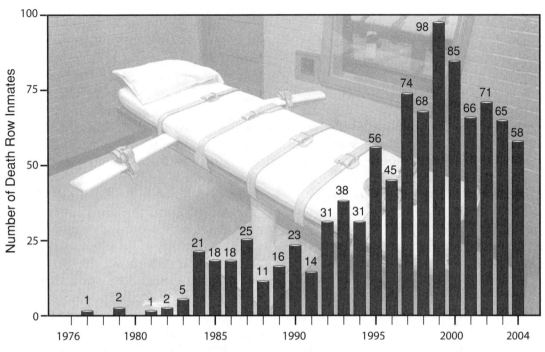

Executions Since 1976
TOTAL: 943

Source: Death Penalty Information Center, www.deathpenaltyinfo.org.

Missouri's death row. **See also** *Furman v. Georgia.*

mitigating circumstances

Mitigating circumstances are facts about a case that tend to lessen the culpability or seriousness of the crime. Mitigating circumstances do not *excuse* a crime, so are never introduced during the guilt phase of a trial; but they may affect the severity of the penalty imposed, so they are presented during the penalty phase of the trial. In two 1978 decisions, *Bell v. Ohio* and *Lockett v. Ohio*, the U.S. Supreme Court ruled that the defense could ask a court to consider any circumstances that might be considered mitigating regardless of whether those circumstances are specifically mentioned in a state's death-penalty statute. For this reason, some states do not bother to list mitigating circumstances in their death-penalty statutes at all. (By contrast, an aggravating circumstance cannot be presented by the prosecution as a reason for imposing the death penalty unless the state statute specifically lists it for that purpose.) However, most states do provide a list of mitigating circumstances that should be considered if appropriate. These lists tend to be fairly short and quite similar to each other.

Six mitigating circumstances are included on nearly every list. They are (1) that the defendant has little or no prior history of violent criminal activity; (2) that the defendant was reasonably young; for example, many jurisdictions encourage leniency in the sentencing of defendants who were under twenty-one at the time of their crime; (3) that the defendant was under extreme mental or emotional distress; (4) that the act was performed under duress or under the domination of another person; (5) that the defendant was only an accomplice to the murder, with a relatively minor degree of participation; and (6) that the victim somehow participated in the crime, either by consenting to the murder itself (i.e., requesting to be killed) or by being engaged with the defendant in the criminal actions that resulted in his or her death.

Some other common mitigating circumstances include that the defendant was suffering from an impaired ability to appreciate the wrongness of his or her actions or to conform his or her behavior to the law; that the defendant had a good-faith (but mistaken) belief that the crime was morally justified; that the defendant cooperated with law enforcement officers (perhaps in the apprehension of another felon); or that the defendant is likely to be rehabilitated or poses little continued threat to society. A few mitigating circumstances are unique to a single state. Kansas lists as a mitigating circumstance that the defendant was suffering from post-traumatic stress due to violence caused by the victim, which might be relevant in the case of a battered wife who murdered her husband. New Hampshire lists as a mitigating circumstance that another defendant who is equally culpable was *not* sentenced to death, which is intended to ensure that defendants involved in the same crime get comparable sentences, **See also** aggravating circumstances; *Bell v. Ohio; Lockett v. Ohio; Mills v. Maryland.*

Model Penal Code

The Model Penal Code is a suggested ideal model for criminal laws in the United States. The code is only a model and has no legal force. Jurisdictions with penal codes are welcome to borrow language from the Model Penal Code at their own discretion, but are under no obligation to do so.

The project of developing such a model was begun in 1951 by the American Law Institute. The American Law Institute is a group of eminent lawyers, judges, and legal scholars who regularly issue "restatements" of law aimed at providing guidance on how laws should be interpreted and applied. In 1951 criminal laws in most states consisted of a conglomeration of statutes enacted at one time or another as particular crimes gained political prominence. The statutes lacked a consistent theoretical underpinning and lacked coherent organizational principles. The members of the American Law Institute decided that a mere "restatement" would not be sufficient to bring order to the chaos of American criminal law. Instead, they decided to conduct the more ambitious project of attempting to create a model code. The head of the project was Herbert Weschler, a professor of law at Columbia University and one of the lawyers who had participated in the Nuremberg Trials at the end of World War II. He put together an advisory committee made up of distinguished judges, lawyers, and prison officials, as well as experts in criminal psychology and criminology. They worked together for over a decade on the project. A final draft of the Model Penal Code was published in 1962.

The Model Penal Code includes an extensive section on capital crimes. The code recommends that capital trials be separated into two phases: a guilt phase, at which the question of the defendant's guilt is settled, and a penalty phase, at which the question of the appropriate sentence is settled if the defendant is found guilty. The Model Penal Code suggests a list of eight aggravating circumstances for consideration during the penalty phase of the trial. At least one of these aggravating circumstances would have to be proved to have accompanied the crime for the death penalty to be imposed. The code also suggests a list of eight mitigating circumstances that might be considered sufficient for leniency in sentencing, despite the presence of aggravating circumstances.

The Model Penal Code has been extremely influential in American law. Many states began reforming their penal codes as soon as the Model Penal Code became available. However, the pace of reform was accelerated in 1972 when the *Furman v. Georgia* decision invalidated death-penalty statutes around the country. In 1976 the *Gregg v. Georgia* decision allowed states that had patterned their death-penalty statutes after the Model Penal Code to resume executions. Although there is still considerable variation from state to state, all death-penalty statutes in the United States now roughly follow the structure of the Model Penal Code. **See also** trial.

"Monsieur New York"

One of the most skillful hangmen in history worked in New York state from roughly 1850 to 1880. His identity was known only to the officials who hired him, and newspaper accounts of his hangings referred to him only as "Monsieur New York" or as "George." He was paid $100 per execution, plus expenses. According to newspaper accounts, he had originally worked as a butcher's assistant. He was hired by the sheriff of New York to conduct hangings when the previous hangman suddenly quit. "Monsieur New York" soon earned a reputation as a capable executioner, known for his "beautiful" work. He was even portrayed as having a bit of an artistic temperament. At an execution in New Jersey, which he was attending only as a spectator, he is reported to have pushed his way onto the gallows and conducted the execution himself rather than see the job bungled.

"Monsieur New York" successfully kept his identity a secret for thirty years, despite rumors and speculation, and it is still not known who he was. Whoever he was, he had a keen sense of the history and traditions of his profession. In choosing to be called "Monsieur New York," he was invoking the customary form of address used for French executioners of the eighteenth century. **See also** executioners; Sanson family.

Montana

Montana has traditionally permitted juries to impose the death penalty, and continues to do so currently. From 1863 to 1889, sixteen executions took place in Montana under territorial jurisdiction, all by hanging. Between 1889, when Montana became a state, and 1943, another fifty-five hangings took place. Thereafter, no executions took place in Montana until 1995.

Following the 1972 *Furman v. Georgia* ruling, which struck down Montana's death-penalty statute, the state passed a new death-penalty statute in 1974. Montana's current death-penalty statute allows jurors to consider the death penalty for homicide under special circumstances. These special circumstances are (1) that the defendant purposely and knowingly caused the death of another or (2) that the homicide occurred in the course of a robbery, sexual intercourse without consent, arson, burglary, kidnapping, escape from custody, or other felony involving the use of force.

The death penalty may be imposed if one of nine aggravating circumstances is proven to have accompanied the crime. The list of aggravating circumstances appears similar to the previous list of special circumstances, but aggravating circumstances are considered during the penalty phase of the trial rather than during the guilt phase. These aggravating circumstances are (1) that the homicide was deliberate and the defendant was under a sentence of imprisonment; (2) that the homicide was deliberate and the defendant was previously convicted of a deliberate homicide; (3) that the homicide was deliberate and involved the use of torture; (4) that the homicide was deliberate and involved lying in wait; (5) that the homicide was deliberate and involved a plan in which more than one person was the victim or intended victim; (6) that the homicide was deliberate and the victim was a police officer acting in the performance of his or her duties; (7) that the death of the victim occurred in the course of a kidnapping and was caused either by the defendant or by a person attempting the rescue of the victim; (8) that the defendant was incarcerated in a penal institution and previously convicted of deliberate homicide or had a record as a persistent felony offender; or (9) that the homicide was deliberate and committed in the course of sexual assault, nonconsensual intercourse, deviate sexual conduct, or incest, or the victim was less than eighteen years old. The jury must also consider any mitigating circumstances that the defense wishes to present.

Under Montana law, a person convicted of a capital offense cannot be executed if he or she was under the age of eighteen at the time of the crime. Montana does provide for life imprisonment without parole as an alternative to the death penalty. The governor has the authority to grant clemency only if he or she receives a favorable recommendation from the Board of Pardons, but the governor is not required to grant clemency on the board's recommendation.

In 1983 Montana made lethal gas an optional method of execution, allowing condemned prisoners to choose between lethal gas and hanging. However, no executions by either method took place. In 1995 convicted murderer Duncan McKenzie was executed by lethal injection. A bill making lethal injection Montana's sole method of execution was passed in 1997; the state executed Terry Langford by this method in 1998. As of June 2005, four people were awaiting execution on Montana's death row. **See also** Beidler, John X.; Regulators and Moderators.

Montesquieu, Baron de (Charles-Louis de Secondat) (1689–1755)

Charles-Louis de Secondat, Baron de Montesquieu, was a French social philosopher whose influential writings during the eighteenth century were largely responsible for changing the way people thought about the relationship between crimes and their punishments. His writings eventually changed the way people thought about capital punishment as well.

Montesquieu was born to aristocratic but not wealthy parents in Labrede, near Bordeaux. His mother died when he was seven, and he was put under the care of a childless uncle, from whom he inherited his title, estate, and the office of deputy president of the regional parliament of Bordeaux. In 1713 he married an heiress, Jeanne de Lantique, whose sizeable dowry made Montesquieu a wealthy man for life.

Well educated in the spirit of Enlightenment ideas and an avid student of the sciences and law, Montesquieu became a noted man of letters at the age of thirty-two with the publication of his first book, *Persian Letters*, in 1721. The book is presented as a correspondence between two visitors from Persia traveling separately through France who write to each other about the curious customs of the French. The book comments on and satirizes French society. In 1748 Montesquieu published *The Spirit of the Laws*, a rambling philosophical investigation of the reasons behind the laws of society. In general, the book argues that the laws of society can best be justified by appealing to "nature" or "natural law." Most modern philosophers dismiss Montesquieu's views on the grounds that he does not provide a clear understanding of "nature" and often uses "natural laws" to mean merely his own predilections and preferences. However, the book was enormously influential in its time. Among the important ideas to emerge from it are the idea of thwarting the tendency of societies to fall into tyranny by instituting a system of checks and balances (an idea that is fundamental to the U.S. Constitution) and the idea that punishments should be proportional to the crime being punished, an idea that sparked a movement to abolish the death penalty to punish robbery, burglary, and other crimes against property. **See also** opposition to capital punishment, history of (1648–1870); proportionality.

moratorium movement

Following the 1976 *Gregg v. Georgia* decision, which reinstated capital punishment in the United States, opponents of capital punishment were left to regroup and determine what direction their cause should take next. Capital punishment enjoyed broad popular support, so there was not much point in working for the abolition of capital punishment by trying to pass laws at the state level. At the same time, the Supreme Court was limiting the use of habeas corpus petitions, thus making it more difficult to bring constitutional challenges to capital punishment in the courts. However, the abolitionist movement was invigorated by evidence that a surprisingly large number of people on death row are innocent of the crime for which they were sentenced to death. New techniques for the analysis of DNA, the reliability and accuracy of which were established in the mid-1990s, have made it possible for investigators to reopen and reexamine evidence in some cases. This has resulted in a significant number of exonerations of death row inmates, although certainly not all exonerations involve DNA evidence. In two states, Pennsylvania and Illinois, more people have been taken off of death row since 1973 because of evidence establishing their innocence than because they were finally executed.

In 1999 the Nebraska legislature passed a bill placing a temporary moratorium on executions in the state. The bill also called for a study of the state's criminal justice system to determine whether the system was adequately preventing the conviction of innocent defendants. However, the governor vetoed the bill. In 2000 George Ryan, the governor of Illinois, used his executive authority to impose a moratorium on executions in Illinois. He then appointed a commission to study the problem.

The Illinois commission on capital punishment had fourteen members, including many prominent lawyers who had served either as prosecutors or as defenders (or both) on capital cases. It even included one person whose father had been murdered and whose grandfather had then killed the person responsible. The report returned by the commission made several recommendations. The commission noticed that a large number of convictions had been obtained based on false confessions. These confessions had been made under duress, and even in some cases under torture. The commission recommended that interrogations in capital cases be videotaped. The commission also recommended banning the death penalty when a conviction is based solely on the eyewitness testimony of a single individual or solely on the testimony of jailhouse informants who may be hoping for a lighter sentence. The commission recommended that the death penalty be available for only five specific categories of crime: multiple murder,

On December 26, 1862, thirty-eight Sioux warriors were hanged after being convicted of murder during an Indian uprising. It is the largest multiple execution in U.S. history.

murder of a police officer or firefighter, murder in prison, murder for the purpose of obstructing justice, and murder involving torture. In all, eighty-five changes in Illinois penal statutes were recommended. However, not all of the recommendations have so far been enacted, and Illinois's current governor, Rod Blagojevich, has chosen to keep the moratorium in place.

Supporters of the moratorium argue that the Illinois system of criminal justice is no less reliable than the system in any other state and that a possibly significant number of the death row inmates in other states are also innocent. With this in mind, people opposed to capital punishment are now trying to pressure other states to adopt moratoriums on execution at least while evidence, including DNA evidence, from old cases is reevaluated. **See also** DNA evidence; Ryan, George H.

Morgan v. Illinois

This was a case heard by the Supreme Court of the United States in 1992 concerning whether a court may refuse to allow prospective jurors to be asked whether they would automatically impose a sentence of death for the crime of murder, and whether prospective jurors should be excused for replying affirmatively to this question. The defendant in the case, Derrick Morgan, was charged with murder in Illinois. During jury selection, the judge did not permit defense attorneys to ask prospective jurors if they would automatically vote to impose the death penalty if they found the defendant guilty. Morgan was convicted and sentenced to death. The case was appealed on the grounds that the defense should have been permitted to question prospective jurors on whether they would automatically impose the death penalty and have them excused if they would. However, the Illinois Supreme Court upheld the conviction and sentence. The U.S. Supreme Court agreed to review the case.

In a 6-to-3 decision, the Supreme Court overturned Morgan's sentence and ordered that a new sentencing trial be held. Writing for the majority, Justice Byron White concluded that a juror who would automatically impose a sentence of death, without considering relevant aggravating and mitigating circumstances, was incapable of performing his or her duties as instructed by the trial court. Such a juror should be excused, and the defense was entitled to ask questions that would have revealed a prospective juror's opinions on this matter. **See also** death-qualified jury; *Wainwright v. Witt; Witherspoon v. Illinois.*

multiple executions

For various reasons, it has been common for more than one person to be executed on the same occasion. In some cases this has occurred merely because it was more efficient to conduct a joint execution rather than individual executions. For example, California's gas chamber (which is no longer in use) was built to accommodate two condemned prisoners at a time, and prisoners were often executed in pairs to reduce costs. Hangings, though less expensive than a gas chamber, were also often performed jointly to make the process more efficient. Since gallows were usually built for a particular occasion, it was not difficult to build a gallows that could accommodate as many people as necessary. One of the most notorious multiple hangings in U.S. history took place in the Arkansas territory in 1875 when six men were hanged together for unrelated crimes. The gallows on which they were hanged was a permanent gallows built by executioner George Maledon. It was designed to handle up to twelve at a time, but never had to accommodate more than six.

On other occasions, multiple executions occurred because multiple defendants accused of the same crime were tried, sentenced, and executed together. The following is a list of some of the largest multiple executions:

On January 27, 1689, eight men were hanged together for piracy in colonial Massachusetts.

On July 7, 1692, nine people (mostly women) were hanged for witchcraft in colonial Massachusetts as part of the infamous Salem witchcraft trials. Two months later, ten more people were hanged, on September 22, 1692.

On April 15, 1712, seven slaves were hanged in colonial New York for participating in a slave revolt. Twenty slaves were eventually hanged in connection with the revolt, but not all on the same day.

On November 8, 1718, twenty men were hanged for piracy in colonial South Carolina.

On July 19, 1723, twenty-six men were hanged for piracy in colonial Rhode Island.

Louisiana had several slave revolts that led to multiple hangings. Slave revolts took place in 1795, 1811, 1837, and 1840. Following the last revolt, twenty-seven people were executed, but the exact dates of the executions are not recorded.

On June 18, 1862, Confederate Georgia hanged seven men as Union spies.

On August 25, 1945, near the end of World War II, seven German prisoners of war who were being held at Fort Leavenworth were hanged for the beating and murder of a fellow inmate.

The largest multiple execution in U.S. history took place in Minnesota on December 26, 1862. On that day, thirty-eight Native Americans were hanged by the U.S. military on murder charges for participating in an Indian uprising. Initially, over three hundred Sioux warriors were captured and tried for participating in the uprising. Of these, 303 were sentenced to death, but President Abraham Lincoln, considering this number impossibly large, commuted the sentences of all but thirty-eight. A special gallows was built with a platform large enough to accommodate all thirty-eight men at the same time. **See also** Maledon, George; Minnesota.

murder

Murder is defined by *Black's Law Dictionary* as "the killing of a human being with malice aforethought." Murder is virtually the only crime that is still punishable by death in the United States, and not all forms of murder are now considered to be serious enough to merit the death penalty.

Not all actions that result in someone's death qualify as murder. For example, neither the killing of an enemy soldier in time of war nor the killing of a condemned prisoner by the designated executioner at the designated time are acts of murder. In legal contexts, *malice* means the intent to cause someone injury without justification or valid reason. The killing of an enemy soldier or a condemned prisoner does not count as murder because the killing is done for recognizably valid reasons, and so does not involve malice. Killing someone for money is not a recognizably valid reason, so such a killing *does* qualify as murder.

Most states distinguish in their criminal codes between two degrees of murder. However, while these distinctions are common, each state may draw its own distinctions.

First-degree murder. This refers to a deliberate or premeditated killing, one in which some prior planning is involved. The killer forms the intention to cause serious injury and then engages in a series of deliberate actions aimed at bringing that injury about. Poisoning, for example, is first-degree murder, since the killer must obtain the poison and somehow administer it to the victim, which requires considerable advance planning. A killing that involves lying in wait for the victim is also first-degree murder. A killing that occurs in the course of committing some other serious felony, such as rape, kidnapping, robbery, burglary, or arson, is also considered first-degree murder under many state statutes, since, even if the killing itself was not planned in advance, the felony that accompanied it required some degree of prior intention to cause harm.

Second-degree murder. This refers to a killing that is intentional but not willfully planned. In a second-degree murder, the killer forms the intention to kill immediately prior to killing, without formulating any particular plan to do so or without having engaged in prior actions aimed at causing injury. In cases in which the killer is judged to have been provoked, or some other extenuating circumstance is present, this charge is sometimes reduced to "voluntary manslaughter."

In addition to these two degrees of murder, some states identify other types of murder.

Depraved heart murder. This refers to a killing that results from an action showing "complete lack of regard for human life"—in other words, an action very likely to cause someone's death, even if the death of a specific person is not intended. Firing a gun into a crowd or driving a car on a sidewalk would qualify as murder of this type, if someone dies as a result.

Murder by torture. This refers to a killing in which the victim is made to suffer prior to being killed. Since torture requires premeditated action, murder by torture is a form of first-degree murder, but some states define it separately so it can receive a more severe penalty.

Serial murder. This refers to the killing of several victims on separate occasions. Each murder counts separately as a first-degree murder, and would normally be tried as individual crimes. Some states, however, allow a series of murders to be defined as a single, more serious crime to avoid separate trials and allow for a more severe penalty.

When the death of someone results from a criminal action but does not involve "malice aforethought," it is called manslaughter, not murder. Manslaughter is considered a much less serious crime than murder, and no jurisdiction in the United States currently punishes manslaughter with death. **See also** capital crimes.

Murray v. Giarratano

This was a case heard by the Supreme Court of the United States in 1989 concerning whether defendants have a right to an attorney while pursuing state-level appeals. Although a specific defendant is named, this case was brought as a class-action suit on behalf of indigent death row inmates in Virginia. The suit was brought in federal court against various Virginia court officials since Virginia does not provide free legal counsel to defendants who wish to pursue appeals in Virginia appeals courts. Such free legal counsel is provided by the federal government to defendants pursuing federal appeals, and many states provide free legal counsel for state-level appeals as well. Virginia, however, does not. The federal district court ruled in favor of the inmates, but the U.S. Supreme Court agreed to review the case.

In a 5-to-4 decision, the Supreme Court reversed the district court's decision and ruled that Virginia had no constitutional obligation to provide free legal counsel to indigent inmates for state-level appeals. Writing for the Court, Chief Justice William H. Rehnquist argued that states were not obligated under the Constitution to provide for an appeals process at all, and that in the case of a capital trial, the automatic review already required (and for which an attorney is provided, if necessary) should be sufficient to ensure a defendant's right to due process. While states may provide more, they are under no constitutional obligation to do so. **See also** racial discrimination in sentencing.

NAACP Legal Defense and Education Fund

The NAACP Legal Defense and Education Fund (LDEF) was at one time the legal arm of the National Association for the Advancement of Colored People (NAACP), but in 1957 it became an independent organization. In its capacity of providing legal assistance to racial minorities pursuing civil rights claims, the LDEF has been associated with some of the most important legal challenges to the death penalty in the United States.

The LDEF first played a pivotal role in the civil rights movement, helping to bring several landmark cases to the Supreme Court that eventually led to the desegregation of schools and the implementation of affirmative action policies at state-funded colleges and universities. Among these cases was the historic 1954 *Brown v. Board of Education* case. The LDEF also played a pivotal role in litigation leading up to the historic 1972 *Furman v. Georgia* decision that briefly abolished capital punishment in the United States. Although the LDEF was not originally concerned with capital punishment per se, it was clear in the 1950s and 1960s that racial minorities, particularly blacks, were sentenced to death far more frequently than whites, and for far less serious crimes. In taking on the defense of individual black clients, LDEF lawyers soon found that it was necessary to lodge appeals on broad constitutional grounds, whether or not these grounds involved questions of race. Most of the capital punishment cases that reached the Supreme Court between 1962 and 1972 were funded in part by the LDEF.

Today the LDEF continues to oppose capital punishment, chiefly on the grounds that it is still applied in a discriminatory manner that unfairly affects poor and minority defendants. **See also** racial discrimination in sentencing.

National Coalition to Abolish the Death Penalty

The National Coalition to Abolish the Death Penalty (NCADP) is a coalition of regional and national organizations that share the goal of abolishing capital punishment in the United States. The coalition was founded in 1976, and is currently one of the most active and influential anti-death-penalty organizations in the United States. It currently includes approximately 120 affiliated organizations, with a total membership of roughly 3,000. Among other activities, the NCADP distributes a newsletter, *Lifelines/Execution Alert*, which notifies members of upcoming executions. The newsletter has a circulation of about 9,000 and is distributed internationally. **See also** NAACP Legal Defense and Education Fund.

Nebraska

Nebraska has traditionally permitted juries to impose the death penalty, and

Members of the NCADP march in St. Louis in 1998 to protest capital punishment. The coalition represents anti-death-penalty groups nationwide.

continues to do so currently. No executions are recorded in territorial Nebraska or for about twelve years after Nebraska became a state in 1867. However, twenty-four executions by hanging occurred between 1879 and 1913. One of the executed men, William Marion, hanged in 1887, was later given a posthumous pardon when the man he was convicted of killing was seen alive four years after Marion's execution. In 1913 Nebraska replaced hanging with electrocution as its method of execution. Between 1920 and 1959, twelve executions took place using Nebraska's electric chair.

Following the 1972 *Furman v. Georgia* ruling, which struck down Nebraska's death-penalty statute, the state quickly passed a new death-penalty statute in 1973. Nebraska's current death-penalty statute allows jurors to consider the death penalty for homicide under special circumstances. These special circumstances are (1) that the homicide was intentional (i.e., performed with deliberate and premeditated malice); (2) that the homicide occurred in the course of a sexual assault, arson, robbery, kidnapping, burglary, or the hijacking of a public or private means of transportation; or (3) that the homicide was committed by means of poison. It is also a capital offense to commit perjury or the suborning of perjury when this results in the sentencing and execution of an innocent person.

The death penalty may be imposed if one of nine aggravating circumstances is proven to have accompanied the crime. These aggravating circumstances are (1) that the defendant was previously convicted of murder or of a felony involving violence, or that the defendant had a substantial history of criminal activity involving violence; (2) that the homicide was committed in order to conceal a crime or the identity of a person committing a crime; (3) that the homicide was a murder-for-hire and the defendant either performed the murder or solicited another to perform the murder; (4) that the homicide was especially heinous, atrocious, and cruel; (5) that the defendant committed another murder at the same time; (6) that the defendant knowingly created a great risk of death to many people; (7) that the victim was known to the defendant to be a public servant acting in the performance of his or her duties, with lawful custody over the defendant (or someone else); (8) that the homicide was committed in order to disrupt a governmental function or the enforcement of the law; or (9) that the victim was known to the defendant to be a law enforcement officer acting in the performance of his or her duties. The jury must also consider any mitigating circumstances that the defense wishes to present.

Under Nebraska law, a person convicted of a capital offense cannot be executed if he or she was under the age of eighteen at the time of the crime. Nebraska does provide for life imprisonment without parole as an alternative to the death penalty. The authority to grant clemency is vested in a special executive panel on which the governor sits.

Although Nebraska was quick to reinstate the death penalty, executions did not resume until 1994. Between 1994 and 1997, only three executions took place in Nebraska, all by electrocution. Nebraska is the only state that has not adopted lethal injection as at least an optional method of execution, and is currently the only state that still uses an electric chair. In 1999 the Nebraska legislature ordered a study of death-penalty procedures in the state and at the same time tried to place a moratorium on executions until the study could be completed. Nebraska's governor vetoed the moratorium and attempted to veto the study, but that veto was overridden. Nevertheless, no executions have taken place in Nebraska since the study began. As of April 2005, nine people were awaiting execution on Nebraska's death row. **See also** moratorium movement.

Nevada

Nevada has traditionally permitted juries to impose the death penalty, and continues to do so currently. Prior to 1903, executions occurred under the jurisdiction of county governments and were the responsibility of local sheriffs. Consequently, the number of executions performed is uncertain, but between 1861, when the Nevada territory was established, and 1903, at least twenty executions by hanging are known to have occurred. In 1901 the Nevada legislature passed a law requiring that, beginning in 1903, all executions would take place at the state prison in Carson City. The first such execution took place in 1905. Ten people were hanged at the state prison between 1905 and 1921. In 1911 the law was changed to allow a condemned prisoner to choose between hanging and a firing squad. Only one person elected to be shot. That was Andriza Mircovich from Montenegro, who was executed in 1913.

In 1921 Nevada became the first state in the United States to adopt lethal gas as its method of execution. In 1924 a Chinese gangster, Gee Jon, was the first person in the country to be executed by this means. Thirty-two people were executed by lethal gas in Nevada between 1924 and 1961.

Following the 1972 *Furman v. Georgia* ruling, which struck down Nevada's death-penalty statute, the state passed a new death-penalty statute in 1977. Nevada's current death-penalty statute allows jurors to consider the death penalty for (1) homicide perpetrated by means of poison, lying in wait, torture or child abuse, or any other clearly premeditated killing; (2) homicide committed in the course of sexual assault, kidnapping, arson, robbery, burglary, invasion of the home, sexual abuse of a child, or sexual molestation of a child under fourteen years old; or (3) homicide committed to avoid or prevent the lawful arrest of any person by a police officer or to effect the escape of any person from legal custody.

The death penalty may be imposed if at least one of thirteen aggravating circumstances is proven to have accompanied the crime. The list of aggravating circumstances appears similar to the previous list of special circumstances, but aggravating circumstances are considered during the penalty phase of the trial rather than during the guilt phase. These aggravating circumstances are (1) that the defendant was under sentence of imprisonment; (2) that the defendant was convicted of another murder or a felony involving violence; (3) that the defendant knowingly created a great risk of death to more than one person; (4) that the homicide was committed in the course of robbery, arson, burglary, invasion of a home, or kidnapping; (5) that the homicide was committed to avoid lawful arrest or to escape from custody; (6) that the homicide was committed for monetary gain; (7) that the victim was a police officer, corrections officer, or fire-fighter; (8) that the homicide was especially heinous and cruel, involving mutilation or torture; (9) that one or more victims were killed at random, without apparent motive; (10) that the victim was under fourteen years old; (11) that the homicide was a hate crime, committed because of the victim's perceived race, color, religion, national origin, disability, or sexual orientation; (12) that the defendant had been convicted of a previous murder; or (13) that the homicide occurred in the course of a rape. The jury must also consider any mitigating circumstances that the defense wishes to present.

A Nevada law that allows the death penalty for sixteen- and seventeen-year-old offenders was invalidated in March 2005 when the Supreme Court abolished capital punishment for juveniles. Nevada does provide for life imprisonment without parole as an alternative to the death penalty. A special panel on which the governor sits has the authority to grant clemency. The governor must vote with the majority for clemency to be granted.

Nevada resumed executions in 1979 with the execution of Jesse Bishop, who was convicted of murder. Bishop was the last person to be executed by lethal gas in Nevada. In 1983 Nevada replaced lethal gas with lethal injection as its method of execution. Since 1983, there have been nine executions by lethal injection in Nevada. As of June 2005, eighty-six people were awaiting execution on Nevada's death row. **See also** gas chamber; Gee Jon.

New Hampshire

New Hampshire has traditionally permitted juries to impose the death penalty, and continues to do so currently, although the number of executions in New Hampshire has always been quite small. Only four people were executed in colonial New Hampshire, all by hanging and all for the crime of murder. Between 1788 and 1868, eight more hangings took place, carried out by local sheriffs. The New Hampshire State Prison was built in 1810, but executions were not centralized at the state prison until 1869. Between 1869 and 1939, only twelve executions took place. The last execution in New Hampshire was the hanging of Howard Long for murder in 1939.

Following the 1972 *Furman v. Georgia* ruling, which struck down New Hampshire's death-penalty statute, the state did not pass a new death-penalty statute until 1991. New Hampshire's current death-penalty statute allows jurors to consider the death penalty for homicide under special circumstances. These special circumstances are (1) that the victim was a law enforcement officer or a judicial officer acting in the line of duty, or the homicide was in retaliation for actions performed by such an officer acting in the line of duty; (2) that the homicide occurred in the course of a kidnapping; (3) that the homicide was a murder-for-hire and the defendant either performed the murder or solicited another to perform the murder; (4) that the defendant was sentenced to life imprisonment without parole; (5) that the homicide occurred in the course of a felonious sexual assault; or (6) that the homicide occurred in the course of a drug-related offense.

The death penalty may be imposed if one of ten aggravating circumstances is proven to have accompanied the crime. In contrast to special circumstances, aggravating circumstances are considered during the penalty phase of the trial rather than during the guilt phase. These aggravating circumstances are (1) that the homicide was intentional; (2) that the defendant was previously convicted of a homicide punishable by life imprisonment or death; (3) that the defendant was previously convicted of two or more offenses involving serious bodily injury to another and punishable by a sentence of imprisonment for more than one year; (4) that the defendant was previously convicted of two or more offenses involving the distribution of controlled substances and punishable by a sentence of imprisonment for more than one year; (5) that the defendant knowingly created a great risk of death to people other than the victim; (6) that the homicide was committed after substantial planning and premeditation; (7) that the victim was particularly vulnerable; (8) that the homicide was especially heinous, cruel, and depraved, involving torture or physical abuse of the victim; (9) that the homicide was committed for monetary gain; or (10) that the homicide was committed in order to avoid arrest or escape from custody. The jury must also consider any mitigating circumstances that the defense wishes to present.

New Hampshire does provide for life imprisonment without parole as an alternative to the death penalty. The governor has sole authority to grant clemency, but is required to get a nonbinding recommendation from the Governor's Council before making a decision.

In 1986 New Hampshire replaced hanging with lethal injection as its preferred method of execution, although hanging is available for cases in which lethal injection is deemed "impractical." Although New Hampshire has a death-penalty statute in place, no one has been executed in New Hampshire since 1939, and no one is currently awaiting execution on New Hampshire's death row. **See also** *Furman v. Georgia*.

New Jersey

New Jersey has traditionally permitted juries to impose the death penalty, and continues to do so currently. Between 1690 and 1775, sixty-five people were executed in colonial New Jersey. Most of the executions were by hanging, but twelve were executions by burning of black slaves who had murdered their masters. A variety of crimes are represented, including robbery, burglary, arson, horse stealing, rape, counterfeiting, and murder. Between 1780 and 1906, an additional 135 hangings took place in New Jersey.

In 1907 New Jersey replaced hanging with electrocution as its method of execution and centralized responsibility for executions at the New Jersey State Prison. A special Capital Sentence Unit was opened in 1907 large enough to house six inmates. This unit was enlarged in 1932 to house eighteen inmates, and it was enlarged again in 1966 to house twenty-six inmates. However, the last execution in New Jersey took place three years earlier, in 1963. Between 1907 and 1963, 160 executions by electrocution took place in New Jersey.

Following the 1972 *Furman v. Georgia* ruling, which struck down New Jersey's death-penalty statute, the state passed a new death-penalty statute in 1982. New Jersey's current death-penalty statute allows jurors to consider the death penalty for homicide under special circumstances. These special circumstances include that the offender purposely or knowingly caused death or serious injury resulting in death; that the offender procured the commission of the homicide by offering payment; or that the offender was a leader in a drug-trafficking network and ordered the homicide in the course of drug-trafficking activities.

The death penalty may be imposed if one of eleven aggravating circumstances is proven to have accompanied the crime. The list of aggravating circumstances appears similar to the special circumstances noted above, but aggravating circumstances are considered during the penalty phase of the trial rather than during the guilt phase. These aggravating circumstances are (1) that the defendant was previously convicted of another murder; (2) that the defendant knowingly created a great risk of death to someone other than the victim; (3) that the homicide was wantonly vile, involving torture; (4) that the defendant was hired by someone else to commit the homicide; (5) that the defendant hired someone else to commit the homicide; (6) that the homicide was committed in order to escape lawful arrest, detention, trial, or punishment; (7) that the homicide occurred in the course of a murder (of someone other than the victim), robbery, sexual assault, arson, burglary, kidnapping, or the crime of contempt; (8) that the victim was a public servant acting in the performance of his or her duties or that the homicide was committed because of the nature of those duties; (9) that, as part of a narcotics trafficking conspiracy, the defendant ordered the homicide committed or committed the homicide under the direction of someone else; (10) that the homicide was committed by means of an explosion, flood, avalanche, or collapse of a building, or by the release of poison gas, radioactive material, or other harmful substance; and (11) that the victim was under fourteen years old. The jury must also consider any mitigating circumstances that the defense wishes to present.

Under New Jersey law, a person convicted of a capital offense cannot be executed if he or she was under the age of eighteen at the time of the crime. New Jersey does provide for life imprisonment without parole as an alternative to the death penalty. The governor has the authority to grant clemency.

In 1983 New Jersey replaced electrocution with lethal injection as its method of execution. However, no executions have taken place in New Jersey since the death penalty was reenacted. As of June 2005, fifteen people were awaiting execution on New Jersey's death row. **See also** *Furman v. Georgia.*

New Mexico

New Mexico has traditionally permitted juries to impose the death penalty, and continues to do so currently. About forty-six executions by hanging took place in New Mexico under territorial jurisdiction between 1851 and 1907. New Mexico became a state in 1912, but executions continued to be conducted under the jurisdiction of county governments until 1929. Eighteen such executions by hanging are known to have taken place. In 1929 New Mexico adopted the electric chair as its method of execution and ordered that executions take place at the state penitentiary in Sante Fe. The first execution by electrocution took place in 1933. In all, seven executions using the electric chair took place in New Mexico. Then, in 1955, the use of the electric chair was discontinued in favor of execution by lethal gas. In 1960 David Cooper Nelson, convicted of robbery and murder, was the only person to be executed in New Mexico's gas chamber.

New Mexico abolished capital punishment in 1969, so New Mexico did not have a death-penalty statute in effect when the 1972 *Furman v. Georgia* ruling struck down death-penalty statutes around the country. However, following the 1976 *Gregg v. Georgia* decision, which reinstated capital punishment in states with revised death-penalty statutes, New Mexico also reenacted the death penalty, passing a new death-penalty statute in 1979. New Mexico's current death-penalty statute allows jurors to consider the death penalty for homicide under special circumstances. These special circumstances are (1) that the homicide was willful, deliberate, or premeditated; (2) that the homicide occurred in the course of another felony; or (3) that the homicide occurred in the course of activities greatly dangerous to the lives of others, indicating a depraved mind and reckless disregard for human life.

The death penalty may be imposed if one of seven aggravating circumstances is proven to have accompanied the crime. The list of aggravating circumstances appears similar to the previous list of special circumstances, but aggravating circumstances are considered during the penalty phase of the trial rather than during the

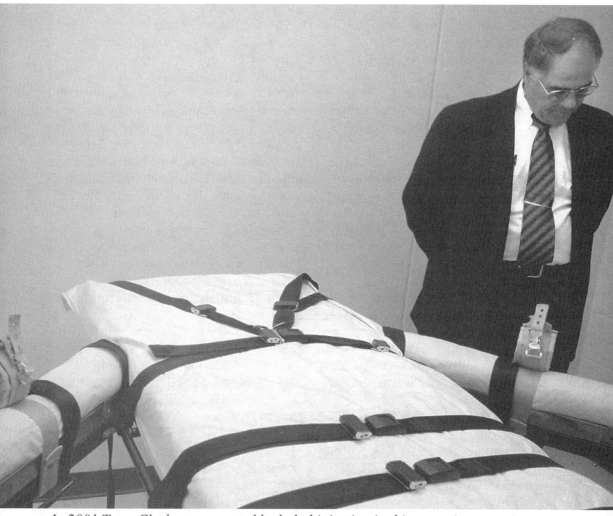

In 2001 Terry Clark was executed by lethal injection in this execution room in a Santa Fe, New Mexico, prison.

guilt phase. These aggravating circumstances are (1) that the victim was a police officer performing his or her official duties; (2) that the homicide occurred in the course of a kidnapping, child molestation, or other sex crime; (3) that the homicide occurred in the course of attempting to escape from a New Mexico penal institution; (4) that the defendant was incarcerated in a New Mexico penal institution and murdered a visitor or another inmate of that institution; (5) that the defendant was incarcerated in a New Mexico penal institution and murdered an employee of that institution; (6) that the defendant was hired to commit the homicide; or (7) that the victim was a witness to a crime and the homicide was committed either to prevent the victim's testimony or in retaliation for that testimony. The jury must also consider any mitigating circumstances that the defense wishes to present.

Under New Mexico law, a person convicted of a capital offense cannot be executed if he or she was under the age of eighteen at the time of the crime. New Mexico does provide for life imprisonment without parole as an alternative to the death penalty. The governor has the authority to grant clemency, but may not grant an unlimited number of reprieves to any given inmate.

In 1980 New Mexico replaced lethal gas with lethal injection as its method of execution. However, it was not until 2001 that an execution took place in New Mexico. So far, Terry Clark, executed by lethal injection on November 6, 2001, has been the only person executed in New Mexico since the resumption of executions. As of June 2005, two people were awaiting execution on New Mexico's death row. **See also** *Furman v. Georgia;* lethal injection.

New York

New York has traditionally permitted juries to impose the death penalty. However, New York's death-penalty statute was declared unconstitutional by the New York Supreme Court in June 2004, so the death penalty is currently in abeyance in New York.

Between 1641 and 1773, ninety-two executions took place in colonial New York. Two major slave revolts account for over half of these executions. A slave revolt in 1712 ended with the execution of twenty black slaves; a slave revolt in 1741 ended with the execution of thirty-two black slaves. Not all of the slaves were hanged. Some were burned, others were displayed on a pillory, and still others were broken on the wheel. For other crimes, which included piracy, counterfeiting, and horse stealing, as well as murder, hanging was the usual method of execution.

Between 1778 and 1889, 330 people were hanged by the state of New York. The executions took place in the county where the crime was committed and were performed by local sheriffs. In 1888 the New York legislature passed a law replacing hanging with electrocution as the state's method of execution for inmates sentenced after the new law took effect. New York was the first state to adopt the electric chair for executions, and was also the first state to abolish executions by county officials and require that all executions take place directly under state jurisdiction at the state penitentiary. The first execution by electrocution took place in 1890 with the execution of William Kemmler. Between 1890 and 1963, 624 people were executed in New York's electric chair, the largest number of executions by electrocution to take place in any state.

New York abolished capital punishment in 1965, so New York did not have a death-penalty statute in effect when the 1972 *Furman v. Georgia* ruling struck down death-penalty statutes around the country. However, New York moved promptly to restore capital punishment following the *Furman* decision, passing a revised death-penalty statute in 1973. New York then abolished capital punishment in 1978, only two years after the 1976 *Gregg v. Georgia* decision reauthorized executions under the revised death-penalty statute. New York remained without a death-penalty statute until 1995, when the legislature again voted to restore capital punishment in New York. New York might have reenacted capital punishment sooner except that from 1982 to 1994 Governor Mario Cuomo vetoed every bill reauthorizing capital punishment that was passed by the state legislature.

New York's death-penalty statute (which was declared unconstitutional in 2004) allows jurors to consider the death penalty for homicide when it is committed under special circumstances. The law then provides a list of twelve such circumstances, which are (1) that the victim was known to the defendant to be a police office performing his or her official duties; (2) that the victim was known to the defendant to be a court officer, parole officer, probation officer, or juvenile corrections officer performing his or her official duties; (3) that the victim was known to the defendant to be an employee of a state or local correctional institution performing his or her official duties; (4) that the defendant was under a sentence of imprisonment for a term of at least fifteen years or longer; (5) that the victim was a witness to a crime and the homicide was somehow connected to the victim's role as a witness; (6) that the homicide was a murder-for-hire and the defendant either performed the murder or solicited another to perform the murder; (7) that the homicide occurred in the course of a robbery, burglary, kidnapping, arson, rape, sodomy, sexual abuse, escape from custody, or murder in the second degree; (8) that the homicide resulted in the death of an additional person who was not an accomplice to the offense; (9) that the defendant was previously convicted of murder; (10) that the homicide was especially wanton and cruel or involved the use of torture; (11) that the defendant had killed two or more other people within the state in the previous two years (i.e., that the defendant was a serial killer); or (12) that the victim was a judge and the homicide was somehow connected to the victim's role as a judge.

The New York statute does not provide a separate list of aggravating circumstances to be considered during the penalty phase of the trial. Whatever special circumstances are proven to have accompanied the crime at the guilt phase of the trial are considered to stand as aggravating circumstances for purposes of the penalty phase. The jury then only needs to consider whether any mitigating circumstances are also present that might lead them to reject a penalty of death.

Under New York law, a person convicted of a capital offense cannot be executed if he or she was under the age of eighteen at the time of the crime. New York does provide for life imprisonment without parole as an alternative to the death penalty. The governor has the authority to commute a death sentence to a sentence of life imprisonment without parole.

In 1995 the New York legislature, besides reenacting the death penalty, also adopted lethal injection as its method of execution. However, no one so far has been executed by lethal injection in New York. New York's Supreme Court invalidated New York's death-penalty statute in June 2004. Two of the four people then on death row in the state have since been resentenced; the remaining two await resentencing. **See also** electric chair; Kemmler, William.

North Carolina

North Carolina has traditionally permitted juries to impose the death penalty, and continues to do so currently. Between 1726 and 1775, ninety-eight executions, mostly by hanging, took place in colonial North Carolina. There were four executions by burning of black slaves accused of murder. Murder was the most common crime punished by execution, although in many cases the precise felony committed is not recorded. Nearly all of those executed were slaves, and this continued to be true following the American Revolution as well. Slave uprisings resulted in twenty-three hangings in 1802. In 1864 twenty-two men were hanged for desertion from the Confederate army, nineteen of them on the same day, April 20. Except for these hangings, which took place under the jurisdiction of the Confederate military, executions were conducted by local county sheriffs until 1910. Between 1777 and 1910, 299 executions by hanging took place in North Carolina. In 1909, besides centralizing executions at Central Prison in Raleigh, North Carolina replaced hanging with electrocution as its method of execution. Between 1910 and 1936, 163 people were executed in North Carolina's electric chair. In 1935 North Carolina replaced electrocution with lethal gas as the state's method of execution, although a few executions by electrocution continued to take place until 1938, for people sentenced before the new law took effect. Between 1936 and 1961, 194 people were executed in North Carolina's gas chamber.

Following the 1972 *Furman v. Georgia* ruling, which struck down North Carolina's death-penalty statute, the state passed a new death-penalty statute in 1977. North Carolina's current death-penalty statute allows jurors to consider the death penalty for homicide under special circumstances. These special circumstances include that the homicide was willful, deliberate, and premeditated—in particular, if it involved poison, lying in wait, imprisonment, starving, or torture—or that the homicide occurred in the course of arson, rape or other sexual offense, robbery, kidnapping, burglary, or any felony involving the use of a deadly weapon.

The death penalty may be imposed if one of eleven aggravating circumstances is proven to have accompanied the crime. The list of aggravating circumstances appears similar to the special circumstances noted above, but aggravating circumstances are considered during the penalty phase of the trial rather than during the guilt phase. These aggravating circumstances are (1) that the defendant was lawfully incarcerated; (2) that the defendant was previously convicted of a capital felony or was previously judged guilty of a juvenile offense that would have been a capital felony if committed by an adult; (3) that the defendant was previously convicted of a felony involving violence or was previously judged guilty of a juvenile offense that would have been a felony involving violence if committed by an adult; (4) that the homicide was committed in order to avoid arrest or escape from custody; (5) that the homicide occurred in the course of another homicide, robbery, rape or other sexual offense, arson, burglary, kidnapping, aircraft piracy, or the unlawful discharge of a destructive device such as a bomb; (6) that the homicide was committed for monetary gain; (7) that the homicide was committed in order to disrupt a governmental function or the enforcement of the law; (8) that the victim was a law enforcement officer, employee of the Department of Corrections, jailer, firefighter, judge, prosecutor, juror, or witness against the defendant; (9) that the homicide was especially heinous, atrocious, and cruel; (10) that the defendant knowingly created a great risk of death to more than one person by means of a device (such as a bomb) that would normally endanger more than one person; or (11) that the homicide occurred in the course of other crimes of violence against people other than the victim. The jury must also consider any mitigating circumstances that the defense wishes to present.

Under North Carolina law, a person convicted of a capital offense cannot be executed if he or she was under the age of eighteen at the time of the crime. North Carolina does provide for life imprisonment without parole as an alternative to the death penalty. The governor has the authority to grant clemency.

In 1983 North Carolina added lethal injection as an optional method of execution, allowing condemned prisoners to choose to be executed by lethal injection or lethal gas. Since 1984, thirty-one executions have taken place in North Carolina. Only two inmates selected lethal gas; the remainder selected lethal injection. In 1998 North Carolina retired its gas chamber and dropped lethal gas as an optional method of execution. As of June 2005, 197 people were awaiting execution on North Carolina's death row. **See also** *Furman v. Georgia.*

North Dakota

North Dakota does not currently permit juries to impose the death penalty. Capital punishment was permitted under the penal code of the Dakota territory, which was patterned after the penal code of New York and adopted by the territory in 1865. This code remained in effect when North Dakota became a state in 1889. However, only eight people were executed between 1865 and 1915, when the state legislature abolished capital punishment for all crimes except the murder of a prison guard by an inmate already serving a life sentence. No one was ever executed under this law, and in 1975 capital punishment was abolished completely in the state. The North Dakota legislature considered a bill reinstating capital punishment in 1995, but the measure was defeated. The last person to be executed in North Dakota was John Rooney in 1905.

Ocuish, Hannah (1774–1786)

Hannah Ocuish is believed to be the youngest person ever executed in the United States. She was twelve years old at the time of her execution. She was described as a mulatto (a term sometimes used to describe people of mixed race) since she was part Native American. She lived on her own in New London, Connecticut, having been abandoned by her parents at an early age. Another child, six-year-old Eunice Bolles, accused her of stealing strawberries. Apparently there was a fight, and Eunice Bolles was killed. Hannah Ocuish was charged with her murder, convicted, and sentenced to death. She was executed by hanging on December 20, 1786. At her execution, at least two preachers delivered sermons on the importance of children being obedient to their parents. **See also** juvenile offenders; repentance.

Ohio

Ohio has traditionally permitted juries to impose the death penalty, and continues to do so currently. Prior to 1885, executions by hanging were conducted by local jurisdictions. Roughly eighty-seven executions are known to have taken place. In 1885 Ohio centralized its executions at the Ohio State Penitentiary in Columbus, but hanging remained the method used. In 1897 Ohio became one of the first states to replace hanging with electrocution. An Ohio prison inmate, Charles Justice, helped to build and install Ohio's electric chair, which came to be known as "Old Sparky." The first person executed in it was a seventeen-year-old juvenile, William Haas, who was convicted of murder. In 1911 Charles Justice, the inmate who had helped build Old Sparky, was arrested on murder charges and executed in the chair he had helped create. Between 1897 and 1963, 315 people were executed in Ohio's electric chair.

Following the 1972 *Furman v. Georgia* ruling, which struck down Ohio's death-penalty statute, the state passed a new death-penalty statute in 1974. However, this statute was declared unconstitutional in 1978. With no death-penalty statute in place, the sentences of all of the one hundred inmates then on Ohio's death row were commuted to life imprisonment. In 1981 the Ohio legislature tried again to reinstate the death penalty and this time was successful. Ohio's current death-penalty statute allows jurors to consider the death penalty for homicide under special circumstances. These special circumstances include that the homicide involved calculation and design; that it occurred in the course of a kidnapping, rape, arson, robbery, burglary, or escape from custody; or that the offender was in detention (or had escaped from detention) having been found guilty of a felony. The intentional killing of a law enforcement officer or of someone under the age of thirteen is also a capital offense. The unlawful termination of another person's pregnancy is a capital offense if it is done either intentionally (involving calculation and design) or in the course of one of the crimes listed above.

The death penalty may be imposed if one of nine aggravating circumstances is proven to have accompanied the crime. The list of aggravating circumstances appears similar to the special circumstances noted above, but aggravating circumstances are considered during the penalty phase of the trial rather than during the guilt phase. These aggravating circumstances are (1) that the victim was the president of the United States, someone in the line of succession to the presidency, the governor or lieutenant governor of Ohio, the president-elect or vice president-elect of the United States, the governor-elect or lieutenant governor-elect of Ohio, or a candidate for any of these offices; (2) that the defendant was hired by someone to commit the homicide; (3) that the homicide was committed in order to escape detection, arrest, trial, or punishment for another offense; (4) that the defendant was under lawful detention or had escaped from detention; (5) that the defendant was previously convicted of a crime involving a killing or attempted killing, or the current offense involves the killing or attempted killing of the two or more people; (6) that the victim was a law enforcement officer; (7) that the homicide was committed in the course of a kidnapping, rape, arson, robbery, or burglary in which the defendant was the principal offender or in which the defendant committed murder with prior planning and design; (8) that the victim was a witness

The state of Ohio's electric chair, nicknamed Old Sparky, was one of the first such devices to be used in the American penal system.

and the homicide was committed to prevent the victim's testimony or in retaliation for the victim's testimony; or (9) that the homicide was intentional and the victim was under the age of thirteen. The jury must also consider any mitigating circumstances that the defense wishes to present.

Under Ohio law, a person convicted of a capital offense cannot be executed if he or she was under the age of eighteen at the time of the crime. Ohio does provide for life imprisonment without parole as an alternative to the death penalty. The governor has the authority to grant clemency for most crimes, but is required to get a nonbinding recommendation from the Adult Parole Authority. In the case of first-degree murder, the governor cannot grant a pardon unless proof is offered establishing innocence beyond a reasonable doubt.

In 1993 the state legislature adopted lethal injection as Ohio's primary method of execution, but retained electrocution as an option. The first person executed in Ohio after the reinstatement of capital punishment was Wilford Berry. Berry, who was thought to be suffering from mental illness, waived his appeals and fired his attorneys, who had been attempting to prevent his execution. He was executed by lethal injection in 1999. In 2001 Old Sparky was retired from service, leaving lethal injection as the sole available method of execution in Ohio. Since 1999, fifteen people have been executed by lethal injection in Ohio. As of April 2005, 198 people were awaiting execution on Ohio's death row. **See also** electric chair; *Furman v. Georgia.*

Oklahoma

Oklahoma has traditionally permitted juries to impose the death penalty, and continues to do so currently. According to surviving records, most of the people executed in early Oklahoma were executed by hanging or shooting for the crime of murder. They were executed under the jurisdiction of Indian tribunals, since Oklahoma was land set aside for Native Americans. Some thirty-four executions are known to have taken place under tribal jurisdiction. In 1899 Oklahoma was taken away from Native American control and became a territory. Eight years later Oklahoma became a state. Only six executions by hanging took place under territorial jurisdiction from 1899 to 1907. In 1907, after becoming a state, Oklahoma adopted electrocution as its method of execution and centralized executions at the state penitentiary. However, executions by hanging continued until 1911. Seven such executions took place. Between 1915 and 1966, eighty-two people were executed by electrocution in Oklahoma. One prisoner under federal jurisdiction was hanged in 1936, since federal law did not provide for execution by electrocution at that time. The last person to be executed by electrocution in Oklahoma was convicted murderer James French in 1966.

Following the 1972 *Furman v. Georgia* ruling, which struck down Oklahoma's death-penalty statute, the state quickly passed a new death-penalty statute in 1973. Oklahoma's current death-penalty statute allows jurors to consider the death penalty for homicide under special circumstances. These special circumstances are (1) that the homicide was committed intentionally (i.e., with malice aforethought); (2) that the homicide occurred in the course of the murder of another person, discharge of a weapon with intent to kill, discharge of a weapon into a building, forcible rape, robbery with a dangerous weapon, kidnapping, escape from custody, burglary, arson, or dispensing or trafficking in controlled substances or illegal drugs; (3) that the victim was a child and the defendant willfully caused, procured, or permitted injury, torturing, or maiming of the child, resulting in the child's death; or (4) that the defendant solicited or caused another's death in the course of illegally manufacturing or distributing controlled substances.

The death penalty may be imposed if one of eight aggravating circumstances is proven to have accompanied the crime. The list of aggravating circumstances appears similar to the previous list of special circumstances, but aggravating circumstances are considered during the penalty phase of the trial rather than during the guilt phase. These aggravating circumstances are (1) that the defendant was previously convicted of a felony involving the threat or use of violence; (2) that the defendant knowingly created a great risk of harm to more than one person; (3) that the homicide was a murder-for-hire and the defendant either performed the murder or solicited another to perform the murder; (4) that the homicide was heinous, atrocious, or cruel; (5) that the homicide was committed to avoid arrest or prosecution; (6) that the defendant was serving a sentence of imprisonment for another felony; (7) that the defendant probably poses a continuing threat to society; or (8) that the victim was a police officer or corrections officer performing his or her official duties. The jury must also consider any mitigating circumstances that the defense wishes to present.

Under Oklahoma law, a person convicted of a capital offense cannot be executed if he or she was under the age of sixteen at the time of the crime. This law was invalidated in March 2005 when the Supreme Court abolished capital punishment for juveniles. Oklahoma does provide for life imprisonment without parole as an alternative to the death penalty. The governor has the authority to grant clemency only if he or she receives a favorable recommendation from the Pardon and Parole Board.

In 1977 Oklahoma replaced electrocution with lethal injection as its method of execution. Oklahoma and Texas were the first two states to adopt this new method of execution. However, while Oklahoma was quick to reinstate capital punishment, executions did not resume until 1990. Since 1990, a total of sixty-seven people have been executed by lethal injection in Oklahoma. As of June 2005, ninety-eight people were awaiting execution on Oklahoma's death row. **See also** *Furman v. Georgia*.

opposition to capital punishment, history of (1648–1870)

Prior to the eighteenth century, there was no organized opposition to capital punishment, an accepted punishment around the world since ancient times. The earliest signs of debate over capital punishment came during the English Revolution of 1648 when the English monarchy was briefly overthrown by liberal Protestants under Oliver Cromwell. Some of the revolutionaries argued that the death penalty was not an appropriate punishment for crimes against property, such as burglary and robbery. One such branch of liberal Protestants, the Quakers, went so far as to question whether a secular government founded on human laws had the authority to put people to death. Only God could decide when to end a life, argued the Quakers, and secular governments could not be presumed to be acting on behalf of God. Hence, secular governments had no authority to put people to death.

In the eighteenth century, resistance to capital punishment began to grow. The French philosopher Montesquieu argued, in *Persian Letters* (1721) and *The Spirit of the Laws* (1748), that contemporary punishments were too harsh, lacking a natural proportion to the crimes they were used to punish. Following Montesquieu, many social philosophers concluded that the use of the death penalty to punish mere property crimes was irrational and a violation of the spirit of enlightened humanity. The most radical and comprehensive critique of capital punishment came in 1764 with the publication of *An Essay on Crimes and Punishments* by the Italian social philosopher Cesare Beccaria. Beccaria's essay was widely read and well received. In the essay, Beccaria argued against the use of capital punishment even for such crimes as murder. He argued on theoretical grounds that civil governments did not possess the authority to take the lives of citizens, but he also argued that capital punishment was not effective in deterring crime in any case.

Beccaria's essay had considerable influence in the young United States. Once the American Revolution was over, the newly independent states saw an opportunity to revise their old colonial criminal codes to bring them in line with the spirit of the eighteenth-century Enlightenment. Many states eliminated capital punishment for property crimes, but did not go so far as to eliminate capital punishment altogether. Pennsylvania led the way in 1786, abolishing capital punishment for burglary and robbery as well as for such "moral" crimes as sodomy and bestiality. In 1794 Pennsylvania went further, eliminating capital punishment for all crimes except murder. Other states, including Virginia and Kentucky, soon followed. Imprisonment rather than death became the usual method of punishment for most serious crimes.

However, even though these reforms were seen as progress, there were some who believed that the reforms did not go far enough. Benjamin Rush, a signer of the Declaration of Independence and a major contributor to the creation of the Constitution of the United States, was the first American social philosopher to entirely oppose capital punishment for all crimes. William Bradford, who served as attorney general to the state of Pennsylvania and later as U.S. attorney general, was another influential voice opposing capital punishment. The arguments of the early abolitionists were based largely on a new view of human psychology under which people were assumed to be by nature virtuous or neutral, rather than naturally sinful and depraved as traditional Christianity had taught. In the new view, criminality was better understood as a disease or disorder than as a moral failing. Criminals should be pitied and, if possible, reformed, not subjected to cruel retributive punishments. In any case, in order to be an effective deterrent, a punishment needed to be long-lasting rather than severe, and certain to be imposed. It was argued that capital punishment—which was severe but over very quickly and in many cases not actually imposed, since juries were often too kindhearted to impose it—was ineffective in deterring crime. Hence, capital punishment was seen as both overly cruel and at the same time an ineffective deterrant.

By the end of the eighteenth century, objections to capital punishment were well known to the general public, and a popular movement to abolish capital punishment was under way, both in Europe and in the United States. However, following the statutory reforms of the 1780s and 1790s, the movement made little progress for several decades. The War of 1812 probably took people's minds away from the subject of social reform. After 1820, though, the abolitionist movement reemerged with new energy and scored some notable victories. More crimes, including rape and arson, were removed from the list of capital crimes in many states. By 1860 only murder and treason were considered capital crimes in the northern states, where the abolitionists were most active.

By the 1840s, the abolitionist movement began to organize into societies for the purpose of disseminating information and lobbying for changes in the law. The elaborately named American Society for the Collection and Diffusion of Information in Relation to the Punishment of Death, founded in 1844, was one such society. It was centered in New York City and actually had little influence outside of New York. It later changed its name to the New York Society for the Abolition of Capital Punishment. The first society with truly national reach was the American Society for the Abolition of Capital Punishment, founded in 1845 and headed by George Mifflin Dallas, who at the time was vice president of the United States. Other important leaders of the abolitionist movement included John L. O'Sullivan, who was active in New York; Charles Spear, who was active in Massachusetts and New England; and Marvin Bovee, who was active in the Midwest, especially in Wisconsin and Iowa.

Abolitionists pressed for the passage of bills abolishing capital punishment at the state level. Bills aimed at abolishing capital punishment were considered by many states during the middle of the nineteenth century. In most cases the bills were not passed. Massachusetts rejected abolitionist bills in 1835, 1836, and 1837. New York rejected bills in 1845, 1846, and 1847. Maine, New Hampshire, New Jersey, and Vermont also considered and rejected abolitionist bills, although Maine did adopt a law requiring a one-year waiting period before executions could be finally authorized. Eventually, three states actually passed abolitionist legislation. In 1846 Michigan became the first state to abolish capital punishment. Rhode Island abolished capital punishment in 1852, and Wisconsin abolished it in 1853.

The Civil War caused the abolitionist movement to stall again. During and after the war, other matters distracted attention away from the issue of capital punishment. Following the war, there was considerable interest in making executions more humane and in stopping the practice of making executions into public spectacles, but there was no consensus that they should be eliminated altogether. Executions were moved out of public sight in many states, so fewer people had the opportunity to witness an execution, but executions continued much as before. **See also** Beccaria, Cesare; Dallas, George Mifflin; Montesquieu, Baron de; O'Sullivan, John L.; Rush, Benjamin; Spear, Charles.

opposition to capital punishment, history of (1870–1963)

In the 1870s there was a resurgence of the movement to abolish capital punishment in the United States after a period of relative inactivity during the Civil War. For the first time, the abolitionists faced not just disagreement and resistance but equally active opposition by retentionists. The result was a period of gains and losses on both sides. Bills to abolish capital punishment were introduced by abolitionists in many states, but in states where these bills succeeded, bills to reenact capital punishment were quickly introduced by retentionists. The public was sharply divided on the issue, and state laws changed frequently. In 1872 Iowa became the fourth state to abolish capital punishment, but in 1878 Iowa reversed its decision and became the first state to reinstate capital punishment. Maine abolished capital punishment in 1876, reinstated it in 1883, and abolished it again in 1887. Colorado abolished capital punishment in 1897 and reinstated it in 1901.

The period of indecision extended into the twentieth century as the abolitionist movement was reinvigorated by a new generation of leaders, many of whom were not merely idealistic social reformers but people with practical experience in the administration of criminal justice. One of these was prominent prison reformer Thomas Mott Osborne, who served as warden of Sing Sing Prison. A few years later Lewis Lawes became warden of Sing Sing, and he, too, was a noted opponent of capital punishment. Many other criminal justice professionals also took a stand against capital punishment. In addition, the influential newspaper magnate William Randolph Hearst published an editorial arguing against capital punishment that ran in newspapers across the country. Clarence Darrow, the best-known criminal lawyer in the country, frequently spoke out against capital punishment and even helped found the American League to Abolish Capital Punishment (a successor to the older American League for the Abolition of Capital Punishment). His defense of the two teenage murderers Nathan Leopold and Richard Loeb kept the issue of capital punishment before the public eye, as did numerous other high-profile murder cases of the period.

Between 1907 and 1917, eight states, Arizona, Kansas, Minnesota, Missouri, North Dakota, Oregon, South Dakota, and Washington, abolished capital punishment. Tennessee abolished it for all crimes except rape (a crime for which only blacks were executed).

However, there was also strong resistance to the abolitionists. By 1920 capital punishment had been restored in Arizona, Missouri, Oregon, Tennessee, and Washington. Kansas and South Dakota restored capital punishment in the 1930s. Only Minnesota and North Dakota did not later restore capital punishment, although bills to restore it were introduced in nearly every legislative session until 1930. Many states that did not actually abolish capital punishment came close at one point or another. The battle was fought in nearly every state. By the 1940s, however, the furor had died down as the issue was again set aside during time of war.

After World War II legislative activity picked up again, perhaps rekindled by several high-profile and highly controversial death row cases, including that of Julius and Ethel Rosenberg, who were executed in 1953, and that of Caryl Chessman, whose death row memoirs made him an international celebrity. The abolitionists again scored some notable successes, but again several of these successes proved temporary.

Well into the 1960s, opposition typically involved state-by-state battles in the legislatures. Alaska and Hawaii abolished capital punishment in 1957, shortly before becoming states. These states still do not allow capital punishment. Delaware abolished capital punishment in 1958 but brought it back in 1961. Oregon abolished capital punishment in 1964 but brought it back after a decade-long court battle in 1984. In 1965 Iowa, New York, Vermont, and West Virginia abolished capital punishment; of these, only New York later restored it in 1973. In 1969 New Mexico abolished capital punishment but brought it back in 1979.
See also Darrow, Clarence; Lawes, Lewis E.; Osborne, Thomas Mott.

opposition to capital punishment, history of (1963–present)

Prior to 1963, people opposed to capital punishment assumed that the best way to work for the abolition of capital punishment was to try to change state laws. In fact, this strategy enjoyed only limited success. However, even if the abolitionists had only a limited effect on state laws, their effect on the number of executions actually performed was more profound. Between 1940 and 1960 the number of executions performed in the United States declined dramatically. A major reason for this decline was simply that juries were becoming increasingly reluctant to impose a sentence of death. In 1935 American juries imposed 158 death sentences nationwide. In 1950 only 79 death sentences were imposed. After 1950 the rate of actual executions declined even more dramatically. By the 1960s, the rate of executions had declined to only one or two a year, and in 1968 no one was executed at all. However, this decline was due not so much to reluctant juries but to the fact that the abolitionist movement had taken the battle into the courts. More capital punishment cases were being appealed, and more appeals were being decided in favor of the defendant. Many of the appeals turned on sweeping constitutional issues that impacted numerous cases and produced significant changes in the criminal justice system.

Two organizations were largely responsible for the most significant of the appeals. The American Civil Liberties Union (ACLU) and the NAACP Legal Defense and Education Fund (LDEF) were both organizations that funded legal appeals for defendants, but the LDEF existed primarily to assist blacks while the ACLU was interested in pursuing civil rights issues regardless of race. Nevertheless, it was the LDEF that was more successful in bringing cases before the Supreme Court. Indeed, the fact that the fight over capital punishment was pushed into the courts was largely a side effect of the civil rights movement. By 1960 it had become abundantly clear that the death penalty was used disproportionately on blacks. However, the equal protection clause of the Fourteenth Amendment had always been interpreted as prohibiting intentional discrimination in specific cases. Mere statistics, no matter how damning, proved only that there was a general pattern of possibly unintentional discrimination; statistics could not prove that there had been intentional discrimination in a particular case. Hence, the Supreme Court regularly rejected appeals lodged on Fourteenth Amendment equal protection grounds.

A turning point came in 1963 when Justice Arthur J. Goldberg wrote a dissent in the Supreme Court's decision *not* to consider the case of *Rudolph v. Alabama*. That dissent signaled to defense attorneys that some members of the Supreme Court were interested in hearing arguments against capital punishment, especially arguments founded on the Eighth Amendment prohibition against cruel and unusual punishment. In an effort to defend their black clients, LDEF attorneys responded by bringing a flurry of appeals on a variety of grounds. By 1967 some of these appeals had worked their way up to the Supreme Court, and a few notable victories were achieved. In *United States v. Jackson* (1967), the Supreme Court overturned a conviction on the grounds that the federal statute under which the defendant was convicted gave defendants too much incentive to give up their right to a trial by jury. In *Witherspoon v. Illinois* (1968), the Supreme Court made it harder to dismiss prospective jurors for expressing qualms about imposing a sentence of death. However, there were also setbacks. In the 1969 *Maxwell v. Bishop* case, the Supreme Court came close to declaring many state death-penalty statutes unconstitutional, but hesitations, disagreements, and the resignation of one of the justices due to a financial scandal, caused the majority

In the 1960s the NAACP worked to save a number of black death row inmates from execution.

to dissolve before a decision could be reached. In *McGautha v. California* (1971), the Supreme Court explicitly rejected several of the arguments that were being raised against the death penalty.

Then in 1972 the abolitionist movement scored a victory that took everyone by surprise. When the case of *Furman v. Georgia* reached the Supreme Court, LDEF attorney Anthony Guy Amsterdam offered a convoluted but brilliant argument for invalidating death-penalty statutes if they were being applied in an arbitrary and capricious manner. He argued that a statute that produced arbitrary or prejudicial sentences should be considered unconstitutional under the Eighth Amendment prohibition against cruel and unusual punishment, since community standards of decency were offended by arbitrary and discriminatory sentences. This was essentially an argument complaining about racial prejudice in sentencing, but it was phrased in a way that appealed to the Eighth Amendment rather than the Fourteenth Amendment. The argument worked. It persuaded some members of the Supreme Court—members who might otherwise have voted in favor of the prosecution—that the capital punishment statutes then in effect in the United States were indeed unconstitutional. The result was a surprising 5-to-4 decision that had the effect of invalidating every death-penalty statute in the United States. It appeared for a while that the abolitionists had won.

The victory, however, proved to be temporary. The justices who had provided the swing votes in the *Furman* decision were not convinced that capital punishmen per se was cruel and unusual. They felt only that it was being imposed under existing statutes in a cruel and unusual manner. The obvious solution was to revise the statutes in a way that gave jurors "guided discretion" to impose the death penalty, forcing them to consider only the nature of the crime, not their various prejudices. In 1976, in the *Gregg v. Georgia* decision, the Supreme Court approved some state statutes that seemed to have been revised in a way that would prevent discriminatory sentencing. States that wanted capital punishment promptly passed death-penalty statutes modeled after the statutes that had passed muster under the *Gregg* decision. Capital punishment was back, and back with an intensity not seen since the 1930s.

From 1976 to 1999, the number of executions performed in the United States grew from one or none per year to nearly a hundred per year. At the same time the Supreme Court made it more difficult for defendants to bring appeals, so the abolitionist strategy of attempting to prevent executions by bringing appeals had become increasingly unsuccessful. In the 1980s and 1990s the abolitionist movement again seemed stalled.

Since 2000 opposition to capital punishment has focused not on outright abolition, but on asking states to impose a moratorium on capital punishment to give investigators time to examine DNA evidence in cases that were originally investigated before genetic technology was available. The hope is to identify prisoners on death row who may have been wrongly convicted. Meanwhile several cases brought before the Supreme Court have resulted in further restrictions on the use of capital punishment: In 2002 the execution of mentally retarded offenders was declared unconstitutional, and in 2005 the execution of juvenile offenders was declared unconstitutional. Polls showing support for capital punishment, while still high, are in decline, and it appears that the abolitionist movement may be regaining some of its momentum. **See also** American Civil Liberties Union; Amsterdam, Anthony Guy; moratorium movement; NAACP Legal Defense and Education Fund; *Roper v. Simmons.*

Oregon

Except for a few brief periods when capital punishment was abolished, Oregon has traditionally permitted juries to impose the death penalty, and continues to do so currently. Prior to 1903, executions by hanging occurred under the jurisdiction of county governments and were carried out by local sheriffs. In 1903 the Oregon legislature passed a law requiring that executions be carried out at the state penitentiary in Salem. This change was made to discourage public viewing of executions. Twenty-four people were hanged in Oregon between 1904 and 1914. In 1914 voters in Oregon adopted an amendment to the state constitution abolishing capital punishment, but six years later, in 1920, voters repealed this amendment and reinstated capital punishment. Fifteen more people were hanged between 1920 and 1931. In 1937 Oregon replaced hanging with lethal gas as its method of execution. Seventeen people were executed in

Oregon's gas chamber between 1937 and 1962.

In 1964 the voters of Oregon again voted to abolish capital punishment by amending the state constitution. So in 1972, while other death-penalty statutes were invalidated by the U.S. Supreme Court's *Furman v. Georgia* decision, Oregon had no death-penalty statute to invalidate. Nevertheless, in 1978, following the 1976 *Gregg v. Georgia* decision approving revised death-penalty statutes, Oregon voters approved a ballot measure reinstating capital punishment in Oregon, this time not as part of the state's constitution but as a criminal statute. However, the statute was declared unconstitutional in 1981 by the Oregon Supreme Court. Under the statute, the trial judge determined the sentence during the penalty phase of the trial without help from a jury, and the Oregon Supreme Court ruled that this violated the defendant's right to trial by jury. In 1984 voters approved a ballot measure amending the statute to provide for a jury during the penalty phase of the trial. This change satisfied the Oregon Supreme Court, which allowed the amended statute to stand. Oregon also replaced lethal gas with lethal injection as its method of execution in 1984.

Oregon's current death-penalty statute allows jurors to consider the death penalty for homicide under special circumstances. These circumstances include that the homicide was intentional and committed personally by the defendant; that the homicide was a murder-for-hire and the defendant either performed the murder or solicited another to perform the murder, or that more than one person was killed. The homicide is also death-eligible if it involved intentional maiming or torture of the victim or if the victim was under fourteen years old. The homicide is death-eligible if the victim was a police officer, corrections officer, parole officer, probation officer, judicial officer, juror or witness in a criminal proceeding, or any person responsible for the control and supervision of convicted persons. The homicide is death-eligible if the defendant was previously convicted of homicide in any jurisdiction, if the defendant was in custody or confined in a correctional facility, or if the defendant had escaped from custody. The homicide is death-eligible if it was committed by means of an explosive device or was committed in order to conceal the commission of a crime or the identity of the defendant.

The Oregon death-penalty statute does not provide a separate list of aggravating circumstances to be considered during the penalty phase of the trial. Whatever special circumstances are proven to have accompanied the crime at the guilt phase of the trial are considered to stand as aggravating circumstances for purposes of the penalty phase. However, at the penalty phase of the trial, the jury must consider whether the defendant poses a continuing threat to society, as well as any mitigating circumstances that may be raised by the defense, before the death penalty can be imposed.

Under Oregon law, a person convicted of a capital offense cannot be executed if he or she was under the age of eighteen at the time of the crime. Oregon does provide for life imprisonment without parole as an alternative to the death penalty. The governor has the authority to grant clemency.

Since 1984, two people have been executed in Oregon, both by lethal injection. They were Douglas Franklin Wright in 1995 and Harry Charles Moore in 1997. As of June 2005, thirty-two people were awaiting execution on Oregon's death row. **See also** *Furman v. Georgia; Gregg v. Georgia.*

Osborne, Thomas Mott (1859–1926)

Thomas Mott Osborne was a prison warden and an important prison reformer of the early twentieth century. He was also a noted opponent of capital punishment.

Osborne was born in Auburn, New York, and graduated from Harvard in 1884. He took over the running of his father's manufacturing company, which produced farm equipment. The company was bought by International Harvester in 1903, and, rather than start another business, Osborne decided to indulge his interest in politics. He ran for mayor of Auburn in 1903, was elected, and served as mayor until 1906. Perhaps because Auburn was the site of New York's oldest prison, Osborne developed an interest in prison administration. At the end of his term as mayor, he addressed the National Prison Association with a stirring call for prison reform. In 1913 New York established a commission to study prison reform, and Osborne was appointed to head it. To research prison conditions, he had himself incarcerated in Auburn Prison for a week under the name Tom Brown. The experience convinced him that prisons primarily served to destroy an inmate's individuality and self-respect, which he thought were the foundations of reform. From 1914 to 1916, Osborne served as warden of New York's Sing Sing Prison. While there he instituted a program known as the Mutual Welfare League, under which prisoners were granted a degree of freedom and self-governance. The idea for the league was suggested to him by an inmate at Auburn Prison during his weeklong incarceration. The program was a notable success, although Osborne's lenient style angered prison staff, who accused him of "coddling prisoners." The complaints eventually produced an indictment on charges of mismanagement, but the case was never brought to trial. In 1917 Osborne was put in charge of the Portsmouth Naval Prison, where he instituted a similar program, again with great success.

Sing Sing Prison warden Thomas Mott Osborne (center), seen here with inmates, promoted prison reform and opposed capital punishment.

Following his retirement in 1920, Osborne continued to write and speak on prison reform. He founded an aid society to assist discharged prisoners. He also founded a national clearinghouse for information on prison conditions. These organizations maintained their headquarters in a building in New York City known as the Tom Brown House. Among the reforms that Osborne sought was an end to capital punishment. His opposition to capital punishment contributed significantly to a revival of the anti–capital punishment movement in the first decades of the twentieth century. **See also** imprisonment; Lawes, Lewis E.; Sing Sing Prison.

O'Sullivan, John L. (1813–1895)

John L. O'Sullivan was one of the most prominent opponents of capital punishment in the decades before the Civil War. He began his career by practicing law in New York but soon turned to journalism. In 1837 he helped found the *United States Magazine and Democratic Review*, a journal dedicated to promoting American expansion and nationalism. O'Sullivan is almost certainly the author of an anonymous article appearing in the *Democratic Review* in which the phrase "manifest destiny" was first used.

O'Sullivan was elected to the New York legislature, and in 1841 presented a report on the ineffectiveness of the death penalty to the legislature, along with a bill to abolish capital punishment in New York. The report, titled *Report in Favor of the Abolition of the Punishment by Death by Law*, discussed the question of scriptural support for capital punishment but then turned to more secular concerns. O'Sullivan argued that the death penalty did not effectively deter crime. He pointed out that in Belgium the number of murders per year actually decreased after 1830, when King Leopold abolished capital punishment. He argued that exposure to executions was more likely to "harden and brutalize" people than turn them away from crime. O'Sullivan also argued that the thought of life in prison would be a more effective deterrent and that juries would be more likely to convict criminals if conviction did not mean condemning them to death. Although O'Sullivan was able to organize an outpouring of opposition to capital punishment, he was not able to convince the state legislature to abolish it.

In 1843 O'Sullivan engaged in highly publicized debates with prominent death-penalty proponent George Barrell Cheever. The debates, held at the Broadway Tabernacle in New York City, continued over three evenings. Newspaper editorials generally reported that Cheever, a fiery Presbyterian preacher, got the upper hand in the debates, and O'Sullivan was furious at what he considered the unfairness of the debates' format. Nevertheless, the debates brought considerable attention to the issue of capital punishment.

After serving in the New York legislature, O'Sullivan was appointed to a diplomatic post in Portugal. During the Civil War, O'Sullivan, who was a Democrat and Southern sympathizer, remained abroad in Spain, France, and England. By 1879, however, he had returned to New York, where he lived in relative obscurity until his death. **See also** Cheever, George Barrell.

Parker, Isaac C. (1838–1896)

Isaac C. Parker was a federal judge in the violent western district of Arkansas. He holds the record for the number of defendants sentenced to death and became notorious for his harsh sentencing. The eastern press gave him the name "Hanging Judge" Parker.

Parker was born near Barnesville, Ohio. Self-educated in the law, he opened a law practice in St. Joseph, Missouri, in 1859. He also became active in politics, first as a Democrat but then becoming a Republican before the outbreak of the Civil War. He was elected to several local offices and was eventually elected to two terms as a U.S. congressman, serving from 1871 to 1875. As a congressman, he supported women's suffrage and was a strong advocate for the rights of Native Americans, although he felt their interests were not being well served by their own tribal governments. After losing his third campaign for Congress, Parker was appointed by President Ulysses S. Grant to the post of federal judge for the U.S. District Court for the Western District of Arkansas.

Parker's court was located at Fort Smith, Arkansas. His jurisdiction included the Indian Territory, which later became the state of Oklahoma. This was a particularly violent jurisdiction. Disputes between Indians were handled by tribal law, but disputes between Indians and whites fell within Parker's purview. Consistent with his views on Native American rights, Parker was scrupulously fair in his administration of justice, generally blaming disputes on whites who often had no business being on Indian land in the first place. Because the Indian Territory had an ambiguous status, falling in some respects outside of legal U.S. jurisdiction, it was a magnet for lawbreakers and desperadoes of all sorts. The U.S. marshal's office, also located at Fort Smith, was kept busy tracking down fugitives who had fled into Indian lands and bringing them back to be tried in Judge Parker's court. The deputies who did this work were known as "Parker's deputies," although they actually worked for the U.S. marshal, not for Parker. It was dangerous work; sixty-five deputies were killed in the line of duty during Parker's tenure.

In 1875, the year Parker took over the district court, six men were hanged at the same time for unrelated crimes. Although none of the hangings would have attracted much attention had they occurred separately, the event was widely reported in the eastern press, and it earned Parker the name "Hanging Judge" Parker, a name and image he was thereafter never able to shake. Parker served as district judge for twenty-one years, from 1875 to 1896. In that time, his court heard 13,490 cases and handed down 9,454 convictions. Of those convicted, 172 were death sentences. Parker sentenced more people to death than any other judge in American history. Of his

172 death sentences, it has been widely reported that 88 resulted in execution. This figure first appeared in a sensationalized 1989 biography of Judge Parker called *Hell on the Border: He Hanged Eighty-Eight Men*, by Samuel W. Harman. Harman's figure is now believed to be in error. The correct number is 79. Parker died in 1896 as he was preparing to retire from the bench anyway. While many were happy to see the end of his harsh justice, the Native Americans under his jurisdiction mourned, and a prominent Creek chieftain even attended his funeral. **See also** Maledon, George.

Payne v. Tennessee

This was a case heard by the Supreme Court of the United States in 1991 concerning whether victim impact statements may be presented during the penalty phase of a trial. The defendant, Pervis Tyrone Payne, was convicted of an assault during which a woman and her two-year-old daughter were murdered. The woman's three-year-old son survived. During the penalty phase of the trial, the woman's mother was allowed to testify regarding the emotional impact of the murders on her grandson. Payne was sentenced to death. He appealed the sentence to the Tennessee Supreme Court on the grounds that the grandmother's testimony violated his right to a fair trial under the Eighth Amendment according to the U.S. Supreme Court decision in *Booth v. Maryland* (1987). Despite this precedent, the Tennessee Supreme Court upheld the sentence, and the case was referred to the U.S. Supreme Court.

In this case, the U.S. Supreme Court also upheld the sentence in a 6-to-3 decision, explicitly reversing its decision in *Booth v. Maryland*. Writing for the majority, Chief Justice William Rehnquist stated merely that the Eighth Amendment did not explicitly prohibit the consideration of victim impact statements.

In a concurring opinion, Justice David Souter offered a more detailed explanation of the reasoning behind the decision. He argued that, contrary to the majority opinion in *Booth v. Maryland*, the amount of harm caused by a crime is relevant to the blameworthiness of the crime, even if that harm was not intended or anticipated by the person committing the crime. For example, a person who runs a red light is guilty of reckless driving whether or not the action causes an accident, but such an action is *more* blameworthy if it does cause an accident than if it does not. Hence, evidence concerning the degree of harm caused by a crime may legitimately be offered during the penalty phase of a trial. **See also** *Booth v. Maryland*; victim impact statements.

peine forte et dure

Also known as pressing, *peine forte et dure* (French for "punishment by pressure and time") is a method of execution in which the condemned prisoner is crushed to death slowly. This method was used as a form of torture to force a confession or other acknowledgment from a prisoner. The prisoner was usually placed face up on the ground underneath a large board. Heavy weights—stones or iron weights—were then piled onto the board. Additional weights were added slowly, so the execution could take several days to complete. The condemned prisoner was even given small amounts of food and water so he would not die of hunger or thirst.

Pressing was used primarily in England, beginning in the fifteenth century. A 1641 law made pressing illegal, but this injunction was not always enforced. The punishment was used in Massachusetts in 1692 on an eighty-year-old man, Giles Cory, who refused to acknowledge the jurisdiction of the court trying him for witchcraft during the Salem witchcraft trials. Apparently the punishment did not succeed in forcing an acknowledgment from him. **See also** Salem witchcraft trials.

Pennsylvania

Pennsylvania has traditionally permitted juries to impose the death penalty, and continues to do so currently. However, Pennsylvania was originally founded by people with strong objections to capital punishment. Quakers in England and other parts of Europe held the view that only God should decide when someone dies; therefore, states did not have the authority to wage war or to put criminals to death. When the Quakers founded colonies in the New World, they attempted to put their principles into practice. In the colony of Pennsylvania, the death penalty was prohibited for all crimes except murder. At that time even the Quakers could not bring themselves to abolish capital punishment for murder. However, by the early 1700s, clashes with native tribes convinced many Quakers that strict pacifist principles were not a practical basis for running a government. Strict Quakers withdrew from government, and in 1718 the penal code of colonial Pennsylvania was revised to resemble more closely the penal codes of other American colonies. The death penalty was introduced for many common crimes. Eighty-eight executions by hanging took place in colonial Pennsylvania between 1693 and 1775. Murder was the crime most frequently punished with death, but there were also many executions for burglary. There were also a few hangings for counterfeiting, robbery, and arson. During the American Revolution, hangings for counterfeiting increased, and there were also executions for espionage and treason.

In 1794, in response to a report on capital punishment by Pennsylvania Supreme Court justice William Bradford, Pennsylvania became the first state to restrict the death penalty to the crime of "murder in the first degree." This was the first law in which first-degree murder was distinguished from less serious crimes resulting in a person's death. In 1834 Pennsylvania also became the second state to abolish public viewing of executions. However, executions continued to he conducted by local officials inside the walls of local county jails. Between 1778 and 1915, 586 people were executed by hanging in Pennsylvania.

In 1913 the Pennsylvania legislature voted to replace hanging with electrocution as its method of execution. However, the electric chair was not ready for use until 1915. Pennsylvania's electric chair was given the nickname "Old Smokey." Between 1915 and 1962, 350 people were executed using Old Smokey.

Following the 1972 *Furman v. Georgia* ruling, which struck down Pennsylvania's death-penalty statute, the Pennsylvania legislature passed a new death-penalty statute in 1974, but the Pennsylvania Supreme Court declared the new law unconstitutional in 1977. In 1978 the legislature again passed a death-penalty statute over the veto of Pennsylvania governor Milton Shapp. This version of the law was upheld. Pennsylvania's current death-penalty statute allows jurors to consider the death penalty for any intentional homicide. The death penalty may be imposed if one of eighteen aggravating circumstances is proven to have accompanied the crime. These aggravating circumstances are (1) that the victim was a firefighter, police officer, or any of a number of specifically named public officials, including the governor, attorney general, state treasurer, and so forth, or an employee or official of a state or federal judicial or corrections system; (2) that the homicide was a murder-for-hire and the defendant either performed the murder or solicited another to perform the murder; (3) that the victim was held for ransom or used as a shield or hostage; (4) that the homicide occurred in the course of an airplane hijacking; (5) that the victim was a witness and the homicide was committed in order to prevent the victim's testimony; (6) that the homicide occurred in the course of committing another felony; (7) that the defendant knowingly created a great risk of death to people other than the victim; (8) that the homicide involved the use of torture; (9) that the defendant had a significant history of convictions for other felonies involving violence; (10) that the defendant was previously convicted of another offense punishable by a sentence of life imprisonment or death; (11) that the defendant was previously convicted of murder; (12) that the defendant was previously convicted of voluntary manslaughter; (13) that the homicide occurred in the course of a felony drug offense; (14) that the defendant and victim were involved, either together or in competition with each other, in various drug-related activities; (15) that the victim was an informant and the homicide was committed in retaliation for information supplied by the victim; (16) that the victim was a child under the age of twelve; (17) that the victim was in the third trimester of a pregnancy and known by the defendant to be pregnant; or (18) that the defendant was under a restraining order restricting the defendant's behavior toward the victim. The jury must also consider any mitigating circumstances that the defense wishes to present.

A Pennsylvania law allowing the death penalty for persons convicted of a capital offense who were at least sixteen at the time of their crime was overturned in March 2005 when the Supreme Court decision in *Roper v. Simmons* outlawed the execution of juveniles. Pennsylvania does provide for life imprisonment without parole as an alternative to the death penalty. The governor has the authority to grant clemency, with the advice of the State Board of Pardons.

In 1990 Pennsylvania replaced electrocution with lethal injection as its method of execution. The first execution in Pennsylvania following the reenactment of the death penalty took place in 1995 with the execution of Keith Zettlemoyer. Since 1995 only three people have been executed in Pennsylvania, all by lethal injection. As of June 2005, 231 people were awaiting execution on Pennsylvania's death row. **See also** Bradford, William.

Penry v. Lynaugh

This was a case heard by the Supreme Court of the United States in 1989 concerning whether the execution of a mentally retarded person is cruel and unusual. The Court was also asked to consider whether a jury should be instructed to consider mental retardation a mitigating circumstance to be weighed during the penalty phase of the trial. The defendant, Johnny Paul Penry, was charged with the rape and murder of a Texas woman. A psychologist testified that Penry was mildly to moderately retarded, with the approximate emotional and intellectual maturity of a six-and-a-half-year-old. Nevertheless, Penry was found competent to stand trial. The jury decided that he was able to distinguish between right and wrong (which meant that he did not meet the legal criterion for being insane) and convicted him of capital murder. During the penalty phase of the trial, the jury was aware of Penry's retardation but were not instructed that they should consider this a mitigating circumstance. Penry was sentenced to be executed. The case was appealed, and eventually the Supreme Court agreed to review the case.

Since the Supreme Court was considering two separate issues, the decision was mixed. Justice Sandra Day O'Connor wrote the decision for the Court. The Court ruled that the execution of a mentally retarded person was not cruel and unusual. Nevertheless, Penry's sentence of death was reversed on the grounds that the jury should have been instructed to consider mental retardation to be a mitigating circumstance. Four justices took the more liberal position that mentally retarded persons should never be executed; four justices took the more conservative position that the judge's instructions to the jury had been adequate. Justice O'Connor was the decisive swing vote on both of the two questions.

Since the jury had decided that Penry was not legally insane, the decision in this case did not overturn the Court's previous decision in *Ford v. Wainwright* (1986) that the execution of a person judged to be legally insane *is* cruel and unusual. However, the *Penry v. Lynaugh* decision was itself overturned by the 2002 *Atkins v. Virginia* Supreme Court decision, which prohibited the execution of mentally retarded offenders in the United States. **See also** *Atkins v. Virginia; Ford v. Wainwright;* mentally retarded offenders.

Phillips, Wendell (1811–1884)

Wendell Phillips was a popular speaker and social reformer in the United States during the nineteenth century. Although best known for his opposition to slavery, he also used his oratorical skill to promote the abolition of capital punishment.

Even as a young student, Phillips distinguished himself in oratory and debate. He attended Harvard Law School and set up a legal practice in Suffolk County, Massachusetts. He was reasonably successful, but did not find the work particularly fascinating. However, at a time before radio and television, there was always a demand for public speakers. Phillips was an entertaining and eloquent speaker and soon had a career speaking on various subjects. Controversial subjects were especially popular. Prior to the Civil War, Phillips established a reputation as an outspoken opponent of slavery. After the Civil War, he became an early advocate

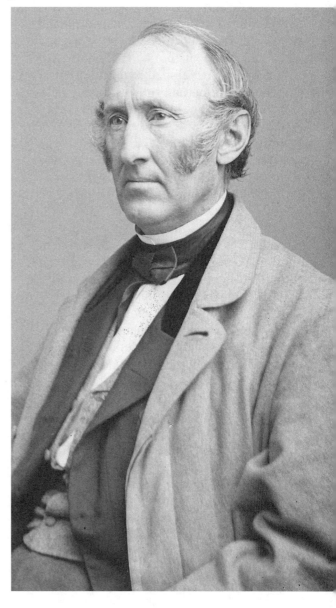

Renowned as an orator, Wendell Phillips often spoke out against slavery and capital punishment.

of women's rights and of the labor movement. Throughout his career, he argued for the abolition of capital punishment. In 1849 Phillips spoke out against the execution of a Boston sailor, Washington Goode, who had been convicted of murder. Phillips's voice helped bring national attention to this case. **See also** Goode, Washington.

phrenology

Phrenology was a popular theory of psychology in the early nineteenth century based on the idea that personality was determined by the shape of the brain and that the shape of the brain was revealed by the shape of the skull. Theories of personality developed by phrenologists played an important role in causing public executions to be discontinued during the 1830s in favor of executions hidden from public view.

The theory behind phrenology was first proposed by Austrian physician Franz Joseph Gall. Gall worked out an elaborate atlas of the human skull, indicating which personality traits were indicated by which skull shapes. He spent years attempting to gather observational data to support his theories and modifying his theories to fit his data. His theories seemed plausible enough that others also began advocating them.

One proponent of phrenology in the United States was George Combe, who was also an advocate of death-penalty reform. Combe used the assumptions of phrenology to argue against holding executions in public. Combe believed that people were predisposed to have certain personality traits, as revealed by their skull shapes. He argued that public executions would naturally frighten and deter people who had little predisposition for violence anyway, but they would tend to encourage violence in those who were already predisposed to violence. Hence, "it will operate with least effect precisely on those on whom it is most needed."

Eventually, phrenology was dismissed as serious science and came to be regarded as a pseudoscience, similar to palmistry. However, the argument that exposure to violence would tend to make those inclined to criminal behavior more violent rather than less violent prevailed. In the 1830s many states banned public executions, and by the 1900s public executions were largely a thing of the past. **See also** viewing of executions.

physician participation in executions

For hundreds of years, physicians have attended executions for the purpose of examining the executed prisoner's body in order to pronounce death. Physicians have traditionally been present at hangings as well as executions using gas and the electric chair. However, physicians do not assist in executions in the capacity of executioners. That is, they do not participate in causing the death of the prisoner.

Physicians are traditionally bound by a code of professional ethics known as the Hippocratic Oath, a statement supposedly written by Hippocrates, the legendary physician of ancient Greece. The central tenet of the Hippocratic Oath is "First, do no harm." American physicians have developed a more comprehensive code of professional ethics issued by the American Medical Association but this code still follows the original spirit of the Hippocratic Oath. American physicians still consider the injunction to do no harm to be the prime directive of medical practice. Most American physicians interpret this injunction as forbidding mercy killing. They also interpret it as forbidding participation in executions.

With the adoption of lethal injection as the standard method of execution in the United States, the question of the physician's role in executions has become a sensitive topic. Physicians still attend executions, but they are careful to limit their role, as before, to pronouncing death and performing an autopsy if one is required. In some cases, a physician may prescribe a mild sedative for the prisoner to relieve anxiety. The physician may prescribe the same sedative for witnesses. **See also** executioners; lethal injection.

Pierrepoint family

From 1901 to 1956, members of the Pierrepoint family served as executioners in England. Three members of the family in succession held the title of chief executioner. Whereas the Sanson family in France were forced by the fears and prejudices of the times to maintain a long family tradition of serving as executioners, no such pressures seem to have forced the Pierrepoint family to maintain the tradition.

Henry Pierrepoint (1874–1922). Henry Pierrepoint learned how to conduct hangings by assisting James Billington, the chief executioner at Newgate Prison, with a hanging in 1901. He assisted James Billington's sons, William and John, with several other hangings. Then, in 1905 William and John Billington resigned, leaving Henry Pierrepoint to be the chief executioner. Henry recruited his older brother, Thomas, to assist him. Henry Pierrepoint conducted 107 executions during his career. He had a reputation as a meticulous hangman who carefully calculated the length of the drop needed. It is said that he never bungled a hanging. Nevertheless, he was dismissed from his post in 1910 for arriving at an execution in Chelmsford "considerably the worse for drink."

Thomas Pierrepoint (1870–1954). Following the firing of Henry Pierrepoint, his brother Thomas took over as chief executioner in England. He served for thirty-seven years and is thought to have executed about three hundred people. During World War II, he also worked as a hangman for the U.S. military, performing executions in Ireland, Germany, and Cyprus as well as in England. He retired in 1946 and died in 1954.

Albert Pierrepoint (1905–1992). Albert Pierrepoint was the son of Henry Pierrepoint and the nephew of Thomas Pierrepoint. He began assisting his uncle with executions at the age of twenty and took over as chief executioner in 1946 upon the death of his uncle. After World War II, many Nazi officers were tried for war crimes, and it was Albert's job to hang them. It is estimated that he hanged as many as two hundred Nazis. He retired from the post in 1956 after executing some 433 people, making him the most prolific and the best-known executioner of the twentieth century. After his retirement, Albert Pierrepoint became an opponent of capital punishment, adding his voice to a growing chorus of opposition in England during the 1950s and 1960s. Nonetheless, he never expressed regret for his life as an executioner. **See also** Billington family; executioners; Sanson family.

Poland v. Arizona

This was a case heard by the Supreme Court of the United States in 1986 concerning whether the introduction of new evidence during a sentencing retrial violates the double-jeopardy clause of the U.S. Constitution. The defendants in the case were two brothers, Michael and Patrick Poland, who were convicted in Arizona of robbery and murder. Posing as police officers, they waylaid an armored car, overpowered the guards and stole $281,000. They then attached weights to the two guards and dumped them into a lake. One of the guards was still alive and died of drowning, as a later autopsy showed. The Polands were sentenced to death by the judge, who ruled that the crime met the standard for being "especially heinous, cruel, or depraved," an aggravating circumstance included in Arizona's death-penalty statute. (At the time, a judge decided the sentence in Arizona's death-penalty cases without the help of a jury.) However, on appeal, the Arizona Supreme Court ruled that the evidence presented at trial was not sufficient to establish that the crime was especially heinous, cruel, or depraved, since it was not proved that the Polands knew one of the guards was still alive. A new trial was ordered. At the retrial, the prosecution argued for the death penalty both because the crime was especially heinous, cruel, or depraved and because the crime was "committed for pecuniary gain," another aggravating circumstance recognized by the Arizona death-penalty statute. New evidence was introduced to support both these arguments. Again, the Polands were convicted and sentenced to death. On appeal, the Arizona Supreme Court again rejected the evidence supporting the first aggravating circumstance but upheld the sentence on the grounds that the second aggravating circumstance, that the crime was committed for pecuniary gain, had been adequately proved. The U.S. Supreme Court agreed to review the case to decide whether a death sentence imposed on substantially new grounds, supported by evidence not introduced at the original trial, violated the constitutional prohibition against subjecting defendants to double jeopardy.

In a 6-to-3 decision, the Supreme Court ruled that the Polands had not been subjected to double jeopardy. Writing for the majority, Justice Byron White pointed out that the principle of double jeopardy is designed to protect a defendant from being prosecuted a second time following an acquittal. However, he argued, the overturning of the death penalty by the Arizona Supreme Court did not constitute an "acquittal," so the resentencing was free to proceed with a "clean slate," allowing both prosecution and defense to introduce fresh arguments.

Michael Poland was executed by lethal injection on June 16, 1999. Patrick Poland was executed by lethal injection on March 15, 2000. **See also** double jeopardy.

Prejean, Helen (1939–)

Sister Helen Prejean is a well-known opponent of capital punishment. Her best-selling 1993 book, *Dead Man Walking*, about her experiences as a spiritual counselor to death row inmates, brought her international attention and made her one of the leading spokespersons for the abolitionist movement.

Prejean was born in Baton Rouge, Louisiana. At the age of eighteen she joined the Sisters of St. Joseph of Medaille. As a member of the order, she attended St. Mary's Dominican College in New Orleans, completing a B.A. in 1962. She then studied religious education at St. Paul's University in Ottawa, Ontario, Canada. She has worked primarily as a teacher at Catholic parochial schools.

In the 1980s Prejean began corresponding with Elmo Patrick Sonnier, who was on death row in Louisiana for killing two teenagers. Eventually Prejean began visiting him in prison as his spiritual adviser. Sonnier was executed in 1984, and Prejean attended the execution in her capacity as his spiritual counsel. She also served as spiritual counsel for Robert Lee Willie, also executed in 1984, and Willie Celestine, executed in 1987.

Prejean's *Dead Man Walking* is a fictionalized account of her experiences counseling death row inmates. Although the book is written as fiction, it is closely based on her actual experiences. The book won a Pulitzer Prize in 1993 and remained on the *New York Times* bestseller list for thirty-one weeks. In 1996 the book was made into a movie starring Sean Penn and Susan Sarandon, who won an Oscar for Best Actress for her role as Helen Prejean. In 2000 the book was even made into an opera and was performed by the San Francisco Opera.

Prejean continues to speak and write in opposition to capital punishment, and she continues to serve as spiritual adviser to death row inmates. She has won numerous humanitarian awards for her work and was nominated four times for the Nobel Peace Prize. **See also** Ingle, Joe.

Proffitt v. Florida

This was a case heard by the Supreme Court of the United States in 1976, and was a companion case to the landmark *Gregg v. Georgia* case, which concerned the constitutionality of a newly enacted state death-penalty statute. The defendant in the case, Charles William Proffitt, was convicted of burglary and murder and sentenced to death under a new Florida death-penalty statute that had been passed to replace the old statute overturned in 1972 by the *Furman v. Georgia* decision. The Florida statute was similar to the statute enacted in Georgia, so the Supreme Court bundled this case with the *Gregg v. Georgia* case. In a 7-to-2 decision, the Supreme Court ruled that the new state death-penalty statutes were constitutional, and it allowed the death sentences to stand. This decision opened the way for a resumption of executions in the United States after a ten-year hiatus. However, Charles William Proffitt was not executed. On a later appeal, his sentence was reduced to life imprisonment without parole. **See also** *Gregg v. Georgia*.

proportionality

Proportionality in the criminal justice system is the concept that the severity of punishment should be roughly equal to the seriousness of the crime; that is, the punishment should fit the crime. This idea is reflected in the earliest known codes of law. For example, the principle of retaliation, or *lex talionis*, as expressed in the Code of Hammurabi, specifies that harm done to a criminal in retaliation for a crime should match (not exceed) the harm done by the crime itself. Hence, the penalty for putting out someone's eye is to have one's own eye put out. The concept of proportionality was codified in English law in 1689 with the passage of the English Bill of Rights, which prohibits "cruel and unusual punishment" (a phrase that was later used in the U.S. Constitution). The prohibition against cruel and unusual punishment is interpreted not only as a prohibition against torture but as a prohibition against punishments that are excessive in relation to the crime they are used to punish.

In Europe during the eighteenth century, the concept of proportionality was also expressly stated by the French philosopher Baron de Montesquieu. In his 1748 essay, *The Spirit of the Laws*, he used the concept to argue that the methods of punishment then in use were too harsh for the crimes they were used to punish. He believed that if a thief were punished in the same way that one would punish a murderer, then the thief was being punished disproportionately, since theft is clearly not as serious a crime as murder. For this reason, many followers of Montesquieu argued that the death penalty should not be used to punish crimes against property, such as burglary and robbery.

One controversial aspect of the proportionality concept is that the degree of punishment that seems proportionate to one person may not seem proportionate to another person. The victim of a crime may feel that a harsh penalty is appropriate while a dispassionate observer may feel that only a mild penalty is justified. A second problem is the problem of incommensurability. Crimes and punishments are fundamentally different kinds of things, like the proverbial apples and oranges. The type of suffering that a victim undergoes in the course of a crime may be quite different than the type of suffering that a prisoner undergoes in the course of being punished. But if there is no common scale on which the seriousness of a crime can be measured against the severity of a punishment, then it is difficult to say how the two could be proportionate to each other. Finally, there are some crimes that are so heinous that providing a proportionate penalty either would not be possible at all or would violate standards of humanity and decency to which we feel bound. In American jurisprudence, such quandaries have traditionally been resolved by appealing to evolving community standards. Judges try to get a sense of what the public considers "proportionate" by looking at jury sentences and by citing laws voted on by representatives of the community. **See also** cruel and unusual punishment; *lex talionis*.

Protocol 6

Protocol 6 is an amendment to the Convention for the Protection of Human Rights and Fundamental Freedoms, also known as the European Convention on Human Rights. This convention was adopted by member states of the Council of Europe in 1950. Protocol 6 was added to the convention in 1983 and is an agreement among the member states to abolish capital punishment except in the case of acts committed during times of war or during times of imminent threat of war. The significance of Protocol 6 is that it makes abolition of the death penalty a condition for membership in the European Union. As a result, nations that wish to be considered for membership in the European Union have had to bring their laws into conformity with Protocol 6. Russia, Ukraine, and Turkey have all recently taken this step, despite traditional support for the death penalty in each of these countries. **See also** international use of capital punishment.

public opinion

Public opinion may be relevant to the debate over capital punishment in ways in which it is not relevant to other moral and ethical debates. In 1958 a Supreme Court decision, *Trop v. Dulles*, declared that the phrase "cruel and unusual punishment," in the Eighth Amendment of the U.S. Constitution, is to be interpreted in light of "evolving standards of decency." In other words, a form of punishment, such as the death penalty, that is not cruel and unusual at one time may become cruel and unusual if its use is considered contrary to community standards of decency by a significant proportion of the public.

Public opinion polls are used to measure what percentage of the population hold certain views. The polls are conducted by selecting a small but representative sample of the population and then recording their answers to certain questions. These polls can be extremely accurate, although no sample can perfectly represent a large and diverse population. Politicians find such polls valuable, since knowing what people think about various subjects can tell them how best to present their own views when running for office. Attitudes about capital punishment are among the views that are regularly tracked using public opinion polls.

The Supreme Court does not use public opinion polls to measure public attitudes toward methods of punishment. Polls do not have any legal status and, unlike elections, cannot be used as an official measure of public sentiment. Instead,

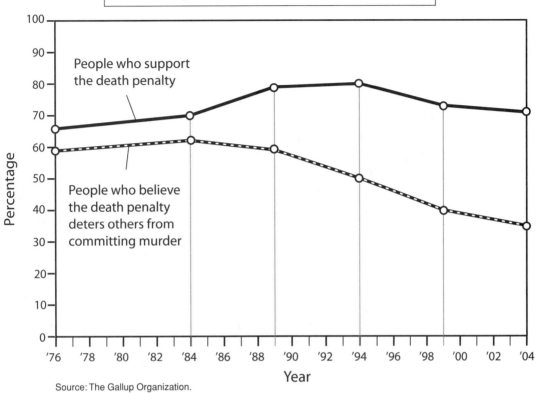

Public Opinion About the Death Penalty

Source: The Gallup Organization.

the Supreme Court tracks jury decisions and laws enacted by state legislators—both of which do have legal status, and both of which also reflect public sentiment. Nevertheless, because of the effect of public opinion on jury decisions and laws, public attitudes toward capital punishment as measured by opinion polls are of considerable interest and importance.

Traditionally, there has been strong support for capital punishment among the American public. Over half the population has consistently answered "yes" when asked, "Are you in favor of the death penalty for a person convicted of murder?" After 1972, when the Supreme Court declared state death-penalty statutes too inconsistent to be used and put a temporary stop to capital punishment in the United States, public support for capital punishment grew, eventually reaching as high as 80 percent approval in 1994. Since then, support for capital punishment has been dropping off, although it remains well above 50 percent.

Two related factors may be responsible for the declining popularity of capital punishment. One is a growing belief that innocent people have been executed. As DNA testing has become available, several convicted prisoners on death row have been able to prove their innocence. However, DNA evidence is not always available, so some wrongly convicted prisoners may never have the opportunity to prove their innocence. Other irregularities in the way capital cases are tried have led to the suspicion that some of those on death row may be innocent. In 2000 Governor George Ryan of Illinois declared a moratorium on executions in his state, declaring that the judicial process was too flawed to be trusted. His action brought national attention to the view that a significant number of death row inmates may be innocent, and raised doubts about the reliability of the process in other states.

A second factor in the declining popularity of capital punishment has been an increase in the availability of the sentence of life imprisonment without parole. When asked to choose between the death penalty and life without parole, Americans currently split about evenly, with only about 50 percent still saying they prefer the death penalty.

Curiously, highly publicized violent incidents, such as the terrorist attack on the World Trade Center on September 11, 2001, and sniper shootings in the Washington, D.C., area in 2002, did not cause support for the death penalty to increase. American opinion on capital punishment seems to be quite stable, not affected by emotional reactions to specific incidents. **See also** DNA evidence; evolving standards of decency.

Puerto Rico

Capital punishment was allowed in Puerto Rico for a brief period, from 1898, when the United States took control of Puerto Rico from Spain following the Spanish-American War, until 1929, when the Puerto Rican government voted to abolish it. Twenty-three executions were performed in Puerto Rico during that period. The last person executed in Puerto Rico was Pasqual Ramos in 1927. The Puerto Rican constitution, ratified in 1952, contains a provision prohibiting capital punishment. **See also** federal death-penalty laws.

Pulley v. Harris

This was a case heard by the Supreme Court of the United States in 1984 concerning whether a state is required to review death sentences to confirm that people who have committed comparable crimes have received comparable sentences. The defendant in the case, Robert Alton Harris, was convicted in California of the 1978 murder of two teenage boys. Harris was out on parole for a previous murder when he and his brother, Daniel Marcus Harris, decided to rob a bank. They saw two sixteen-year-old boys, John Mayeski and Michael Baker, with their car in the parking lot of a fast-food restaurant. Robert Harris forced the two boys at gunpoint to drive to a nearby reservoir, where he shot them to death, and then ate the hamburgers they had bought. Harris and his brother then robbed a bank, planning to use the stolen car to escape. However, they were caught following the robbery and charged with the murders as well as the robbery. Robert Harris was convicted and sentenced to death. His brother, who testified against Robert, was sentenced to a term of imprisonment, of which he served three years.

At the time, death-penalty statutes in some other states, notably Georgia, required that a sentence of death be subjected to what was called a "comparative proportionality" review to ensure that people who had committed comparable crimes had received proportionately severe sentences. California's death-penalty statute required no such review. Harris's lawyers appealed his sentence on the grounds that there was no evidence that his sentence was proportional to the crime committed and that California should be required to perform a comparative proportionality review. When the case reached the U.S. Court of Appeals for the Ninth Circuit, the court agreed that a comparative proportionality review should be required. The case was then appealed by the prosecution to the U.S. Supreme Court, and the Supreme Court agreed to review the case.

In a 7-to-2 decision, the Supreme Court ruled that a comparative proportionality review was not a constitutional right. Writing for the majority, Justice

Byron White agreed that laws should be struck down if it could be shown that they led to sentences that were disproportionate in particular cases. Indeed, this was precisely the reason for the 1972 *Furman v. Georgia* decision. However, in this case it had not been shown that the California statute failed to provide adequate protection "against the evil identified in *Furman*." In a concurring opinion, Justice John Paul Stevens agreed that a comparative proportionality review was not the only possible method that could be used to ensure that sentences were imposed in a manner sufficiently consistent to be deemed constitutional.

Robert Alton Harris was executed by lethal gas on April 21, 1992. He was the first person to be executed in California since 1967. **See also** proportionality.

Purvis, Will (1874–1943)

Will Purvis enjoyed an apparently miraculous escape from the gallows. In the early twentieth century, his story became a favorite with opponents of capital punishment as a cautionary tale about the risk of hanging the wrong man.

In Mercer County, Mississippi, Purvis was a member of an early white supremacist organization known as the White Caps, a group similar to the Ku Klux Klan but not as large or well known. Soon after Purvis joined the group, another member, Will Buckley, was shot to death, and Buckley's brother claimed that Purvis was responsible. Purvis was convicted of the murder, but many people were inclined to believe Purvis's claim that he was innocent. At the hanging, on February 7, 1894, roughly three thousand people came to watch. A preacher in the crowd shouted, "God save this innocent boy!" just as the trapdoor of the gallows was released. Rather than killing Purvis, the noose came unraveled and Purvis fell to the ground, bruised but still alive. Convinced they had witnessed a miracle, the people in the crowd refused to allow the hangman to make a second attempt to hang Purvis. Instead, he was returned to jail. When the Mississippi Supreme Court ordered that the original sentence had to be carried out, friends helped Purvis escape from jail. He then spent two years in hiding.

In 1896 a new governor, A.J. McLaurin, took office, having made clemency for Purvis a central promise of his campaign. Purvis allowed himself to be recaptured. In 1898 McLaurin granted Purvis a full pardon when Buckley's brother, who had originally identified Purvis as the killer, admitted that he was not actually sure who had done it. The murder remained unsolved until 1917, when another White Cap member, Joe Beard, confessed at a religious revival meeting that he and White Cap member Louis Thornhill had shot Will Buckley. Purvis was paid $5,000 in compensation for the false arrest and near execution. **See also** Abbott, Burton; exoneration.

racial discrimination in sentencing

From 1900 to 1970, African Americans made up slightly less than 11 percent of the total population of the United States. During this same period, over half of the inmates on death row, more than 43 percent of the total state and federal prison population, and half of the condemned prisoners who were actually executed were African American. This disparity gave rise to claims that the death penalty was unfairly applied on the basis of race and therefore should be abolished as unconstitutional. This issue remains at the forefront of the death-penalty debate.

The discrepancy could be explained if statistics showed that crime rates, especially murder rates, were five times higher in predominantly black communities than in predominantly white communities. However, this was not the case. Although rates of violent crime in black communities—especially poor urban communities—were significantly higher than in white communities, they were not enough higher to account for the disparity between the death row population and the general population. The implication was that juries were simply more willing to condemn a prisoner to death if he was black.

Prior to 1972, the Supreme Court had upheld the principle that even if it can be proved that a statistical pattern of discrimination exists, that fact does not in itself prove discrimination in a particular case. Moreover, a law cannot be overturned merely because it is applied in a discriminatory fashion: It must be shown that the law was passed for the purpose of discriminating against a group. For these reasons, the obvious pattern of racial discrimination in sentencing could not be used either to overturn individual death sentences or to invalidate the death-penalty statutes according to which those sentences were imposed.

Nevertheless, in the 1972 *Furman v. Georgia* decision, the Supreme Court did accept the argument that laws that permitted "arbitrary and capricious" patterns of sentencing could be declared unconstitutional. The decision asserted that it was cruel and unusual for comparable crimes to be punished with dramatically different sentences. Death-penalty statutes under which African Americans received a death sentence for the same crime for which a white defendant received only a term of imprisonment were therefore unconstitutional. The *Furman* decision required that death-penalty statutes had to be rewritten in such a way that sentencing could not be influenced by a jury's ethnic, social, or racial prejudices. In the 1976 *Gregg v. Georgia* decision, the Supreme Court ruled that several states, including Georgia, had adopted reformed death-penalty statutes that probably met this test by mandating review of sentences in capital cases and by requiring juries to follow new sentencing guidelines that stopped short of mandatory sentences.

Since the adoption by most states of death-penalty statutes similar to the ones approved by the *Gregg* decision, the proportion of African Americans among death row inmates still exceeds 40 percent, and roughly 35 percent of executed inmates are African American. This is still significantly higher than the proportion of blacks in the general population (now at about 12 percent), but given the higher crime rate in poor urban black communities, these numbers cannot be taken as evidence of discriminatory sentencing. Racial prejudice and discrimination are still cited as factors in the social conditions that cause higher violent crime rates in black communities. But some experts argue that this fact cannot be used to establish that death-penalty statutes are discriminatory any more than the fact that divorce rates are higher in black communities could be used to establish that alimony laws are discriminatory.

Nevertheless, researchers claim that race—the race of the victim, not the race of the defendant—is still a factor in death-penalty sentencing. In 1987 University of Iowa law professor David Baldus reported that in Georgia a defendant (regardless of race) was much more likely to receive a death sentence if the victim was white than if the victim was black. This statistic was considered in the case of *McCleskey v. Kemp*, which reached the Supreme Court in 1987. In this case the Supreme Court ruled that, by itself, this statistic was not sufficient to establish that the Georgia death-penalty statute was discriminatory. Since then, Baldus has compiled studies suggesting that, in nearly every state that allows the death penalty, the race of the victim is a significant factor in sentencing; in other

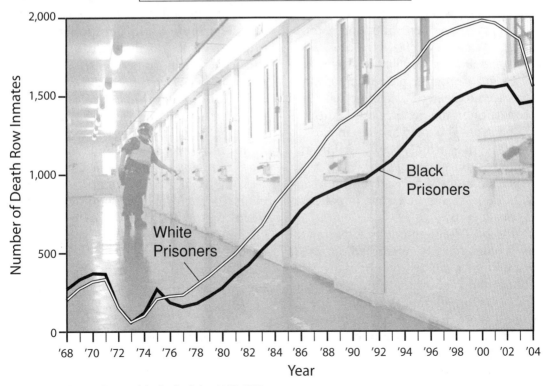

Source: Bureau of Justice Statistics, 1968–2004.

words, the victim's being white serves as an unacknowledged aggravating factor for the crime of homicide, as if juries value the life of white victims more highly than the life of black victims. Whether this conclusion will have an impact on future Supreme Court decisions remains to be determined.

The issue of racism in capital sentencing focuses on African Americans in part because comparable statistical discrimination has not been found among other minority groups.

Asian Americans. Asian Americans make up 3.8 percent of the general population but less than 2 percent of those sentenced to death. Statistically, this means that Asian Americans are significantly underrepresented on death row.

Hispanics. Hispanics make up roughly 12 percent of the general population but just over 7 percent of those sentenced to death. This means that Hispanics are also significantly underrepresented on death row. However, crime rates are higher in Hispanic neighborhoods than in white neighborhoods, and Hispanics make up 18 percent of the general prison population.

Native Americans. Native Americans make up a negligible proportion of those sentenced to death, far smaller than their proportion in the general population of 1.5 percent. This may be due, in part, to the fact that tribal lands within the United States have sovereign status, so crimes committed by Native Americans on those lands fall under the jurisdiction of tribal courts.

Women. Although not a racial minority, women have been singled out as an example of a death-row population far out of their proportion to their percentage of the population. Women make up slightly more than 50 percent of the general population. However, they make up only 14 percent of those convicted of homicide and only about 1.5 percent of those sentenced to death. This is by far the most obvious discrepancy in sentencing patterns. It is clear that women commit far fewer violent crimes than men. Nevertheless, even women who do commit violent crimes are far less likely than men to receive harsh sentences, usually explained as the result of deeply held cultural protections for mothers and cultural biases that women are less responsible than men for their actions. As of April 2005, only ten women had been executed in the United States since 1976. **See also** guided discretion; *McCleskey v. Kemp.*

reanimation of corpses

Early in the discovery and development of electricity, researchers noticed that passing an electric current through a recently dead body could cause muscular responses—twitching, clenching of jaws and fists, and even an occasional breath. In 1786 Luigi Galvani, an Italian biologist who experimented with electricity, speculated that electricity could be used to reanimate a dead body, especially if the electricity could be applied soon after death. It was difficult to perform this experiment on people who died of natural causes, since an experimenter could never know when such an opportunity would present itself. This problem could be solved by doing the experiment on recently executed criminals instead. Throughout the nineteenth century, it was fairly common for curious physicians to perform reanimation experiments on the bodies of recently hanged criminals. None of these experiments produced the intended result, but they were the real-life basis of Mary Shelley's famous horror novel *Frankenstein.* **See also** dissection.

Regulators and Moderators

Vigilante squads in eighteenth- and nineteenth-century America. In frontier

America, where official forms of law enforcement had not yet been established, punishment for crimes was often handled by vigilantes called Regulators. The term was first used in colonial South Carolina following an Indian war in 1767 that left some settlers homeless. The uprooted settlers turned to banditry, which caused other landowners to organize vigilante squads in self-defense. These vigilante squads called themselves Regulators. Having no court system, the Regulators engaged in summary executions. The violence of the Regulators shocked other landowners, who then organized competing vigilante squads known as Moderators. The Moderators also captured suspected lawbreakers, but they administered only floggings rather than hangings. By 1776 the Regulators and Moderators were no longer operating because the land was more settled and the bandits had been driven off.

In the 1840s, Regulators and Moderators again appeared on the Western frontier, notably in eastern Texas. There the Regulators were led by Charles Jackson and, following his death, Watt Moorman, both greedy and ambitious men who used the Regulators as much to enforce their own authority as to fight criminal behavior. A group of Moderators organized to oppose them. Both groups recruited gunfighters from the ranks of the very outlaws they were supposedly organized to stop, and the feud between the two groups grew increasingly violent. By 1844 both sides had formed an army of gunfighters, and an all-out war appeared inevitable. The war was prevented when President Sam Houston of the Republic of Texas (which was not yet part of the United States) sent in the militia to restore order.

In most cases, Regulators and Moderators were local landowners who organized to protect their property. The groups disbanded as soon as more official forms of law enforcement were established. Only a few men made a career of acting as Regulators, moving west with the frontier. Of these, the best known was John X. Beidler, who was active chiefly in the Montana territory. One of the last groups of Regulators, which operated in Montana between 1884 and 1886, was known as the Stranglers. In a brief period of only about a year and a half, they were responsible for hanging some seventy cattle rustlers. **See also** Beidler, John X.; lynching.

Rehnquist, William H. (1924–2005)

William H. Rehnquist was an associate justice of the U.S. Supreme Court from 1971 to 1986 and chief justice from 1986 to 2005. Rehnquist was an influential supporter of capital punishment. As an associate justice, he frequently dissented from opinions that had the effect of limiting capital punishment. As chief justice, he presided over an increasingly conservative Supreme Court. Under Rehnquist's leadership, the Court made numerous decisions that limited the ability of defendants to file habeas corpus appeals.

Rehnquist was born in Milwaukee, Wisconsin, and studied law at Stanford University. Following graduation he served briefly as a law clerk for Supreme Court justice Robert H. Jackson. He then moved to Arizona, where he practiced law in Phoenix. In 1969 Rehnquist became an assistant attorney general in the Richard Nixon administration. In 1971 President Nixon appointed him to the U.S. Supreme Court, against the objections of civil rights organizations, who believed that Rehnquist had a poor record on civil rights issues. Rehnquist proved to be one of the most consistently conservative Supreme Court justices. In 1973 he dissented from the *Roe v. Wade* decision legalizing abortion. He also consistently opposed affirmative action and consistently favored limiting the rights of criminal defendants and suspects.

Rehnquist was one of four justices to oppose the 1972 decision in *Furman v. Georgia*, which overturned the country's death-penalty statutes. In 1976 Rehnquist joined the majority in *Gregg v. Georgia*, ruling that death-penalty statutes could be reinstituted provided they gave juries sufficient guidance on when a death sentence could be imposed. In 1985 Rehnquist wrote the majority opinion in *Wainwright v. Witt*, which, modifying an earlier decision, made it easier for courts to exclude from death-penalty cases jurors who are inclined to be hesitant to impose the death penalty. Under Rehnquist's leadership, the Supreme Court took a more conservative stance on capital punishment, ruling in 1987 in *McCleskey v. Kemp* that statistics alone are not enough to prove that death-penalty statutes are being applied unfairly. Rehnquist died of thyroid cancer on September 3, 2005. **See also** Supreme Court; *Wainwright v. Witt.*

relativism

Relativism is a theory of ethics according to which the difference between right and wrong is taken to have no objective basis, either in the observable consequences of actions or in objective duties. Relativists believe that an action is right or wrong solely because some person or group of people *say* it is right or wrong, and for no other reason. For this reason relativists usually feel that capital punishment is acceptable in countries where it is permitted.

There are two types of relativism, individual and cultural. Individual relativism is the view that each individual decides for him- or herself what is right and wrong. Although this view is popular with beginning philosophy students, it is not taken seriously by most philosophers, since the view is really equivalent to saying that there is no such thing as morality and people may do as they please. Cultural relativism is the view that right and wrong is decided for each community by the consensus of opinion within that community. Since different communities may develop different conventional opinions, it follows that right and wrong may differ from community to community.

Cultural relativism is sometimes offered as a justification for the claim that countries should respect and tolerate other countries' different customs and practices. Different practices concerning the treatment of criminals would certainly be included. A cultural relativist would maintain that capital punishment is legitimate in one country, provided the social consensus favors it, but not legitimate in another country where the social consensus opposes it. Moreover, different methods of execution may be legitimate from country to country for different crimes. In one country, stoning may be acceptable for the crime of adultery; in another country, stoning may not be acceptable at all. In one country, the execution of juveniles may be acceptable; in another country, it may not be acceptable.

Against cultural relativism, critics argue that the view cannot be used to defend universal respect and toleration without violating the very principle upon which the argument rests. According to cultural relativism, moral judgments can be made only within the scope of a specific society, and they apply only to the members of that society. Therefore, if a society in which the consensus of opinion favors toleration, it may be valid to claim that the members *of that society* should respect and tolerate the practices of other societies. But the universal rule that *all societies* should respect and tolerate each other's practices reaches beyond the scope of a specific society, so it cannot be consistently maintained by a cultural relativist. Indeed, if the consensus within a particular society favored interfering in the practices of other societies, the cultural relativist would have to admit that such interference was morally justified. **See also** justification of punishment; utilitarianism.

religious views

The views that people hold about capital punishment are often influenced, if not determined, by their religious beliefs, which are closely tied to individual moral values. The earliest opposition to capital punishment came from liberal Protestant denominations, such as the Quakers, the Puritans, and the Mennonites, who came to question the authority of civil governments to act on behalf of God in putting people to death.

In early America, the debate over capital punishment largely turned on religious conceptions of the nature of the human soul. Conservative religious groups, such as the Congregationalists and the Presbyterians, held that humans were by nature depraved and sinful. According to this view, all people had an inclination toward criminal behavior, but those who maintained a proper hold on Christian teachings could resist the fall into criminality. People who failed to resist had only their own depraved nature to blame, and were properly punished for their failings, even by being put to death. By contrast, liberal religious groups, such as the Unitarians and the Universalists, rejected the doctrine of original sin and the accompanying view that all people are by nature depraved. People were presumed to be essentially well meaning. People who became criminals were thought to be victims of a harsh environment who turned to crime out of anger or desperation. According to this view, the chief purpose of punishment should be to reform rather than to punish. In particular, the Universalists, who believed in universal salvation (i.e., that no soul would ultimately be consigned to hell), believed that criminals could be redeemed and that it was the responsibility of society to try to redeem them. Naturally, the liberal religious movements saw little value in capital punishment, and members of these groups were leaders in the movement to abolish capital punishment. Interpretation of the Bible also played a major role in the debate, with different denominations giving different interpretations of scripture. Congregationalists and Presbyterians interpreted the Bible as explicitly endorsing capital punishment, citing Genesis 9:6, "Whoso sheddeth man's blood, by man shall his blood be shed." Unitarians and Universalists interpreted the Bible as offering little or no support for the continued use of capital punishment.

Most American religious denominations have adopted resolutions or issued position statements on capital punishment. These statements do not generally have the force of doctrine, and it would not be fair to assert that all members of a religious group agree with the position expressed by the organization to which they belong. Nevertheless, it is possible to make some general comments about the status of the capital punishment debate in the major world religions.

Christianity. Protestant Christians are still divided, much as they were in early America. Denominations that consider themselves to be fundamentalist or Pentecostal tend to strongly endorse capital punishment and claim biblical support for their view. For example, at its 2000 session the Southern Baptist Convention adopted a resolution in support of capital punishment that states that capital punishment is "a legitimate form of punishment for those guilty of murderous or treasonous acts that result in death," when used by civil authorities. On the other hand, many other denominations, including many that have historically supported capital punishment, have shifted their position. Recent resolutions opposing capital punishment have been passed by the American Baptists (who are not the same group as the Southern Baptists), the Episcopalians, the Lutherans, the Methodists, the Presbyterians, and the United Church of Christ. The Catholic Church has traditionally supported capital punishment as a legitimate exercise of the authority of the state. However, sentiment among church leaders has recently become more critical of capital punishment. In 1995 Pope John Paul II issued an encyclical titled *Evangelium Vitae* that takes the view that, while capital punishment may be acceptable in principle, it is not the best way in practice to achieve the goals of punishment and therefore should not be used. Orthodox Christian organizations, such as the Russian Orthodox Church and the Greek Orthodox Church, have also come out against capital punishment.

Islam. Like Christianity, Islam is a large and diverse religious movement, and no single statement can capture the beliefs of all Muslims. There are Muslims who oppose capital punishment and others who support it, and a lively debate rages on the issue within Muslim society. However, it is generally acknowledged that the Koran does not forbid capital punishment when it is imposed through appropriate legal channels, and sharia (traditional Islamic law) provides for the imposition of the death penalty for such crimes as robbery, adultery, and apostasy. Nearly all Islamic countries permit the use of the death penalty.

Judaism. Judaism is also a large and diverse religion, and American Jews are divided on the issue along much the same lines as American Christians. Reform Jews and conservative Jews are more inclined to oppose capital punishment, whereas the Orthodox branch of Judaism finds scriptural support for capital punishment in the Torah. However, rather than taking an official stand, Jewish organizations deem the issue of capital punishment to be a matter for the conscience of individuals. Israel, which is officially a Jewish state, has renounced the use of capital punishment except for crimes committed during time of war.

Buddhism. Certain major sects of Buddhism take a strong stand against capital punishment. The Dalai Lama, leader of the important Vajrayana sect, has stated his opposition to capital punishment. The Tendai sect in Japan has also issued a statement declaring capital punishment incompatible with Buddhist principles. However, countries where Buddhism is practiced are among those in which executions are quite common. China is the most obvious example, but Southeast Asian countries that frequently employ the death penalty are also strongly influenced by Buddhism.

Hinduism. Hinduism does not have a central institutional authority, so there can be no official position on the issue of capital punishment. Nevertheless, certain sects of Hinduism practice forms of extreme pacifism, attempting to refrain from killing even such minor creatures as insects. The eating of meat is forbidden for most Hindus. This would seem to suggest that Hindus would oppose the use of the death penalty. However, India, the country most strongly influenced by Hinduism, continues to practice capital punishment. **See also** Bible; Koran.

repentance

In early America, criminal trials were usually quite brief—several could be held in the course of a single day—and there were no appeals courts, so a sentence of death, once pronounced, could be considered final. Nevertheless, between pronouncing a sentence of death and carrying it out, courts would typi-

A confessed murderer prays with a priest in his cell. Some spiritual advisers specialize in ministering to death row inmates.

cally allow a delay of one or two weeks, and in some cases even up to several months. This delay was allowed even though it cost money to feed and house the condemned prisoner and even though it increased the chance of an escape. The delay was regarded as necessary to allow the condemned prisoner time to repent in preparation for death.

According to widely held Christian belief, all humans are sinners, but they may be saved from hell by accepting God's forgiveness before death. For condemned prisoners, this doctrine was considered both good news and bad news. A condemned prisoner was considered fortunate in that he knew the precise time of his death and could focus his mind on accepting divine forgiveness ahead of that time, but, of course, he was considered unfortunate in that time was short. To facilitate the prisoner's acceptance of divine forgiveness, it was not unusual for a parade of ministers, preachers, and even well-intentioned citizens to visit the condemned prisoner with spiritual advice, exhortations, and prayers. In some cases this had the intended effect. Prisoners who gave a full confession of their sins and professed to feel forgiven by God were sent to the gallows with much rejoicing that a soul had been saved. In some cases, if the appropriate authorities felt the repentance was genuine, the sentence of death could then be lifted. However, in other cases prisoners regarded the visitors as meddlers and a nuisance that they would gladly have been spared. Rose Butler, a nineteen-year-old slave condemned for arson, complained that one clergyman's only words of comfort to her were to assure her that she would burn in hell. Hannah Ocuish, a twelve-year-old girl whose parents had abandoned her, had to endure a steady stream of visitors telling her that her fault lay in not being more obedient to her parents.

Today, access to condemned prisoners is more limited, but prisoners are still allowed frequent visits by spiritual advisers of their choice. Death row repentance does still occur, although the delay between sentencing and execution now has to do with the time it takes for legal appeals rather than concern for the condemned prisoner's soul. Karla Faye Tucker, who was executed for murder in 1998, underwent a conversion experience while on death row in Texas. She claimed to be "born again," a term used by some branches of Protestant Christianity to refer to the religious experience of divine forgiveness.

Some spiritual advisers specialize in ministering to death row inmates. Among the best known are Sister Helen Prejean and United Church of Christ minister Joe Ingle. Both are staunch opponents of capital punishment. **See also** Ingle, Joe; Ocuish, Hannah; Prejean, Helen; Tucker, Karla Faye.

retentionists

In the context of the debate over capital punishment, a retentionist is someone who favors capital punishment or someone who is opposed to abolishing the use of capital punishment. Unlike the abolitionist movement, retentionists have never been highly organized. Capital punishment has been, at least until the twentieth century, an accepted practice not subject to dispute, so there was little incentive for a movement in support of capital punishment. However, retentionists have provided strong resistance to the abolitionist movement at all stages of its history, and in any generation there have been important spokesmen for the retention of capital punishment. During the nineteenth century, George Barrell Cheever distinguished himself as a proponent of capital punishment by debating the issue with prominent abolitionists. In the twentieth century, philosopher Walter Berns was one of the most articulate defenders of capital punishment. **See also** Berns, Walter; Cheever, George Barrell; opposition to capital punishment, history of.

Rhode Island

Rhode Island does not currently permit juries to impose the death penalty. However, thirty-two people were hanged for piracy in colonial Rhode Island, as well as a handful for murder and other crimes. (Twenty-six people were hanged for piracy on the same day, July 19, 1723.) In 1833 Rhode Island became the first state to formally abolish public viewing of executions. In 1852 Rhode Island became the second state to abolish capital punishment altogether (preceded by Michigan in

1846). However, capital punishment was reinstated twenty years later, in 1872, for murder committed by a prisoner serving a life sentence. No one was executed under this law. In fact, the last execution in Rhode Island took place in 1845.

In 1972 all state death-penalty statutes, including Rhode Island's, were declared unconstitutional by the U.S. Supreme Court decision in *Furman v. Georgia.* The Rhode Island legislature has not so far bothered to replace it, so there is currently no death-penalty statute in Rhode Island. **See also** *Furman v. Georgia;* multiple executions.

rights of the accused

To prevent the conviction of innocent people, and to prevent governments from abusing their powers by harassing and intimidating citizens, people who are accused of crimes are guaranteed certain rights. Among the most important rights in capital prosecutions are the following.

The right to counsel. Because criminal law can be quite complex, any person charged with a crime has the right to be advised by, and represented by, someone with expertise in the law. Initially, this right meant only that a defendant could not be prevented from hiring legal counsel if he or she wished to do so. It did not necessarily mean that the government was obligated to provide counsel to defendants. However, in the 1963 *Gideon v. Wainwright* decision, the Supreme Court ruled that state governments as well as the federal government must provide adequate counsel for defendants too poor to hire their own counsel, since the law is so complex that people who lack the financial means to hire an attorney would not otherwise be guaranteed due process of law.

The right to refrain from self-incrimination. The Fifth Amendment to the U.S. Constitution says that no one may be compelled to be a witness against himself. This means that the prosecution may not call the defendant to testify in court. Indeed, a defendant may decline to testify altogether, and neither the judge nor the prosecutor is allowed to imply (to jurors) that such a refusal to testify suggests that the defendant is guilty. The right to refrain from self-incrimination applies even outside the courtroom. Defendants may not be compelled to answer questions by investigators, and may demand the presence of an attorney during interrogation. Furthermore, defendants must be told that they have these rights. On the other hand, the right to refrain from self-incrimination applies only to verbal testimony. Investigators *may* collect evidence, including DNA samples, fingerprints, and voice and handwriting samples from a defendant, and they may compel a defendant to participate in a lineup.

The right to trial by jury. To prevent prosecution by government officials (including judges) who may have political reasons to find a defendant guilty, the Sixth Amendment guarantees that criminal defendants have the right to be tried by a jury of impartial citizens. The Sixth Amendment does not specify the size of the jury, but a jury of twelve is required for capital trials in every jurisdiction in the United States, except the military. To ensure impartiality, the selection of jurors is a carefully controlled process, and numerous cases involving the selection of jurors have come before the Supreme Court. A defendant may waive the right to trial by jury, and this has been done in rare cases, notably the trial of Nathan Leopold and Richard Loeb in 1924. **See also** Constitution of the United States; trial.

Ring v. Arizona

This was a case heard by the Supreme Court of the United States in 2002 concerning whether a sentence of death may be imposed by a judge alone, without the help of a jury. The defendant, Timothy Ring, was convicted of felony murder during the commission of an armed robbery, although the jury deadlocked on the charge of premeditated murder. Under Arizona law, the penalty phase of a trial was presented before a judge who determined, without the help of a jury, which aggravating and mitigating circumstances were present. At least one aggravating circumstance had to be present for the penalty of death to be imposed, and there could be no mitigating circumstances sufficient to call for leniency. In this case, the judge determined that two aggravating circumstances were present, and, while Ring's minimal criminal record was a mitigating factor, the judge did not consider it sufficient to call for leniency. The judge sentenced Ring to death. Ring's sentence was then appealed on the grounds that the Arizona death-penalty statute, under which no jury is present at sentencing, violated the Sixth Amendment guarantee of a defendant's right to trial by jury. Two previous Supreme Court decisions, *Jones v. United States* (1999) and *Appendi v. New Jersey* (2000), had offered conflicting decisions on this matter. To clear up confusion, the Supreme Court agreed to review Ring's appeal.

In a 7-to-2 decision, the Court ruled that, to the extent that a sentencing hearing involved the determination of facts not decided by the jury during the guilt phase of the trial, a judge alone could not impose a sentence. Writing for the majority, Justice Ruth Bader Ginsburg held that the Sixth Amendment guarantees a defendant the right to have all questions of fact decided by a jury. The presence or absence of aggravating and mitigating circumstances relevant to the nature of the crime are matters of fact and should therefore be decided by a jury. Only if these facts have been sufficiently determined in the guilt phase of the trial may a judge impose a sentence without the help of a jury. In Ring's case, the judge had made substantial findings of fact beyond what had been decided by the jury, so Ring's sentence was overturned. **See also** Arizona; trial.

Roberts v. Louisiana
This was a case heard by the Supreme Court of the United States in 1976, and was a companion case to the landmark *Woodson v. North Carolina* case, which considered the constitutionality of state death-penalty statutes that make the death penalty a mandatory sentence. The defendant in the case, Harry Roberts, was convicted of the murder of a police officer and sentenced to death under a new Louisiana death-penalty statute that had been passed to replace the old statute overturned in 1972 by the *Furman v. Georgia* decision. The new statute was similar to the statute in North Carolina, under which a sentence of death was mandatory for certain crimes, so the Supreme Court bundled the case with the *Woodson v. North Carolina* case. The Court ruled that laws requiring a mandatory death sentence were unconstitutional, being too severe to be consistent with the Eighth Amendment's prohibition of cruel and unusual punishment. **See also** mandatory sentencing; *Woodson v. North Carolina.*

Romano v. Oklahoma
This was a case heard by the Supreme Court of the United States in 1994 concerning whether information made available to a penalty-phase jury about a defendant's previous death sentence violated the defendant's right to a fair sentencing. In 1985 John Joseph Romano and his accomplice, David Wayne Woodruff, robbed and murdered Roger Sarfaty, an acquaintance of Romano's who worked as a jeweler. About nine months later, in 1986, they robbed and murdered another man, Lloyd Thompson. They were arrested and tried jointly

for Thompson's murder. Both were initially sentenced to death. They were later given separate trials at which Romano was again sentenced to death, but Woodruff was sentenced to life imprisonment without parole. However, following the joint trial for Thompson's death, Romano was convicted of Sarfaty's murder. During the penalty phase of the trial, the jury was told of Romano's death sentence from the previous trial. Romano was given a second death sentence. The sentence was appealed on the grounds that information about the previous death sentence was irrelevant to the present case and should have been withheld from the jury. The Oklahoma Criminal Court of Appeals rejected this argument, and the U.S. Supreme Court agreed to review the case.

In a 5-to-4 decision, the Supreme Court ruled that the defendant's rights had not been violated and that the sentence should be allowed to stand. Writing for the Court, Chief Justice William H. Rehnquist admitted that information about the previous death sentence was indeed irrelevant. However, he argued that the defendant's rights could be violated only by the admission of evidence that misleads the jury or impairs their ability to perform their duty. He concluded that since there was no reason to suppose that knowing about a previous death sentence would make the jury either more or less inclined to impose a sentence of death, the defendant's rights in this case were not violated. John Romano was executed by lethal injection on January 29, 2002. **See also** *South Carolina v. Gathers.*

Roper v. Simmons

This landmark 2005 Supreme Court decision abolished the death penalty for juveniles; that is, for persons younger than eighteen at the time of their offense. The ruling is based on the presumption, based on evolving community standards, that juveniles lack the maturity to be fully responsible for their actions.

The defendant in the case, Christopher Simmons, was convicted in Missouri of the 1993 murder of Shirley Crook, by tying her up with electrical cable, leather straps, and duct tape, and throwing her into the Meramac River. He was seventeen years old at the time. At the time of his conviction in 1997, Missouri permitted the execution of offenders who were under the age of eighteen, and Simmons was sentenced to death. The Missouri Supreme Court initially upheld the conviction. However, Simmons' attorneys filed a second appeal following the U.S. Supreme Court's 2002 *Atkins v. Virginia* decision, in which the execution of mentally retarded offenders was declared to be cruel and unusual. This time the Missouri Supreme Court agreed that execution of juvenile offenders should no longer be considered constitutional in Missouri. The court argued that the 1989 *Stanford v. Kentucky* decision, in which the Supreme Court upheld the execution of juvenile offenders, could no longer be considered binding in light of changes in community standards since the time of that decision. The prosecution appealed this decision, and the U.S. Supreme Court agreed to review the case.

In a 5-to-4 decision issued in March 2005, the Supreme Court upheld the Missouri Supreme Court's ruling, bringing an end to the execution of juvenile offenders in the United States. Writing for the majority, Justice Anthony Kennedy explained that the criterion used by the courts in determining community standards involves objective evidence; specifically, laws enacted by state legislatures and decisions reached by juries. He illustrated this point by noting that, following the 1989 *Penry v. Lynaugh* decision upholding the execution of mentally retarded offenders, several states changed their laws to prohibit the execution of the mentally retarded, which then led to the 2002 Supreme Court decision, in *Atkins v. Virginia*, in which the execution of mentally retarded offenders was declared unconstitutional. Kennedy then pointed out that, since the 1989 *Stanford v. Kentucky* decision, several states had also changed their laws on the execution of juvenile offenders, and that in that time juries had rarely sentenced juvenile offenders to death, even in states in which such decisions were permitted. He concluded that a national consensus against the execution of juvenile offenders had emerged. Moreover, he wrote, because juveniles are less mature and responsible than adults, and are more susceptible to outside influence, juvenile offenders could not be reliably included among the worst offenders, for whom the death penalty should be reserved. Finally, he pointed out that there was a strong international consensus against the execution of juvenile offenders, expressed in such treaties and declarations as the United Nations Convention on the Rights of the Child. This emerging consensus, Kennedy argued, provided sufficient reason to conclude that execution was a disproportionate penalty for juvenile offenders.

Writing in dissent, Justice Sandra Day O'Connor challenged Kennedy's arguments, claiming that the number of changes in state laws, and the number of jury decisions, was not sufficient to establish clear evidence of a national consensus against the execution of juvenile offenders. She also challenged the view that there is a significant and universal difference in maturity between adults and juveniles. While she agreed with Kennedy that international law should be considered relevant to the question of community standards, she did not think it was sufficient by itself to justify overturning the precedent set in the *Stanford* decision. Justices Antonin Scalia, Clarence Thomas, and Chief Justice William Rehnquist also dissented from the majority opinion. However, unlike O'Connor, they specifically disagreed with Kennedy's use of international law, asserting, "'Acknowledgment' of foreign approval has no place in the legal opinion of this Court."

The *Roper* decision overturned the sentences of seventy-two condemned inmates convicted of their crimes as juveniles, and invalidated the statutes of twenty-three states that permitted the death penalty for juveniles as young as sixteen. The decision—both majority and dissenting opinions—is likely to be pivotal to future discussions of community standards in "cruel and unusual punishment" cases. **See also** juvenile offenders; *Stanford v. Kentucky*.

Rosenberg, Julius (1918–1953) and Ethel (1915–1953)

Julius and Ethel Rosenberg were the last people executed for espionage in the United States. Although they were charged with helping to pass information to the Soviet Union on how to build nuclear weapons, surely one of the most serious breaches of national security of the twentieth century, their executions provoked considerable sympathy and sparked worldwide protests and claims that the executions amounted to political persecution for the couple's leftist politics.

As a young man in the 1930s, Julius Rosenberg was a member of the Communist Party of the United States. He met Ethel Greenglass at a labor union event and married her in 1939. During the 1940s, while the Soviet Union was allied with the United States against Nazi Germany, some sympathy for the Soviets was to be expected among Americans, and Julius Rosenberg was undoubtedly sympathetic to Soviet interests. In 1944 Ethel's brother, David

In 1953 Ethel and Julius Rosenberg became the last people to be executed for espionage in the United States.

Greenglass, who was serving as a soldier in the U.S. military, was assigned to work as a machinist on the Manhattan Project, a highly secret program to develop a functioning nuclear weapon. Julius Rosenberg asked Greenglass to provide him with information on the progress of the research. Greenglass agreed to do so. Greenglass supplied handwritten notes and drawings with critical information on the workings of a nuclear bomb. In most cases, Greenglass passed this information to a courier, Harry Gold, who identified himself as working for Rosenberg by showing one piece of a Jell-O box that had been neatly cut into two pieces, the other piece having been given to Greenglass's wife, Ruth. Gold then passed the information on to Anatoli Yakovlev, the head of Soviet intelligence operations in the United States. The spy ring was broken up when Klaus Fuchs, a German-born physicist who was also working on the Manhattan Project, was arrested in England for passing information to the Soviets. Fuchs's contact had also been Harry Gold. When Gold was captured, he confessed to espionage and implicated Greenglass, who in turn implicated Julius Rosenberg. Rosenberg himself denied any involvement in spying, but two more members of the ring, Morton Sobell and Max Elitcher, were eventually captured and Elitcher agreed to testify against Rosenberg and Sobell.

There was no clear evidence against Ethel Rosenberg, but charges were brought against her nevertheless in the hope that this would pressure Julius Rosenberg into providing more information. To build a case against Ethel, the FBI threatened to bring charges against Ruth Greenglass. At trial, David Greenglass testified that his sister, Ethel, had spent an evening typing sensitive information that he had supplied. This was the only evidence presented at trial implicating Ethel Rosenberg in the espionage operations. In an interview in 2001, David Greenglass admitted that his testimony against his sister had been a lie, which he had told in order to get the FBI to drop its charges against his wife. At the time, he did not realize that his testimony would result in his sister's death.

The trial of Julius and Ethel Rosenberg on federal charges of conspiracy to commit wartime espionage took place in March 1951. Morton Sobell was tried at the same time. The Rosenbergs continued to deny the charges against them, but both were found guilty and sentenced to death. Sobell was found guilty and sentenced to thirty years in prison (of which he served eighteen). After two years of legal appeals and pleas for clemency failed to result in reduced sentences, the Rosenbergs were executed on June 19, 1953. Since that time, others have been charged with and convicted of espionage, but none have been sentenced to death.

After the fall of the Soviet Union in 1989, some KGB (the Soviet intelligence agency) documents were released to the West. These documents confirm that Julius Rosenberg was spying for the Soviets. However, there is no mention of Ethel Rosenberg's involvement, and Russian officials familiar with the case have stated that, in their opinion, her execution was unjustified. **See also** capital crimes; Sacco, Nicola, and Bartolomeo Vanzetti.

Rudolph v. Alabama

This was a case that was *not* heard by the Supreme Court of the United States, although it was considered for review in 1963. The defendant in the case, Frank Lee Rudolph, was a black man sentenced to death for rape. The sentence was appealed on the grounds that the death penalty was disproportionately severe for the crime committed. In a 6-to-3 ruling, the Supreme Court refused to hear the case (thus allowing the decision of the appeals court to remain in effect). However, the dissent issued by the three justices who had voted to hear the case, Arthur J. Goldberg, William Brennan, and William O. Douglas, proposed several constitutional issues that they believed were raised by the case. The issues they suggested went well beyond the rather narrow argument made by Rudolph's attorney, including whether state death-penalty statutes were allowing sentences to be imposed too arbitrarily. The dissent signaled to defense lawyers around the country that at least some members of the Supreme Court were willing to consider challenges to capital punishment based on the arbitrary and discriminatory way in which the death penalty was being imposed. In response, numerous appeals were filed along these lines. Eventually, many of these appeals worked their way up to the Supreme Court, ultimately changing the way capital punishment is practiced in the United States. **See also** *Furman v. Georgia;* Goldberg, Arthur J.; *Maxwell v. Bishop.*

Rush, Benjamin (1745–1813)

Benjamin Rush was one of the founding fathers of the United States, and the first vocal opponent of capital punishment in the United States. Rush was born near Philadelphia in 1745 and educated at the College of New Jersey (which later became Princeton University). He then went to Scotland to study medicine at the University of Edinburgh. He received further training in medicine at St. Thomas Hospital in London. While he was in London he became acquainted with fellow American Benjamin Franklin, who was visiting England at the time. When he returned to America, Rush practiced medicine and took a position as professor of chemistry at the College of Philadelphia, where he established himself as a leading scientist and physician.

In the years leading up to the American Revolution, Rush developed an interest in social philosophy and began associating with revolutionary leaders Thomas Paine and John Adams. Rush proposed the title for Thomas Paine's pamphlet *Common Sense.* He was among those elected to represent Pennsylvania at the Continental Congress and so became one of the signers of the Declaration of Independence. In 1777, with the establishment of the Continental army under George Washington, Rush was made surgeon general of the army, but controversies led to his resignation soon afterward. After the Revolution, Rush was influential in the writing and ratification of the Constitution of the United States. It was Rush who insisted to John Adams that a republic must have *three* branches of government to ensure a proper balance of power.

Rush was involved in numerous reform movements in an attempt to improve the moral character of the citizens of the new United States. He supported improved education for women and served as one of the founding trustees of Dickenson College, a Presbyterian college for women. He was opposed to slavery and served as president of the Pennsylvania Society for Promoting the Abolition of Slavery. In addition, his writings on temperance are credited with starting the American temperance (anti-alcohol) movement.

Among Rush's chief crusades was an attempt to reform the treatment of criminals. Rush first presented his ideas in a talk at the home of Benjamin Franklin. This talk was prompted by the passage in 1786 of a new criminal law in Pennsylvania known as the "wheelbarrow law." Under this law, many crimes that had previously been punishable by death were now punishable by hard labor, intended both to humiliate criminals publicly and to reap the benefits of their forced labor. Within a few months, it became clear that the punishments were only serving to create a class of hardened criminals. In opposing these laws, Rush argued that the purpose of punishment should be the *reform* of criminals, not merely deterrence or the exacting of retribution. For this purpose, he argued that criminals should be sent not to prisons for the purpose of incarceration but to "penitentiaries," or houses of repentance, where they could be reeducated to become reformed and useful members of society. Rush proposed that criminals should not be sentenced to fixed periods of imprisonment but should be given indefinite sentences and held as long as necessary to achieve their reform. Since a dead criminal cannot be reformed, Rush drew the conclusion that the death penalty had no place in a system of justice.

Rush's talk was published as part of a larger essay titled *An Enquiry into the Effect of Public Punishments upon Criminals and upon Society*, which was widely read. A second essay, *Considerations on the Injustice and Impolicy of Punishing Murder by Death*, focusing specifically on arguments against capital punishment, opened a flood of controversy. To answer his critics, Rush revised the essay twice, finally publishing it in 1798 as *An Enquiry into the Consistency of the Punishment of Murder by Death, with Reason and Revelation*.

In this essay, Rush was the first to use many of the arguments that are still raised against capital punishment today, from scriptural and religious objections to arguments on the ineffectiveness of the death penalty as a deterrent. Rush argued that murderers were rarely habitual criminals but more likely to have been motivated by brief, violent passions. As such, they were more likely to feel remorse and be amenable to reform than criminals who were habitually guilty of less serious crimes.

Rush's views were extremely influential. Although he was not able to convince any states to abandon the death penalty, his essay did result in the repeal of the wheelbarrow law in 1789 and the conversion in 1790 of the Walnut Street Jail in Philadelphia into the world's first penitentiary. The modern practice of giving variable sentences, with a possibility of parole for prisoners who show evidence of having reformed, is due to Rush's influence on American criminal justice. **See also** Beccaria, Cesare; imprisonment; opposition to capital punishment, history of (1648–1870).

Ryan, George H. (1934–)

As governor of Illinois, George Ryan declared a moratorium on executions in his state. He then appointed a commission to study problems within the Illinois death penalty system and to make recommendations for solving those problems. When the Illinois legislature failed to act on the commission's recommendations, Ryan commuted the sentences of all 167 prisoners awaiting execution on Illinois' death row. His actions as governor are among the most bold and dramatic by any politician in the history of capital punishment.

Ryan was born in Manquoketa, Iowa, in 1934. One year later his family moved to Kankakee, Illinois, where his father had taken a job as a pharmacist. In 1948 Ryan's father started his own pharmacy business in Kankakee. After serving in the U.S. Army in Korea, Ryan followed in his father's footsteps, studying pharmacy at Ferris State College (now Ferris State University) and then going to work in the family pharmacy in 1961.

While still working in the pharmacy, Ryan became involved in politics. In 1962 he served as campaign manager for Republican state senator Edward McBroom. In 1966 he was appointed to a seat on the Kankakee County Board, and two years later he won the seat in an election. In 1972 he ran for and won a seat in the Illinois House of Representatives. As a state representative, Ryan was known as a social conservative, opposing abortion and gun control. He also successfully worked to defeat ratification of the Equal Rights Amendment by Illinois. By 1977, Ryan had become House minority leader, and when the Republicans became the majority party in 1981, Ryan became speaker of the House. However, in 1982 Ryan left the state legislature to serve for eight years as lieutenant governor under Republican governor James R. Thompson.

In 1990 Ryan and his father sold the family pharmacy, and Ryan devoted himself to politics full-time. Ryan ran for and won the office of secretary of state in Illinois. As secretary of state, he supported legislation that could be characterized as "tough on crime," including a bill to reduce the legal blood alcohol limit for drunk driving from 0.1 percent to 0.08 percent.

After two terms as secretary of state, Ryan announced that he would run for governor. Ryan's opponent was Democratic congressman Glenn Poshard from southern Illinois. Poshard held views that were in some cases more conservative even than Ryan's. For example, Ryan's "tough on crime" stance had led him to support tough penalties on crimes committed with guns. He had also come to support strong gun-safety laws. Poshard opposed even these restrictions on guns and received higher marks from the National Rifle Association than did Ryan. With support from many moderate Democrats, as well as support from his own party, Ryan won the election by a healthy margin.

Not long after taking office, Ryan became aware of serious problems in the Illinois criminal justice system, especially in the prosecution of capital cases. Since 1977, when Illinois reinstated the death penalty following the *Furman v. Georgia* decision, only twelve prisoners on death row had been executed, but thirteen death row prisoners had been released because it had been discovered that they were innocent. In September 1998, Anthony Porter was released from death row just forty-eight hours before his scheduled execution when a university journalism class turned up evidence proving his innocence. Horrified by the state's record of sentencing innocent people to death, Ryan announced on January 31, 2000, that no one else would be executed in Illinois until factors leading to the conviction of the innocent were discovered and fixed. Ryan then appointed a blue-ribbon commission to study the problem and make recommendations. When the commission returned its recommendations, Ryan pressured the state legislature to have them enacted.

At first there appeared to be broad support for the commission's recommendations. However, many state legislators were unwilling to vote in ways that could be characterized by opponents as "soft on crime," so no action was taken. Meanwhile, Governor Ryan had become embroiled in a major scandal resulting from evidence that inspectors responsible for issuing driver's licenses had given licenses to unqualified drivers in exchange for contributions to Ryan's campaign fund. Because of the scandal, Ryan decided not to run for reelection in 2002, but he was also unwilling to leave office with the death-penalty issue unresolved. Since the legislature had failed to act, Ryan decided to commute the sentences of all prisoners still awaiting execution in Illinois. On January 11, 2003, ten days before leaving office, he announced that all 167 Illinois death row inmates would have their sentences reduced. Three had their sentences reduced to forty years, the same as codefendants who had been convicted of the same crime but not sentenced to death. The remaining 164 had their sentences reduced to life in prison without parole.

There was surprisingly little negative response to Governor Ryan's actions. Indeed, polls showed that roughly half of the voters of Illinois agreed that Ryan had been forced to grant clemency because of the inaction of the legislature. The result was that the incoming legislature was much more willing to consider death-penalty reforms. Several of the commission's recommendations were eventually passed and signed into law by the new governor, Rod Blagojevich, who had campaigned as a supporter of capital punishment. However, the moratorium on the death penalty imposed by Governor Ryan has yet to be lifted, and Blagojevich has hinted that it may not be lifted while he is in office. **See also** Illinois; moratorium movement.

Sacco, Nicola (1891–1927), and Bartolomeo Vanzetti (1880–1927)

The executions of Nicola Sacco and Bartolomeo Vanzetti were among the most controversial executions in the history of the United States. Sacco and Vanzetti were Italian immigrants who came to the United States in 1908. Sacco worked in a shoe factory near Medford, Massachusetts, and Vanzetti worked as a fish peddler. The two men were active anarchists (i.e., they believed that society would be more just and peaceful if governments did not exist), and Vanzetti sometimes gave talks promoting his political views. At the time, anarchists were widely feared as radicals who were seeking the violent overthrow of democratic governments.

On April 15, 1920, a gang of five men robbed a shoe factory in South Braintree, Massachusetts. The paymaster and his guard were killed, and the payroll—over $15,000—was taken. Witnesses said the men looked Italian. It is hard to understand precisely how Sacco and Vanzetti were connected to this crime. Police, in an unrelated investigation, had a car under surveillance because the owner was suspected of being part of an Italian gang that had attempted a holdup a few months before. The car was in a garage for repairs. When a group of Italian men showed up to claim the car, the garage owner attempted to stall them until the police could arrive in force. Becoming suspicious, the men scattered. Two boarded a streetcar. A few minutes later police stopped the streetcar and arrested Sacco and Vanzetti. Sacco and Vanzetti were each found to be carrying unlicensed guns and a flyer announcing an anarchist meeting at which Vanzetti was scheduled to speak. Sacco's gun appeared to be similar to the gun used in the South Braintree robbery, so Sacco and Vanzetti were charged with the crime.

The trial, which began in May 1921, was followed closely by the press. Most historians describe the trial as degenerating into a debating forum on Sacco and Vanzetti's unpopular political views. Their political views came up because they claimed they were picking up the car, with the permission of the owner, in order to use it to transport literature supporting their cause. Sacco and Vanzetti believed they were being persecuted for their political beliefs, and Vanzetti was willing to use the trial as a forum for his ideas. Some sources claim that the judge and prosecutor made every effort to keep the trial focused on the question of their guilt, but the press at least were chiefly interested in the political debate. The evidence against Sacco and Vanzetti came down to the fact that the bullets used in the South Braintree robbery and murders matched the kind of ammunition used by Sacco's pistol. The ballistics expert who testified at the trial left jurors with the impression that he had actually matched the bullets used in the robbery to Sacco's gun, but he later claimed that he only meant it was possible for Sacco's gun to fire that kind of ammunition. The judge in the trial, Webster Thayer, had a particular dislike of Italians and hated anarchists. Few historians are willing to claim that Sacco and Vanzetti received a fair trial. They were convicted, and Judge Thayer sentenced them to death by electrocution.

The sentencing of Sacco and Vanzetti sparked worldwide protests. There were demonstrations, and even riots, in front of U.S. embassies around the world. Numerous celebrities stated their opinions, and pleas were made to the state of Massachusetts to commute their sentences. Meanwhile, lawyers filed appeals for a new trial, but the appeals were turned down. Even in 1925 when another inmate, Celestine Madieros, who was on

Nicola Sacco (center, right) and Bartolomeo Vanzetti (center, left) are shackled together as they make their way to the courthouse. Executed in 1927 for murder, the pair has since been exonerated.

death row for a separate murder, confessed to the South Braintree killings, Sacco and Vanzetti still were not granted a new trial. Madieros claimed that he and a gang from Rhode Island were responsible, but his story was full of inconsistencies and was dismissed.

On August 23, 1927, Sacco and Vanzetti, and—coincidentally—Madieros, were executed in sequence on the same day. With his dying breath, Madieros continued to maintain that Sacco and Vanzetti were innocent. Vanzetti also used his last words to proclaim his innocence. Sixty years later, on August 23, 1987, Governor Michael S. Dukakis belatedly used his authority as governor to pardon Sacco and Vanzetti. **See also** Rosenberg, Julius and Ethel.

Salem witchcraft trials

In 1692 the town of Salem, in Massachusetts colony, underwent a hysterical panic during which some two hundred people, mostly women, were accused of witchcraft. Nineteen of the accused were hanged, and one person was executed by *peine forte et dure* (pressing). This incident was similar to witch hunts that had taken place in Europe over the previous three centuries.

The Salem witch hunt was started when a Carib Indian slave named Tituba, who belonged to Reverend Samuel Parris, entertained several village girls with an exhibition of fortune-telling. Among the girls at the fortune-telling was Reverend Parris's nine-year-old daughter, Betty. Later, Betty and her cousin, eleven-year-old Abigail Williams, began falling into trances and making odd noises and gestures. It has been suggested that the girls were hysterical because they believed that the fortune-telling had put their souls at risk of eternal damnation. In any case, it was decided that the girls were bewitched, and the girls named Tituba and two other women who rarely attended church as those responsible for bewitching them. Tituba confessed to the crime, but insisted she had been forced into it by others, including some she could not identify.

This set off an avalanche of accusations that continued through the spring of 1692. The first trial was of the tavern keeper Bridget Bishop. She was convicted on the testimony of Samuel Gray that he had seen a specter with Bishop's appearance hover over his child's cradle and that the child had subsequently sickened and died. Bishop was hanged on June 10. Too late, several respected religious leaders from out of town, including the renowned preacher Cotton Mather, pointed out that "spectral evidence" was unreliable, since specters may take any appearance, including "the shape of the innocent." In later trials such spectral evidence was discounted. However, by the time the trials concluded in May 1693, nineteen people had been convicted and hanged. One eighty-year-old man named Giles Cory was executed by the slower and more painful method known as *peine forte et dure*, which was illegal in England at the time. Cory was executed in this manner in an attempt to force him to acknowledge the jurisdiction of the court. (None of the accused were burned at the stake, a popular misconception, as burning of witches was not practiced in England or its colonies.)

Even before the trials were concluded, people had begun to realize that all, or nearly all, of the accused were innocent. At the final trial, only three of the fifty-two people who stood accused were convicted, and these three were immediately pardoned. Eventually, in response to petitions, nearly all of the earlier convictions were also reversed by the Massachusetts legislature, and compensation was paid to the families of victims. Seven convictions remain on record, for people for whom no one submitted a petition. **See also** burning at the stake; Massachusetts; *peine forte et dure*.

San Quentin State Prison

San Quentin State Prison is the oldest correctional facility in California and was for many years the main maximum-security prison in California. It is famous for housing California's gas chamber.

San Quentin was built during the 1850s, soon after California became a state. It was built using the labor of the convicts who were eventually housed there. As they built the prison, the convicts lived on a prison ship that was anchored just off the coast. Prior to 1893, executions in California were performed chiefly by local county sheriffs, but then San Quentin became the site for most of the executions in the state. (A few executions were also carried out at Folsom Prison.) Executions at San Quentin were originally carried out by hanging. In 1938 a gas chamber was constructed, and the last hanging at San Quentin took place in 1942. From then until 1994, all executions in California were carried out using the gas chamber at San Quentin. In 1994 California began using lethal injection to execute prisoners. However, the gas chamber is still functional, and condemned prisoners have the option of execution by gas if they wish.

All California executions still take place at San Quentin. However, death row prisoners are often held at other institutions, since San Quentin's death row is too small to hold all the prisoners currently awaiting execution in California. **See also** California; gas chamber.

Sanson family

From 1687 to 1847, members of the Sanson family served as executioners in Paris, and throughout France their name became virtually synonymous with the word *executioner*. Six members of the family in succession held the title of chief executioner of Paris through some of the most turbulent periods of French history. Branches of the family served as executioners in Reims, Blois, Provins, Montpellier, and Tours, and female members of the family married executioners who served in Versailles, Melun, and elsewhere. No other family in history has maintained such a long tradition of service as professional executioners or been more famous for their association with the profession. The family tradition continued for so many generations primarily because of the fear and prejudice that was directed against executioners and those who were related to executioners. Some descendants of the Sanson family tried to avoid being executioners. One tried to be a blacksmith and another tried to be a locksmith. However, their businesses failed because few people were willing to do business with them.

Charles Sanson (1635–1707). The first Sanson to hold the title of chief executioner in Paris became an executioner for love. As a young man, he served as an officer in a regiment in the town of Dieppe. He was injured in a riding accident and found on the road by Pierre Jouenne and his daughter Marguerite. Marguerite Jouenne nursed him back to health, and he fell in love with her. She agreed to become his mistress, but would not agree to marry him. He later discovered that her father was the executioner for Dieppe, and that by custom Marguerite was forbidden to marry anyone but another executioner. When their liaison was discovered, Charles resigned his military commission, married Marguerite, and became his father-in-law's apprentice. It is reported that at his first public execution, where his task was only to administer a beating with a club (prior to the prisoner being broken on the wheel by the senior executioner), he fainted and was jeered by the crowd. He apparently did better at subsequent executions. Marguerite died in 1681 giving birth to their second son, also named Charles. In 1685 Charles Sanson moved with his children to Paris, and in 1687 he purchased the commission to be the executioner for the city of Paris. He held the position for eleven years and retired in 1699. When not performing executions, he supplemented his income with the practice of medicine. He was well liked and had a reputation for being polite and as merciful as possible with the people he was required to execute.

Charles Sanson (1681–1726). The first Charles Sanson was always a reluctant executioner, ashamed of his profession. However, he saw no option for his son but to practice the same profession. The second Charles Sanson was sent to Pontoise to apprentice with the executioner of that city. On completing his apprenticeship, he returned to Paris to assist his father. At their first and only execution together, the elder Sanson found himself unable to perform his duty, the beheading of a young woman accused of plotting to kill her husband. The younger Sanson stepped in and performed the execution in his place. That evening the elder Sanson resigned, passing the title of executioner to his son. The second Charles Sanson held the position for twenty-seven years, until his death in 1726. Like his father, he had a gentle nature, practiced medicine to supplement his income, and was respected for his kindness to the people he executed. However, unlike his father, he was not ashamed of his profession or upset by the violence it involved.

Jean-Baptiste Sanson (1719–1788). When the second Charles Sanson died in 1726, his eldest son, Jean-Baptiste, was only seven years old. Nevertheless, according to his father's will—and some pressure applied to the public prosecutor's office by his mother, Anne-Marthe Dubut, who was a forceful and strong-minded woman—the title of executioner of Paris passed to Jean-Baptiste. For the next eleven years, executions in Paris were carried out by deputy executioners, but Jean-Baptiste was present on the scaffold to make the proceedings legal. Given his official position, he had no opportunity to train under a provincial executioner as his father had done. Instead, he and his younger brother Charles-Gabriel were trained by their mother. Charles-Gabriel later became executioner for the city of Reims. At the age of eighteen, Jean-Baptiste, with his mother proudly looking on, performed his first execution. Like his grandfather, Jean-Baptiste had a gentle nature and despised his profession. Early in his career he was known for taking long rides in the countryside following each execution to regain his composure. He is also known to have occasionally disobeyed orders by strangling prisoners prior to breaking them on the wheel so they would not suffer as much. He continued to perform executions until 1754 when, at the age of thirty-five, he suffered a stroke that temporarily left him paralyzed on the right side. Following a period of rest in the countryside, he eventually recovered the use of his limbs and occasionally returned to Paris on visits.

Jean-Baptiste married twice. By his first wife he had two children, a daughter, Madeleine-Claude-Gabrielle, who married the executioner of Melun, and a son, Charles-Henri, who succeeded him as executioner of Paris. His second wife was Jeanne-Gabrielle Berger. The Berger family were executioners in the province of Touraine. By his second wife he had eight more children, including six sons who, following the Sanson/Berger tradition, became executioners in various cities around France. Through them, the Sanson name came to be associated with executions not only in Paris but throughout the country. At family dinners, the men referred to each other formally by the name of the city in which they were employed. Jean-Baptiste Sanson was called "Monsieur Paris" and Nicholas-Charles-Gabriel Sanson was called "Monsieur Reims."

Charles-Henri Sanson (1739–1806). In 1755, at the age of sixteen, Charles-Henri Sanson took over from his father the task of officiating at executions. Again, Anne-Marthe Sanson, his grandmother, applied some pressure to make sure the commission remained in the family. Charles-Henri became the best known and most historically important of the Sanson family since he presided over executions for the longest period of time and served during the bloody period of the French Revolution.

Charles-Henri had a long career as executioner in the period before the French Revolution, serving for over thirty years. As the person responsible for carrying out the harsh sentences imposed by the monarchy, Charles-Henri came to be an obvious symbol of the tyrannical rule of the king. In 1788 he was ordered to execute a young revolutionary named Louschart by breaking him on the wheel. Louschart was accused of murdering his father, but in fact the killing was widely believed to be accidental. At the execution the crowd rioted, destroying the scaffold and releasing Louschart. Charles-Henri fled for his life as a blacksmith held back the mob with a bullwhip. As a result of the incident, the penalty of breaking on the wheel was abolished and other judicial reforms were made, but it was too little and too late to prevent the Revolution.

As the Revolution progressed, Charles-Henri was inclined to support the monarchy, since many revolutionaries opposed not just torture but capital punishment in any form. Charles-Henri feared that under the new government he would be out of work. Instead, he was approached by Joseph-Ignace Guillotin, a prominent member of the revolutionary Constituent Assembly, with a proposal that the two of them should design and build a machine that could guarantee quick and humane executions, To assist them, Charles-Henri approached a friend, harpsichord maker Tobias Schmidt, to do the actual building. Guillotin sought advice from a physician, Antoine Louis, who is generally credited with designing the device. By 1792 the device, which eventually came to be known as "le guillotine," was ready for use. Meanwhile, power in the Constituent Assembly shifted away from the moderates like Guillotin to far more radical revolutionaries headed by Jean-Paul Marat and Robespierre. Robespierre's brutal regime came to be known as the Reign of Terror, and it was the busiest period in Charles-Henri's long career. During that time, Charles-Henri used the guillotine to execute many political prisoners, including the former queen, Marie-Antoinette; the king, Louis XVI; the revolutionary Charlotte Corday for the murder of fellow revolutionary Jean-Paul Marat; and eventually Robespierre himself when he was removed from power in 1794. During that period, Charles-Henri made repeated attempts to resign his post. Finally in 1795, after the Reign of Terror was over, his resignation was accepted.

Henri Sanson (1767–1840). When Charles-Henri's resignation was accepted, his son Henri became the executioner of Paris. Henri Sanson was an educated man with cultured tastes. He played the piano well and frequently attended the opera. However, following the Revolution and the Reign of Terror, executions became increasingly infrequent. Even though Henri supplemented his income with the practice of medicine, as his predecessors had done, it was still very difficult to make a living as an executioner. Unfortunately, as past generations of the Sanson family had learned, their reputation made it impossible to make a living at anything else. Reluctantly, Henri began grooming his own eldest son, Henri-Clement, to continue the family tradition. In 1819 Henri developed pleurisy and remained in ill health for the remainder of his life. He continued to officiate at executions, but his son assisted. After twenty years of ill health, Henri Sanson finally died in 1840.

Henri-Clement Sanson (1799–1889). Having assisted his father at executions for over twenty years, Henri-Clement became the executioner of Paris in 1840 upon the death of his father. Like earlier members of his family, he loathed his profession, but knew he was trapped in it. Unlike his predecessors, he had difficulty accepting his station with wise resignation. Instead, he turned to drink, gambling, and general profligacy. He collected fine art, dressed extravagantly, and maintained mistresses. He soon exhausted the little money he had inherited from his father and could not earn enough to keep up with his debts. He was arrested in 1846 and sent to the debtors' prison on Clichy Street. In order to buy his release, he pawned the guillotine, giving it to his chief creditor, who agreed to hold it until a debt of 3,800 francs was paid. Then in March 1847 Henri-Clement received orders to perform an execution. He was, of course, unable to comply, as the creditor refused to loan back the guillotine. In the end, the Ministry of Justice was forced to pay off the debt to have the guillotine returned. Henri-Clement performed one last execution and was promptly dismissed from his post. Indigent and abandoned by his wife, he retired to the country with his mother. For the rest of his life, he lived primarily on the charity of relatives.

Henri-Clement's only son died in infancy, and his two daughters managed to marry outside the family profession. The Sanson dynasty had come to an end. **See also** breaking on the wheel; executioners; guillotine.

Sawyer v. Whitley

This was a case heard by the Supreme Court of the United States in 1992 concerning the circumstances under which a defendant may file a second habeas corpus petition alleging actual innocence when the second petition is judged to be "successive, abusive, or defaulted." The defendant in the case, Robert Wayne Sawyer, was convicted in Louisiana of participating in a particularly brutal murder in which the victim was beaten, scalded with boiling water, and set on fire. Sawyer was sentenced to death, and the standard state-level appeals were concluded in 1984. The case was then appealed to the federal courts on the grounds that the prosecution's closing statement was in violation of a new rule announced by a 1985 Supreme Court decision. Sawyer's appeal reached the Supreme Court in 1990 as *Sawyer v. Smith*, but in that case the Supreme Court upheld Sawyer's conviction and sentence. New attorneys then filed a second habeas corpus petition on the grounds that the prosecution had failed to disclose evidence that Sawyer had actually attempted to prevent the victim from being set on fire, and on the grounds that Sawyer had received inadequate representation at trial since his trial attorneys had failed to introduce into evidence mental health records indicating that Sawyer was mentally retarded due to fetal alcohol syndrome. However, the federal district court rejected this petition as "successive, abusive, or defaulted," since these issues should have been raised as part of the first habeas corpus petition. The Supreme Court agreed to review the case.

In a unaminous decision, the Supreme Court agreed with the district court that Sawyer's petition failed to meet the standard for a second habeas corpus petition. Writing for the Court, Chief Justice William H. Rehnquist stated that, in a second habeas corpus petition, the petitioner must show "by clear and convincing evidence that, but for a constitutional error, no reasonable juror would have found him or her eligible for the death penalty under the applicable State law." Sawyer's appeal fell short of this standard, so the district court was right not to grant the habeas corpus petition.

Robert Wayne Sawyer was executed by lethal injection on March 15, 1993. Only two years later, the Supreme Court reversed its decision, ruling in *Schlup v. Delo* that the standard for appeals created by the *Sawyer* decision was too difficult to meet. **See also** habeas corpus; *Schlup v. Delo*.

Schlup v. Delo

This was a case heard by the Supreme Court of the United States in 1994, and decided in 1995, concerning the circumstances under which a defendant may file a second habeas corpus petition alleging actual innocence. The defendant in the case, Lloyd E. Schlup, was accused of participating in the stabbing death of a fellow prison inmate at the Missouri State Penitentiary. Two prison guards identified Schlup as one of three white inmates who assaulted a black inmate, Arthur Dade, as the prisoners were filing out of their cells for lunch. However, no other witnesses identified Schlup, and no physical evidence linked Schlup to the crime. Nevertheless, Schlup was convicted and sentenced to death. After exhausting standard state-level appeals, Schlup filed a federal habeas corpus petition claiming that he had been inadequately defended since his trial attorney had failed to call witnesses who could testify that he had not been one of the assailants. The appeal was decided against Schlup. The district court ruled that Schlup's lawyers had reviewed the testimony of relevant witnesses and made a reasonable decision not to present it at trial on the grounds that the testimony would be "repetitive." In 1992 Schlup filed a second habeas corpus petition, again claiming inadequate representation at trial, and also claiming that the prosecution had failed to disclose evidence tending to prove Schlup's innocence. Numerous affidavits from inmates who had been present at the murder were submitted with the petition. All claimed that Schlup was not one of the assailants. Nevertheless, the district court dismissed the petition without considering the merits of the case, saying that it failed to meet the standard of evidence required under the 1992 *Sawyer v. Whitley* Supreme Court decision that a second petition must be supported by "clear and convincing evidence that, but for a constitutional error, no reasonable juror would have found [the defendant] eligible for the death penalty." The Supreme Court agreed to review the case.

In a 6-to-3 decision, the Supreme Court explicitly reversed its earlier *Sawyer v. Whitley* ruling. Writing for the majority, Justice John Paul Stevens claimed that the standard of proof required by the *Sawyer* decision was too strict to prevent obvious miscarriages of justice—in other words, that such a strict standard might result in the execution of people who were actually innocent. Stevens argued that a more appropriate standard of proof, stated in the 1986 *Murray v. Carrier* decision, was that the petition must be supported by evidence sufficient to establish that a constitutional error "probably resulted in the conviction of one who is actually innocent." The Supreme Court returned the case to the district court for reconsideration under the looser standard of evidence. **See also** actual innocence; *Sawyer v. Whitley*.

Scottish Maiden

The Scottish Maiden was a device used for decapitation. It was similar to the guillotine except that it used a curved rather than an angled blade and did not have a collar for securing the condemned prisoner in place. The first such device was built around 1286 in Halifax, England, and was known as the Halifax gibbet. It continued to be used for executions until 1650. In 1565 Lord James Douglas, the Earl of Morton, saw the Halifax gibbet in use and was so impressed that he had another one constructed in Edinburgh. This one became known as the Scottish Maiden. Ironically, Morton himself was executed by this device in 1581. The Scottish Maiden continued to be used until 1710. **See also** decapitation; guillotine.

Scottsboro Boys

The Scottsboro Boys were a group of nine black youths ranging in age from twelve to twenty who were arrested in March 1931 near Scottsboro, Alabama, for raping two white girls who were riding a freight train with them. The boys were Charlie Weems, 20; Clarence Norris, 19; Haywood Patterson, 19; Andy Wright, 19; Willie Roberson, 17; Olin Montgomery, 17; Ozie Powell, 16; Eugene Williams, 13; and Roy Wright, 12. The two girls were Ruby Bates and Victoria Price.

Since the boys could not afford counsel, the judge in the case, Alfred E. Hawkins, offered the job to any lawyer willing to take it. The job went to Tennessee attorney Stephen R. Roddy, an alcoholic who admitted he was not familiar with Alabama law and who was drunk during most of the proceedings. At trial, the evidence clearly did not support the charges. Ruby Bates testified that she was beaten and bruised by the repeated rapes and that she lost consciousness, regaining consciousness only when she found herself on the way to the Scottsboro jail. In fact, numerous witnesses and the arresting officers saw her fully conscious when she and the boys were taken off the train. The physician who examined the two girls testified that they showed evidence of recent sexual activity, but not recent enough to match the time of the alleged rapes, and they showed no evidence of bruising or violent treatment. Despite this contrary evidence, eight of the defendants were found guilty and sentenced to death. In the case of twelve-year-old Roy Wright, the judge declared a mistrial, since seven of the jurors insisted on a death sentence even though the prosecution had asked for only a sentence of life imprisonment.

The convictions outraged people around the country, including liberal politicians and academics, civil libertarians, and members of the radical American Communist Party. Lawyers working for the Communist Party appealed the case on behalf of the defendants. The Alabama Supreme Court upheld seven of the eight convictions, overturning only the conviction of thirteen-year-old Eugene Williams. The U.S. Supreme Court, however, overturned the remaining seven convictions on the grounds that the accused had not been adequately defended. New trials were ordered.

Haywood Patterson was tried ahead of the others. His lawyer, hired by the Communist Party, was Samuel Leibowitz, a respected New York lawyer. At Patterson's second trial, the same lack of physical evidence was presented. Ruby Bates even took the stand to recant her previous testimony, saying that she and Victoria Price had lied to avoid being arrested for vagrancy. The country was scandalized by evidence that Bates and Price

The Scottsboro Boys were falsely accused of rape in 1931 in Alabama. Their cases highlighted the racist bias that dominated American jurisprudence since the Civil War.

were actually prostitutes who regularly serviced a black clientele. Nevertheless, the jury again convicted Patterson and sentenced him to death. Apparently they were persuaded by prosecuting attorney Wade Wright, who urged them not to let Alabama justice "be bought and sold with Jew money from New York." Without even waiting for an appeal, the judge set the verdict aside and ordered a new trial.

Patterson's third trial was also a fiasco, with abuses on both sides. Blacks were systematically excluded from the jury, and signatures were forged to hide this abuse. At the same time, lawyers working for the Communist Party were caught trying to bribe jurors. Leibowitz threatened to resign unless the Communist lawyers withdrew from the case. Patterson was again convicted and sentenced to death, but the U.S. Supreme Court overturned the conviction on the grounds that blacks had been intentionally excluded from the jury. A fourth trial was ordered.

At his fourth trial, which took place in January 1936, Patterson was convicted for a fourth time, but this time only sentenced to imprisonment for a term of seventy-five years. Following Patterson's conviction, Clarence Norris, Andy

Wright, and Charlie Weems were given separate trials. All were convicted. Norris was sentenced to death (but the sentence was later commuted), Wright received a sentence of ninety-nine years, and Weems received a sentence of seventy-five years. The charges against the remaining defendants were dropped when a new Alabama district attorney, who felt the charges were not worth pursuing, took office.

It seemed patently unfair to many that some of the Scottsboro Boys were convicted while the rest were not. At one point, Alabama governor Bibb Graves agreed to pardon the four who had been convicted, but changed his mind in the face of public opinion. Weems was eventually paroled in 1943. Wright and Norris were paroled in 1944, but both broke parole and were sent back to prison. Wright was paroled again in 1950. Norris was not. Patterson escaped from prison in 1948 and fled to Detroit, where he was apprehended. However, Michigan governor G. Mennen Williams refused to allow him to be extradited to Alabama, and he was set free. He was later convicted of manslaughter in a separate incident and died in prison of cancer in 1952. Norris remained in jail until 1976, when he was finally pardoned by Alabama governor George C. Wallace. **See also** racial discrimination in sentencing.

Shays' Rebellion

Shays' Rebellion began in 1786 as an attempt by overtaxed and impoverished Massachusetts farmers to prevent the courts of Massachusetts from trying and imprisoning debtors. The rebellion was put down by government troops in 1787. This was the first opportunity after the American Revolution for the newly independent states to consider the appropriateness of the death penalty for the crime of treason. In a letter to James Madison, Thomas Jefferson was inclined to be sympathetic to the rebels, pointing out that Massachusetts owed its independence to just such a public uprising. He noted that many prominent current leaders of the state would have been executed for treason themselves if the American Revolution had failed, and argued that, while a monarchy might execute rebels for treason, a republic, founded on the consent of the governed, had to be more lenient with public uprisings and should impose only mild punishments so as "not to discourage them too much." Samuel Adams, meanwhile, objected that a republic was even more justified in protecting itself from violent insurrections than a monarchy and declared "the man who dares to rebel against the laws of a republic ought to suffer death."

In the end, most of the fifteen hundred rebels, including their leader, Daniel Shays, were pardoned. Only two men, John Bly and Charles Rose, were executed for participating in the rebellion, and they were charged not with treason but with various robberies committed in the course of the rebellion. Bly and Rose were hanged in 1787. **See also** capital crimes.

Simmons v. South Carolina

This was a case heard by the Supreme Court of the United States in 1994 concerning whether a penalty-phase jury should be informed that a defendant would be ineligible for parole if sentenced to life imprisonment. The defendant in the case, Jonathan Dale Simmons, was convicted of sexually assaulting three elderly women, one of whom was his own grandmother, and of beating a fourth woman to death. Under South Carolina law, this pattern of violent behavior, and the determination that Simmons was likely to be dangerous in the future, made Simmons ineligible for parole. However, the judge refused to instruct the penalty-phase jury about this aspect of

South Carolina law, even after the defense attorney requested that they be so instructed and even after the jury, during deliberations, requested information about the possibility of parole for Simmons. Having been told by the judge not to consider the issue of parole, the jury sentenced Simmons to death. The sentence was appealed on the grounds that Simmons's right to due process was violated by the judge's failure to adequately explain the law to the jury. The South Carolina Supreme Court upheld the sentence, and the U.S. Supreme Court agreed to review the case.

In a 7-to-2 decision, the Supreme Court ruled that the jury should have been instructed that Simmons was not eligible for parole. Writing for the Court, Justice Harry Blackmun pointed out that the jurors probably felt they had been presented with a choice between imposing a death sentence or allowing the defendant to be released at some future time. However, this was a misconception, and the defendant had been given no opportunity to correct this misconception. According to the principle of due process, a defendant must have the right to correct or rebut information that will form the basis of punishment. The Court ordered that Simmons be resentenced. **See also** due process; life imprisonment without parole.

simulated hangings

Simulated hangings were a form of punishment common in Europe and colonial America during the eighteenth century. In a simulated hanging, the prisoner sits on the gallows for an hour, usually wearing the noose. This is followed by a whipping or other corporal punishment, and possibly by a term of time spent in jail. The chief purpose of the simulated hanging was to allow the prisoner time to reflect on the possible consequences of future transgressions. Crimes nominally considered to be capital offenses could be punished by a simulated hanging if the defendant was young or a first-time offender. Simulated hangings were also used as a substitute for actual hangings as criminal codes were revised to make fewer crimes subject to the death penalty. For example, New Hampshire replaced actual hanging with simulated hanging for the crime of blasphemy in 1718. In 1749 Rhode Island made the crimes of adultery and bigamy punishable only by simulated hanging. Dueling (provided no one was killed) and incest were also punished by simulated hangings in some states. **See also** gallows reprieve.

Sing Sing Prison

Sing Sing Prison is the site of the first and most frequently used electric chair in the United States. The Sing Sing correctional facility was built in 1825–1826 using the labor of the convicts who were eventually housed there. It was the first prison facility built with convict labor, although it later became common practice for prisons to be built in this way. The prison was originally named Mt. Pleasant Prison, but it was always known as "Sing Sing" after the town of Ossining, New York, where it was located. It was not until 1985 that the name of the prison, bowing to common practice, was officially changed to Sing Sing. Located up the Hudson River from New York City, Sing Sing is the source of the expression "sent up the river," meaning sent to prison.

When the state of New York commissioned three electric chairs to be built, one was kept at Sing Sing, and that chair was first put to use in 1891 to execute J.J. Slocum. From 1914 to 1963, all executions in the state of New York were performed at Sing Sing using the electric chair. By 1963 more people, 695 in all, had been executed at Sing Sing Prison than at any other prison. However, when New York reenacted its death-penalty statute in 1995, it changed its method of execution to lethal injection and designated Clinton Prison as the site of executions. As of July 2005 none have yet taken place at Clinton. **See also** electric chair; Lawes, Lewis E.

Singleton, Charles (1960–2004)

Charles Singleton was executed for murder in Alabama in 2004. His execution is notable because he was diagnosed as suffering from severe paranoid schizophrenia, which developed while he was on death row. He was given antipsychosis drugs to make him legally competent to undergo execution.

At the age of nineteen, Singleton murdered Mary Lou York by stabbing her to death in the course of an armed robbery of a grocery store in Hamburg, Arkansas. He was tried for the murder and sentenced to death in 1979. He then spent eighteen years on death row as various appeals worked their way through the system. In 1997 a prison psychiatrist diagnosed Singleton as suffering from paranoid delusions. Singleton claimed that his cell was inhabited by demons and he reported having his "thoughts stolen" as he read his Bible. The psychiatrist prescribed antipsychosis drugs that seemed to treat Singleton's symptoms successfully. However, once it became clear that the state of Arkansas intended to proceed with his execution, Singleton's lawyers sued to prevent the prison from administering the antipsychosis drugs. The lawyers' argument was that Singleton should not take the drugs on the grounds that it was not in his medical best interest to take them. While suffering from delusions, Singleton could not be judged competent to undergo execution. By mitigating the effect of his mental illness, the drugs made Singleton competent to be executed, but since it was clearly not in Singleton's interest to be executed, it followed that it was not in his best interest to take the drugs. This argument was, of course, intentionally ironic. The real purpose of the argument was to point out the absurdity of treating a person for mental illness only so he could be executed. Seeing the irony of the argument, a panel of the Eighth U.S. Circuit Court of Appeals agreed that Singleton should be resentenced to life imprisonment without parole. The panel placed a stay on Singleton's execution and allowed the prison to continue administering his medications. However, the full Eighth U.S. Circuit Court, in a sharply divided and highly controversial decision, reversed the panel's ruling. It lifted the stay of execution and allowed prison officials to continue to administer Singleton's medications. The U.S. Supreme Court refused to review the case, and on January 7, 2004, Singleton was executed by lethal injection. **See also** competence; *Ford v. Wainwright*; mentally ill offenders.

Skipper v. South Carolina

This was a case heard by the Supreme Court of the United States in 1986 concerning whether testimony about a defendant's good behavior while in jail may be excluded from the penalty phase of a trial. The defendant in the case, Ronald Skipper, was convicted in South Carolina of rape and murder. At the penalty phase of the trial, Skipper's attorney asked to introduce testimony from three witnesses, including two guards at the jail where Skipper was being held, that Skipper had been a model prisoner. The judge ruled the issue irrelevant and did not permit the witnesses to testify. Skipper was sentenced to death. Skipper's sentence was then appealed on the grounds that he had not been permitted to offer evidence in support of all relevant mitigating circumstances. The South Carolina Supreme Court upheld the sentence, and the U.S. Supreme Court agreed to review the case.

In a 9-to-0 decision, the Supreme Court ruled that, as in the earlier *Eddings v. Oklahoma* (1982) and *Lockett v. Ohio* (1978) decisions, a defendant must be allowed to present evidence for any mitigating circumstance that the jury might consider relevant. Writing for the Court, Justice Byron White remarked that it was reasonably likely that the jury might have imposed a different sentence if they had heard evidence from impartial witnesses of Skipper's good behavior while in jail. The Court ordered Skipper to be resentenced. **See also** *Eddings v. Oklahoma; Lockett v. Ohio*.

slavery

Societies that have practiced slavery generally have special death-penalty laws pertaining to slaves. Some of these laws concern crimes committed by slaves; other laws concern crimes of free citizens that involve slaves.

Societies that have practiced slavery almost invariably have applied a harsher penal code to slaves than to free citizens. Slaves could be executed for more crimes, and the method of execution could be far more cruel. For example, under the Roman Empire only slaves and foreigners could be crucified. In Louisiana and South Carolina before the Civil War, crimes for which a free white could only be hanged could be punished by burning or by gibbeting if the perpetrator was a slave. In colonial New York, slaves could be executed not only for murder and rape but also for attempted murder and attempted rape. In colonial South Carolina, slaves could be executed for destroying the commercial goods that they were engaged in producing, such as grains, manufactured items, and other commodities. In Georgia, a slave could be executed merely for striking a white person twice, or once if the blow caused a bruise. Slaves also did not receive a full trial. In Virginia and South Carolina, a local justice of the peace had the authority to sentence slaves to death. No jury trial was needed. However, as harsh and unfair as these laws seem, they were actually a significant step toward more humane and law-governed treatment of slaves. Prior to the passage of such laws, slaves were accorded no rights whatsoever and could be treated however their masters deemed necessary. The brutal torture and execution of slaves was common, but since slaves were considered to be a form of property, their treatment fell outside the concerns of the law.

On the other hand, because a slave was a valuable piece of property, there were harsh laws governing theft of slaves. Since horse stealing was a crime punishable by death in some states, it is not surprising that the kidnapping of slaves was also punishable by death. Helping a runaway slave to escape was considered tantamount to slave stealing, so it was also punishable by death in some states; however, as states limited the death penalty to the crime of murder, assisting a runaway slave ceased to be a capital offense. It was briefly made a capital offense again in territorial Kansas in 1858 by a group of laws known as the Black Code, but these laws were not enforced and were repealed by the time Kansas became a state. **See also** Black Code.

Snyder, Ruth (1894–1928)

Ruth Snyder and her lover Judd Gray were executed in New York in 1928 for the murder of Snyder's husband. The execution is notable not only because the trial was a media sensation but because a journalist, Thomas Howard, managed to get a photograph of Snyder as she was being executed in the electric chair. Ruth Snyder was married to Albert Snyder, the

The executions of Snyder and Gray were front-page news on January 13, 1928. An unauthorized photo of Snyder's electrocution caused great controversy.

art editor of a boating magazine, in what was apparently a boring and loveless relationship. She began an affair with Judd Gray, a corset salesman, and after taking out a double-indemnity insurance policy on her husband, began urging Gray to kill him on the grounds that he was abusing her. Gray eventually agreed, but Albert Snyder proved hard to kill. One night Ruth Snyder let Gray into the house and, as Albert slept, Gray attempted to crush his skull with a window sash weight. The blow only woke him up. Ruth Snyder had to finish the job herself as her husband attacked Gray and Gray shrieked for help. Gray and Snyder then tried to make the crime look like a robbery, but investigating police quickly found the items that were alleged to have been stolen hidden under a mattress. Caught red-handed, Snyder confessed, but blamed the murder on Gray. Gray, in turn, blamed it on Snyder. The trial soon became a media circus attended by noted mystery writers, novelists, moralists, and even movie mogul D.W. Griffith. (Two movies, *Double Indemnity* and *Body Heat*, were later inspired by the incident.) Both Gray and Snyder were found guilty and sentenced to death.

At Snyder's execution, on January 1, 1928, journalist Thomas Howard, a photographer with the *New York Daily News*, attended with a hidden camera strapped to his ankle. As the executioner threw the switch, Howard crossed his ankle over his knee and snapped a picture. The picture ran on the front page of the *Daily News* the next day. Demand for the paper was so great that an extra 750,000 copies had to be printed. The state of New York tried unsuccessfully to prosecute the paper and Howard for taking the picture, but public sentiment so strongly favored the paper that the case was dropped. Thereafter, journalists began to be carefully searched before being permitted to witness executions in New York. The photograph remains one of only two photographs ever taken of an electric chair in use. **See also** censorship of reporting on executions; viewing of executions.

social contract theory

Social contract theory is a theory of social justice that was developed in England during the seventeenth century and was extremely influential during the eighteenth century, having a particular influence on the American Revolution and on the development of American democracy. As a theory of social justice, social contract theory has been important in discussions of the justness of capital punishment. The earliest objections to capital punishment were founded on social contract theory. In contrast to the older theory that governments derive their legitimacy from divine authority, social contract theory takes the view that governments derive their legitimacy from the consent of the governed. This consent is granted in the form of a "social contract," or agreement by the people to be obedient to the laws.

Social contract theory was originally developed by two British philosophers, Thomas Hobbes and John Locke. Both believed that humans originally lived in a state of complete freedom, able to do whatever they pleased. Unfortunately, of course, this meant that acts of theft and violence went unpunished, so, in practice, this state of complete freedom amounted to what Hobbes called "a war of all against all." In order to achieve peace and prosperity, people agreed—entered into a contract—to give up some of their freedom in exchange for better conditions. Governments are in place to ensure that the social contract is maintained for the benefit of all.

Interestingly, Hobbes and Locke had opposing agendas in proposing social contract theory. During the rebellion against King Charles I, 1642 to 1646, Hobbes supported the monarchy. He portrayed the social contract as an agreement *among* the people to obey the laws. The king was not, strictly speaking, a party to the contract, and so could not do anything to violate the contract. For the people to overthrow the king, however, was a violation of the contract, since it broke faith with other citizens. Therefore, rebellion was not morally justified. Locke, by contrast, supported rebellion—specifically the 1688 rebellion against King James II. Locke portrayed the social contract as an agreement *between* the people on the one hand and the government on the other hand. The people pledged obedience to the laws, but the government in turn pledged to provide just governance. According to this view, the king *was* a party to the contract and could violate the contract by failing to govern justly. Overthrowing a king who failed to govern justly was, therefore, morally justified. Locke's view forms the basis of the American Declaration of Independence.

According to social contract theory, crimes cannot be understood as moral transgressions but only as exercises of freedom beyond what is consistent with the peace and prosperity of society, and therefore not permitted by the "social contract." Since crimes are actions that tend to undermine the structure of society, the seriousness of crimes can be defined by the extent to which they threaten that structure. On this account, treason and crimes directly attacking the state are the most serious; crimes against the property of individuals are among the least serious. It is perhaps because of the continued influence of social contract theory that treason and espionage are considered capital crimes under federal law, even if no death results from them.

Italian philosopher Cesare Beccaria used social contract theory to develop an argument against the death penalty. He argued that no person would enter into a contract from which he did not benefit, and no one would benefit from a contract in which he agreed to forfeit his life. Hence, no citizen would agree to grant the state the power to put him to death. Beccaria's argument, however, was not particularly influential, even among other social contract theorists. **See also** Beccaria, Cesare; justification of punishment; Locke, John.

Socrates (469–399 B.C.)

The ancient Greek philosopher Socrates, one of the great philosophers in world history, was executed in 399 B.C. by the leaders of Athens. The crimes of which he was convicted were "corrupting the youth" by teaching philosophy and "failing to honor the gods of the city." It is probable that these charges were brought against him because of his connection with members of the Thirty Tyrants, a widely hated and short-lived puppet government imposed on Athens by Sparta after Athens's defeat in the Peloponnesian War.

Under Athenian law, a convicted criminal was entitled to propose his own punishment. The jury would then decide whether that punishment was appropriate or whether death (the only available alternative) would be imposed instead. Most convicted criminals proposed sentences that could be deemed reasonable by the jury, such as banishment from the city, so they rarely received death sentences. However, when Socrates was asked to propose his punishment, he proposed that he should be "punished" by being allowed to feast at public expense, an honor generally given to winning Olympic athletes and recognized public benefactors. Socrates was making the point that his "crimes" actually benefited the public. At the insistence of his friends, he then suggested a modest fine instead. His proposals gave the jury no choice but to condemn him to death. A month after his trial, Socrates was executed by voluntarily drinking an infusion of hemlock, a poisonous herb. The philosopher Plato, Socrates' student, used the story of the trial and execution of Socrates as a framework for many of his philosophical dialogues, which are regarded as some of the most influential writings in the history of philosophy. **See also** Draconian Code; Joan of Arc.

solitary confinement
Solitary confinement means isolating a prisoner from contact with other prisoners and allowing only minimal contact with prison guards. The original idea of solitary confinement was to give prisoners isolation and quiet so they could reflect on their crimes in the hope that this would lead to repentance. The Quakers, in particular, believed that allowing time for meditation and reflection should be an effective and humane way to rehabilitate criminals. Solitary confinement was an integral part of the design for the Walnut Street Jail in Philadelphia, widely considered the first American "penitentiary." The Walnut Street Jail was an attempt to put Quaker principles into practice by emphasizing rehabilitation over punishment. However, when it was first used, no one realized that extended time in isolation would lead to severe mental distress and even insanity. The use of solitary confinement to facilitate meditation and reflection was quickly abandoned. It continues to be used only as a method of disciplining prisoners and for temporarily isolating especially violent prisoners. **See also** imprisonment.

South Carolina
South Carolina has traditionally permitted juries to impose the death penalty, and continues to do so currently. Between 1718 and 1775, seventy-three people were executed in colonial South Carolina. On November 8, 1718, twenty men were hanged for piracy. There were also hangings for robbery, rape, horse stealing, burglary, poisoning, aiding runaway slaves, and murder. While whites were invariably hanged, black slaves were sometimes executed by more cruel methods, including burning and gibbeting. Between 1777 and 1911, 324 people were executed under state jurisdiction in South Carolina, mostly by hanging, although there were a few instances of slaves being burned. In 1822 a slave revolt, led by a former slave named Denmark Vesey, ended with the hanging of Vesey and thirty-four others. In 1912 South Carolina replaced hanging with electrocution as its method of execution. Between 1912 and 1962, 240 people were executed in South Carolina's electric chair.

Following the 1972 *Furman v. Georgia* ruling, which struck down South Carolina's death-penalty statute, the state passed a new death-penalty statute in 1974. South Carolina's current death-penalty statute allows jurors to consider the death penalty for any intentional homicide (i.e., any homicide committed with "malice aforethought"). The death penalty may be imposed if one of eleven aggravating circumstances is proven to have accompanied the crime. These aggravating circumstances are (1) that the homicide occurred in the course of criminal sexual conduct, kidnapping, burglary, robbery, larceny, killing by poison, drug trafficking, torture, or dismemberment of the victim; (2) that the defendant was previously convicted of murder; (3) that the defendant knowingly created a great risk of death to more than one person; (4) that the homicide was committed for monetary gain; (5) that the victim was a judicial officer,

South Carolina college students voice their support for the death penalty as a convicted murderer is executed in the electric chair in 1986.

solicitor, or other officer of the court; (6) that the defendant directed another to commit the homicide or was directed to commit the homicide by someone else; (7) that the victim was a law enforcement officer, corrections employee, or firefighter; (8) that the victim was a family member of a judicial officer, solicitor, officer of the court, law enforcement officer, corrections employee, or firefighter; (9) that more than one person was killed at the same time or following the same criminal plan; (10) that the victim was eleven years old or younger; (11) that the victim was a witness and the homicide was committed to prevent the victim's testimony. The jury must also consider any mitigating circumstances that the defense wishes to present.

Under South Carolina law, a person convicted of a capital offense cannot be executed if he or she was under the age of sixteen at the time of the crime. This provision was invalidated by the Supreme Court's decision in 2005 that abolished the death penalty for persons younger than eighteen. South Carolina does not provide for life imprisonment without parole as an alternative to the death penalty. The governor has the authority to grant reprieves and to commute a death sentence to life imprisonment.

The first execution following the reenactment of the death penalty took place in 1985 with the execution of Joseph Shaw. Between 1985 and 1994, four people were executed by electrocution in South Carolina. In 1995 South Carolina added lethal injection as an optional method of execution, allowing condemned prisoners to choose between electrocution and lethal injection. Since 1995 there have been thirty-two executions in South Carolina, all but one by means of lethal injection. As of April 2005, seventy-seven people were awaiting execution on South Carolina's death row. **See also** multiple executions; *South Carolina v. Gathers.*

South Carolina v. Gathers

This was a case heard by the Supreme Court of the United States in 1989 concerning whether the prosecution may introduce personal information about a defendant during the penalty phase of a trial. The defendant in the case, Demetrius Gathers, was convicted in South Carolina of the beating and stabbing of a mentally handicapped victim. During sentencing, the prosecuting attorney informed the jury that Gathers was deeply religious. The jury sentenced Gathers to death. His sentence was appealed on the grounds that personal information about Gathers's religious views might have inclined the jury to be more willing to impose a sentence of death. The South Carolina Supreme Court agreed that the information might have been prejudicial and vacated the sentence. The U.S. Supreme Court agreed to review the case.

In a 5-to-4 decision, the Supreme Court ruled that the South Carolina Supreme Court was right to vacate the sentence in this case. Writing for the Court, Justice William Brennan argued that personal characteristics of the defendant that were neither relevant to a statutory aggravating circumstance nor introduced by the defense as a mitigating circumstance could only serve to prejudice the jury and make their task of rational decision making more difficult. The Court ordered Gathers to be resentenced. **See also** *Romano v. Oklahoma.*

South Dakota

South Dakota has sometimes permitted juries to impose the death penalty, and does so currently, although the number of executions in South Dakota has always been quite small. Only three people were executed in South Dakota under territorial jurisdiction, all by hanging. Between 1892 and 1913, another seven people were executed under state jurisdiction. In 1915 South Dakota abolished capital punishment altogether. In 1939 the South Dakota legislature reenacted a death-penalty statute under which electrocution was adopted as the state's method of execution. However, South Dakota's electric chair was used only once, in 1947, to execute George Stitts for murder. That was the last execution to take place in South Dakota.

Following the 1972 *Furman v. Georgia* ruling, which struck down South Dakota's death-penalty statute, the state passed a new death-penalty statute in 1979. South Dakota's current death-penalty statute allows jurors to consider the death penalty for homicide under special circumstances. These special circumstances include that the homicide was premeditated or that it was committed in the course of arson, rape, robbery, burglary, kidnapping, or the unlawful use of a destructive or explosive device. Homicide is also a capital offense if it was committed in the course of attempting to avoid detection or prevent prosecution for one of these crimes.

The death penalty may be imposed if one of ten aggravating circumstances is proven to have accompanied the crime. The list of aggravating circumstances appears similar to the special circumstances noted above, but aggravating circumstances are considered during the penalty phase of the trial rather than during the guilt phase. These aggravating circumstances are (1) that the defendant was previously convicted of a felony; (2) that the defendant knowingly created a great risk of death to more than one person in a public place by means of a device (such as a bomb) that would normally endanger more than one person; (3) that the homicide was committed for monetary gain; (4) that the victim was a judicial officer or prosecutor acting to perform his or her duties, or the homicide was motivated by the nature of those duties; (5) that the defendant ordered someone else to commit the homicide or committed the homicide under the direction of someone else; (6) that the homicide was wantonly vile, involving torture or beating of the victim, or in which the victim was under thirteen years old; (7) that the victim was a law enforcement officer, employee of a corrections institution, or firefighter acting in the performance of his or her duties; (8) that the defendant was in the custody of a law enforcement officer or a correctional facility or had escaped from such custody; (9) that the homicide was committed in order to avoid the arrest or aid the escape from custody of either the defendant or someone else; or (10) that the homicide occurred in the course of manufacturing or distributing narcotics. The jury must also consider any mitigating circumstances that the defense wishes to present.

Under South Dakota law, a person convicted of a capital offense cannot be executed if he or she was under the age of eighteen at the time of the crime. South Dakota does provide for life imprisonment without parole as an alternative to the death penalty. The governor has the authority to grant clemency. The governor may ask for a nonbinding recommendation from the Board of Pardons but is not required to do so.

In 1984 South Dakota replaced electrocution with lethal injection as its method of execution. However, no one so far has been executed in South Dakota since the reinstatement of capital punishment. As of June 2005, four people were awaiting execution on South Dakota's death row. **See also** *Furman v. Georgia.*

Spaziano v. Florida

This was a case heard by the Supreme Court of the United States in 1984 concerning whether a judge can override the recommendation of an advisory jury in imposing a sentence of death. The defendant in the case, Joseph Robert Spaziano, who was a member of a biker gang known as the Outlaws, was convicted by a Florida court of kidnapping, torturing, and eventually killing a young woman, Laura Lynn Harberts, in 1973. A friend of Spaziano's, Tony DiLisio, led police to the body and testified that Spaziano had committed the crime. However, more than two years had gone by since the crime, so Spaziano could not be charged with kidnapping and assault since the statute of limitations had run out for those crimes. On the basis of DiLisio's testimony, Spaziano was also charged with the rape and mutilation of a second woman, Vanessa Croft, and sentenced to a term of imprisonment for that crime. The jury hearing the Harberts murder case did not have access to Spaziano's entire criminal record and recommended a sentence of life imprisonment. The judge, who had access to a presentencing report that detailed Spaziano's complete criminal record, including crimes Spaziano had only been accused of but not tried for, overrode the jury's recommendation and imposed a sentence of death. The case was appealed on the grounds that the judge was wrong to consider information in the presentencing report that had not been shared with the defense and to which the defendant had been given no opportunity to respond. The Florida Supreme Court agreed that Spaziano's right to due process had been violated. The conviction was upheld, but a new sentencing trial was ordered. At the new sentencing trial, Spaziano was again sentenced to death, and this time the Florida Supreme Court upheld the sentence. However, Spaziano's lawyers then appealed in federal court on the grounds that the judge at the initial sentencing trial should not have been permitted to override the jury's recommendation. The U.S. Supreme Court agreed to review the case.

In a 6-to-3 decision, the U.S. Supreme Court ruled that the use of an advisory jury was constitutional and that it was reasonable to expect a judge to override a jury's recommendation based on his own examination of the facts. Writing for the majority, Justice Harry Blackmun noted that, while the judge had been given access to information not available to the advisory jury, it was appropriate under Florida law for the judge to consider this information. Spaziano's sentence was upheld.

In 1994 DiLisio recanted his testimony in an interview given to the *Miami Herald*. In 1996 Spaziano's conviction and sentence were vacated (declared invalid). However, in 1997 Spaziano was reindicted for the murder of Laura Harberts based on evidence other than DiLisio's testimony. To avoid another trial, he and his lawyers agreed to plead "no contest," which is not an admission of guilt but merely an agreement not to contest the charges, in exchange for a sentence of time already served plus two years. By this time, Spaziano had already been in prison for over twenty years. After serving the additional two years, Spaziano was still not released; he remains in prison because of his conviction in the Vanessa Croft case. **See also** *Harris v. Alabama.*

Spear, Charles (1801–1863)

Charles Spear was the most prominent opponent of capital punishment in New England in the pre–Civil War period. As a young man, Spear was an enthusiastic convert to Universalism (an American religious denomination that believed in universal salvation, or that no souls are irrevocably sent to hell), and began his career as a minister of a Universalist church in Brewster, Massachusetts. However, Spear was unsatisfied with the settled life of a parish minister, and perhaps did not possess the right combination of talents for it. He then became a professional reform activist, making his living by speaking and writing.

Spear's best-known work was the widely read *Essays on Capital Punishment*, published in 1844. Typical of discussions of capital punishment of that period, the book was divided into two sections. The first section dealt with secular arguments, including the argument developed by the earlier opponent of capital punishment Cesare Beccaria that no person would consent to enter into a "social contract" in which he agreed to forfeit his own life. The second section dealt with religious and scriptural issues. Consistent with his Universalist principles, Spear argued that humans were fundamentally moral, rational, and redeemable, not, as the more conservative Christian denominations taught, sinful and corrupt. According to Universalist principles, even murderers were entitled to a chance at reform.

In 1844 Spear helped found the Massachusetts Society for the Abolition of Capital Punishment. A year later he began publishing a weekly newspaper, the *Hangman*, devoted to the abolition of capital punishment. The newspaper later changed its name to the *Prisoner's Friend* and became a monthly publication. With the outbreak of the Civil War, Spear became a hospital chaplain with the Union army, where he contracted an infectious illness and died. **See also** Beccaria, Cesare; religious views.

special circumstances

In order to prevent the death penalty from being imposed arbitrarily, the U.S. Supreme Court requires that death-penalty statutes clearly spell out the circumstances under which a crime is sufficiently serious to be punishable by death. In most statutes, a list of special circumstances is used to satisfy this requirement. For a crime to be death-eligible, it must be proved, during the guilt phase of the trial, that the defendant was guilty of the crime (almost always some form of murder) and that at least one of the special circumstances listed in the statute accompanied the commission of the crime. Some typical special circumstances for homicide include that the homicide was committed by someone already serving a sentence on another offense; that the homicide was committed in the course of a violent crime, including attempting to flee or evade arrest for that crime; that the victim was a police officer, firefighter, or other public official engaged in the performance of official duties; that the homicide endangered the lives of many people; that the homicide was done for hire or at the direction of another person; or that the homicide was especially heinous, cruel, or inhuman.

Since the purpose of special circumstances is to define when a crime is sufficiently serious to merit the death penalty, special circumstances tend to be quite similar to aggravating circumstances, which are considered during the penalty phase of a trial. Indeed, in its 1990 *Walton v. Arizona* decision, the U.S. Supreme Court ruled that there was nothing unconstitutional in using substantially the same circumstances as both special circumstances used to determine a crime as death-eligible and aggravating circumstance used to decide whether a death sentence is warranted in a specific case. Consistent with this ruling, some states, including Texas and Utah, do not provide a separate list of aggravating circumstances at all but simply specify that the same list is to be used for both purposes.

The lists of special circumstances vary widely from state to state. The longest list of special circumstances occurs in Utah's death-penalty statutes, which defines no less than seventeen special circumstances that make a homicide death-eligible. The shortest lists belong to the states of Missouri, Pennsylvania, and South Carolina, each of which define only a single special circumstance. However, that circumstance is very broad: Each of these states allow consideration of the death penalty for any intentional or premeditated killing. In recent years, there has been a tendency of states to attempt to toughen their penal codes. Often this is done by adding new items to the list of special circumstances by which homicides are made death-eligible. **See also** aggravating circumstances; capital crimes.

Stanford v. Kentucky

This was a case heard by the Supreme Court of the United States in 1989 concerning whether the execution of a juvenile offender (a person who was under the age of eighteen at the time of his or her crime) is cruel and unusual. The case was decided concurrently with *Wilkins v. Missouri*, which concerned the same issue. Kevin Stanford was seventeen years old when he committed murder in

Kentucky; Heath Wilkins was sixteen years old when he committed murder in Missouri. Both were subsequently convicted as adults and sentenced to death. The sentences were appealed on the grounds that the defendants were too young at the time of their crimes to be executed, but both sentences were upheld by the respective appeals courts. The U.S. Supreme Court agreed to hear the two cases.

In a 5-to-4 decision, the Court ruled that the appeals courts were right to uphold the sentences. Writing for the majority, Justice Antonin Scalia held that the best evidence of "national consensus" on the execution of juveniles is to be found by considering state laws. Since only fifteen states prohibited the death penalty for sixteen-year-olds, and only twelve states prohibited the death penalty for seventeen-year-olds, he argued that there was no national consensus opposing the death penalty for people as young as sixteen or seventeen. Hence the death penalty for sixteen- and seventeen-year-olds could not be considered cruel and unusual by current standards of decency.

The decision in this case, along with the 1988 decision in *Thompson v. Oklahoma* in which it was decided that the execution of a fifteen-year-old *was* cruel and unusual, had the effect of setting the minimum age for execution in the United States at sixteen. This minimum was raised to eighteen in 2005 by the Supreme Court's decision in *Roper v. Simmons*. **See also** juvenile offenders; *Roper v. Simmons; Thompson v. Oklahoma.*

stay of execution

A stay is an order issued by a court that delays or suspends some other legal procedure or action. The purpose of a stay is to ensure that legal procedures are carried out correctly and in their proper order. A court-ordered sentence of execution is an example of the kind of legal action that may be subject to a stay, known as a stay of execution. A stay of execution is not the same thing as an executive reprieve, which also results in the delay of an execution but is issued by a governor or president rather than by the courts.

In death-penalty cases, defendants are entitled to an automatic review of their case by an appeals court. However, a sentence of death carries with it the requirement that an execution date be set. For this reason, an execution date is set, but a stay of execution is immediately put into effect until the initial review has been completed. Further appeals may then result in further stays, but courts are under no obligation to issue a stay of execution merely because a defendant has filed an appeal. If they were, it would be possible for a defendant to put off an execution indefinitely, merely by filing new (and frivolous) appeals. Thus, upon receiving an appeal, a court will not issue a stay of execution unless it is convinced that the appeal has sufficient merit to warrant further consideration. **See also** *Barefoot v. Estelle;* clemency.

Stewart, Potter (1915–1985)

Potter Stewart was an associate justice of the U.S. Supreme Court from 1958 until 1981. Stewart was a centrist on the subject of capital punishment, not opposed to the death penalty in principle but insisting that it be applied fairly. As a result of his centrist views, Stewart has been the single most influential justice on this subject, writing several landmark decisions and effectively establishing the strictures with which the death penalty in the United States must be practiced.

Stewart was born in Jackson, Michigan, and studied law at Yale University. After graduation he took a position with a New York law firm, but his legal career was somewhat interrupted by World War II. Stewart joined the navy and served as an officer. His duties included assisting at military trials. After the war, Stewart moved to a law firm in Cincinnati. He ran for city council and served two terms, from 1950 until 1953, also serving as vice mayor from 1952 to 1953. In 1954 President Dwight Eisenhower appointed him to the U.S. Sixth Circuit Court of Appeals, and then in 1958 Eisenhower appointed him to the Supreme Court. As a member of the Supreme Court, Stewart joined in, and even wrote, a number of liberal opinions on desegregation and the right to engage in peaceful protest. However, he also dissented from some liberal opinions, notably on the decision barring prayer in public schools.

Stewart is the author of the Supreme Court's most important decisions on capital punishment, and it is fair to say that his views represent the current law of the land on the subject. Stewart's first significant capital punishment opinion was written in 1968 in *Witherspoon v. Illinois*, which concerned whether people who were inclined to be reluctant to impose a sentence of death could be excluded from juries charged with deciding capital cases. Writing for the majority, Stewart argued that people opposed to capital punishment made up a significant proportion of the population and that excluding them from juries would make juries unrepresentative of the community. (However, this decision was later overturned in 1985.) In 1972 Stewart joined the majority in the *Furman v. Georgia* decision, which invalidated all of the nation's death-penalty statutes. Each justice wrote a separate opinion, but Stewart's opinion was particularly significant since it was later used as the basis for the 1976 *Gregg v. Georgia* decision, which reauthorized the use of the death penalty in the United States. In the *Furman v. Georgia* decision, Stewart took the view that the death-penalty statutes then in effect were too arbitrary and were being applied in a manner that permitted undue influence of social prejudice. However, he refrained from saying that the death penalty per se was unconstitutional. In 1976 the majority of the Court agreed with Stewart, in *Gregg v. Georgia*, that new, less arbitrary death-penalty statutes could be considered constitutional. Writing for the majority, Stewart wrote, "We hold that the death penalty is not a form of punishment that may never be imposed." States were entitled to have death-penalty statutes provided that those statutes gave juries clear guidelines on when a death sentence could be imposed. However, in 1976 Stewart joined the majority ruling in *Woodson v. North Carolina*, saying that states could not make the death penalty mandatory. Death-penalty statutes passed since 1976 have carefully followed the strictures laid out by Stewart's decisions.

Stewart retired from the Supreme Court in 1981 and died four years later.
See also *Furman v. Georgia; Gregg v. Georgia;* Supreme Court; *Witherspoon v. Illinois.*

stoning

Stoning is an ancient method of execution in which the victim is pelted with stones, usually thrown by a large group of people. The condemned prisoner is generally placed next to a wall, traditionally the wall surrounding a fortified village. Death results from contusions to the head, which cause internal bleeding and injuries to the brain.

As a method of punishment, stoning is mentioned in the Bible and in the Koran. It is the recommended punishment for adultery and prostitution. As such, women have been executed by stoning far more frequently than men. In the Bible (Numbers 15:32–36), stoning is also the recommended penalty for failing to keep the Sabbath. In the modern era, stoning is practiced in only a few Muslim countries. In 1996 in Afghanistan, the stoning of a couple accused of adultery caused worldwide outrage against the fundamentalist Taliban government, which was in power at the time. In Iran, where the practice is also permitted, laws prohibit the use of large stones to ensure that death does not occur too rapidly due to a crushed skull. **See also** breaking on the wheel; crucifixion; torture.

Supreme Court

The Supreme Court of the United States is the highest court in the United States, with jurisdiction to review cases from federal courts, all lower state courts, and military courts. The Supreme Court has ultimate authority to interpret the meaning of the Constitution of the United States.

The Supreme Court is made up of nine justices, one of whom presides over the Court as chief justice. The justices are appointed by the president of the United States, but their appointment must be

The nine judges of the Supreme Court are pictured in 1972, the year in which the Court ruled that the death-penalty statutes then in effect in the United States were unconstitutional.

confirmed by the Senate. In rare cases, the Senate has refused to confirm an appointment and the president has been forced to select someone else. Once appointed, a justice may not be removed except by being impeached (accused of a crime) by the House of Representatives and found guilty by the Senate. Otherwise, Supreme Court justices serve until they die or until they voluntarily step down.

The Supreme Court was established under Article III of the Constitution, but its powers are only sketchily defined there. The chief power of the Supreme Court was established by the Supreme Court itself in an 1803 case, *Marbury v. Madison*. In that case, the Supreme Court ruled that it has the power to invalidate laws by declaring them "unconstitutional" (i.e., in conflict with the principles articulated in the U.S. Constitution). This decision effectively made the judiciary a third branch of government, balancing the power of Congress to make laws. In its role of interpreting and applying the Constitution, the Supreme Court can overturn laws viewed as inconsistent with established principles of justice or in violation of the rights of individuals, even when such laws represent the will of the majority at a particular time or on a particular issue.

Although the Supreme Court has the power to declare laws unconstitutional, it cannot merely overturn a law as soon as it is passed. The Supreme Court can declare a law unconstitutional only in the context of an actual court case involving that law. For example, in the case of criminal law, a person must first be charged with a crime, convicted, and sentenced. Then the conviction or sentence must be appealed for review by a higher court on the grounds that some law or procedure was not correctly followed, or on the grounds that some law or procedure, even if correctly followed, violates the defendant's rights. Once the appeals court has made its decision, the Supreme Court may then choose to review that decision. If the members of the Supreme Court feel that an injustice has occurred (i.e., that the defendant's rights have been violated), they may vote to overturn the law or require that a different procedure be followed. Because the process is so involved, it often takes several years after the passage of a law before it can be declared unconstitutional. Indeed, some laws may remain in effect for decades simply because no case in which they are involved is brought before the Supreme Court.

Decisions of the Supreme Court must be supported by a majority of the members of the Court. The decision itself is a statement to the effect that some action must be taken (e.g., that a defendant must be released, retried, or resentenced). The decision is always accompanied by a careful explanation of the reasons for that decision. These reasons are known as an opinion. Typically, one justice takes on the responsibility of writing an opinion. If there is a disagreement among the members of the Court as to which action should be taken, a second justice takes on the responsibility of writing a contrary opinion. The other justices read the opinions and decide which opinion best expresses their own views of the matter. The opinion that is backed by the majority of the Court becomes the opinion of the Court, but the dissenting opinion is also issued. Dissenting opinions have no immediate legal force, but they are carefully studied by legal scholars, and the reasoning in them often becomes the basis for later decisions.

In some cases, a member of the Court may agree with the action to be taken but disagree with the reasons for that action. In that case, the justice may write a separate opinion called a concurring opinion. Likewise, in some cases a member of the Court may disagree with the action to be taken and disagree with the dissenting opinion written by another justice. Each justice may write his or her own concurring or dissenting opinion in each case, if the justice wishes to do so. In some rare cases, none of the justices can agree on the wording of an opinion, and each will write a separate opinion. In such cases, the action to be taken is issued as a brief separate statement called a per curiam decision. The important *Furman v. Georgia* decision is an example of a per curiam decision.

The Supreme Court has made many landmark decisions pertaining to capital punishment. The earliest was the case of *Wilkerson v. Utah* (1878), in which the Supreme Court ruled that laws providing for execution by firing squad were *not* unconstitutional. However, most of the Supreme Court's decisions on capital punishment came after 1963 when Justice Arthur Goldberg prepared a memo listing several important arguments that he believed could be used to challenge the constitutionality of capital punishment laws. The Court's most important decision came in the 1972 *Furman v. Georgia* decision in which the Court ruled that all of the death-penalty statutes then in effect in the United States were unconstitutional. This ended capital punishment in the United States for a period of four years. However, some of the justices who voted to invalidate the capital punishment statutes suggested in their opinions that the statutes could be satisfactorily revised to meet their objections. In 1976 the *Gregg v. Georgia* decision restored capital punishment for states that had revised their statutes along the suggested lines. Since then, the Supreme Court has made some additional refinements. For example, in the 2002 *Ring v. Arizona* decision, the Court ruled that a sentence of death could be imposed only on the basis of aggravating circumstances determined to be present by a jury; in other words, a judge acting independently of a jury may not impose a death sentence. In the 2002 *Atkins v. Virginia* decision, the Court declared the execution of mentally retarded offenders to be unconstitutional.

Among the most important trends in recent years is that the Court has made it much more difficult for inmates on death row to bring appeals. Most appeals take the form of a petition for a writ of habeas corpus, which is a request that an appeals court review the legitimacy of the laws and procedures under which a defendant was tried and sentenced. During the 1990s, the Supreme Court made several decisions that made it more difficult to petition for a writ of habeas corpus. The 1991 *McCleskey v. Zant* decision and the 1996 *Felker v. Turpin* decision were among the most important of these. **See also** appeals process; Constitution of the United States; habeas corpus.

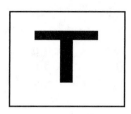

Tennessee

Tennessee has traditionally permitted juries to impose the death penalty, and continues to do so currently. Prior to 1796, when Tennessee became a state, only four executions are recorded, and three of these took place on the same day when three men were hanged for stealing horses. Between 1800 and 1908, 189 people were executed by hanging. These hangings were carried out by local authorities. In 1909 Tennessee centralized executions at the state prison. Between 1909 and 1913, sixteen more executions by hanging took place at the Tennessee state prison. In 1913 Tennessee replaced hanging with electrocution as its method of execution. The first execution using Tennessee's electric chair took place in 1916 with the execution of Julius Morgan, a black man convicted of rape. Between 1916 and 1960, 125 people were executed in Tennessee by electrocution.

Following the 1972 *Furman v. Georgia* ruling, which struck down Tennessee's death-penalty statute, the Tennessee state legislature attempted to reenact a new death-penalty statute in 1974. However, this statute was found unconstitutional the same year by the Tennessee Supreme Court. The legislature tried again in 1976, but the Tennessee Supreme Court ruled this statute unconstitutional in 1977. Finally, in 1979 the legislature enacted a death-penalty statute that proved acceptable. Tennessee's current death-penalty statute allows jurors to consider the death penalty for homicide under special circumstances. These special circumstances are (1) that the homicide was premeditated or intentional; (2) that it was committed in the course of first-degree murder (of someone else), arson, rape, robbery, burglary, theft, kidnapping, child abuse, child neglect, or aircraft piracy; or (3) that it occurred as the result of the unlawful use of a destructive or explosive device.

The death penalty may be imposed if one of fourteen aggravating circumstances is proven to have accompanied the crime. The list of aggravating circumstances appears similar to the previous list of special circumstances, but aggravating circumstances are considered during the penalty phase of the trial rather than during the guilt phase. These aggravating circumstances are (1) that the victim was under twelve years old and the defendant was eighteen years or older; (2) that the defendant was previously convicted of one or more felonies involving violence; (3) that the defendant knowingly created a great risk of death to two or more people other than the victim; (4) that the homicide was a murder-for-hire and the defendant either performed the murder or solicited another to perform the murder; (5) that the homicide was especially heinous, atrocious, or cruel, involving torture or physical abuse beyond what was necessary to produce death; (6) that the homicide was committed in order to avoid the arrest or aid the escape from custody of the defendant or of someone else; (7) that the homicide was committed in the course of a first-degree murder, arson, rape, robbery, burglary, theft, kidnapping, aircraft piracy, or unlawful discharge of an explosive device; (8) that the defendant was in custody or had escaped from custody; (9) that the victim was a law enforcement officer, corrections official, corrections employee, emergency medical or rescue worker, emergency medical technician, paramedic, or firefighter; (10) that the victim was a judge, district or state attorney general, or a district or state assistant attorney general acting in the performance of his or her duties, or the homicide was motivated by the nature of those duties; (11) that the victim was known to the defendant to be an elected official; (12) that the defendant killed three or more people during the same criminal episode or at different times within a two-year period; (13) that the defendant knowingly mutilated the victim's body after death; or (14) that the victim was seventy years of age or older, or was otherwise particularly vulnerable due to a physical or mental handicap or disability. The jury must also consider any mitigating circumstances that the defense wishes to present.

Under Tennessee law, a person convicted of a capital offense cannot be executed if he or she was under the age of eighteen at the time of the crime. Tennessee does provide for life imprisonment without parole as an alternative to the death penalty. The governor has the authority to commute a death sentence to life imprisonment provided that the state supreme court finds that commutation of the sentence is justified.

In 1999 Tennessee replaced electrocution with lethal injection as its method of execution. Electrocution was left available as an option for prisoners sentenced prior to the adoption of the new method. The only execution to take place in Tennessee since the reinstatement of capital punishment was the execution of Robert Coe by lethal injection in 2000. As of April 2005, 107 people were awaiting execution on Tennessee's death row. **See also** *Furman v. Georgia.*

Texas

Texas has traditionally permitted juries to impose the death penalty, and continues to do so currently. Between 1846 and 1923, 368 people were executed under state jurisdiction in Texas. The executions were by hanging and were conducted by local sheriffs. In 1923 Texas ordered that executions be carried out at the state penitentiary in Huntsville. At the same time, Texas replaced hanging with electrocution as its method of execution. Between 1924 and 1964, 361 people were executed by electrocution in Texas.

Following the 1972 *Furman v. Georgia* ruling, which struck down Texas's death-penalty statute, the state passed a new death-penalty statute in 1974. The current death-penalty statute in Texas allows jurors to consider the death penalty for homicide under special circumstances. These special circumstances are (1) that the victim was a police officer or firefighter engaged in his or her official duties; (2) that the homicide occurred in the course of a kidnapping, burglary, robbery, sexual assault, arson, obstruction of the criminal justice system, or retaliation against it; (3) that the homicide was a murder-for-hire and the defendant either performed the murder or solicited another to perform the murder; (4) that the homicide occurred in the course of attempting to escape from a penal institution; (5) that the defendant is incarcerated in a penal institution and the victim was an employee of that institution; (6) that the defendant is incarcerated in a penal institution and the victim was another inmate; (7) that the homicide involved the killing of more than one person; or (8) that the victim was under six years old.

The Texas death-penalty statute does not provide a separate list of aggravating circumstances to be considered during the penalty phase of the trial. Whatever special circumstances are proven to have accompanied the crime at the guilt phase of the trial are considered to stand as aggravating circumstances for purposes of the penalty phase. However, at the penalty phase of the trial the jury must consider whether the defendant poses a continuing threat to society. If the defendant was an accomplice not directly responsible for causing the death of the victim, the jury must also consider whether the defendant *also* intended to kill the victim. Finally, the jury must consider any mitigating circumstances that may be raised by the defense before the death penalty can be imposed.

Under Texas law, a person convicted of a capital offense cannot be executed if he or she was under the age of eighteen at the time of the crime. Texas does not provide for life imprisonment without parole as an alternative to the death penalty. The governor has the authority to grant clemency, provided he or she receives a favorable recommendation from the Board of Pardons and Paroles. Even with a favorable recommendation, the governor is not obligated to grant clemency. The governor also has the authority to grant reprieves of up to thirty days.

In 1977 Texas replaced electrocution with lethal injection as its method of execution. Texas and Oklahoma were the first two states to adopt this new method of execution. The first execution in Texas following the reenactment of the death penalty took place in 1982, when Charles Brooks became the first person in the United States to die by lethal injection. Since 1982, there have been 322 executions in Texas, all by lethal injection. Since the 1972 *Furman v. Georgia* decision, Texas has conducted more executions than any other state. In fact, over one-third of all executions in the United States since 1972 have been conducted in Texas. In that time Texas has executed over three times as many people as Virginia, which has conducted the second largest number of executions (91). As of April 2005, 441 people were awaiting execution on Texas's death row. **See also** *Branch v. Texas;* Brooks, Charles; Foreman, Percy.

thirty-day rule

The thirty-day rule limits to just thirty days the time during which a defendant may file a motion for a new trial based on the discovery of new evidence. The purpose of the rule is to prevent defendants from filing innumerable appeals based on the discovery of allegedly new evidence, thereby stretching out the appeals process indefinitely. In Texas and thirteen other states, the period during which a defendant may sue for a new trial is thirty days, but other states have set longer periods of time. Only two states, New York and New Jersey, place no limit on motions for new trials based on new evidence.

Since evidence of a defendant's innocence might conceivably be discovered long after the thirty-day period has expired, it has been argued that the thirty-day rule violates a defendant's right to due process under the Fourteenth Amendment. However, in the 1993 *Herrera v. Collins* decision, the Supreme Court ruled that it was reasonable for states to place limits on the introduction of new evidence. **See also** actual innocence; *Herrera v. Collins*.

Thompson v. Oklahoma

This was a case heard by the Supreme Court of the United States in 1988 concerning the age at which a person who committed a crime is too young to be eligible for the death penalty. The defendant, William Wayne Thompson, was fifteen years old when he participated in the brutal murder of his brother-in-law. Three other people also participated in the murder. Thompson was tried as an adult, convicted, and sentenced to death. An appeals court upheld the sentence on the grounds that if Thompson was tried and convicted as an adult, he should be sentenced as an adult. Eventually, the U.S. Supreme Court agreed to review the case.

In a 5-to-3 decision, (Justice Anthony Kennedy did not participate) the Court ruled that Thompson was too young at the time of his crime to be subject to the death penalty. Writing for the Court, Justice John Paul Stevens offered the opinion that Oklahoma law did not give fifteen-year-olds other responsibilities of adulthood and therefore could not hold fifteen-year-olds to an adult standard of culpability for crimes. He pointed out that juries, who represent the conscience of their communities, generally refuse to give death sentences to defendants as young as fifteen. He concluded that a national consensus exists that the execution of fifteen-year-olds violates common standards of decency. Hence, the execution of fifteen-year-olds is "cruel and unusual," and prohibited by the Eighth Amendment to the Constitution. Thompson's sentence was overturned.

This ruling established that fifteen was too young to be eligible for the death penalty; it did not clarify at what age a person becomes old enough to commit a death-eligible crime. However, the next year, in 1989, the Supreme Court issued two additional rulings, *Stanford v. Kentucky* and *Wilkins v. Missouri*, that established that a defendant as young as sixteen could be eligible for the death penalty. This minimum has been raised to eighteen by the 2005 Supreme Court decision in *Roper v. Simmons*. **See also** juvenile offenders.

time between sentencing and execution

In ancient Athens, the execution of the philosopher Socrates was unusual because the execution was delayed for a whole month following the end of the trial while a delegation from the city was busy consulting with the Oracle at Delphi. In ancient times it was expected that an execution would follow immediately after sentencing, and most people believed that part of the deterrent value of an execution came from the fact that it quickly followed the commission of the crime. Justice, it was believed, should be both sure and swift.

In colonial America, some delay between sentencing and execution was allowed for religious reasons. It was felt that criminals should be given a little time to prepare their souls for death. Even so, the time allowed for this purpose was measured in weeks, and almost never exceeded two months. By the twentieth century, however, the time between sentencing and execution began to lengthen, because, under the "due process" clause of the Fourteenth Amendment, trials were being scrutinized much more carefully. More appeals were being filed, and the consideration of those appeals was taking longer. In 1911 a Pennsylvania judge, Robert Ralston, complained that, because of the length of the appeals process, a criminal might spend *years* on death row. At the time this was true in only a few cases, but by 1959 it was typical for inmates to be on death row for up to two years following sentencing. At least one person had spent nine years on death row. Now the average time spent on death row is between ten and eleven years, and several people have been on death row for over twenty-four years. **See also** Antiterrorism and Effective Death Penalty Act; death row.

torture

Torture traditionally means the infliction of pain on a prisoner for the purpose of eliciting information and/or breaking down a prisoner's resistance. Torture was used during the Middle Ages to extract confessions of guilt. This was done because, without better techniques for investigating crimes, proof of guilt was thought to be impossible unless there were at least two witnesses to a crime or the guilty party confessed. Since it was rarely possible to find two witnesses, it was usually more practical to try to get a confession, through torture if necessary. During the fourteenth century, torture was used by investigators known as "inquisitors of moral depravity" to get prisoners to admit to such crimes as heresy and witchcraft. Torture is still used by some governments on political prisoners to extract intelligence information, although this practice is universally condemned as a violation of human rights.

When the infliction of pain is used to extract information or a confession, it is not considered to be an aspect of punishment. However, if no information is being sought, the infliction of pain can be used solely for the purpose of punishment. This may be referred to as torture in some cases, but not all. For example, the spanking of children is not considered a form of torture. The infliction of pain as an aspect of punishment is considered torture only if it is "cruel and unusual," that is, that it (a) shocks the conscience of the court; (b) violates standards of decency as they have evolved in our society; (c) is disproportionate to the offense; (d) is wanton and unnecessary; or (e) shows indifference to the health and safety of the person being punished. Since the Eighth Amendment to the U.S. Constitution prohibits cruel and unusual punishment, it follows that American courts do not permit the use of torture. However, what qualifies as torture must be decided by considering "evolving standards of decency."

Under ancient legal codes, torture was sometimes an aspect of capital punishment. Some methods of execution were intentionally designed to be slow and painful. Stoning, crucifixion, and breaking on the wheel are all examples of intentionally painful methods of execution. In any case, executions were frequently preceded by a flogging or other form of physical abuse. Such methods were used to punish particularly serious crimes or to punish slaves and the lower classes. The use of torture as an aspect of capital punishment disappeared (in most countries) during the eighteenth century, since it seemed to serve no purpose other than encouraging brutality in the people who inflicted and witnessed the torture. Death itself was the ultimate punishment. Since the eighteenth century, there has been an effort to perform executions with as little pain inflicted as possible. Hanging was adopted because it seemed fairly quick and painless. Electrocution and lethal gas were adopted later because they appeared to be equally painless and were more reliable. Finally, lethal injection has replaced electrocution and lethal gas, again because it can be reliably performed without the infliction of pain. **See also** breaking on the wheel; corporal punishment; crucifixion; cruel and unusual punishment.

trial

A trial is the formal examination of evidence by a judicial authority in order to settle a matter in dispute. Some disputes can be settled by a judge alone, so a trial need not necessarily involve a jury. Such a trial is called a bench trial. However, when a defendant is accused of a crime, the defendant has the right to be tried by a jury. A defendant may waive the right to be tried by a jury, but such a choice is rarely made. When a jury is present, the jury decides all questions of fact, leaving only questions of how to interpret the law to the judge. In a criminal trial, the court considers evidence in order to determine whether or not a person who has been charged with a crime is guilty of the crime, and if so, what punishment should be imposed. If a capital crime is involved (i.e., if there is a possibility that the death penalty could be imposed), then the trial may differ from ordinary criminal trials in several important respects.

Under the constitutional requirement that every defendant (a person accused of a crime) is entitled to due process of law, a trial may not be conducted unless the defendant is able to participate in the process. All defendants have the right to know that they have been charged with a crime, to hear the charges against them, and to respond to those charges. Hence, if a defendant is missing, or too ill to participate, or in a state of mind that prevents him or her from understanding the significance of the proceedings, then a trial cannot be held. Since understanding

During a trial, a witness (left) is questioned by an attorney, while a judge (center) presides over the proceedings.

the nature of the proceedings is important, and legal proceedings can often be complex and difficult to understand, it is now recognized that every defendant has the right to be represented by an attorney, who uses his or her knowledge of law to act in the best interest of the defendant. This attorney is known as the defense attorney. In some states the defendant at a capital trial is represented by at least two defense attorneys. The two attorneys share the workload of the case, but they also act as a check on each other. Each can make sure that the other is truly acting in the defendant's best interest, not making mistakes that might later cost the defendant his or her life.

In a criminal trial, the defendant is charged with committing an act that is illegal under the laws of some jurisdiction, usually the state. This jurisdiction is represented by attorneys who are called prosecuting attorneys. At a capital trial, there will probably be two or more prosecuting attorneys. Since the defendant is presumed to be innocent, most of the work must be done by the prosecution. It is the responsibility of the prosecution to present the evidence that proves the defendant to be guilty. Since there may be a great deal of evidence involved, the workload for the prosecution is likely to be quite heavy. Several attorneys may be necessary to keep it all straight.

Responsibility for conducting a trial is in the hands of a judge. The judge makes sure that procedures are followed correctly, and if disputes arise in the course of the trial, the judge will resolve them by making rulings. However, the judge does *not* decide whether the defendant is guilty or innocent. The judge is assisted in the courtroom by various people. A clerk acts as the judge's secretary, scheduling the judge's time and making sure that important papers are kept in order. A court reporter records what is said in the courtroom. A bailiff acts as a security officer, making sure that everyone in the courtroom is safe.

The first step in a criminal trial is the selection of the jury. The job of the jury is to decide all questions of fact, the most important of which is whether or not the defendant actually committed the crime with which he or she is charged. It is important that the members of the jury be willing to decide this question with an open mind. The selection process begins with a pool of prospective jurors who are picked randomly from the local community. Every citizen has a duty to be available for jury service, although people who are in poor health or who would suffer some other hardship (such as loss of income) are generally excused. From this initial pool, prospective jurors are then excused in two ways. First, some prospective jurors are excused "for cause." The prospective jurors are asked a series of questions aimed at determining whether they have any prejudices that might make it impossible for them to be fair and open-minded. This process of questioning is known as voir dire. These questions will certainly include whether any of the prospective jurors personally know the defendant or any of the witnesses, or the attorneys on either side. If the defendant is a member of a racial minority, the prospective jurors may be asked to reveal any racial prejudices that they harbor. The prospective jurors will be asked if they have been involved with a crime similar to the one the defendant is charged with. In the case of a capital trial, the prospective jurors will be asked if they have fixed opinions on the issue of the death penalty itself— if they believe it should never be imposed or if they believe it should always be imposed for certain crimes. Prospective jurors who answer yes to any of these questions will be dismissed from the jury because there is reason to believe that such jurors could not be open-minded in deciding the issues that they will be asked to decide.

Following voir dire, some prospective jurors may then be dismissed in a second way. Both the prosecution and the defense may dismiss a certain number of prospective jurors on "peremptory challenges." That is, they may ask that the prospective jurors be dismissed and give no reason for the dismissal. This gives the attorneys on both sides the ability to remove prospective jurors that they *suspect* may be prejudiced against their case even though the process of questioning revealed no concrete evidence of prejudice.

A capital trial is divided into two phases, known as the guilt phase and the penalty phase. During the guilt phase of the trial, the jury is asked to decide whether or not the defendant is guilty. The prosecution begins by providing evidence to show that the defendant is guilty. The evidence is presented by witnesses who explain what the evidence means and how it was collected. As each item of evidence is presented, the defendant (usually through his or her attorney) has the right to challenge the evidence by cross-examining the witness who presented it. Once all the evidence has been provided by the prosecution, the defendant may then choose to mount an "affirmative defense" by providing evidence aimed at proving that he or she is not guilty. As this evidence is presented, the prosecution may challenge it. It is not required, however, that the defendant mount an affirmative defense. Because the defendant is presumed to be innocent unless proven guilty, the defense may rely solely on challenging the evidence provided by the prosecution.

Once all the evidence is presented, the jury is asked to render a verdict, or decide whether the defendant is guilty or not guilty. If the jury decides that the defendant is not guilty, the trial ends. On the other hand, if the jury decides that the defendant is guilty, then the defendant must be sentenced. In an ordinary trial, the judge will impose the sentence immediately, or after a break of a few days to give the judge some time to think. In the case of a capital trial, however, the trial then moves to its second phase, the penalty phase.

Capital trials have a separate penalty phase because the question of whether the death penalty should be imposed turns on a careful consideration of the factors surrounding the crime. Factors that tend to make a crime more serious are called aggravating circumstances; factors that tend to make a crime less serious are called mitigating circumstances. Whether or not any of these factors are truly present is a question of fact and must, therefore, be decided by the jury. The second phase of the trial proceeds in much the same way as the first phase. The prosecution begins by providing evidence of aggravating circumstances. The defense may challenge this evidence as it is presented. The defense may then provide evidence of mitigating circumstances, and the prosecution may challenge the evidence as it is presented. Once all the evidence is presented, the jury is asked to decide whether any of the aggravating circumstances were present and, if so, whether enough mitigating circumstances were also present to counterbalance them. The jury does not, technically speaking, impose the sentence. This is still the responsibility of the judge. However, the judge may impose a sentence of death only if the jury decides that aggravating circumstances were present and that there were not enough mitigating circumstances to counterbalance them. In practice, the judge is largely bound by the jury's recommendation.

Condemned murderer Karla Faye Tucker points to symbols of her newfound Christian faith. Despite appeals for clemency from religious leaders, Tucker was executed in 1998.

Once the sentence is imposed, the trial ends. However, this may be only the beginning of the legal process in a capital case. The trial will inevitably be carefully reviewed by an appeals court, and any errors that were committed in the course of the trial may lead to the conviction or the sentence (or both) being overturned, which may then lead to a new trial. To avoid this possibility, judges and prosecutors are extremely careful in the conduct of trials. **See also** affirmative defense; aggravating circumstances; appeals process; mitigating circumstances.

Trop v. Dulles

This was a case heard by the Supreme Court of the United States in 1958 concerning whether Congress had the power to revoke a person's citizenship as punishment for desertion from the military in time of war. This was not a capital case, but it is highly relevant to the issue of capital punishment since it was in this case that the phrase "evolving standards of decency" was first used. In a 5-to-4 decision, the Court ruled that Congress did not have the power to revoke a person's citizenship without his or her consent, since doing so would constitute cruel and unusual punishment. In the majority opinion, Chief Justice Earl Warren wrote that the phrase "cruel and unusual" in the Eighth Amendment "must draw its meaning from the evolving standards of decency that mark the progress of a maturing society." Warren meant that punishments not considered to be cruel and unusual at one time might later come to be regarded as cruel and unusual. Since this decision, it has been understood by legal scholars that the question of whether the death penalty is cruel and unusual must be settled by determining whether it is considered "decent" by society at the time the question is asked. A similar ruling occurred in a much earlier Supreme Court decision, *Weems v. United States* (1910), in which Justice Joseph McKenna held that whether a punishment was cruel and unusual should be decided based on "current sensibilities." **See also** cruel and unusual punishment; public opinion.

Tucker, Karla Faye (1959–1998)

Karla Faye Tucker was the first woman to be executed in Texas since 1863. Her execution gained attention because she had become a repentant born-again Christian while on death row.

Tucker was convicted, along with her boyfriend, Daniel Ryan Garrett, of the 1983 murder of Jerry Lynn Dean. Tucker and Garrett broke in to Dean's home and killed him with a pickax. They also killed Deborah Thornton, who was in Dean's home at the time. Both Tucker and Garrett were sentenced to death. Garrett died of liver disease in 1993 while awaiting execution. Tucker, meanwhile, underwent an apparently sincere religious conversion experience and expressed remorse for the killings. Because of her religious conversion, conservative religious leaders who normally support capital punishment, including the Reverend Pat Robertson, made pleas for her to receive clemency. However, Texas governor George W. Bush declined to grant clemency, and the U.S. Supreme Court refused to consider a last-minute appeal. Tucker was executed by lethal injection on February 3, 1998. **See also** clemency; repentance.

United Nations Commission on Human Rights

The principal organ of the United Nations responsible for monitoring and issuing position statements on human rights. The commission was created in 1947 and comprises representatives from fifty-three nations. Since 1993 the office has been headed by a high commissioner for Human Rights.

Since 1997 the commission has included capital punishment as a human rights concern, citing Article 3 of the Universal Declaration of Human Rights, which states that everyone has a right to life. In 1998 the commission issued a resolution calling for a moratorium on the use of capital punishment in the United States on the grounds that those defendants who were sentenced to death in the United States were not necessarily those who had committed the most heinous crimes. In 1999 the commission issued a resolution calling for a worldwide moratorium on the use of capital punishment, and since then has regularly issued statements urging nations to work toward the eventual abolition of capital punishment. **See also** Universal Declaration of Human Rights.

United States v. Jackson

This was a case heard by the Supreme Court of the United States in 1967, and decided in 1968, concerning the wording of the Federal Kidnapping Act, which made interstate kidnapping a capital offense under federal law. The defendants in the case, Charles Jackson, Glenn Motte, and John Albert Walsh Jr., were indicted by a federal grand jury for violating the Federal Kidnapping Act. However, the Federal Kidnapping Act states that the death penalty may be imposed "if the kidnapped person has not been liberated unharmed, and if the verdict of the jury shall so recommend." This phrase had been interpreted to mean that the death penalty could not be imposed unless it was imposed by a jury. Therefore, if the defendant were to forgo a jury trial, either by pleading guilty or by requesting a bench trial, then the defendant could not be sentenced to death. The convictions of Jackson, Motte, and Walsh were appealed on the grounds that defendants had too much incentive to give up their right to a jury trial in order to avoid a sentence of death. The Supreme Court eventually agreed and declared the Federal Kidnapping Act unconstitutional. **See also** federal death-penalty laws.

Universal Declaration of Human Rights

Passed by the United Nations in 1948, this declaration is the first international document to use the phrase "human rights," and is considered to be the founding document in international law for the notion of human rights. In thirty brief articles, it spells out the rights of individuals as recognized under international law, including the right to "life, liberty and security of person" (Article 3) and the right not to be subjected to "torture or to cruel, inhuman or degrading treatment or punishment" (Article 5). The document makes no specific mention of capital punishment, but the UN Commission on Human Rights cites Articles 3 and 5 as the basis for considering capital punishment a human rights concern. **See also** United Nations Commission on Human Rights.

Utah

Utah has traditionally permitted juries to impose the death penalty, and continues to do so currently. Utah is the only state that has traditionally used a firing squad as its method of execution. Under territorial law, three methods of execution were available to a condemned prisoner: hanging, beheading, and the firing squad. The firing squad was the primary method used, and was mandated if the prisoner did not select an alternative. While available under the law, beheading was never used, and in 1888 it was removed from the list of options. Only three hangings and seven executions by firing squad took place under territorial jurisdiction, which ended in 1896 when Utah became a state. Prior to 1903, executions occurred under the jurisdiction of county governments and were performed locally. In 1903, to limit public viewing, executions were moved to the Sugar House prison. In 1951 a new state prison was built at Point of the Mountain, and this became the site for executions. However, executions continued to be carried out by local law enforcement officers. Firing squads were made up of volunteer law enforcement officers from the county in which the crime had occurred. Between 1896 and 1960, thirty-three people were executed in Utah, thirty-one by firing squad and two by hanging.

Following the 1972 *Furman v. Georgia* ruling, which struck down Utah's death-penalty statute, the state passed a new death-penalty statute in 1974. Utah's current death-penalty statute allows jurors to consider the death penalty for homicide under special circumstances. The law then provides a list of seventeen statutorily defined special circumstances, the longest list provided by any state law. These special circumstances are (1) that the defendant was incarcerated in a correctional institution; (2) that the defendant killed or attempted to kill two or more people during the same criminal episode; (3) that the defendant knowingly created a great risk of death to people other than the victim; (4) that the homicide was committed in the course of a robbery, rape (including rape of a child and rape with an object), sexual assault, child abuse, arson, burglary, or kidnapping; (5) that the homicide was committed in order to prevent someone's arrest or effect someone's escape from custody; (6) that the homicide was committed for monetary gain; (7) that the homicide was a murder-for-hire and the defendant either performed the murder or solicited another to perform the murder; (8) that the defendant was previously convicted of murder or of a felony involving violence or the threat of violence; (9) that the homicide was committed in order to prevent a witness from testifying, to prevent a person from providing evidence or otherwise participating in legal proceedings, to retaliate against a witness for testifying or for providing evidence, or otherwise hindering governmental functions or the enforcement of law; (10) that the victim was (or had been) a public official or candidate for public office and the homicide was related to or motivated by the victim's position; (11) that the victim was known by the defendant to be a law enforcement officer, prosecutor, jailer, prison official, firefighter, judge or other court official, juror, probation officer, or parole officer, and the homicide was related to or motivated by the official duties of the victim; (12) that the homicide was committed by means of a destructive or explosive device such as a bomb; (13) that the homicide was committed during the hijacking of a train, airplane, or any other public means of transportation; (14) that the homicide employed the use of poison; (15) that the victim was used as a hostage or shield or was held for ransom; (16) that the defendant was under sentence of life imprisonment or death; or (17) that the homicide was especially heinous and cruel, involving torture or physical abuse prior to the victim's death.

The Utah death-penalty statute does not provide a separate list of aggravating circumstances to be considered during the penalty phase of the trial. Whatever special circumstances are proven to have accompanied the crime at the guilt phase of the trial are considered to stand as aggravating circumstances for purposes of the penalty phase. However, the jury must consider any mitigating circumstances that may be raised by the defense before the death penalty can be imposed.

Under Utah law, a person convicted of a capital offense cannot be executed if he or she was under the age of eighteen at the time of the crime. Utah does provide for life imprisonment without parole as an alternative to the death penalty. The authority to grant clemency is vested in a special panel on which the governor sits as a member.

With the execution of Gary Gilmore in 1977, Utah became the first state to resume executions following the 1976 *Gregg v. Georgia* Supreme Court decision allowing executions to continue in the United States under revised death-penalty statutes. Gilmore was executed by firing squad, and was the last execution by firing squad in Utah. In 1980 Utah replaced hanging with lethal injection as one method of execution that may be selected by a condemned prisoner. However, the firing squad was retained as the method to be used if the prisoner does not make a choice. There have been five executions in Utah since 1980. All have been by lethal injection. In March of 2004, despite decades of tradition, Utah discontinued its use of firing squads as an available method of execution. As of June 2005, ten people were awaiting execution on Utah's death row. **See also** Gilmore, Gary.

utilitarianism

Utilitarianism is a theory of ethics that was developed in England during the nineteenth century. It remains one of the most important and influential ethical theories in the world today, and is widely invoked in discussions of the ethical basis of capital punishment. Utilitarianism can be defined by its three central doctrines:

1. Whether an action is right or wrong depends on the consequences of that action.
2. An increase in happiness is a desirable consequence, and an increase in unhappiness is an undesirable consequence.
3. Everyone's happiness (or unhappiness) matters equally.

These three central doctrines can be summarized in a slogan called the principle of utility, which states that we should act to produce the greatest possible happiness for as many people as we can. An action is wrong if, on balance, it produces greater unhappiness than happiness. Jeremy Bentham, the English philosopher who first proposed and named this theory, was a social reformer concerned with the poverty and poor working conditions of British factory workers in the early days of the industrial revolution. He used the principle of utility to argue for laws requiring minimum wages for workers and limiting the number of hours they had to work each day. He also succeeded in getting the British Parliament to outlaw child labor.

Utilitarianism has significant implications for the theory of punishment in general and capital punishment in particular. According to utilitarianism, the morality of any action (including the punishment of criminals) is determined by the consequences of that action, not on events that happened previously. Utilitarianism is entirely forward looking. Since a crime occurs prior to the punishment, the nature or seriousness of the crime is not germane to the nature or severity of the punishment. Clearly, punishing people will make them unhappy. In fact, if it did not make them unhappy, it would not be a punishment. However, according to the principle of utility, it is morally wrong to cause people to be unhappy, so punishment, including the death penalty, can be justified only if it somehow produces enough happiness to outweigh the unhappiness that it causes. The death penalty clearly cannot be justified on the grounds that it results in the reform of the criminal, so it must be justified either on the grounds that it has a strong deterrent effect or on the grounds that it is the best way to prevent criminals from doing further harm. Neither reason seems entirely convincing. The evidence that the death penalty has a deterrent effect is unclear, or at best controversial, and it appears that imprisonment is just as effective as execution for preventing criminals from doing further harm. Hence, utilitarianism does not provide strong support for capital punishment, and it is not surprising that the use of the death penalty diminished as utilitarianism became influential in ethical debates.

Philosophers often criticize utilitarianism for its exclusively forward-looking perspective. They point out that a utilitarian might reasonably favor the punishment of an innocent person on the grounds that this would deter crime just as effectively as the punishment of a guilty person (provided, of course, that the general public *believed* the innocent person to be guilty). A utilitarian might also favor imprisoning (or executing) people *likely* to commit serious crimes on the grounds that this would not only deter crime but prevent the harm caused by the crime in the first place. In short, critics of utilitarianism argue that utilitarianism would warrant what most people would consider serious miscarriages of justice and violations of human rights. Utilitarians have attempted to modify their theory to meet these criticisms. Nevertheless, utilitarianism remains an influential ethical theory despite its difficulty in accounting for concepts of justice. **See also** Bentham, Jeremy; justification of punishment.

Vermont

Vermont does not currently permit juries to impose the death penalty. Although Vermont has historically permitted the death penalty, the number of executions there has been quite small. From 1791, when Vermont became a state, until 1919, only nineteen people were executed by hanging in Vermont. In 1919 Vermont adopted the electric chair as its method of execution, but from 1919 until 1954 only five people were executed. The last person to be executed was Donald DeMag in 1954. In 1965 capital punishment in Vermont was abolished for most crimes, and it was abolished entirely in 1984. However, in July 2005 a Vermont jury convened under federal jurisdiction convicted a defendant, Donald Fell, of an interstate carjacking and murder. The jury recommended Fell be put to death under the federal death-penalty law. **See also** federal death-penalty laws.

victim impact statements

Victim impact statements are statements entered into evidence at various legal proceedings that report on the financial, physical, and psychological impact of a crime on the victim, interpreted to mean the victim's family as well. Such statements may be considered at parole hearings, for example. In 1978 California law was changed to allow the introduction of victim impact statements as evidence during the penalty phase of criminal trials, including those involving the death penalty. Numerous other states quickly followed suit, and in 1982 the U.S. Congress approved the use of victim impact statements in federal trials as well. However, in 1987 the U.S. Supreme Court ruled in *Booth v. Maryland* that facts about the victim's life and about the suffering of survivors were not relevant to the nature of the crime and therefore should not be available to a jury considering a sentence of death. In 1991 a differently constituted Supreme Court reversed this decision in *Payne v. Tennessee*. Victim impact statements are now regularly included during the penalty phase of death-penalty trials, and the opportunity to submit such statements is often considered an aspect of victims' rights. **See also** *Booth v. Maryland; Payne v. Tennessee;* victims' rights.

victims' rights

After a crime has been committed, the criminal justice system finds itself mostly concerned with the offender, who must be arrested, charged, jailed, tried, and punished. The victim and the victim's family often seem to have no clearly defined role in the process and often complain that, rather than being seen as central to the crime, they are marginalized and forgotten. In response to such complaints, many states, in the past twenty years, have passed laws and even amendments to their constitutions granting specific rights to the victims of crimes and, especially in the case of homicide, to the members of the victim's family.

In most states, victims have been granted the right to attend legal proceedings, including those not open to the general public, such as parole hearings. As appropriate, victims and their families have a right to provide victim impact statements as evidence at legal proceedings. These rights imply the right to be informed where and when such legal proceedings are scheduled to take place. Many states have broadened this right to be informed to include other status information about the offender such as transfers between facilities, temporary release information, and even information about an offender's escape and recapture, should such events occur. Victims generally identify the right to be informed as the most important of their rights, both because it provides the most emotional comfort and because it is a prerequisite for the exercise of other rights.

Studies show that many state correctional systems do a poor job of complying with victims' rights requirements. As a result, victims' rights advocates have been pressuring for stricter enforcement of laws mandating victims' rights, including the levying of fines and other penalties against officials who fail to keep victims and their families adequately informed. In 1993 the Arizona Supreme Court overturned a parole board's decision to grant parole to a prisoner, and ordered a new hearing, on the grounds that the victim had not been informed of the time and place of the original hearing. At the second hearing, the victim submitted a victim impact statement, based on which the parole board denied parole. **See also** victim impact statements.

viewing of executions

Prior to the nineteenth century, executions in America were frequently conducted in an outdoor public place, and crowds were welcome, or even encouraged, to attend. Since part of the purpose of executions was to deter crime, it seemed obvious that this deterrent effect could best be achieved if people saw the consequences of crime for themselves. For this reason, whole families, including children, would attend. In fact, it was often for the sake of the children that families made an effort to attend an execution, since witnessing an execution was considered a necessary part of a child's moral education.

In colonial America, hangings were extremely popular. It is estimated that more people assembled for hangings than for any other public purpose. For some hangings, people traveled from as far away as fifty miles. The hangings of women convicted of infanticide drew especially large crowds, although the hanging of convicted murderer John Johnson in New York City in 1824 is said to have drawn the largest crowd recorded for a public execution: fifty thousand people. Local residents near the gallows later sued the city of New York for damage done to their trees, fences, and lawns by the exceptionally large crowd.

It would be a mistake to characterize public hangings as rowdy or bloodthirsty events. They were, in fact, solemn events, more like large public funerals than like sporting events. They were conducted with a great deal of ceremony, beginning with a somber procession from the jail to the gallows. Prior to the execution, at least one minister, and sometimes more, delivered a sermon. Often the condemned prisoner would give a brief speech, ideally one expressing repentance and urging others not to follow his or her example. It is likely that the crowd turned out for the sermons and speeches as much as for the execution itself. In a time before radio and television, a public sermon given by a

Two black men accused of murder are lynched in the town square of Marion, Indiana, in full view of white townspeople.

well-known minister could draw a large audience even without an execution. The execution, though, served to make such sermons especially poignant and moving, and ministers undoubtedly saved their best sermons for these special occasions.

At the beginning of the nineteenth century, attitudes toward public executions began to change. For one thing, opposition to capital punishment itself was beginning to grow. The idea began to spread that it was insensitive and vulgar to watch—and enjoy watching—the execution of a fellow human being. While the majority of executions were conducted with dignity and decorum, people tended to remember and talk about the ones that were not. Ministers complained that the crowd was not absorbing the moral lesson that the occasion was intended to impart, and the notorious presence of pickpockets in the crowd suggested that public executions actually did more to promote crime than to deter it. This view was encouraged by a new theory of psychology, associated with the "science" of phrenology, under which the viewing of violent acts was thought to appeal to people who were already predisposed to violence and was likely to incline them to further violence. It was also thought that executions were making martyrs and folk heroes of the condemned, and that this, too, had a tendency to promote crime and rebellious behavior. Accounts of early-nineteenth-century executions frequently remark on the surprisingly large number of women present. It was considered ironic that women, who were thought to have more delicate sensibilities than men, would so eagerly attend such abhorrent spectacles. More and more public executions came to be seen as a form of vulgar entertainment, not worthy of civilized people.

These attitudes were especially widespread in northern states. In 1830 Connecticut was the first state to move executions out of sight of the general public. In 1833 Rhode Island became the first state to prohibit by law the public viewing of executions. By 1860 all of the northern states and several southern states had passed laws requiring that executions be held in locations where they could not be viewed by the general public. In most cases, this meant the jail's exercise yard. By 1900 most southern states had also banned public executions. Executions for the crime of rape continued to be held in public in Arkansas until 1906, and in 1920 Kentucky restored public executions for this crime, having originally banned all public executions in 1880. Typically, only blacks were executed for rape. In other southern states, illegal lynching of blacks for the crime of rape continued to be practiced, and continued to draw large crowds. However, this was the only form of public execution available to most people after 1900.

By 1923, the few states that still held public executions switched their method of execution from hanging to electrocution. Since an electric chair cannot easily be set up for public display, practical considerations brought a final end to legal public executions. The last legal public execution in the United States took place in Owensboro, Kentucky, in 1936 when a black man, Rainey Bethea, was hanged for rape. The execution was anything but decorous. Vendors sold drinks and hot dogs, the crowd was unruly, and, even before he was declared dead, the hood that covered Bethea's face was snatched and torn up to provide mementos of the event. Editorials and letters around the nation condemned the event as barbarous and uncivilized. Embarrassed officials canceled a public hanging that had been planned for a few days later (in a different county) and held it discreetly in private inside the jail. Even reporters were barred. Two years later, in 1938, Kentucky joined the rest of the nation in banning all public executions.

However, moving executions inside the walls of a jail did not end the participation of crowds. Dignitaries and other people with influence were invited into the jail yard to witness executions, and the competition for invitations was often intense. The size of the audience was limited primarily by the space available for viewing, and some jail yards could host an audience of several hundred. Meanwhile, larger crowds would gather outside the jail. Sometimes trees and rooftops would afford a view of the proceedings, but crowds gathered even if there was nothing to see. The public's habit of attending executions never entirely died out, and even today it is common for vigils to be held outside of prisons on days that executions are scheduled to take place.

Today, only a select group of people are allowed to witness executions. Naturally the prison officials responsible for conducting the execution must be present, as well as a physician to pronounce the time of death. Beyond that, a few reporters, elected officials, or other dignitaries may be present as representatives of the public, including in some cases the district attorney, the judge who presided over the case, and the prosecutor. A few members of the condemned prisoner's family may be present, as well as a minister or other spiritual adviser and the condemned prisoner's attorney. In many states, members of the victim's family may also be present, if they so request. Oklahoma permits all adult members of the victim's family to attend; other states limit the number of members of the victim's family to five or fewer. It is becoming an increasingly popular notion that a primary reason for executing murderers is to bring about a feeling of closure for the victim's family. It is argued that allowing family members to witness the execution contributes to this feeling of closure, which suggests that members of the victim's family may have a special right to witness executions, if they choose to. At the 2001 execution of Timothy McVeigh, who was responsible for the deaths of 168 people, so many members of the victims' families asked to be present at the execution that the rather small viewing facility could not accommodate them all. A few were permitted to view the execution in person. For the rest, prison officials arranged for the execution to be carried on closed-circuit television to a viewing room at a federal facility in Oklahoma City. About 250 people watched the execution in this way. Prior to the execution, both advocates and opponents of capital punishment argued that, since the execution was being carried on video anyway, it should be broadcast to the general public. U.S. attorney general John Ashcroft turned down this suggestion. **See also** censorship of reporting on executions; closure.

Virginia

Virginia has traditionally permitted juries to impose the death penalty, and continues to do so currently. The first execution in colonial America took place in Virginia, and more people have been executed in Virginia than in any other state. Between 1608 and 1776, 202 people were executed in colonial Virginia. Most executions were by hanging, but there were also a couple of burnings. In 1700 three people were hung on a gibbet for piracy, and in 1720 four people were executed for piracy by the same method. Virginia was the only colony to use this particularly cruel form of execution, and only for the crime of piracy.

The last public execution in Virginia took place on March 25, 1879, when two black men, Julius Christian and Patrick Smith, were hanged for robbery and murder. The circus atmosphere at the execution was an embarrassment to public officials, and a week later the Virginia General Assembly voted to ban public viewings of executions. Executions continued to be conducted by local sheriffs but were held behind the walls of local jails until 1908. Between 1777 and 1908, some 830 people were hanged in Virginia. In 1908 Virginia replaced hanging with electrocution as its method of execution. At the same time the state moved all executions to the state penitentiary. Between 1908 and 1962, 236 executions by electrocution took place in Virginia.

Following the 1972 *Furman v. Georgia* ruling, which struck down Virginia's death-penalty statute, the state passed a new death-penalty statute in 1974. Virginia's current death-penalty statute allows jurors to consider the death penalty for homicide under special circumstances. The law provides a list of twelve statutorily defined special circumstances, all of which specify that the killing must be willful, deliberate, and premeditated. These special circumstances are (1) that the homicide occurred in the course of an abduction for ransom; (2) that the homicide was a murder-for-hire; (3) that the defendant was in custody or incarcerated in a correctional facility; (4) that the homicide occurred in the course of a robbery; (5) that the homicide occurred in the course of rape, forcible sodomy, or rape with an object; (6) that the victim was a law enforcement officer; (7) that more than one person was killed at the same time; (8) that the defendant has killed more than one person within a three-year period; (9) that the homicide occurred in the course of a drug-related offense; (10) that the homicide was ordered by someone engaged in a continuing criminal enterprise (i.e., someone involved in organized crime); (11) that the victim was a pregnant woman and the goal of the homicide was to terminate the pregnancy without the woman's consent; or (12) that the victim was under fourteen years old and the defendant twenty-one or older.

The death penalty may be imposed if one aggravating circumstance can be proven to have accompanied the crime. The one aggravating circumstance is that, based on the defendant's past history or on the circumstances surrounding the present crime, the defendant probably poses a continuing threat to society, or the present offense involved conduct that was outrageously or wantonly vile, involving torture or physical abuse of the victim. The jury must also consider any mitigating circumstances that the defense wishes to present.

Until the Supreme Court abolished the death penalty for juveniles under the age of eighteen in its 2005 *Roper v. Simmons* decision, Virginia law permitted imposition of a death sentence if the convicted was at least sixteen at the time of the crime. Virginia does provide for life imprisonment without parole as an alternative to the death penalty. The governor has the authority to grant clemency.

Following the reenactment of the death penalty, executions in Virginia resumed in 1982. Between 1982 and 1994, twenty-four people were executed in Virginia's electric chair. In 1995 Virginia added lethal injection as an optional method of execution, allowing condemned prisoners to choose either electrocution or lethal injection. Since 1995 there have been sixty-seven executions in Virginia, all but one by means of lethal injection. In 1998 Kenneth Stewart elected to be executed by means of electrocution instead. Since 1972, Virginia has had the second largest number of executions of any state. Only Texas has had more. As of June 2005, twenty-three people were awaiting execution on Virginia's death row. **See also** Kendall, George.

visitation privileges

Normally, incarcerated people are allowed to receive visits from family members and friends, under varying conditions. There are three main types of visits. Noncontact visits are those in which the prisoner and visitor are separated by a screen or glass to prevent exchange of weapons, drugs, and other contraband. Contact visits are those in which the prisoner and the visitor meet at a table and are permitted a quick hug at the beginning and end of the visit. Both types of visits are closely monitored by prison personnel. Conjugal, or "family weekend," visits are those in which the prisoner and visitor are permitted to spend a weekend together without being closely watched. Such visits are generally available only to prisoners who are not considered to be a security risk.

Studies have shown that prisoners who receive frequent visits from family and friends are less likely to commit new crimes and are therefore less likely to return to prison. For this reason, prison policies on visitation have tended to become more lenient in recent decades. Prisons have tended to allow longer visits and more frequent visits. Prisons have also become much more lenient in allowing contact and conjugal visits. However, since one of the primary reasons for encouraging visitation is to promote prisoner rehabilitation, and since rehabilitation is not an issue for death row prisoners, more lenient visitation privileges might not be expected to be a priority for prisoners on death row. This is certainly the view held in Japan, and Japanese prisons have been criticized by the international community for not permitting death row inmates comparable visitation, correspondence, and exercise privileges as other prisoners.

In the United States, prisons generally treat death row inmates in the same manner that maximum-security prisoners are treated. This means that death row inmates have some visitation privileges but are frequently not permitted contact, let alone conjugal visits. It is sometimes argued that, since death row inmates are often not a significant security risk, they should be permitted more lenient visitation privileges. In the same humanitarian spirit that has led to the custom of the last meal, some believe that death row inmates should be permitted at least one unsupervised (conjugal) visit with family members to give them a chance to say goodbye. No state currently provides for conjugal visits by death row inmates.

In various cases, courts have ruled that visitation is a privilege, not a right. This means that visitation policies can be set by prison officials and vary from institution to institution. Access to visitors can be based on a prisoner's behavior. By contrast, consultation with an attorney is a right, not a privilege, so it cannot be restricted based on behavior. Visits from ministers and members of the press are treated like visits with friends and must conform to the prison's usual visitation policies. However, death row inmates tend to receive more such visits because of their special circumstances. **See also** death row.

volunteers

The term *volunteer* is sometimes used to refer to a defendant who actually requests a sentence of death during the penalty phase of a capital trial. A defendant is entitled to request a death sentence and has, in any case, no obligation to mount a defense during the penalty phase of trial. However, the court must inform the defendant of the potential merit of any mitigating circumstances that might be presented on the defendant's behalf. Since 1976, some seventy-five defendants (about 12.5 percent of all those executed) have requested a death sentence at trial. Other defendants have refused to exercise their right to an appeal once a penalty of death has been imposed. Westley Allan Dodd, a confessed child molester and killer executed in 1993, insisted on being put to death, saying he would rape and kill again if given the chance. Gary Gilmore, the first person executed after the *Furman v. Georgia* decision brought a temporary halt to executions in the United States, even demanded that appeals filed by his attorneys without his permission be withdrawn. Carl Panzram, a brutal serial killer who was executed in 1930, was even more vehement in his demand that he be put to death. He wrote to anti-death-penalty activists saying, "I wish you all had one neck, and I had my hands on it." **See also** Gilmore, Gary.

Wainwright v. Witt

This was a case heard by the Supreme Court of the United States in 1985 concerning when prospective jurors may be excluded from hearing a case involving a possible death sentence because of their views on the death penalty. The defendant in the case, Johnny Paul Witt, was convicted of murder and sentenced to death by a jury from which several people had been excluded for expressing opposition to the death penalty. Following the conviction, Witt's lawyers appealed the conviction and sentence on the grounds that the exclusion of those prospective jurors violated the principles of jury selection laid out in the U.S. Supreme Court's 1968 *Witherspoon v. Illinois* decision. The Florida Supreme Court reaffirmed the conviction and sentence, but a federal appeals court agreed that one of the prospective jurors had been improperly excluded. The U.S. Supreme Court agreed to review the case.

In a 7-to-2 decision, the Supreme Court reversed the federal appeals court's decision and allowed Witt's conviction and sentence to stand. Writing for the Court, Justice William Rehnquist explained that the correct criterion for excusing a prospective juror was that the juror held views that would substantially impair the juror's ability to perform his or her duties as instructed by the court. The trial judge in this case was convinced that the juror in question was sufficiently biased to warrant being excused on these grounds, and no evidence had been presented to suggest that the trial judge's opinion should not be presumed correct. Hence, the prospective juror was properly excused. Writing in dissent, Justice William Brennan worried that this decision went too far in weakening the *Witherspoon* decision, making it too easy to excuse prospective jurors who represented the segment of the community who were inclined to be more circumspect in the imposition of the death penalty. **See also** death-qualified jury; *Morgan v. Illinois; Witherspoon v. Illinois.*

Walton v. Arizona

This was a case heard by the Supreme Court of the United States in 1990. Several issues were considered. The defendant in the case, Jeffrey Alan Walton, was convicted of kidnapping and murder in Arizona after he and two associates abducted a marine for the purpose of robbing him. Following the robbery, they shot him in the head and left him stranded in the desert to die. Under Arizona law at the time, a judge oversaw the penalty phase of the trial without a jury being present. The judge heard arguments from the prosecution that the crime was done "for pecuniary gain" and was "especially heinous, cruel, or depraved," both of which are listed as aggravating circumstances under the Arizona death-penalty statute. The judge agreed and sentenced Walton to death. Walton's lawyers appealed the sentence on four grounds: (1) that by a defendant's right to trial by jury, only a jury may make findings of fact, and since the aggravating circumstances by virtue of which the death penalty was imposed are matters of fact, a jury should have been involved in the penalty phase of the trial; (2) that during the penalty phase of the trial, defendants have the burden of establishing "by a preponderance of the evidence" that there are sufficient mitigating circumstances to call for leniency (which seems to violate the principle that a defendant is "innocent unless proven guilty"); (3) that the Arizona death-penalty statute creates a presumption, at the penalty phase, that the death penalty should be imposed unless sufficient mitigating circumstances are proven (rather than allowing sentences to be weighed equally, without presumption); and (4) that the phrase "especially heinous, cruel, or depraved" is too vague. Eventually, the U.S. Supreme Court agreed to review the case, and to rule on all four questions.

In a 5-to-4 decision, the Supreme Court upheld Walton's sentence. On the first issue, the Supreme Court ruled that a judge, acting without a jury, was competent to make findings of fact. (This decision was later reversed in 2002 in *Ring v. Arizona.*) On the second issue, the Court ruled that "a preponderance of the evidence" was a reasonable burden of proof to place upon the defense during sentencing, especially since the prosecution still had to meet a similar burden of proof in establishing the presence of aggravating circumstances. On the third issue, the Court ruled that making the death penalty the presumed penalty did not preclude the trial court from imposing a lesser penalty, if a lesser penalty is justified. Finally, on the fourth issue, the court ruled, in support of its earlier 1980 *Godfrey v. Georgia* decision, that the phrase "especially heinous, cruel, or depraved" is not unconstitutionally vague and that in this case it was correctly understood and appropriately applied. **See also** *Godfrey v. Georgia; Ring v. Arizona.*

war crimes

War crimes refer to actions taken during time of war that violate the usual standards governing the conduct of war. It is, of course, recognized that war involves the killing of enemy soldiers and that sometimes civilians are inadvertently killed as well. Such actions cannot be considered crimes, since they are a normal and inevitable aspect of war. However, actions that go beyond the normal conduct of war may be considered crimes. Such actions include the intentional killing of hostages; the abuse of civilians in occupied territory, including genocide of civilian populations; the abuse of prisoners of war; and mass destruction on a wanton and unnecessary scale. Traditionally, people found guilty of war crimes have been sentenced to death, presumably because, to stand out from the normal violence of war, war crimes must be especially heinous. At the end of the Civil War, one Confederate officer, Henry Wirz, was found guilty of war crimes for abuse of prisoners of war at the Andersonville Prison and was hanged. At the end of World War II, many Nazi leaders, including Hans Frank, Wilhelm Frick, and Hermann Göring, were found guilty of war crimes by a war crimes tribunal held at Nuremberg, Germany, and were executed for their crimes. However, since the Nuremberg trials, the international community has largely renounced the use of capital punishment. The International Criminal Tribunal that is currently trying Serbian dictator Slobodan Milosevic for war crimes in connection with Serbian aggression against Croatia does

Nazi war criminals stand trial before a tribunal at Nuremberg in 1945. Of the eight defendants pictured here, four were put to death.

not have the authority to sentence defendants to death. **See also** international use of capital punishment; Wirz, Henry.

Washington

Except for a brief period at the beginning of the twentieth century, Washington has traditionally permitted juries to impose the death penalty, and continues to do so currently. Between 1849 and 1888, fifteen people were hanged in Washington under territorial jurisdiction. Washington's territorial death-penalty statute remained in effect after Washington became a state in 1889, and thirty-two people were executed under state jurisdiction between 1889 and 1911. In 1913 the state legislature revised the criminal code, abolishing capital punishment. Five years later the code was revised again, this time reinstating capital punishment. Capital punishment remained in effect until the state's death-penalty statute was invalidated by the U.S. Supreme Court's 1972 *Furman v. Georgia* ruling. Between 1921 and 1963, fifty-eight people were executed by hanging.

In response to the *Furman v. Georgia* ruling, the state legislature abolished capital punishment altogether in 1975, but later that same year a ballot initiative was passed requiring the state to adopt a new death-penalty statute. The legislature passed the new statute in 1977. For the crime of aggravated first-degree murder, the new law provided for the mandatory imposition of the death penalty if the defendant was convicted by a jury, but defendants who pled guilty to the same crime—thus avoiding a trial—could be sentenced only to life imprisonment. The Washington Supreme Court declared the law unconstitutional under the state constitution since it gave defendants too strong an incentive to forgo their right to due process. It was not until 1981 that the legislature passed a death-penalty statute that met constitutional requirements.

Washington's current death-penalty statute allows jurors to consider the death penalty for homicide under special circumstances. The law then provides a list of fourteen special circumstances. These special circumstances are (1) that the victim was a law enforcement officer, corrections officer, or firefighter; (2) that the defendant was under a sentence of imprisonment; (3) that the defendant was in custody, having been judged guilty of a felony; (4) that the defendant was hired to commit the homicide; (5) that the defendant hired someone else to commit the homicide; (6) that the homicide was committed to improve the defendant's standing in a gang or criminal organization; (7) that the homicide involved firing a gun from a motor vehicle or *near* a motor vehicle used to transport the defendant or the weapon (or both) to the scene of the shooting; (8) that the victim was a judge, juror, witness, prosecuting attorney, defense attorney, member of the indeterminate sentencing review board, probation officer, or parole officer; (9) that the defendant committed the homicide to conceal a crime or the identity of someone committing a crime; (10) that there was more than one victim; (11) that the homicide was committed in the course of a robbery, rape, burglary, kidnapping, or arson; (12) that the victim was a journalist and the killing was an attempt to hinder journalistic activities (investigation, research, or reporting); (13) that the defendant was under a restraining order not to contact or disturb the victim; or (14) that the defendant had engaged in a persistent pattern of harassment or criminal assault on the victim (whether or not these incidents had resulted in conviction).

The Washington death-penalty statute does not provide a separate list of aggravating circumstances to be considered during the penalty phase of the trial. Whatever special circumstances are proven to have accompanied the crime at the guilt phase of the trial are considered to stand as aggravating circumstances for purposes of the penalty phase. However, the jury must consider any mitigating circumstances that may be raised by the defense before the death penalty can be imposed.

Under Washington law, a person convicted of a capital offense cannot be executed if he or she was under the age of eighteen at the time of the crime. Washington does provide for life imprisonment without parole as an alternative to the death penalty. The governor is authorized to commute a sentence of death to a sentence of life imprisonment with hard labor.

Washington's 1981 death-penalty statute added lethal injection to hanging as an optional method of execution, but hanging remained the method to be used if the prisoner makes no choice. Washington has had only four executions since passing its new statute. In 1993 Westley Allan Dodd became the first person to be hanged in Washington, or the United States, since 1963. Charles Campbell was hanged in 1994. In 1996 Washington made lethal injection the preferred method of execution, although hanging remained an available choice. Washington's two subsequent executions have been by lethal injection. As of April 2005, eleven people were awaiting execution on Washington's death row. **See also** hanging.

West Virginia

West Virginia does not currently permit juries to impose the death penalty, although West Virginia has historically permitted capital punishment. Prior to 1899, executions occurred under the jurisdiction of county governments and were the responsibility of local sheriffs. However, the unruly behavior of an unusually large crowd at the 1897 hanging of John F. Morgan attracted national attention and embarrassed the state. In response, the legislature transferred responsibility for executions to officials at the state penitentiary and ordered that executions be conducted away from public viewing. From 1899, when this law took effect, until 1959, ninety-four executions took place in West Virginia. In 1949 West Virginia replaced hanging with electrocution as its means of execution. However, the law specified that persons sentenced prior to the change should still be hanged. As a result, the first electrocutions did not take place until 1951. The West Virginia electric chair saw little use. Only nine people were executed by electrocution. The last person to be executed in West Virginia was Elmer David Brunner, who was executed in 1959. In 1965 West Virginia abolished capital punishment. **See also** hanging.

Wilkerson v. Utah

This was a case heard by the Supreme Court of the United States in 1878 concerning whether execution by firing squad was cruel and unusual and therefore a violation of the Eighth Amendment of the U.S. Constitution. The defendant in the case, Wallace Wilkerson, was convicted of killing a man, William Baxter, in a saloon shootout in Utah in 1877. The jury found that the killing was malicious and premeditated and sentenced Wilkerson to death. At the time, territorial Utah carried out executions by means of a firing squad. Wilkerson's lawyers appealed the sentence on the grounds that death by firing squad was cruel and unusual. At the time, humane methods of execution were being widely discussed, and even hanging was being criticized as unnecessarily cruel. Certainly, few jurisdictions used firing squads, so it was a reasonable time to make the argument that firing squads were cruel and unusual. When the Supreme Court of the Territory of Utah denied Wilkerson's appeal, the U.S. Supreme Court agreed to review the case.

In a unanimous decision, the Supreme Court ruled that execution by firing squad was not cruel and unusual. Writing for the Court, Justice Nathan Clifford pointed out that firing squads were the usual method of execution in the military and that this was sufficient to establish that the method was not cruel and unusual by the intended meaning of the Eighth Amendment. The Supreme Court has never revisited this issue and indeed may never have a chance to do so, since firing squads are no longer the exclusive method of execution in any U.S. jurisdiction. Wilkerson was executed by firing squad on May 16, 1879. The marksmen in this case were apparently not at their best, and newspapers reported that Wilkerson died slowly, leading many people to question the wisdom of the Supreme Court's decision. **See also** firing squad; Gilmore, Gary.

Wirz, Henry (1823–1865)

Henry Wirz was the only Confederate soldier to be executed after the Civil War on charges of war crimes. Wirz was born

Henry Wirz, the Confederate commander of a prisoner-of-war camp in Georgia, was convicted of war crimes and executed in 1865.

in Zurich, Switzerland, in 1823 and immigrated to the United States in 1849 following his divorce. He worked briefly in a factory in Massachusetts and then moved to Kentucky, where he joined a medical practice, claiming to have had medical training in Europe (which was apparently not true). When the Civil War began, Wirz enlisted as a sergeant in the Fourth Louisiana Infantry. He received a debilitating wound at the Battle of Seven Pines and was thereafter reassigned to a staff position. Eventually he was put in charge of the Andersonville Prison in Georgia.

The Andersonville Prison was a prisoner-of-war camp for captured Union soldiers. Conditions at the camp were deplorable. Some historians have even compared Andersonville to the worst of the Nazi concentration camps of World War II. Toward the end of the war, the Confederate army was impoverished and short of supplies. Nothing could be spared for captured soldiers. Hence the Union soldiers at Andersonville had little to eat and lived in tents that barely provided shelter from the sun. Clothing and sanitation were also inadequate. Nearly thirteen thousand Union soldiers died at Andersonville, mostly of starvation. Those that survived were little more than skeletons. After the camp was liberated, Northerners were furious.

Wirz was captured and brought in chains to Washington, D.C., where he was tried for war crimes. Wirz defended himself by claiming that he was only following orders. He was executed by hanging on November 10, 1865. **See also** war crimes.

Wisconsin

Wisconsin does not currently permit juries to impose the death penalty. Capital punishment was abolished in Wisconsin in 1853 when the legislature passed a bill introduced by social reformer and death-penalty opponent Marvin Bovee. This made Wisconsin the third state to abolish capital punishment (preceded by Michigan and Rhode Island). However, Wisconsin claims to be the jurisdiction with the world's longest permanent ban on capital punishment for all crimes. Other far-flung jurisdictions, including Russia, Tuscany, Austria, and Rhode Island, abolished capital punishment before Wisconsin but later reinstated it. Michigan also abolished capital punishment before Wisconsin, but retained a technical exception for the crime of treason. The only person ever executed by the state of Wisconsin was John McCaffry in 1851, for the crime of drowning his wife in a water barrel. **See also** Bovee, Marvin H.; Michigan.

Witherspoon v. Illinois

This was a case heard by the Supreme Court of the United States in 1968 concerning whether a person who expresses reservations about the death penalty may be excluded from a jury charged with deciding a capital case. The defendant in the case, William C. Witherspoon, was charged with murder in Illinois in 1960. At the time, Illinois law allowed for the dismissal of prospective jurors who "might hesitate" to impose a sentence of death when considering a capital case. Following this law, the prosecutor dismissed nearly half of the prospective jurors under consideration because they had expressed some qualms about imposing a sentence of death. Hence, all of the jurors eventually seated strongly favored the death penalty. Witherspoon was convicted and sentenced to death. His lawyers appealed the case on the grounds that the Illinois law created bias in the jury selection process. After the Illinois Supreme Court refused to overturn the conviction and sentence, the U.S. Supreme Court agreed to review the case.

In a 5-to-4 decision, the Supreme Court overturned Witherspoon's sentence, but not his conviction for murder. Writing for the Court, Justice Potter Stewart argued that there was no evidence to suggest that the jury was predisposed to find the defendant guilty, so the conviction could be allowed to stand. However, Stewart argued that the jury selection process had clearly resulted in a jury that was predisposed to impose a sentence of death, whether such a sentence was warranted or not, and a jury that did not, in any case, represent the whole of the community. Therefore, the defendant's right to due process had been violated. Stewart drew a distinction between people who expressed conscientious scruples about imposing a sentence of death but were willing to impose a death sentence if they felt the facts in the case warranted such a sentence and people who were altogether opposed to capital punishment and would not impose a sentence of death regardless of the facts. While people altogether opposed to the death penalty could be excluded from juries in capital cases, people in the first group could not be excluded, since doing so would produce juries that did not reflect the conscience of the community. The dissenting opinion, written by Justice Hugo Black, agreed that the purpose of jury selection was to produce an unbiased jury. However, he argued that people who had expressed conscientious scruples about imposing the death penalty had expressed a bias on a question to be decided by the jury and should, therefore, be excluded. On the other hand, Black argued, people who expressed a bias in favor of imposing the death penalty, and certainly people who felt a moral or religious obligation to impose the death penalty for certain crimes, should also be excluded. **See also** death-qualified jury; *Morgan v. Illinois; Wainwright v. Witt.*

Woodson v. North Carolina

This was a case heard by the Supreme Court of the United States in 1976 concerning whether a state law may require the death penalty as a mandatory sentence. The defendants, James Tyrone Woodson and Luby Waxton, were convicted of killing a convenience store clerk during an armed robbery in North Carolina. Under the North Carolina death-penalty statute, "murder committed in perpetrating or attempting to perpetrate a felony" carried a mandatory sentence of death. Following this law, Woodson and Waxton were sentenced to death. In 1976 no executions were being performed in the United States, since the Supreme Court decision in *Furman v. Georgia* (1972) had declared state death-penalty statutes too arbitrary to be consistent with the right to due process. Mandatory sentencing, however, is not arbitrary and might be expected to meet the standards laid out in *Furman*. For this reason, the Supreme Court agreed to review the case, along with a similar case, *Roberts v. Louisiana*, which concerned the same issue.

In a complex decision, the Court ruled that mandatory imposition of the death penalty is unconstitutional. Writing for the Court, Justice Potter Stewart pointed out that, when given a choice, juries impose the death penalty only rarely, even in cases of first-degree murder. From this, he drew the conclusion that the imposition of the death penalty in *all* such cases would frequently violate the community's sense of decency and would therefore be "cruel and unusual." Although consistency is desirable in a death-penalty statute, consistency cannot be achieved through mandatory sentencing in the case of capital crimes. This case was decided at the same time as the landmark *Gregg v. Georgia* case, which opened the way for a continuation of executions in the United States. **See also** *Gregg v. Georgia;* mandatory sentencing; *Roberts v. Louisiana.*

Wyoming

Wyoming has traditionally permitted juries to impose the death penalty, and continues to do so currently. From 1864 to 1890, four executions took place under territorial jurisdiction, all by hanging. Between 1890, when Wyoming became a state, and 1933, another thirteen hangings took place. In 1935 Wyoming replaced hanging with lethal gas as its method of execution. Five people died in Wyoming's gas chamber between 1937 and 1965, one under federal rather than state jurisdiction.

Following the 1972 *Furman v. Georgia* ruling, which struck down Wyoming's death-penalty statute, the state passed a new death-penalty statute in 1977. Wyoming's current death-penalty statute allows jurors to consider the death penalty for homicide under special circumstances. These special circumstances include that the homicide was premeditated or that it was committed in the course of any sexual assault, arson, robbery, burglary, escape from custody, resisting arrest, kidnapping, or abuse of a child under the age of sixteen.

The death penalty may be imposed if one of twelve aggravating circumstances is proven to have accompanied the crime. The list of aggravating circumstances appears similar to the special circumstances noted above, but aggravating circumstances are considered during the penalty phase of the trial rather than during the guilty phase. These aggravating circumstances are (1) that the defendant was confined in a jail or correctional facility, was on probation or parole, had escaped custody, or was released on bail; (2) that the defendant was previously convicted of a first-degree murder or of a felony involving violence; (3) that the defendant knowingly created a great risk of death to two or more people; (4) that the homicide occurred in the course of aircraft piracy or the unlawful discharge of an explosive device such as a bomb; (5) that the homicide was committed in order to avoid arrest or to escape from custody; (6) that the homicide was committed in order to collect insurance benefits or for other monetary gain; (7) that the homicide was especially atrocious or cruel, involving torture; (8) that the victim was a judicial official, district attorney, defense attorney, police officer, juror, or witness acting in the performance of his or her duty, or the homicide was motivated by the nature of that duty; (9) that the victim was known to the defendant to be under seventeen years old or older than sixty-five; (10) that the victim was known to the defendant to be particularly vulnerable due to a physical or mental disability; (11) that the defendant poses a continuing threat or is likely to commit future acts of criminal violence; or (12) that the homicide occurred in the course of a robbery, sexual assault, arson, burglary, kidnapping, or abuse of a child under the age of sixteen. The jury must also consider any mitigating circumstances that the defense wishes to present.

Under Wyoming law, a person convicted of a capital offense cannot be executed if he or she was under the age of eighteen at the time of the crime. Wyoming does provide for life imprisonment without parole as an alternative to the death penalty. The governor has the authority to grant clemency.

In 1984 Wyoming replaced lethal gas with lethal injection as its method of execution. Only one person has been executed in Wyoming since the reenactment of capital punishment. That was Mark Hopkins, who was executed by lethal injection in 1992. As of June 2005, two people were awaiting execution on Wyoming's death row. **See also** *Furman v. Georgia.*

FOR FURTHER RESEARCH

Books

James R. Acker, Robert M. Bohm, and Charles S. Lanier, eds., *America's Experiment with Capital Punishment: Reflections on the Past, Present, and Future of the Ultimate Penal Sanction.* 2nd ed. Durham, NC: Carolina Academic Press, 2003.

Robert M. Baird and Stuart E. Rosenbaum, eds., *Philosophy of Punishment.* Buffalo, NY: Prometheus, 1988.

Stuart Banner, *The Death Penalty: An American History.* Cambridge, MA: Harvard University Press, 2002.

Lawrence C. Becker and Charlotte E. Becker, eds., *Encyclopedia of Ethics.* 2nd ed. New York: Routledge, 2001.

Hugo Adam Bedau and Paul Cassell, eds., *Debating the Death Penalty: Should America Have Capital Punishment? The Experts on Both Sides Make Their Best Case.* New York: Oxford University Press, 2003.

Craig Brandon, *The Electric Chair: An Unnatural American History.* Jefferson, NC: McFarland, 1990.

Corey Lang Brettschneider, *Punishment, Property, and Justice: Philosophical Foundations of the Death Penalty and Welfare Controversies.* Burlington, VT: Ashgate/Dartmouth, 2001.

John D. Carlson, Eric P. Elshtain, and Eric C. Owens, eds., *A Call for Reckoning: Religion and the Death Penalty.* Grand Rapids, MI: Eerdmans, 2004.

Judy Culligan, *Villains and Outlaws.* New York: Simon & Schuster, 1998.

Joshua Dressler, ed., *Encyclopedia of Crime and Justice.* 2nd ed. New York: Macmillan Reference, 2002.

R.A. Duff, *Punishment, Communication, and Community.* New York: Oxford University Press, 2001.

R. Shannon Duval, ed., *Encyclopedia of Ethics.* New York: Facts On File, 1999.

Raphael Goldman, *Capital Punishment.* Washington, DC: Congressional Quarterly, 2002.

Mark Grossman, *Encyclopedia of Capital Punishment.* Santa Barbara, CA: ABC-CLIO, 1998.

Gardner C. Hanks, *Against the Death Penalty: Christian and Secular Arguments Against Capital Punishment.* Scottdale, PA: Herald, 1997.

Harry Henderson, *Capital Punishment.* New York: Facts On File, 2000.

Peter Hodgkinson and Andrew Rutherford, eds., *Capital Punishment: Global Issues and Prospects.* Winchester, UK: Waterside, 1996.

Peter Hodgkinson and William A. Schabas, eds., *Capital Punishment: Strategies for Abolition.* New York: Cambridge University Press, 2004.

Roger Hood, *The Death Penalty: A World-Wide Perspective.* 2nd ed. New York: Oxford University Press, 1996.

Rachel King, *Don't Kill in Our Names: Families of Murder Victims Speak Out Against the Death Penalty.* New Brunswick, NJ: Rutgers University Press, 2003.

Edward W. Knappman, ed., *Great American Trials*. Detroit: Gale Research, 1994.

Michael Kronenwetter, *Capital Punishment: A Reference Handbook*. 2nd ed. Santa Barbara, CA: ABC-CLIO, 2001.

Barbara Levy, *Legacy of Death*. Englewood Cliffs, NJ: Prentice-Hall, 1973.

Marie J. MacNee, *Outlaws, Mobsters, and Crooks from the Old West to the Internet*. Detroit: Gale, 1998.

Desmond Manderson, ed., *Courting Death: The Law of Mortality*. Sterling, VA: Pluto, 1999.

J. Michael Martinez, William D. Richardson, and D. Brandon Hornsby, eds., *The Leviathan's Choice: Capital Punishment in the Twenty-First Century*. Lanham, MD: Rowman & Littlefield, 2002.

Louis P. Masur, *Rites of Execution: Capital Punishment and the Transformation of American Culture, 1776–1865*. New York: Oxford University Press, 1989.

Marilyn D. McShane and Frank P. Williams, eds., *Encyclopedia of American Prisons*. New York: Garland, 1996.

———, *Encyclopedia of Juvenile Justice*. Thousand Oaks, CA: Sage, 2003.

Hayley R. Mitchell, ed., *The Compete History of the Death Penalty*. San Diego: Greenhaven, 2001.

Jay Robert Nash, *Bloodletters and Badmen: A Narrative Encyclopedia of American Criminals from the Pilgrims to the Present*. New York: Evans, 1991.

Stephen Nathanson, *An Eye for an Eye: The Immorality of Punishing by Death*. 2nd ed. Lanham, MD: Rowman & Littlefield, 2001.

Michael Newton, *The Encyclopedia of Serial Killers*. New York: Checkmark, 2000.

Louis J. Palmer, *Encyclopedia of Capital Punishment in the United States*. Jefferson, NC: McFarland, 2001.

Louis P. Pojman and Jeffrey Reiman, *The Death Penalty: For and Against*. Lanham, MD: Rowman & Littlefield, 1998.

Philip L. Reichel, *Corrections: Philosophies, Practices, and Procedures*. Boston: Allyn and Bacon, 2001.

Peter G. Renstrom, *Constitutional Rights Sourcebook*. Santa Barbara, CA: ABC-CLIO, 1999.

George E. Rush, *The Dictionary of Criminal Justice*. 6th ed. New York: Dushkin/McGraw-Hill, 2004.

William A. Schabas, *The Abolition of the Death Penalty in International Law*. 2nd ed. New York: Cambridge University Press, 1997.

———, *The Death Penalty as Cruel Treatment and Torture: Capital Punishment Challenged in the World's Courts*. Boston: Northeastern University Press, 1996.

Thorsten Sellin, *The Penalty of Death*. Thousand Oaks, CA: Sage, 1980.

Leon Shaskolsky Sheleff, *Ultimate Penalties: Capital Punishment, Life Imprisonment, Physical Torture*. Columbus: Ohio State University Press, 1987.

Carl Sifakis, *The Encyclopedia of American Crime*. 2nd ed. New York: Facts On File, 2001.

Rita J. Simon and Dagny A. Blaskovich, *A Comparative Analysis of Capital Punishment: Statutes, Policies, Frequencies, and Public Attitudes the World Over*. Lanham, MD: Lexington, 2002.

Eliza Steelwater, *The Hangman's Knot: Lynching, Legal Execution, and America's Struggle with the Death Penalty*. Boulder, CO: Westview, 2003.

Lloyd Steffen, *Executing Justice: The Moral Meaning of the Death Penalty*. Cleveland: Pilgrim, 1998.

Symposium on Capital Punishment. Notre Dame, IN: Thomas J. White

Center on Law and Government, Notre Dame Law School, 1994.

Scott Turow, *Ultimate Punishment: A Lawyer's Reflections on Dealing with the Death Penalty*. New York: Farrar, Straus & Giroux, 2003.

Bryan Vila and Cynthia Morris, eds., *Capital Punishment in the United States: A Documentary History*. Westport, CT: Greenwood, 1997.

Paul A. Winters, ed., *The Death Penalty: Opposing Viewpoints*. 3rd ed. San Diego: Greenhaven, 1997.

Franklin E. Zimring, *The Contradictions of American Capital Punishment*. New York: Oxford University Press, 2003.

Web Sites

Criminal Justice Legal Foundation, www.cjlf.org. Founded in 1982, this nonprofit public-interest organization supports capital punishment and works to expedite the appeals process in death-penalty cases and disseminate information about the effectiveness of and justification for the death penalty.

Death Penalty Information Center, www.deathpenaltyinfo.org. Authoritative clearinghouse of information about the death penalty, with links to state-by-state statutes, death row statistics, and ongoing research into the application of, support for, and opposition to capital punishment.

A Student Guide to the Death Penalty, www.deathpenaltyinfo.msu.edu. Maintained by the Michigan State University Comm Tech Lab and Death Penalty Information Center, this interactive site offers arguments for and against the death penalty, state-by-state comparisons, and discussion of the stages in capital trials.

World Coalition Against the Death Penalty, www.worldcoalition.org. International coalition of bar associations, unions, governments, and human rights organizations, founded in 2002 to advocate the worldwide abolition of capital punishment. Web site offers comprehensive links to anti-death-penalty member organizations.

INDEX

Abu-Jamal, Mumia, 173
Accusing Finger, The (film), 101
actual innocence, 13
Adams, John, 261
Adams, Robert, 181
Adams, Samuel, 274
affirmative defense, 13–14
African Americans, as death row inmates, 246, 247
aggravating circumstances, 15–17
 in federal death-penalty laws, 98–99
Alabama, 17–18
Alaska, 18
Aldridge, Alfred Scott, 18–19
Aldridge v. United States (1931), 18–19
alibi, 14
American Bar Association (ABA), 19
American Civil Liberties Union (ACLU), 19–20, 227
American League to Abolish Capital Punishment, 19, 69, 226
American Medical Association, 238
American Society for the Abolition of Capital Punishment, 19, 67
American Society for the Collection and Diffusion of Information in Relation to the Punishment of Death, 225
Amnesty International, 19, 149, 150
Amsterdam, Anthony Guy, 20–21, 228

Anderson, Esther, 183
Andersonville Prison, 318
anesthesia, 21
Angels with Dirty Faces (film), 101
Antiterrorism and Effective Death Penalty Act (1996), 21–22, 128
appeals process, 22
Appendi v. New Jersey (2000), 256
Applequist, Otto, 137
Arizona, 23–25
Articles of War, 192
Ashcroft, John, 310
Asian Americans, as death row inmates, 248
Assyrian Code, 26
Atkins, Daryl Renard, 26, 27
Atkins v. Virginia (2002), 26, 66, 192, 257, 258
Auburn Prison, 143, 231

Bailey, William, 73, 132
Baldus, David, 187, 247
Barefoot, Thomas, 28
Barefoot v. Estelle (1983), 28
Barney, Jeffrey, 167
Bates, Ruby, 272, 273
Baudricourt, Robert de, 151
Baxter, William, 317
Beard, John, 145
Beccaria, Cesare, 28–30, 48, 53, 155, 224
 social contract theory and, 280, 285
Beck, Gilbert, 30
Beck v. Alabama (1976), 30
Bedau, Hugo Adam, 30–31
Beidler, John X., 31
Bell, Willie Lee, 31

Bell v. Ohio (1978), 31–32
benefit of clergy, 32
Bennett, John A., 194
Bentham, Jeremy, 32–33, 304–305
Berger, Leo, 124
Berns, Walter, 33–34, 254
Bethea, Rainey, 309
Beyond a Reasonable Doubt (film), 101
Bible, 34, 171, 251, 288
Billington, James, 239
Billington, John, 34, 239
Billington, Thomas, 34
Billington, William, 34, 239
Bishop, Bridget, 266
Bishop, Jesse, 166, 212
Black, Hugo
 in *Maxwell v. Bishop*, 186
 in *Witherspoon v. Illinois*, 319–20
Black Code, 34–35, 277
Blackmun, Harry A., 35–36
 in *Callins v. Collins*, 47
 in *Furman v. Georgia*, 109
 in *Herrera v. Collins*, 136
 in *Maxwell v. Bishop*, 187
 in *Mills v. Maryland*, 196
 in *Simmons v. South Carolina*, 275
 in *Spaziano v. Florida*, 285
Blagojevich, Rod, 141
Blakeley, David, 88
Bloodworth, Gervis, 115
Bly, John, 274
Bolles, Eunice, 220
Booth, John, 36
Booth v. Maryland (1987), 35, 234, 306
Bovee, Marvin H., 36, 150, 225, 319

Bradford, William, 36–37, 48, 224, 235
Branch, Elmer, 37, 109
Branch v. Texas (1972), 37, 108
branding, 61
breaking on the wheel, 37–38
Brennan, William J., 38–39
  in *Coker v. Georgia,* 55
  in *Furman v. Georgia,* 108
  in *Maxwell v. Bishop,* 186
  in *McCleskey v. Kemp,* 187
  in *McGautha v. California,* 189
  in *Rudolph v. Alabama,* 260
  in *South Carolina v. Gathers,* 283
  in *Wainwright v. Witt,* 313
Bridge, Warren, 167
Briggs, George, 120
Brooks, Charles, 39, 171, 294
Brown, Edmund, 53
Brown, Harold, 86, 87
Brown v. Board of Education (1954), 89, 208
Brunner, Elmer David, 317
Bryan, Stephanie, 12
Buchanan, James, 67
Buckley, Will, 245
Buddhism, 252
Buenoano, Judais, 39–40
Bundy, Theodore, 40, 167
burden of proof, 41–42
Burger, Warren, 118
  in *Bell v. Ohio,* 31–32
  in *Furman v. Georgia,* 109
  in *Lockett v. Ohio,* 176
  in *Maxwell v. Bishop,* 187
burning at the stake, 42–43
Burton, Abbott, 12
Bush, George W., 126, 301
Bushnell, Edward, 153
Butler, Rose, 254

Cabana, Donald A., 173
Calcraft, William, 44, 183
California, 44–47
Callins v. Collins (1987), 35, 47
Calloway, Thomas, 181
Campbell, Charles Rodman, 132, 316

caning, 60
Cannon, Robert, 45
capital crimes, 47–49
capital punishment, 291
  cost of, 62–63
  film treatment of, 100–101
  history of opposition to
    1648–1870, 223–25
    1870–1963, 225–26
    1963–present, 226–29
  international use of, 149–50
  in literature, 172–73
Carvel, Elbert N., 72
Carver, Frank, 182
Categorical Imperative, 74, 161
Catherine II (empress of Russia), 149
Cell 2455, Death Row (Chessman), 52, 173
Cell 2455, Death Row (film), 101
censorship of reporting on executions, 49–50
Champion, Jane, 129
Cheever, George Barrell, 34, 50–51, 232, 254
Chessman, Caryl, 51–53, 147–48, 173, 226
Childers, Erskin, 166
Christ and the Gallows; or, Reasons for the Abolition of Capital Punishment (Bovee), 36
Christensen, Soren, 137
Christian, Julius, 310
Christianity, 251–52
Clark, Steven, 53
Clark, Terry, 216
clemency, 53–55
Clement, Bill, 39
clergy. *See* benefit of clergy
Cleveland, Grover, 36
Clifford, Nathan, 317
closure, 55
Cocker, Ehrlich Anthony, 55
Cockran, W. Bourke, 87
Coker v. Georgia (1977), 48, 55–56, 65
Coleman v. Thompson (1991), 128

Colorado, 56–57
Combe, George, 238
competence, 57
Compulsion (film), 101
Connecticut, 57–58
Considerations on the Injustice and Impolicy of Punishing Murder by Death (Rush), 262
Constitution, U.S., 58–60, 126, 290
  see also Eighth Amendment; Fifth Amendment; Fourteenth Amendment
Convention for the Protection of Human Rights and Fundamental Freedoms, 252
Cooper, Paula, 146
corporal punishment, 60–62
Cory, Giles, 234, 266
cost of capital punishment, 62–63
counsel, right to, 255
court-martial, 193
Crabtree, Larry, 84
Crampton, James E., 188
Croft, Vanessa, 284
Cromwell, Oliver, 223
Crook, Shirley, 257
crucifixion, 63–64
cruel and unusual punishment, 64–65
  see also Eighth Amendment
cultural relativism, 250–51
Cuomo, Mario, 216

Dallas, George Mifflin, 19, 67, 225
Dance with a Stranger (film), 101
Darrow, Clarence, 20, 68–69, 168, 226
Davis, Edwin F., 88, 94
Dead Man Walking (film), 101
Dead Man Walking (Prejean), 173, 240–41
Dean, Jerry Lynn, 301
Death at Midnight: The Confessions of an Executioner (Cabana), 173

Death Blossoms: Reflections from a Prisoner of Conscience (Abu-Jamal), 173
death penalty, 159, 242–43
Death Penalty in America, The (Bedau), 30
Death Penalty Information Center (DPIC), 69–70
death-qualified jury, 70, 154
death row, 24, 70–72, 106, 247
  average time spent on, 295–96
Debs, Eugene V., 69
decapitation, 72
defense, affirmative, 13–14
Defense of Capital Punishment (Cheever), 50–51
DeMag, Donald, 306
deontology, 74
depraved heart murder, 207
Dershowitz, Alan, 74–75
determinism, 75–76
deterrence, 76–77, 155
DiLisio, Tony, 284
Diocletian, 183
dissection, 77–78
District of Columbia, 78
divine authority, 78–79
DNA evidence, 79–81
Dodd, Westley Allan, 132, 312, 316
Domingues, Michael, 148
double jeopardy, 81
Douglas, James (earl of Morton), 272
Douglas, William O.
  in *Furman v. Georgia,* 109
  in *Maxwell v. Bishop,* 186
  in *McGautha v. California,* 189
  in *Rudolph v. Alabama,* 260
Draco, 82
Draconian Code, 47, 81–82
Dracula (Stoker), 142
drawing and quartering, 82
Drug Kingpin Statute (1988), 97
due process, 82–83
Dugan, Eva, 130

Dukakis, Michael S., 266
Dulles, John Foster, 148
Durkheim, Emile, 155

Eddings, Monte Lee, 84, 158
Eddings v. Oklahoma (1982), 84, 158
Edison, Thomas, 85, 86
Ehrlich, Isaac, 76
Eighth Amendment, 55, 84–85, 108, 227–29
Eisenhower, Dwight D., 35, 39, 288
electric chair, 17–18, 85–88
Elliott, Robert, 94
Ellis, Edward, 167
Ellis, Ruth Neilson, 88
Engel, George, 135, 136
English Bill of Rights, 64, 241
Enmund, Earl, 88–89
Enmund v. Florida (1982), 88–89
"Enquiry How Far the Punishment of Death Is Necessary in Pennsylvania, An" (Bovee), 37
Enquiry into the Consistency of the Punishment of Murder by Death, with Reason and Revelation, An (Rush), 262
Enquiry into the Effect of Public Punishments upon Criminals and upon Society, An (Rush), 262
equal protection, 89–90
  see also Fourteenth Amendment
ESPY file, 90
Essay on Crimes and Punishment, An (Beccaria), 28, 29, 224
Essays on Capital Punishment (Spear), 285
Estelle, W.J., Jr., 28
European Convention on Human Rights. *See* Convention for the Protection of Human Rights and Fundamental Freedoms

Evangelium Vitae (John Paul II), 90–91, 252
Evans, Franklin, 78
evidence, DNA, 79–81
evolving standards of decency, 91–92, 192
executioners, 92–95
Executioner's Song, The (film), 101
execution, 199, 287
  censorship of reporting on, 49–50
  multiple, 205–206
  physician participation in, 238–39
  time between sentencing and, 295–96
  viewing of, 307–10
exoneration, 95
Ex parte Milligan (1866), 126
expiation theory, as justification of punishment, 156
extradition, 95–96

Face of Justice (Chessman), 52
Farr, Edward, 165
Fay v. Noia (1963), 127–28
federal death-penalty laws, 97–100
Federal Kidnapping Act (1932), 302
Felker v. Turpin (1996), 22, 100, 128
Fell, Donald, 306
Fell, George, 85
Fielden, Samuel, 135–36
Fifth Amendment, 81, 82, 120, 255
Figuer, Victor Harry, 150
firing squad, 101–103, 317
Fischer, Adolph, 135, 136
flogging, 60
Flores, Mariano, 135
Florida, 103–104
For Capital Punishment: Crime and the Morality of the Death Penalty (Berns), 33
Ford, Alvin Bernard, 104
Ford v. Wainwright (1986), 104–105, 191

foreign nationals, 105–106, 148
Foreman, Percy, 106
Fortas, Abe, 186
Fort Leavenworth Penitentiary, 107–108
Fourteenth Amendment, 82, 227
Fowler, Rebecca, 183
Francis, Willie, 65
Frank, Daniell, 129
Frank, Hans, 314
Frankenstein (Shelley), 248
Frankfurter, Felix, 19–20, 179
Franks, Bobby, 168
French, James, 222
Frick, Wilhelm, 314
Fuchs, Klaus, 260
Fuller, Melville Weston, 144–45
Furman, William Henry, 108, 109
Furman v. Georgia (1972), 37, 65, 108–109, 291
    Amsterdam's argument in, 21, 228
    distinction of death-eligible homicides and, 49
    mandatory sentencing and, 183
    military justice and, 193
    role of NAACP Legal Fund in, 208

Gacy, John Wayne, 110
Gall, Franz Joseph, 238
Gallatin, Albert, 67
gallows, 110–11, 138
gallows reprieve, 111
Galvani, Luigi, 248
Garrett, Daniel Ryan, 301
garrote, 111
Gary, Joseph Eaton, 135
gas chamber, 111–14
Gathers, Demetrius, 283
Gee Jon, 113, 114, 211
Gentry, John, 40
Georgia, 115–16
gibbet, 116
Gibbs, Charles, 131

Gideon v. Wainwright (1963), 255
Gilbert, William, 94
Gilmore, Gary, 103, 116–18, 166, 304, 312
Ginsberg, Ruth Bader, 256
Glass, Jimmy, 167
Godfrey, Robert Franklin, 118
Godfrey v. Georgia (1980), 118
Gold, Harry, 259
Goldberg, Arthur J., 74, 118–19, 227, 260
Goode, Washington, 119–20, 238
Goodyear, James, 39
Göring, Hermann, 314
grand jury, 120
Grant, Ulysses S., 233
Graunger, Thomas, 158
Graves, Bibb, 274
Gray, Judd, 277
Gray, Samuel, 266
Great Writ. *See* habeas corpus
Greenglass, David, 259, 260
Greenglass, Ruth, 260
Gregg, Troy Leon, 121–22
Gregg v. Georgia (1976), 18, 21, 121–22, 153, 230
Gregory, David, 39
Griffin v. Illinois (1956), 89
guided discretion, 122
Guillotin, Joseph-Ignace, 122–23, 124
guillotine, 72, 123–25

Haas, William, 220
habeas corpus, 126–28
Hagglund, Joel. *See* Hill, Joe
Hammurabi, Code of, 26, 43, 47–48, 128–29, 171
hanging, 110–11, 129–32, 275
Hangman (newspaper), 286
hara-kiri, 132
Harberts, Laura Lynn, 284
Harding, Donald E., 24
Harding, Thomas, 119
Harlan, John M., II, 186, 188–89

Harman, Samuel W., 234
Harper, Edward L., 163
Harris, Louis, 132
Harris, Robert Alton, 47, 50, 167, 244, 245
Harris v. Alabama (1995), 132–33
Harrison, Carter, 135
Hauptmann, Bruno, 133–35
Hawaii, 135
Hawkins, Alfred E., 272
Haymarket Square riot, 135–36
Hearst, William Randolph, 226
Hell on the Border: He Hanged Eighty-Eight Men (Harman), 234
Herrera, Raul, Sr., 136
Herrera v. Collins (1993), 13, 22, 54, 136, 294
Hill, David Bennett, 85
Hill, Joe (Joel Hagglund), 136–37, 166
Hilton, Orrin, 137
Hinckley, John, 15
Hinduism, 252
Hippocratic Oath, 238
Hispanics, as death row inmates, 248
Hobbes, Thomas, 279–80
Hold Back Tomorrow (film), 101
Hopkins, Mark, 321
Horn, Tom, 137–38
Howard, Thomas, 277, 279
Hulbert, John, 94

I Want to Live (film), 101
Idaho, 139–40
Illinois, 140–41
impalement, 141–42
imprisonment, 142–44
    life, without parole, 171–72
In Cold Blood (film), 101
In re Kemmler (1890), 144–45, 162
incapacitation, as justification of punishment, 156
Indiana, 145–46
individual relativism, 250

Industrial Workers of the World (IWW), 137
Ingle, Joe, 146, 254
Innocence Project, 81, 146–47
insanity, 14–15
intoxication, 15
Introduction to the Principles of Morals and Legislation (Bentham), 32–33
Iowa, 150
Islam, 252

Jackson, Lucius, 109
Jackson, Robert H., 249
Jackson v. Georgia (1972), 108, 141
James II (king of England), 64
Jefferson, Thomas, 176, 274
Jesus, 64
Joan of Arc, 43, 151–53
John Paul II (pope), 90, 252
Johnson, Edward Earl, 167
Johnson, John, 307
Jones, William, 26
Jones, Willie, 115
Jones v. United States (1999), 256
Jouenne, Marguerite, 267
Judaism, 252
Judy, Steven T., 146
Jurek, Jerry Lane, 153
Jurek v. Texas (1976), 28, 121, 153
jury, 70, 120, 255
  selection of, 298–99
jury nullification, 153–54
Justice, Charles, 220
Justice for All, 154
justification of punishment, 157
Justinian, Code of, 157–58
juvenile offenders, 148, 158–59

Kansas, 160–61
Kant, Immanuel, 74, 161
Kee, Tom Quong, 113, 114
Keller, Helen, 19, 137
Kelly, Charles, 150

Kemmler, William, 87, 144, 161–62
Kendall, George, 103, 162
Kennedy, Anthony M.
  in *Loving v. United States*, 179
  in *McCleskey v. Zant*, 188
  in *Roper v. Simmons*, 257–58
Kennedy, John F., 119
Kentucky, 162–63
Ketch, Jack, 94, 164–65
Ketchum, Thomas "Black Jack," 130, 165, 166
Knight, Goodwin J., 12
Knox, Clark, 160
Koran, 165, 252, 288
KQED, Inc. v. Vasquez (1991), 50
Ku Klux Klan, 181

Landry, Richard, 171
last meal, 166
Last Mile, The (film), 101
Law of the Twelve Tables, 167
Lawes, Kathryn, 167
Lawes, Lewis E., 20, 167–68, 226
LeGrand, Karl, 148
LeGrand, Walter, 148
Leopold, Nathan F., 69, 168–69, 226, 255
Leopold I (king of Belgium), 76, 232
Leopold II (grand duke of Tuscany), 29–30
lethal injection, 94, 169–71
lex talionis (law of retaliation), 156–57, 165, 171, 241
Liebowitz, Samuel, 272, 273
life imprisonment without parole, 171–72
Lincoln, Abraham, 126, 206
Lindbergh kidnapping, 133
Lingg, Louis, 135, 136
literature, 172–73
Livingston, Edward, 173–74
Locke, John, 174, 279–80
Lockett, Sandra, 176

Lockett v. Ohio (1978), 31, 84, 176
Lockhart v. McCree (1986), 70, 176
Loeb, Richard A., 69, 168–69, 226, 255
Long, Howard, 212
Louis, Antoine, 124, 125
Louisiana, 177–78
Louisiana ex rel. Francis v. Resweber (1947), 178–79
Louis XVI (king of France), 124, 125
Love, W.H., 165
Loving, Dwight J., 179
Loving v. United States (1996), 179
Lowenfield, Leslie, 179–80
Lowenfield v. Phelps (1988), 179–80
Lynch, Charles, 181
lynching, 131, 181, 309

Madieros, Celestine, 265–66
Magna Carta, 153
Maine, 182
Maledon, Ann, 182
Maledon, George, 94, 182, 205
mandatory sentencing, 183, 320
Marbury v. Madison (1803), 290
Marshall, Thurgood
  in *Coker v. Georgia*, 55
  in *Ford v. Wainwright*, 105
  in *Furman v. Georgia*, 108
  in *Maxwell v. Bishop*, 186
martyrs, 183
Marwood, William, 183
Mary (queen of England), 64
Maryland, 183–84
Mason, David, 47
Mason, Ed, 17
Massachusetts, 184–86
Mather, Cotton, 266
Matthews, Ryan, 147
Maxwell, William, 186
Maxwell v. Bishop (1970), 35, 186–87, 227–28
McCaffry, John, 319

McCleskey, Warren, 187
McCleskey v. Kemp (1987), 35, 187, 247
McCleskey v. Zant (1991), 128, 187–88
McCree, Andria, 176
McGautha, Dennis, 188
McGautha v. California (1971), 188–89, 228
McKenna, Joseph, 65, 92
McKenzie, Duncan, 202
McLaurin, A.J., 245
McQueen, Harold, 163
McVeigh, Timothy, 21, 99–100, 189–90
Means, Gaston, 133
mens rea (guilty mind), 190
mentally ill offenders, 191
mentally retarded offenders, 191–92
Mercer, George, 198
M (film), 100–101
Michigan, 192
Mikado, The (Gilbert and Sullivan), 94
military justice, 192–94
Mill, James, 194
Mill, John Stuart, 154, 194–95
Mills, Ralph, 195
Mills v. Maryland (1988), 195
Milosevic, Slobodan, 314
Minnesota, 196
minors. *See* juvenile offenders; *Roper v. Simmons*
Mircovich, Andriza, 211
Mississippi, 196–97
Missouri, 197–98
mitigating circumstances, 199–200
  see also Bell v. Ohio; Lockett v. Ohio
M'Naghten test, 14–15
Model Penal Code, 200–201
Moderators, 248–49
  see also Regulators
Monge, Louis, 56
"Monsieur New York," 201
Montana, 201–202

Montesquieu, Baron de (Charles-Louis de Secondat), 202–203, 223–24, 241
Montgomery, Olin, 272
Moore, Harry Charles, 230
moratorium movement, 203–204
Morelli, James "Mad Dog," 49
Morgan, Derrick, 205
Morgan, John F., 317
Morgan, Julius, 292
Morgan v. Illinois (1992), 70, 204–205
Morris, Bobbie Joe, 40
Morrison, John G., 137
Muhammad (the Prophet), 165
multiple executions, 205–206
murder, 206–207
Murphy, James, 130–31
Murray v. Carrier (1986), 271
Murray v. Giarratano (1989), 207
mutilation, 61

NAACP Legal Defense and Education Fund (LDEF), 20, 21, 208, 227
Napoléon I, 53
National Coalition to Abolish the Death Penalty (NCADP), 208
Native Americans, as death row inmates, 248
Nebraska, 208, 210–11
Neene, Oscar, 135
Nelson, David Cooper, 214
Nesbitt, Eric, 26
Neufeld, Peter J., 146
Nevada, 211–12
New Hampshire, 212–13
New Jersey, 213–14
New Mexico, 214–16
New York, 216–17
Nichols, Terry, 190
Nixon, Richard, 35, 249
Norris, Clarence, 272–74
Norris v. Alabama (1935), 89
North Carolina, 217–19

North Dakota, 219
Nuremberg trials, 314

Oak Street Jail, 281
O'Connor, Sandra Day
  in *Enmund v. Florida,* 89
  in *Harris v. Alabama,* 133
  in *Roper v. Simmons,* 258
Ocuish, Hannah, 158, 220, 254
Ohio, 220–22
Oklahoma, 222–23
On Liberty (John Stuart Mill), 194–95
Oregon, 229–30
Osborne, Thomas Mott, 226, 230–32
O'Sullivan, John L., 51, 225, 232

Paine, Thomas, 261
Panzrum, Carl, 166, 312
pardons, 53, 54
Paris, Betty, 266
Paris, Samuel, 266
Parker, Isaac C., 94, 182, 233–34
Parsons, Albert, 135, 136
Patterson, Haywood, 272, 273, 274
Payne, Pervis Tyrone, 234
Payne v. Tennessee (1991), 234, 306
Peck, G.W., 21
peine forte et dure, 234–35
Penn, Sean, 241
Penn, William, 153
Pennell, Steven Brian, 73
Pennsylvania, 235–36
Penry v. Lynaugh (1989), 26–27, 65, 192, 257–58
peremptory challenges, 299
Persian Letters (Montesquieu), 202, 223–24
Phillips, Wendell, 237–38
phrenology, 238, 309
physician participation in executions, 238–39
Pierrepoint, Albert, 239
Pierrepoint, Henry, 239
Pierrepoint, Thomas, 239

Pierrepoint family, 94, 239
pillory, 60
Plato, 155, 281
Plessy v. Ferguson (1896), 89
Poland, Michael, 239
Poland, Patrick, 239
Poland v. Arizona (1986), 239–40
Polk, James K., 67
Popish Plot (1678), 164
Porter, Anthony, 263
Poshard, Glenn, 263
Powell, Lewis
  in *Booth v. Maryland*, 36
  in *Eddings v. Oklahoma*, 84
  in *Furman v. Georgia*, 109
  in *McCleskey v. Kemp*, 187
Powell, Ozie, 272
Prejean, Helen, 173, 240–41, 254
Price, Victoria, 272, 273
Prisoner's Friend (newspaper), 286
Proffitt, Charles William, 241
Proffitt v. Florida (1976), 121, 241
proportionality, 241–42
Protocol 6, 242
Public Enemy, The (film), 101
Public Justice, Private Mercy (Edmund Brown), 53
public opinion, 242–43
Puerto Rico, 244
Pulley v. Harris (1984), 244–45
punishment, justification of, 157
Purvis, Will, 245

Quakers, 223, 235

racial discrimination in sentencing, 246–48
Ralston, Robert, 295
Rasul v. Bush (2004), 126
Ray, James Earl, 106
Read, James, 162
Reagan, Ronald, 179, 193
reanimation of corpses, 248
recidivism rate, 144

Reed, Stanley R., 178–79
Regulators, 31, 248–49
rehabilitation theory, as justification of punishment, 155–56
Rehnquist, William H., 65, 249
  in *Booth v. Maryland*, 234
  in *Furman v. Georgia*, 109
  in *Herrera v. Collins*, 54, 136
  in *Lockett v. McCree*, 177
  in *Lowenfield v. Phelps*, 180
  in *Murray v. Giarratano*, 207
  in *Romano v. Oklahoma*, 257
  in *Roper v. Simmons*, 258
  in *Sawyer v. Whitley*, 270–71
  in *Wainwright v. Witt*, 313
relativism, 250–51
religious views, 251–52
reparation theory, as justification of punishment, 157
repentance, 252–54
Report in Favor of the Abolition of the Punishment of Death by Law (O'Sullivan), 232
Resnover, Gregory, 146
retaliation. See *lex talionis*
retentionists, 254
retribution theory, as justification of punishment, 156–57
Rhode Island, 255
Ridley, Alice, 115
rights of the accused, 255, 297–98
Ring, Timothy, 255–56
Ring v. Arizona (2002), 22, 132–33, 255–56
Roberson, Willie, 272
Roberts, Harry, 256
Roberts v. Louisiana (1976), 122, 256
Robertson, Pat, 301
Robinson v. California (1962), 65
Roddy, Stephen R., 272
Roe v. Wade (1973), 249

Romano, John Joseph, 256
Romano v. Oklahoma (1994), 256–57
Rooney, John, 219
Roper v. Simmons (2005), 18, 66, 148, 159, 257–58
Rose, Charles, 274
Rosenberg, Ethel, 147, 226, 258–59
Rosenberg, Julius, 147, 226, 258–59
Rudolph, Frank Lee, 260
Rudolph v. Alabama (1963), 119, 227, 260–61
Rush, Benjamin, 48, 142–43, 224, 261–62
Russell, William, 164
Ryan, George H., 141, 203, 243–44, 262–63
Rye House Plot (1685), 164

Sacco, Nicola, 264–65
Salem witchcraft trials, 185, 205, 234–35, 266–67
San Quentin State Prison, 267
Sanson, Charles, 267–68
Sanson, Charles, Jr., 268
Sanson, Charles-Henri, 124, 269
Sanson, Henri, 269–70
Sanson, Henri-Clement, 270
Sanson, Jean-Baptiste, 268–69
Sanson family, 94, 267–70
Sarandon, Susan, 241
Sarfaty, Roger, 256
Savonarola, Girolamo, 43
Sawyer, Robert Wayne, 270
Sawyer v. Whitley (1992), 270–71
Scalia, Antonin, 258, 287
Scheck, Barry C., 146
Schlup, Lloyd E., 271
Schlup v. Delo (1995), 271–72
Schmidt, Tobias, 124
Schnaubelt, Rudolph, 135
Schwab, Michael, 135–36
Scopes, John T., 69
Scott, James, 164
Scottish Maiden, 124, 272

Scottsboro Boys, 272–74
Sebastian, Saint, 183
Second Treatise on Government (Locke), 175
self-defense, 14
self-incrimination, right to refrain from, 255
  see also Fifth Amendment
sentencing
  mandatory, 183, 320
  racial discrimination in, 246–48
  time between execution and, 295–96
September 11, 2001, attacks, 244
Servetus, Michael, 43
Shapp, Milton, 235
Shays, Daniel, 274
Shays' Rebellion, 274
Shelley, Mary, 248
Simmons, John Dale, 274, 275
Simmons v. South Carolina (1994), 274–75
Simpson, O.J., 42, 75
simulated hangings, 275
Sing Sing Prison, 167–68, 275–76
Singleton, Charles, 191, 276
Skipper, Ronald, 276
Skipper v. South Carolina (1986), 276–77
slavery, 277
Slocum, J.J., 275
Smith, John, 162
Smith, Patrick, 310
Snyder, Albert, 277, 279
Snyder, Ruth, 49, 277–79
social contract theory, 29, 279–80
Socrates, 280–81, 295
solitary confinement, 281
Souter, David, 234
South Carolina, 281–83
South Carolina v. Gathers (1989), 283
South Dakota, 283–84
Southwick, Alfred, 85
Sparf and Hansen v. United States (1895), 154

Spartacus, 64
Spaziano, Joseph Robert, 284
Spaziano v. Florida (1984), 284–85
Spear, Charles, 285–86
special circumstances, 286
  in federal death-penalty laws, 97–98
Spenkelink, John, 166
Spies, August, 135, 136
Spirit of the Laws, The (Montesquieu), 202–203, 223–24, 241
Spry, William, 137
Stanford, Kevin, 286–87
Stanford v. Kentucky (1989), 66, 159, 257, 286–87, 295
stay of execution, 287
Stephen, Saint, 183
Stevens, John Paul
  in *Atkins v. Virginia*, 26, 27
  in *Beck v. Alabama*, 30
  in *Pulley v. Harris*, 245
  in *Schlup v. Delo*, 271
  in *Thompson v. Oklahoma*, 295
Stewart, Kenneth, 311
Stewart, Potter, 287–88
  in *Furman v. Georgia*, 109
  in *Godfrey v. Georgia*, 118
  in *Maxwell v. Bishop*, 186
  in *Witherspoon v. Illinois*, 319
  in *Woodson v. North Carolina*, 320
Stitts, George, 283
stocks, 60
Stoker, Bram, 142
stoning, 288–89
Sullivan, Arthur S., 94
Supreme Court, 289–91
  see also specific cases and justices

Taborsky, Joseph, 57
Tennessee, 292–93
Tepes, Vlad, 142
Tesla, Nikola, 86
Texas, 293–94
Thayer, Webster, 265
Theodosius, Code of, 158

Thin Blue Line, The (film), 101
thirty-day rule, 294
Thomas, Andrew, 178
Thomas, Clarence, 258
Thomas, Saint, 183
Thompson, Jimmy, 94, 196
Thompson, Lloyd, 256
Thompson, William Wayne, 159, 295
Thompson v. Oklahoma (1988), 159, 295
Thornhill, Louis, 145
Thornton, Deborah, 301
time between execution and sentencing, 295–96
Tommey, Charles, 78
Traveling Executioner, The (film), 101
treason, 48–49, 82
trial, 296–99, 255, 301
Trial by Ordeal (Chessman), 52
Trop v. Dulles (1958), 65, 91
Tucker, Karla Faye, 254, 301
Turner, Delos A., 113
20,000 Years in Sing Sing (film), 101
Two Seconds (film), 101

Uniform Code of Military Justice, 179, 193
United Nations Commission on Civil Rights, 302
United States, international criticism of, 147–48
United States Magazine and Journalism Review (journal), 232
United States v. Jackson (1967), 227, 302
Universal Declaration of Human Rights, 302–303
Utah, 303–304
utilitarianism, 32, 304–305

Vanzetti, Bartolomeo, 264–65
Vasquez, Daniel B., 50
Vermont, 306
Vesey, Denmark, 281

victim impact statements, 234, 306
victim's rights, 306–307
Vienna Convention on Consular Relations (VCCR), 105, 106
viewing of executions, 307–10
Virginia, 310–11
visitation privileges, 311–12
voir dire, 298–99
volunteers, 312

Wainwright v. Witt (1989), 154, 313
Walnut Street Jail, 143
Walton, Jeffrey Allan, 313
Walton v. Arizona (1990), 286, 313–14
war crimes, 314–15
Warren, Earl, 91, 92
  in *Maxwell v. Bishop,* 186, 187
Washington, 315–17
Washington, D.C. *See* District of Columbia
Waxton, Luby, 320
Weems, Charlie, 272, 274
Weems v. United States (1910), 92

Weschler, Herbert, 200
Westinghouse, George, 85, 87
West Virginia, 317
wheelbarrow law, 261
whipping, 60
White, Byron, 240
  in *Barefoot v. Estelle,* 28
  in *Coker v. Georgia,* 55
  in *Enmund v. Florida,* 89
  in *Furman v. Georgia,* 109
  in *Maxwell v. Bishop,* 186
  in *Morgan v. Illinois,* 205
  in *Pulley v. Harris,* 245
  in *Skipper v. South Carolina,* 277
White Caps, 245
Wilkerson, Wallace, 317
Wilkerson v. Utah (1878), 103, 317
Wilkins, Heath, 287
Wilkins v. Missouri (1989), 66, 159, 295
William of Orange, 175
William III (king of England), 64
Williams, Abigale, 266
Williams, Ann, 119
Williams, Eugene, 272
Williams, Robert, 178
Williams, William, 196

Wilson, Jimmy, 148
Wingfield, Edward Maria, 162
Wirz, Henry, 314, 317–19
Wisconsin, 319
Witherspoon, William C., 319
Witherspoon v. Illinois (1968), 70, 154, 187, 227, 313, 319–20
  affirmation of, 176–77
Witt, Johnny Paul, 313
women, as death row inmates, 248
Woodruff, David Wayne, 256, 257
Woodson, James Tyrone, 320
Woodson v. North Carolina (1976), 122, 183, 256, 320
Wright, Andy, 272–74
Wright, Douglas Franklin, 230
Wright, Roy, 272
Wright, Wade, 273
Wyoming, 320–21

Yakolev, Anatoli, 259–60
Yarris, Nicholas, 147
York, Mary Lou, 276
Yu-ha-gu, 196

Zettlemoyer, Keith, 236
Ziegler, Tillie, 161–62

PICTURE CREDITS

Cover: © Greg Smith/CORBIS
AP/Wide World Photos, 147, 170, 209, 215
© Archivo Iconografico, S.A./CORBIS, 123
© Bettmann/CORBIS, 12, 17, 33, 41, 52, 59, 68, 93, 102, 112, 117, 134, 152, 164, 169, 221, 231, 253, 273, 282, 289, 308
Paul Buck/EPA/Landov, 199
© CORBIS, 86, 189
© CORBIS SYGMA, 75
Corel Corporation, 91
Digital Stock, 130
© J. Patrick Forden/CORBIS SYGMA, 46
Getty Images, 80
Hulton Archive/Getty Images, 38
Chris Jouan, 24, 71, 199, 243, 247
© Ron Kuntz/CORBIS SYGMA, 300
Library of Congress, 175, 180, 185, 204, 228, 237, 259, 265, 278, 318
© Clay McLachlan/Reuters/CORBIS, 247
National Archives, 315
North Wind Picture Archives, 195
PhotoDisc, 297
Photos.com, 63, 71, 141
Time Life Pictures/Getty Images, 107

ABOUT THE AUTHOR

Bruce E.R. Thompson has a PhD in philosophy, and teaches philosophy at Cuyamaca College and at Southwestern College in Southern California. He also holds a degree in library science and works as a reference and instruction librarian at California State University, San Marcos. He has edited and written several books on history and critical thinking, including *Evolution: Fact or Fiction* for Greenhaven Press and *An Introduction to the Syllogism and the Logic of Proportional Quantifiers* for Peter Lang Press. He lives in Southern California with his wife and twin sons, a dog, two cats, and a snake.

ABOUT THE CONSULTING EDITOR

Mary Jo Poole teaches criminology and sociology at California State University, San Marcos. She has a master's degree in applied sociological practice and is working toward a PhD in sociology at the University of California, Riverside. Her chief area of research is the incarceration of women; she is the coauthor of an article on this subject published in the journal *Social Justice*. She lives with her family in Southern California.